Antislavery, Abolition, and the Atlantic World
R. J. M. Blackett and James Brewer Stewart, Editors

If
We Must
DIE

Shipboard Insurrections in the Era of the Atlantic Slave Trade

ERIC ROBERT TAYLOR

Louisiana State University Press
Baton Rouge

Published by Louisiana State University Press
Copyright © 2006 by Louisiana State University Press
All rights reserved
Manufactured in the United States of America
First Printing

Designer: Michelle A. Garrod
Typeface: Rotis Serif
Printer and binder: Edwards Brothers, Inc.

Library of Congress Cataloging-in-Publication Data

Taylor, Eric Robert, 1971–
  If we must die : shipboard insurrections in the era of the Atlantic slave trade / Eric Robert Taylor.
      p. cm. – (Antislavery, abolition, and the Atlantic world)
  Includes bibliographical references and index.
  ISBN-13: 978-0-8071-3181-7 (cloth : alk. paper)
  ISBN-10: 0-8071-3181-4 (cloth : alk. paper)
  1. Slave trade—Africa—History. 2. Slave trade—America—History. 3. Slave insurrections—History. I. Title. II. Series.
HT1322.T38 2006
306.3ʹ62096–dc22

                                                                  2006005860

The paper in this book meets the guidelines for permanence and durability of the Committee on Production Guidelines for Book Longevity of the Council on Library Resources. ∞

To
Sean and Drew

If we must die, let it not be like hogs
Hunted and penned in an inglorious spot,
While round us bark the mad and hungry dogs,
Making their mock at our accursèd lot.
If we must die, O let us nobly die,
So that our precious blood may not be shed
In vain; then even the monsters we defy
Shall be constrained to honor us though dead!
O kinsmen we must meet the common foe!
Though far outnumbered let us show us brave,
And for their thousand blows deal one deathblow!
What though before us lies the open grave?
Like men we'll face the murderous, cowardly pack,
Pressed to the wall, dying, but fighting back!

—Claude McKay, "If We Must Die"

Contents

Illustrations and Tables   xi
Acknowledgments   xiii

Introduction   1
1. Enslavement, Detention, and the Middle Passage   15
2. Conditions Favorable for Revolt   41
3. Precautions against Revolt   67
4. Revolt   85
5. Unsuccessful Revolts   104
6. Successful Revolts   119
7. Shipboard Revolts in the Americas: A New Wave   139
Conclusion   164

Appendix: Chronology of Shipboard Slave Revolts, 1509–1865   179
Notes   215
Bibliography   241
Index   259

Illustrations and Tables

ILLUSTRATIONS

"Stabbed one of the Negroes" 40
Shipboard revolts on the African coast by region 65
"Insurrection on board a slave ship" 75
"Révolte sur un bâtiment négrier" 97
"La révolte" 126
"Death of Capt. Ferrer, the Captain of the Amistad, July, 1839" 153

TABLES

1. Weapons used by slaves and number of times mentioned 96
2. Percentage of revolts at known times of day 100
3. Slave deaths resulting from shipboard revolts 116

Acknowledgments

This book is the product of more than ten years of research and writing that began when I entered UCLA as a master's student in African American studies. Over that time, a great many individuals have provided encouragement, assistance, and guidance. To each of these individuals, I wish to express my heartfelt appreciation.

My thesis and dissertation committee members deserve a great deal of thanks. These individuals include Ellen DuBois, Robert Edgerton, Robert Hill, and William Worger, each of whom was a great source of support. However, the two professors who deserve the lion's share of appreciation are my dissertation committee cochairs, Edward A. Alpers and Brenda Stevenson, each of whom helped mold me from an enthusiast into a historian. Their advice, editorial suggestions, and overall guidance were invaluable and contributed greatly to this book. To both I offer my sincerest gratitude.

I would also like to acknowledge other individuals at UCLA who helped me throughout my many years of graduate school. Barbara Bernstein and Shela Patel of the History Department were always helpful and encouraging. My appreciation also goes to the faculty and staff of the Center for African American Studies and to the staff of the Young Research Library. I would also like to specially acknowledge James Diego Vigil, formerly of UCLA's Center for the Study of Urban Poverty, who graciously provided me not only friendship and support but financial assistance toward the completion of my research as well.

There were also numerous scholars who kindly responded to my many queries with both advice and information, including Steven Deyle, Gwendolyn Midlo Hall, Herbert S. Klein, Winston McGowan, Clarence J. Munford, Johannes M. Postma, David Richardson, Stuart Schwartz, Verene A. Shepherd, Richard B. Sheridan, and Richard H. Steckel. Each of these individuals graciously took the time to reply to my letters, faxes, and e-mails, often giving me extremely useful guidance and suggestions for further research. Joseph C. Miller and Jerome S. Handler also gave me wonderful advice and engaged me in much-appreciated correspondence. I would also like to thank David Eltis for first bringing to my attention the remarkable Mettas and Daget *Repertoire* of eighteenth-century French slaving voyages, Stephen D. Behrendt for sending me a very nice and detailed letter with references to a number of revolts that were unknown to me at the time, and Robert Harms, who was generous enough to send me information on a fascinating case of shipboard resistance from the eighteenth-century French trade. I cannot begin to adequately express my gratitude to each of these individuals.

I am also indebted to those who helped me with the translation of material written in foreign languages. Of primary importance to me in this respect was Nikol Hodges, who translated each of the 140 or so paragraphs dealing with shipboard insurrections on French voyages included in the Mettas and Daget *Repertoire*. Nikol was a graduate student herself when she completed this job, but still found time to do remarkable work, enabling me to access a very important source for the study of shipboard revolts. I thank her very much for her excellent translations. Similarly, I would like to express my gratitude to Jeanette Fischer for her assistance in translating other French documents. Finally, Tim Tangherlini of UCLA's Scandinavian studies department deserves thanks for his assistance in translating an eighteenth-century Danish document regarding the revolt on board the *Fridericus Quartus* in 1709.

I would also like to acknowledge the numerous individuals at the various archives that I contacted and visited who provided me with great assistance. These include Gail Saunders, director of the Bahamian National Archives, and Karen Schafer, county archivist of the Breckinridge County Archives in Hardinsburg, Kentucky, who provided some wonderful court records regarding the revolt aboard an unnamed vessel in the Ohio River in 1826. More generally, I would like to thank the staff of the Public Record Office in Kew, England, for running a smooth and well-organized operation. The staff of the other archives I visited, notably the Newport Historical Society, the Rhode Island State Archives, and the Rhode Island Historical Society, were all extremely helpful and friendly as well.

Great appreciation also goes to Louisiana State University Press and the wonderful support its staff showed for my work from the very start.

From my initial communication with Maureen Hewitt and Sylvia Rodrigue through the editorial process, which was made smooth and enjoyable by the consistent help and encouragement of Rand Dotson and the expert editorial guidance of George Roupe, my experience with LSU Press has been nothing less than outstanding. Furthermore, professors Richard Blackett and James Stewart, coeditors of the Press's Abolition, Antislavery, and the Atlantic World series, both provided editorial commentary and guidance. They were always extraordinarily helpful and responsive, and I am greatly appreciative of their support for my work.

I also owe a special debt of gratitude to George Skoch, who worked closely with me in creating the map illustrating the regional occurrence of shipboard revolts on the African coast, and to David denBoer for his excellent work assembling the book's index. I would also like to extend my thanks to Liezl Lao at Corbis, Martin Mintz at the British Library, and the staff of the Prints and Photographs Division of the Library of Congress for their kind assistance in helping me acquire the illustrations that appear in the book.

In addition to those listed above, my work would never have been finished without the continual support of my family. I would like to thank my parents, Dianne Jerome and Robert Taylor, for everything they have done for me, and for their unwavering commitment to me, my education, and my research in every step of my journey through college and graduate school. Words cannot convey the love, respect, and appreciation I have for both of them. My father also became my primary research assistant, traveling with me to both England and Rhode Island to do research. A number of the revolts considered in this book are included thanks to his efforts and his willingness to spend eight hours a day in the Public Record Office methodically analyzing difficult-to-read seventeenth- and eighteenth-century documents. He also served as a sounding board for many of the questions I had concerning the best possible way to construct and present my work. In short, he played an extraordinarily important role in the completion of this book, and I am extremely grateful to him.

Finally, I would like to express my deepest gratitude to my wife, Crissy Thomas-Taylor, without whom I never would have pursued a graduate career in the first place. She has been the single greatest motivating force in my life for more than seventeen years, and she was there for me every second of every day. In addition to assisting me with my research at the Public Record Office, she provided editorial guidance as I struggled with how best to interpret and present the material. More importantly, however,

Crissy encouraged me when I was feeling frustrated, inspired me when I needed it most, and constantly impressed me with her own remarkable intelligence, character, and strength. But her greatest gift came to me in October of 2004 with the delivery of our twin sons. For the pride we feel in them every day, the indescribable joy they bring to our lives, and the limitless possibilities we see in their future, I dedicate this book to our boys, Sean and Drew.

IF WE MUST DIE

Introduction

In August 1764, the sensational case of a slaving voyage struck by multiple shipboard insurrections was widely reported in the American press, filling newspaper columns in port cities throughout the Northeast. The vessel in question was the *Hope* of New London, Connecticut, which limped into port at the Caribbean island of St. Thomas after a harrowing voyage from West Africa. Explaining the death of Captain Gould and two seamen, the surviving sailors described a deadly slave revolt that they said occurred while the *Hope* was still on the Senegal coast. According to the crew, the forty-three slaves on board at the time suddenly revolted as the vessel was weighing anchor to sail to the nearby island of Goree. In the ensuing fight, the Africans managed to kill the captain and two of his crew before anyone had time to react. However, the rebels then made the fateful mistake of fleeing below deck, where the remainder of the sailors were quickly able to confine them and put an end to the deadly incident. After order was restored, the *Hope* finally managed to leave the African coast bound for the West Indies, this time under the watch of a new commander, George Taggart, who replaced the fallen Gould. However, the passage was not to be a smooth one, for at some point during the voyage the slaves rose once again, this time killing the ship's carpenter. The crew opened fire on the rebelling slaves, killing seven or eight and thus ending the insurrection. Finally, after the remaining Africans had been placed in double irons to avoid a third rebellion, the vessel made its way to St. Thomas, and the troubled slaving voyage of the *Hope* came to an end.[1]

While certainly a tragic and fascinating case, the slave rebelliousness that plagued the voyage of the *Hope* was just one example of hundreds—perhaps thousands—of similar incidents that took place throughout the history of the slave trade. What makes this particular case especially interesting and significant, however, is that the story the sailors recounted was, at least in part, a lie. While it is true that the slaves rose against the crew during the Middle Passage, the earlier incident at Senegal never happened. The truth came out in the press some seven months later when it was revealed that it was in fact the crew who had staged a mutiny while the ship was on the coast. While the particulars are unclear, it appears that on the night of May 15, the vessel's second mate, with the aid of another crew member, struck Captain Gould in the head with a musket while he slept, after which they and at least one other man threw the captain's body overboard. The truth came to light when one of these men, William Preest, was jailed in Boston for his role in the murder.[2] The most significant aspect of this story with regard to an exploration of shipboard slave resistance is not what truly happened but the lie that was told to cover it up.

These men attempted to cover the murder of their captain by blaming the crime on the slaves. The significance of this ploy on the part of the sailors is that shipboard slave insurrection, even when alleged to have been powerful enough to claim the lives of three crew members, was a highly believable alibi. Not only did the sailors have enough confidence in their lie to present it as the truth, instead of claiming that Gould and the two seamen died from other plausible causes such as disease, a shipboard accident, or even an attack by a pirate ship or privateer, but the plethora of newspapers that reported the story had full confidence that such an incident had occurred. This strongly suggests that shipboard revolt was an ordinary occurrence during the trade. Case after case of shipboard rebellion had come to light and had become a part of the collective consciousness. The imagination of the Western world, so deeply implicated in the slave trade, was open to and familiar with the notion of slave resistance and accepted the story of the *Hope* without hesitation or suspicion. Slaves were rebellious, and people knew and accepted it as an inevitable consequence of the slave trade. Africans did not succumb to a life of enslavement without a struggle, and this struggle had been well documented for generations. When newspapers reported the incidents on the *Hope,* there was no reason to question the story's accuracy or authenticity. Sailors had been telling similar stories since the early days of the trade. Newspapers had reported dozens of similar incidents over the years, and the educated public had read those tales time and time again. The *Hope* was just one more case of shipboard revolt. It wasn't the first and it wouldn't be the last.

Throughout the eighteenth century, shipboard insurrections were continually occurring throughout the transatlantic system. In the research for this book, more than four hundred cases of rebellion have been identified during this century alone, and the true numbers no doubt significantly surpass this figure.[3] It is highly likely that revolts of varying magnitude and success occurred on slave ships at least once a month on average. A great number of these, perhaps even the majority, were minor and went unrecorded. The slave trade was nothing more than a business for those involved in the enslavement of Africans, and ship owners, underwriters, and company executives did not look favorably on irresponsible or careless captains.[4] And while slaves found ways to rise in rebellion regardless of the relative competence of a ship's officers or crew, captains nevertheless received much of the blame. There was great incentive to keep certain things quiet, since a substantial part of a captain's reputation in the slave trade, and thus his likelihood of being rehired for subsequent voyages, depended on his ability to control the Africans aboard his vessel and keep losses to a minimum. When captains failed to cover their tracks, they sometimes suffered consequences that could be damaging to their careers, as the case of a 1721 revolt on board a British vessel attests. After the seventeen Africans who were out of irons revolted and killed two of the sailors, the captain was relieved of his command.[5] So when a revolt was minor enough that few or no lives were lost and no major damage was done to the ship that could not be explained in some other fashion, it is reasonable to conclude that the captain might well choose not to report it. Therefore many revolts probably went unrecorded, and the details surrounding hundreds of shipboard insurrections will never be known.

Nevertheless hundreds of insurrections have survived in the historical record, providing the basis for a detailed exploration of the history of shipboard slave resistance. In addition to documents such as the published writings of slave ship captains and crew members and the records of slave trading companies like the Royal African Company of England, a great deal of information can be found in the eighteenth- and nineteenth-century press. Combining records such as these with the literature on slavery and the slave trade, this book seeks to explore shipboard slave revolt in detail and in so doing shed greater light on its frequency, magnitude, and rate of success. Accordingly, the chapters that follow analyze the phenomenon of shipboard resistance in detail, focusing first on the setting in which this resistance occurred, primarily in the Middle Passage. Insurrection is shown to have been one of the only viable options for resistance open to slave rebels on ships, in spite of the seemingly overwhelming array of obstacles set up to defeat it. Bonds were established within the holds of slave ships that helped infuse Africans with the confidence and determination they needed to mount effective rebellions. Each side waged a war of manipulation, deception, and observation throughout a vessel's voyage. For every condition that made rebellion seem promising, the Africans found themselves beset by an equally significant barrier put in place by the sailors. Such was the context in which rebellion brewed. With this background established, the central part of this book examines the revolts themselves, breaking them down by such factors as location, timing, and the roles of women and children. A discussion then follows contrasting successful and unsuccessful insurrections and the vastly different consequences of each. The final part of this study looks at the second wave of shipboard resistance, which occurred not during the Middle Passage but in the international and domestic slave trades within the Americas. A number of powerful rebellions are profiled in this section and compared with shipboard resistance during the transatlantic voyage. A comprehensive chronology of shipboard slave insurrections that charts all the revolts uncovered in the research for this book is provided as an appendix.

Altogether, this information places the relatively unstudied history of shipboard slave resistance in a new and perhaps surprising light. It becomes clear that shipboard revolts were not at all uncommon but in fact plagued slave traders every step of the way throughout the long history of the trade. They stand as important predecessors to the many revolts that subsequently occurred in the plantation societies of the Americas and add a new perspective to our understanding of slave resistance in general. The remarkable level of success that shipboard rebels attained challenges the notion that African and African American slave resistance was ineffective. When shipboard rebellions are considered along with the later tradition of plantation-based resistance, there is a compelling argument for historians to redefine their conception of slave insurrection and acknowledge a level of success heretofore largely unappreciated. The history of shipboard resistance emerges as not a minor and relatively insignificant aspect of the slave trade but one of the most fundamental characteristics of the trade. And this tradition of resistance helped to define, minimize, and ultimately end the traffic in African slaves.

* * *

Until recently, much of the work that has been done, not only regarding slavery as a whole, but also on slave resistance itself, rarely acknowledged evidence of resistance prior to the arrival of slaves in the New World. When one examines the literature on resistance, shipboard revolt is largely absent. Herbert Aptheker, Eugene Genovese, and Michael Craton, for example, have each written excellent books on the history of slave revolts, yet each explicitly omits any detailed discussion of shipboard resistance. Aptheker, for instance, makes little extensive reference to shipboard insurrection, acknowledging that his groundbreaking *American Negro Slave Revolts* "excludes, with a few exceptions, the scores of outbreaks and plots that occurred upon domestic or foreign slave traders."[6] Genovese, similarly, completely omits an examination of revolts during the slave trade from his *From Rebellion to Revolution,* stating that their inclusion "would only extend the text without essentially affecting the argument."[7] And Craton, in his *Testing the Chains,* includes only a few brief paragraphs about shipboard revolts, suggesting that general uprisings "were no more than occasional episodes."[8]

However, as I hope to show, the inclusion of shipboard insurrections is crucial to any comprehensive analysis of slave resistance. Indeed, shipboard revolt was a very unique form of revolt, and its occurrence was far more than occasional. The slaves who found themselves locked below deck were in a vastly different environment from that of plantation slaves. The greater language barriers Africans encountered on slave ships, combined with a total lack of knowledge regarding their destination or eventual destiny, meant that such things as the emergence of a rebel leadership occurred in a completely different context than plantation slaves in the Americas faced. In addition, the fact that slave ships were essentially closed authoritarian environments akin in many ways to such totalitarian institutions as Nazi concentration camps meant that the choices for resistance on ships were severely limited. There was little opportunity for flight and absolutely no room for the more subtle forms of resistance practiced by plantation slaves. There were no tools to break, no hideaways to run to, no garden plots to cultivate for one's own sense of self-worth, and no work regimen to manipulate by feigned laziness or sickness. The choices for resistance open to Africans during the Middle Passage essentially boiled down to suicide or revolt.

Surely this special environment is just as worthy of study as are New World plantations, and surely shipboard slaves' decision to revolt cannot be considered merely an unimportant detail in the already studied history of slave resistance. Indeed, awareness of the unique circumstances of shipboard revolt is absolutely crucial to a full understanding of the varied ways in which slaves responded to their enslavement. A neglect of shipboard insurrection consequently trivializes the actions of Africans during the slave trade, and considering that the research for this book has yielded evidence of nearly five hundred cases of shipboard revolt, there is a strong case to be made for recognizing the actions of those Africans historians have tended to leave out of their analyses. At the very least, the evidence demonstrates beyond a doubt that shipboard insurrections were far more than merely episodic. Rather, they were part and parcel of the trade, rising and falling with its overall volume over time, and threatening every slave ship that crossed the Atlantic with the potential for disaster.

While many books such as the ones mentioned acknowledge that slaves revolted at sea, most tend to move quickly through a brief discussion based on a few of the half dozen or so relatively well-known revolts, rarely crediting shipboard resistance as a significant and unique phenomenon. Furthermore, many of these authors construct their narratives from the very few sources written specifically about shipboard resistance, citing no new evidence and relying exclusively on secondary sources. Thus old errors are repeated time and again. In one book about slave resistance published in 1996, for instance, the author mistakenly asserts that no shipboard revolt was successful until the nineteenth century.[9] However, my research has identified well over one hundred revolts prior to the nineteenth century in which at least some of the slaves regained their freedom. Errors of fact, widely divergent estimates of the scale and significance of shipboard revolt, and above all a general neglect of the phenomenon as a whole all hamper our understanding of slavery and the slave trade and offer an incomplete portrait of slave behavior. As a result of such misinformation, many of the theories regarding slave revolts in the Americas imply that the tactics utilized by slaves spontaneously emerged once Africans set foot in a plantation environment, ignoring the tradition of resistance that began on the other side of the Atlantic, which was first tried and tested, attempted and occasionally perfected, on the ships of the transatlantic slave trade. Previously published studies are valuable, of course, for expanding our knowledge of slavery and of the varied ways in which slaves adapted, resisted, and survived, but they nevertheless tell only part of the story. This book aims to add a new dimension to the historiography by demonstrating that comprehensive histories of slavery cannot ignore the tradition of revolt that developed prior to the arrival of Africans in the Americas.

Other historians have attempted to look at the issue of shipboard resistance more fully, but efforts to undertake a comprehensive and systematic analysis did not begin until recently. In 1927, George Francis Dow included a chapter on the revolts of the slave trade in his book on slave ships, but it was essentially limited to quoting the journal of Captain William Snelgrave.[10] Over the next decade, Elizabeth Donnan's four-volume documentary work on the slave trade was published and included a number of valuable references to shipboard revolt.[11] In 1931, Gaston Martin produced a study of slaving from Nantes, France, between 1714 and 1744 and determined that revolts struck about one out of every fifteen trips, or a little more than 1.5 per year.[12] In 1937, Harvey Wish provided a useful listing of revolts during the trade and concluded that shipboard revolts between 1699 and 1750 occurred at a rate of approximately two per year.[13] The first detailed discussion, however, came from the African American scholar Lorenzo J. Greene in 1944, who focused largely on resistance aboard New England vessels.[14] These studies were followed by those of Darold Wax in 1966, Okon Uya in 1976 and 1993, a chapter by Daniel Mannix and Malcolm Cowley in 1978, and an excellent chapter entitled "The Middle Passage: Resistance on the Waves" by Clarence Munford in 1991.[15] Additional historians, such as Winston McGowan in both 1990 and 2002, as well as Richard Rathbone, Joseph Inikori, and Vincent Bakpetu Thompson, have touched on resistance by Africans prior to their arrival in the Americas, including shipboard insurrection.[16]

In addition, some writers have included significant, though limited, discussions or accounts of shipboard insurrection as part of their broader analyses of the slave trade. Examples include Johannes Postma in his examination of the Dutch trade; Jay Coughtry in his study of the Rhode Island trade; Joseph Miller with regard to the Portuguese trade; David Richardson in exploring the trade from Bristol, England; and Serge Daget in his analysis of the nineteenth-century French trade.[17] Until recently, the single most important secondary source of this sort for the study of shipboard rebellion was unquestionably the two-volume catalog of eighteenth-century French slaving voyages compiled by Jean Mettas and edited by Serge Daget, in which shipboard revolt is one of numerous areas of inquiry that the authors investigate. In this analysis, the authors present evidence of some 140 cases of shipboard revolts.[18] None of these sources, however, attempts to provide a comprehensive account of revolts on the slave trading ships of different nations. Each presents valuable parts of the puzzle, but one remains left with a fragmented and uncertain understanding of shipboard insurrection as a historical phenomenon.

In 1999, David Eltis and others published what is by far the most comprehensive analysis of the transatlantic slave trade to date. These historians have collected the work of many different scholars into one large, searchable CD-ROM database containing records of more than 27,000 slaving voyages. For each voyage, the editors extracted information for 226 different fields of information, including shipboard revolts. In the end, this database yielded evidence of 338 insurrections.[19] In the years since the publication of this database, the authors have continued to examine the issue of shipboard resistance and have produced a number of scholarly articles on the subject. With their most recent published findings, the total number of shipboard revolts they have documented has risen to 388, including 22 conspiracies and 8 ambiguous cases of slave ships being "cut off."[20]

Other authors have chosen to analyze particular revolts in detail. These include essays written on the voyages of the Danish *Patientia* and on the American vessels *Sally* and *Nancy*.[21] The best known examples of such scholarship are the works written on the cases of the *Amistad* in 1839 and the *Creole* in 1841, both of which involved rebellions not during a transatlantic voyage but during slave trading voyages within the Americas. The attention given to the case of the Spanish slaver *Amistad* in recent years is particularly noteworthy. More than a dozen historical works, as well as novels, an opera, a major motion picture, and even a full-scale replica of the ship, have chronicled the events that occurred aboard this vessel. It is obviously valuable that an otherwise neglected aspect of African American history has been brought to light with such vigor. The actions of these shipboard rebels were certainly significant and deserve a prominent place in history, and the fact that the case went to the Supreme Court of the United States and became a vital part of the antislavery movement is highly meaningful as well. In addition, the nature of the evidence regarding the *Amistad*—more than exists for any other shipboard revolt—makes it an obvious choice for attention.

However, there is another side to consider. For one, the concentration on any single revolt tends to diminish one's understanding of how widespread shipboard insurrection actually was. Similarly, and perhaps more importantly, the fact that the *Amistad* case so prominently involved whites makes it particularly misleading. Concentration on the *Amistad* to the exclusion of other cases diminishes the role of Africans while overemphasizing the role of whites, thus distorting the historical record. The case of the *Amistad* is particularly significant for the events which occurred *off* the ship. This is precisely why it is such a misleading representative of shipboard resistance. While the details of this particular revolt once it entered the court system are obviously very significant, the case of the *Amistad* stands essentially alone in this regard. In the overall picture of shipboard resistance, it is what occurred *on* the ships that is important. In short, the tendency to emphasize the case of the *Amistad* above all other revolts may have a distorting influence for those attempting to see it as part of a much larger tradition. This study hopes to aid in correcting this potential distortion by providing a more complete view of the phenomenon of shipboard revolt. I do, of course, discuss the *Amistad* case in chapter 7, but by that time I hope that the reader will have developed an appreciation for the larger tradition of which it is merely a part.

One of the main difficulties in investigating the history of shipboard slave insurrections is the scarcity of evidence. While 493 cases of shipboard revolt have been identified in the research for this book, many of these are documented only in passing comments in the historical record. For instance, the records of the Royal African Company are filled with abstracts of letters regarding slave ships on the African coast. However, many of these abstracts offer only the briefest of details. From one letter written at Cape Coast Castle in 1681, agents abstracted simply "Branfill Sick, Desires goods, His Negroes rose."[22] All we know from this is that there was a slave revolt on a vessel commanded by Captain Branfill. Although the location can reasonably be determined to be in the vicinity of Cape Coast, the date, time, ship name, mortalities, and ultimate fate of the slaves and crew remain unknown.

Reports in the press, another key source of information on insurrections, are also often sketchy. For example, a London paper in 1749 reported merely that "The Scipio, Stewart, of Leverpool, from Africa for America, was blown up on the Coast, occasion'd by an Insurrection of the Negroes."[23] We do not know where on the African coast this incident took place, what precipitated the revolt, or whether any of the crew or slaves survived the explosion. In 1765, the same paper reported simply that "the Sloop Sisters, Jackson, had an Insurrection on board, and several were kill'd on both Sides."[24] While this is somewhat more information than was provided about the 1681 revolt noted above, it still leaves us very little to work with. There is no indication of where or when the incident occurred, how many were killed, or whether the revolt was successful.

Evidence taken from the press presents other problems, for while early eighteenth-century newspapers tended not to editorialize blatantly, there is no way to be certain that information was not either added or omitted according to the personal motivations of the editor. Later, of course, the problem becomes much more acute. Revolts in the domestic slave trade of the United States were often simultaneously reported in newspapers with very clear anti- and pro-slavery biases. Arriving at the truth from such a tangled web of politics is clearly problematic. Newspapers regularly contradicted each other, and often themselves, regarding details such as the spelling of captains' names. For example, the slave rebellion aboard the English ship *Clare* was first reported by two London papers on August 2, 1729. One spelled the captain's name "Morell" and the other listed him as "Murrel." The next month, readers saw yet another version of the captain's name, this time spelled "Murrell." In the months to come, this man was variously referred to as both "Murel" and "Morrell," thus giving him a total of five different names in the press.[25] While this example does not seem extremely important, it does illustrate that the eighteenth- and early-nineteenth-century newspaper evidence relied on for many of the insurrections in this analysis is sometimes flawed.

As these examples indicate, the history of shipboard slave insurrection is often marked by a general lack of precisely detailed information from which to reconstruct events. As a result, while every effort has been made not to overgeneralize or unnecessarily speculate, the relatively thin nature of the evidence encourages a certain amount of informed speculation in order to achieve the fullest possible understanding of the circumstances under which these revolts unfolded. However, in spite of these limitations, hundreds of separate pieces of information, some actually very detailed, are available for the study of shipboard revolt. There is enough evidence regarding such factors as the timing and location of revolts, the mortality rate for slave rebels, and the frequency of successful insurrections to make well-founded assertions regarding these and other elements of the phenomenon. It is this evidence, gleaned from archival materials, early newspapers, and secondary sources, upon which this analysis is based.

The language of source material is also a problem, for there were so many different countries involved in the slave traffic that a thorough investigation of all relevant archival material would require one to be versed in English, French, Spanish, Portuguese, Dutch, Danish, and other languages. Therefore, this study does not claim to present an exhaustive catalog of all known shipboard slave insurrections but represents a concerted effort to consider as many cases of revolt as ten years of research has led me to uncover, regardless of the time period or nationality of the vessel on which the insurrection occurred. It is my hope that this evidence will encourage further research on the history of shipboard revolts. Because of the bulk of the primary sources consulted for this book, as well as the focus of most of the pioneering studies that historians have undertaken on the slave trade over the past half century and more, the vast majority of the evidence considered herein comes from the English, French, and North American slave trades.

Perhaps the biggest problem of all, however, is that, whether from newspapers, letters, or ships' logs, virtually all of the surviving evidence regarding shipboard slave revolts is written by whites. Therefore, all of this material becomes highly problematic in any attempt to fully understand a tradition of resistance that involves Africans at its very core. With the exception of some brief comments in the writings of figures such as Ottobah Cugoano, Mahommah Baquaqua, and Olaudah Equiano,[26] almost never do we find the voice of an African commenting on his or her experiences during the Middle Passage, much less specifically referring to shipboard revolts or conspiracies. Finding a way to adequately consider the inherent biases of these documents while still relying on them for a historical representation of what actually occurred has been one of the most difficult challenges of writing this book. Of course, historians of the slave experience run into this problem all the time, but it becomes even more troublesome when one looks at the transatlantic slave trade, which very few survivors ever discussed in detail in later narratives or autobiographies.

The voices of the millions of Africans who crossed the Atlantic can only be approximated by looking at their actions, and their actions, in turn, can only be comprehended by recognizing that whites were the chroniclers of the slave trade. Any representation we have of slave behavior must be filtered through this reality. For example, Captain William Snelgrave wrote of a revolt on board the *Eagle* in 1704 that the insurrection ended when one of the slaves was shot. At this point, according to Snelgrave, "all the Men-negroes on the Forecastle threw themselves flat on their Faces, crying out for Mercy."[27] This comment must be considered cautiously, however. After all, the slaves on board had just seen one of their ranks shot, and this would very likely have frightened them, perhaps to the point of surrender as suggested. The startling sound of a pistol shot and the sight of a dead African bleeding on the ship's deck would have been unnerving, and the psychological effect of such an incident should not be underestimated. However, the tone of Snelgrave's comment sounds overly boastful and self-aggrandizing. This was not the captain's private journal that nobody would ever see. Instead, Snelgrave was writing an adventurer's tale and surely constructed his narrative in whatever manner would present him in the most heroic light. His victory here over rebelling Africans would have accomplished such a purpose nicely. This one-sided perspective on the event is a typical example of the way in which the African voice is silenced in the historical record. Such are the kinds of problems the historian encounters when using sources written from a white perspective to reconstruct African and African American history. Despite this caveat, however, I am confident that a careful analysis of the evidence uncovered for this book still provides valuable and compelling details of the history of shipboard slave insurrections.

Additionally, it should be explained just what is meant by the term "shipboard slave revolt" in this book. Reference to an "insurrection," "rebellion," "uprising," or "revolt," indicates that a group of at least two slaves rose together and took active and aggressive steps to change the balance of power on board a particular ship with the intent of reclaiming their freedom. Instances of resistance such as suicide and escape, which were not aimed at overthrowing the system but singularly concerned with personally rejecting it, are not included. Thus, when some one hundred slaves on board the *Prince of Orange* suddenly decided to jump overboard in an apparent mass suicide attempt in 1737, my interpretation of their actions is that they were resisting, but not revolting.[28] Similarly, when Africans aboard the English vessel *Guinea* had to be resecured after prying open a window and attempting to escape, I do not consider this an insurrection.[29] Both of these incidents are therefore excluded from my analysis. As will be discussed in greater detail in chapter 6, ambiguous accounts of slave ships being "cut off" on the African coast in which it is impossible to determine whether the events were slave revolts or acts of violence committed by free Africans are similarly excluded. Furthermore, those rare cases in which evidence exists of a single slave attempting to attack one or more members of the crew of a slave ship also fall beyond the scope of my definition. In one case aboard the *Diligent,* a slave who had been pushed to the breaking point attempted to stir his fellow Africans to rebellion. When they refused, he became enraged, biting anyone who came near him before he was finally subdued by the crew and subsequently strung up and shot by a firing squad assembled on deck in front of the rest of the Africans to teach them a bloody lesson the sailors hoped they would not soon forget.[30] This event is more akin to a suicide than a revolt, and although it says a lot about the effect enslavement had upon the Africans, the varied ways in which Africans lashed out against their bondage, and the brutal methods by which captains chose to deal with intractable slaves, it does not meet the definition of an insurrection as used herein.

Lastly, while plots and conspiracies are discussed in this book as interesting components of the larger history of shipboard insurrection, they are not included as cases of revolt themselves. To take one example, a conspiracy was discovered on board the French ship *Le Courrier de Bourbon* in 1723 while the ship was leaving the West Indian island of Grenada. In this case, the crew found out from a young African on board that the slaves were planning to rise up and slaughter the sailors. In an effort to find out more about this potentially disastrous situation, the crew whipped a number of the slaves until they gave in and revealed the identity of the leader of the plot. As an example to the others, this man was promptly hoisted into the ship's rigging and shot to death.[31] Once again, while valuable for understanding the full nature of shipboard slave resistance, the context in which it unfolded, and the consequences attending its failure, such incidents that never developed beyond the planning stages are excluded as cases of shipboard revolt.

By collecting information from a widely dispersed assortment of primary and secondary source material, it is the intent of this study to bring the much-neglected history of shipboard rebellion to greater light and to challenge the assumption that it was merely a minor, rare, and relatively insignificant aspect of the broader history of slave resistance. It offers a different view from that of those who maintain that the Middle Passage was so psychologically traumatic—such a "shock," as Stanley Elkins has written—that it crushed the spirit of rebelliousness and led to a mere "cargo" of broken and largely passive slaves. This investigation will provide powerful evidence to the contrary, demonstrating the means by which slaves found ways to triumph over the emotional burden of their enslavement.[32] This book serves as an exploration and a celebration of the thousands upon thousands of Africans and African Americans who refused to let the slave trade beat them into submission. It is an investigation into how these men, women, and children gathered their courage, mobilized their fellow captives, and struck boldly and often for their freedom.

1

Enslavement, Detention, and the Middle Passage

In about April of 1794, a group of young African men were bought by South Carolinian slave trader Joseph Hawkins, who was trading in the rivers north of Sierra Leone. Hawkins had arrived in Africa the year before on a slaving expedition and resided inland for some time. Having finally purchased his slaves, he now faced the task of getting these men to his ship, the *Charleston,* which was anchored off the coast. When the day came for Hawkins and his slaves to begin their journey, the Africans found themselves restrained with poles tied around their necks for the march to the river. It was clear that the Africans were agitated by their new bondage, and in an attempt to calm them, Hawkins promised that such treatment was intended only to keep them from running away and that he was taking them to a place where they would be free of their bonds and have complete liberty. However, once the slaves arrived at the river to board boats that would take them to the coast and their loose wicker bonds were replaced with iron shackles, they quickly realized that Hawkins's promise had been a lie. Hawkins's crew soon managed to board all of the captives onto two small boats despite the Africans' heightened state of unrest.

As the boats made their way down the river, the Africans became more restless with each passing hour. In an attempt to pacify them, Hawkins ordered that they be given alcohol. For a brief time this tactic worked, and there was no trouble that night when the boats anchored. By daybreak, the Africans' alcohol-induced contentment was gone and the terror of their situation set in again as the journey downriver continued. By noon, the two boats met up with a larger shallop into which all of the Africans were to be loaded for the final leg of the journey to the waiting *Charleston.* To most safely and easily accomplish this transfer, all three vessels were positioned beside one another in the center of the river. The Africans, who now appeared calmer to the crew, were unshackled in groups of six and moved into the locked hold of the vessel. Running out of space below, Hawkins allowed the last group of Africans to remain on deck.

As the shallop set sail, it must have seemed to Hawkins and his crew that the worst part of their journey to the coast was behind them. But when two of the Africans on deck suddenly jumped overboard as the vessel sailed through a narrow part of the river, it became clear that the captives would not give up without a fight. Although one of these men probably escaped to shore, the other was quickly recaptured, and the ensuing commotion generated by the cries of the slaves on deck set in motion a concerted effort by all the slaves to stage a full insurrection. Several of the Africans attempted to throw two of the sailors overboard, while five others below had freed themselves and were attempting to unshackle the rest. Several crew members had been asleep when the revolt broke out, but they were quickly roused and seized firearms and bayonets. Hawkins, however, was caught unarmed. When he noticed that an African was attempting to take a gun from one of the sailors, Hawkins tried to intervene but was struck so hard by an oar that it severed his little finger. Undeterred, he joined the fight again, this time enabling the sailor to recover his bayonet and kill his African foe. All the while, the rest of the slaves below were shouting encouragement to their fellow rebels above. Those who could not get out of their shackles did the best they could, reaching through the open hatch and holding the legs of the sailors. But in spite of the collective effort of the insurrectionists, the armed crew managed to prevail over the rebelling Africans. By the time the sailors regained control of the vessel, nine Africans and five sailors had been seriously wounded.[1] As this incident suggests, constant vigilance on the part of slave traders was required from the very start. From the march to the water to the voyage down river to the Atlantic crossing, slave traders like Hawkins quickly learned that the least bit of laxity in security measures could mean death.

In order to investigate the nature of shipboard resistance, it is imperative to understand, at least as far as possible so many generations after the fact, what the traumatic experiences of enslavement and life aboard the ships of the Middle Passage must have been like for the countless Africans who made the long voyage across the ocean. Only with the knowledge of these experiences can we truly comprehend the motivations, methods, and strategies of rebelling slaves. Furthermore, without an appreciation of the true enormity of the forces arrayed against slaves during the Atlantic passage, the remarkable tradition of resistance that these men and women mounted cannot be fully valued. An understanding of the experiences of capture, enslavement, and the Middle Passage are fundamental precursors to the story, enabling the history of shipboard resistance to emerge in all of its complexity, power, and importance.

CAPTURE

The Africans who ultimately boarded the *Charleston* for their voyage to South Carolina were brought to the coast by small boats that carried them down the river. Slaves were sometimes captured quite some distance inland, and slave traders regularly used this quick and efficient method of transporting Africans to the coast. Others were carried down local rivers in canoes, forced to lie in the bottom of the vessel with their hands bound. In certain regions of West Africa, convoys of dozens of canoes would sometimes arrive at the coast to offer their slaves to the waiting ships. Anywhere from just a few to thirty or more Africans would be in each canoe with their arms tied behind their backs. The strongest Africans would be additionally tied at the knees. As Alexander Falconbridge noted in 1788, "[The Africans'] allowance of food is so scanty, that it is barely sufficient to support nature. They are, besides, much exposed to the violent rains which frequently fall here, being covered only with mats that afford but a slight defence; and as there is usually water at the bottom of the canoes, from their leaking, they are scarcely ever dry."[2] When rivers were not accessible or boats were not available, Africans instead made the journey to the coast on foot. Whether sold into slavery as debtors or criminals, captured in raids, or enslaved as prisoners of war, Africans often endured a long trek to the coast chained together in coffles of anywhere from ten or twenty to as many as a thousand or more. In the eighteenth century, coffles ranging from twenty to a hundred slaves were probably typical. A European who accompanied one such slave caravan reported in 1799 that a typical coffle in the Senegal River area would march some twenty miles in seven or eight hours every day.[3]

Chained by the legs and even fastened together at the necks in some cases, these groups would endure inclement weather, scant provisions, and mounting sickness until they eventually arrived at their coastal destinations.[4] The networks from which men and women were taken extended hundreds of miles inland in certain areas like West Central Africa, necessitating unbearably long treks for some. As time went on and slaving frontiers were exhausted, Africans were captured from increasingly distant locations extending inward toward the center of the continent. To maintain discipline and discourage resistance on these long journeys, slaves were manacled, whipped, and sometimes laden with heavy weights such as pieces of wood weighing as much as thirty pounds attached to their wrists or ankles to prevent flight. Guards would sometimes even keep the entire group awake for days on end, "seating them each night around a large fire, and kicking any who managed to doze off back to wakefulness."[5] When they were allowed to sleep, it was not restfully. As one Portuguese doctor wrote, "The night is passed in a state of half sleep and watchfulness, because even during the hours intended for rest and sleep, they are constantly aroused by their black guards, who, fearing an uprising, scream at them and frighten them."[6] The Africans may not have known exactly where they were being taken or what was to happen to them once they got there, but it was clear from the start that anything they could do to avoid their coming fate was worth the effort. The minds of many of these men and women quickly turned to resistance, and they carefully watched for any opportunity they might get to spark a rebellion. Those who guarded the Africans were ever aware of this potentiality, and they did whatever they could to avoid it. As Joseph Hawkins wrote, the African captives "were tied to poles in rows, four feet apart; a loose wicker bandage round the neck of each, connected him to the pole, and the arms being pinioned by a bandage affixed behind above the elbows, they had sufficient room to feed, but not to loose themselves, or commit any violence."[7] Of course, such precautions were far from foolproof. In one case in about 1755, for example, a coffle of slaves revolted against the two men who had marched them to the coast, and two slaves regained their freedom.[8]

Just as they were at all stages of the slaving process, however, the odds were against the Africans, and most rebellions were unsuccessful. For others, the chance for rebellion never even presented itself. As much as the slaves wanted to escape, the guards diligently sought to protect their own safety, and this was usually sufficient to stifle most conspiracies before they materialized. For most, the march continued, with each agonizing day bringing them closer and closer to the anchored slave ships awaiting their arrival. Barely sustained by poor supplies of food and water, the latter being scarce toward the end of the dry season, these slaves often suffered from severe malnutrition and dehydration. Suffering from hunger and thirst and forced to bear heavy loads of supplies and to sleep without shelter or sufficient clothing, captives were progressively weakened by their trek. As one Luanda merchant noted, slave traders in the latter half of the eighteenth century expected to lose approximately 40 percent of their slaves to either flight or death before reaching the slave ships.[9] In the illegal era of the mid-nineteenth century, when the presence of naval patrols made the loading of slaves more difficult, captives were sometimes forced to walk forty miles or more along the coast to meet secretly with a slave ship's canoes.[10] Not all slaves who boarded ships endured such a long and traumatic ordeal, but very few Africans who were shipped across the Atlantic were captured from the immediate area in which they boarded the slave ships, and therefore most endured some sort of forced journey either by foot or by boat to reach the coast.

THE BARRACOON EXPERIENCE

Once at the coast, enslaved Africans continued to suffer, as they were now imprisoned for an indefinite amount of time, awaiting the arrival of slave ships to carry them off. Depending on European wars, the presence of pirates in the Atlantic, the demand for slaves in the Americas, outbreaks of disease on the African coast, and any number of other factors, slave ships could either be plentiful or incredibly scarce at any given time. When ships were scarce, Africans could spend a considerable amount of time either imprisoned in the dark slave pen of a West African trade castle waiting for a ship from one of the chartered European companies to arrive or confined in a makeshift pen constructed on the beach waiting to be sold to the captain of a private trader. Regardless of which of these fates the Africans faced, the wait was intolerable. Describing the barracoons of the major West Central African slave trading ports of Luanda and Benguela, for example, Joseph Miller writes, "Large numbers of slaves accumulated within these pens, living for days and weeks surrounded by walls too high for a person to scale, squatting helplessly, naked, on the dirt and entirely exposed to the skies except for few adjoining cells where they could be locked at night. They lived in a 'wormy morass' . . . and slept in their own excrement, without even a bonfire for warmth."[11] At Benguela, the slave pens sometimes held 150 to 200 slaves, along with pigs and goats, leaving only about two square meters for each captive. This experience would have been both disgusting and disheartening, and Africans were sometimes forced to suffer these conditions for months on end. Probably having already endured a prolonged journey to the coast, many Africans would not survive this phase of their enslavement. As another observer noted, "[The slaves] are confined in prisons or dungeons, resembling dens, where they lie naked on the sand, crowded together and loaded with irons. In consequence of this cruel mode of confinement, they are frequently covered with cutaneous eruptions. Ten or twelve of them feed together out of a trough, precisely like so many hogs."[12] This dehumanizing experience certainly took its toll on the Africans and must have been extraordinarily confusing and distressing. Not knowing what lay ahead, hearing strange languages all around them as traders bartered with Europeans, catching glimpses of white faces and giant slave ships unlike anything they had ever seen before, close enough perhaps to hear the cannon salutes of ships as they came into port or to smell the cauldrons of food cooking on nearby vessels, many must have become paralyzed with fear and dread.

To make matters worse, disease periodically ravaged the dirty and crowded slave pens, and Africans became progressively weakened by their extended confinement. Death rates were extremely high—probably at least 10–15 percent in the mid- to late-eighteenth-century trade in Angola, for example. When slaves died, traders would unceremoniously bury them or simply throw their bodies onto the beach to rot or to be picked over by animals. Such practices continued in certain locations until the very end of the eighteenth century.[13] At the Royal African Company's Cape Coast Castle, mortality was so high that officials in London complained. In 1718, the Castle's surgeon recommended constructing raised platforms on which the slaves could sleep, proposed the building of separate quarters for the quarantine of sick slaves, and suggested that tubs be placed in the underground dungeon "for the slaves to ease themselves at night."[14] His statements imply that none of these practices was currently in use, revealing the true nature of what must have been a horrifying place to be confined. As one observer wrote of the conditions at Anomabu Fort on the Gold Coast, "Surrounded on every Side with high Walls, without a possibility of being refreshed with either Sea Breezes or Land Winds, The Slaves [some 450] not over & above cleanly; The Country of itself naturally hot sultry & unwholesome; what other effect can result from such a situation, but to render the place more disagreeable and unhealthy than any Gaol in Europe?"[15] These conditions prevailed wherever slave trading ports sprang up along the African coast, regardless of the nationality of those buying or selling the slaves. In the Dutch castle at Elmina, captives were spared constant imprisonment, as they were instead put to work during their detention. Dutch officials felt that work was better than confinement for the health, and thus the profitability, of the Africans. However, these concerns were only valid when it was considered safe for the slaves to be out of their cells. When darkness fell, the three to four hundred slaves typically held at the castle would be packed into their communal cell for a long and depressing night.[16]

In spite of efforts to control the captives, here again Africans did not passively submit to their situation. As on the march to the coast, both flight and insurrection were ever-present possibilities for the slaves, in spite of the slim chances for success. In some barracoons, guards smartly anticipated revolts and cut openings into the walls through which they could thrust muskets and fire upon slaves who became rebellious.[17] But just as handcuffs, neck weights, and psychological torment failed to keep Africans from rebelling in slave coffles, efforts to keep them in check while imprisoned on the coast were similarly insufficient at times. As early as 1667, for instance, slaves killed all but one of a garrison of thirty-two men at an English fort during an insurrection.[18] In August 1727, another group of slaves in Danish Fort Christiansborg on the Gold Coast ambushed and killed the overseer of the fort and temporarily escaped. When half of them were later recaptured, the ringleader was broken on the wheel and subsequently beheaded.[19] Occasionally, slaves would rebel when taken out of the building for fresh air.[20] As one official reported in 1820, "[In spite of] precautions, insurrections, as on board the slave ships, were not uncommon. . . . On one occasion . . . armed only with the irons and chains of those who were so confined the slaves audaciously attacked the lock-up keeper, at the moment he made his entre to return them to their dungeons after a few hours of basking in the sun."[21] And in the 1830s, an African was executed after staging several unsuccessful attempts to escape from and burn down a slave fort near Sierra Leone.[22] Still others resisted in different ways. One remarkable slave known as Captain Tomba, who will be discussed in greater detail later in connection with his leadership of the revolt aboard the *Robert* in 1721, is described as being of a "tall, strong Make, and bold, stern aspect" and as having "seemed to disdain his Fellow-Slaves for their Readiness to be examined." He "scorned looking at" whites and "refus[ed] to rise or stretch his Limbs, as the Master commanded; which got him an unmerciful Whipping."[23] For hundreds of years, Africans like Captain Tomba simply refused to be enslaved without putting up a fight. While such defiance rarely led to slaves' regaining their freedom, the Africans never stopped trying, and revolt remained an ever-present potentiality in the dungeons and barracoons of the African coast. Beaten but not broken—such was the condition of many slaves who boarded the ships of the Middle Passage. The mortality due to illness during the transatlantic voyage is often attributed in part to ailments first contracted in the long march to and detention periods on the coast before the ships ever sailed.

When a ship at last arrived to pick up slaves, the Africans were herded out of their cells and assembled on the beach to embark on the next terrifying leg of their journey. At this time, either on shore or sometimes after having been brought to the ship, they were forced to undergo a humiliating physical inspection and often a painful branding so that they could later be identified by those who claimed to own them. During the physical examination, the slaves encountered perhaps their first sign that this new form of slavery into which they were being sold was unlike anything in their experiences: the customary rights and privileges that governed domestic slavery in African societies were replaced by strict lines of ownership, profit, and race. Like the most lowly of livestock, slaves were poked and prodded, had their limbs and teeth checked, and were inspected for any signs of disease. In the late seventeenth century, Willem Bosman described this process as follows: "They are thoroughly examined, even to the smallest Member, and that naked too both Men and Women, without the least Distinction or Modesty . . . the lame or faulty are set by as *Invalides.* . . . These are such as are above five and thirty Years old, or are maimed in the Arms, Legs, Hands or Feet, have Lost a Tooth, are grey-haired, or have Films over their Eyes; as well as all those which are affected with any Vener[e]al Distemper, or with several other Diseases."[24] Falconbridge echoed Bosman's observations when he wrote: "If they are afflicted with any infirmity, or are deformed, or have bad eyes or teeth; if they are lame, or weak in the joints, or distorted in the back, or of a slender make, or are narrow in the chest; in short, if they have been, or are afflicted in any manner, so as to render them incapable of much labour; if any of the foregoing defects are discovered in them, they are rejected."[25] The inspections were embarrassing and infuriating, but with armed guards on hand, the Africans had no choice. An eighteenth-century Dutch slaving handbook recommended that traders check the hearing and speaking ability of slaves by making them scream. And in order to avoid purchasing older slaves, captains were advised to check their teeth, examine their hair, and test the firmness of women's breasts.[26] According to a well-known

Danish slave trader, the Portuguese were especially picky in their examination of slaves, spending as much as four hours inspecting each African, smelling their throats, making them laugh and sing, and finally licking the chins of the men to find out whether they had beards and thereby gauge their age.[27] Even well into the nineteenth century, little had changed. As Theophilus Conneau described the procedure in 1826, "Every joint was made to crack; hips, armpits, and groins were also examined. The mouth was duly inspected, and when a tooth fell short it was noted down as a deduction. The eyesight was minutely observed, the voice and speech was called into request. Nothing was forgotten; even the fingers and toes had to undergo similar inspection."[28]

Once declared acceptable, slaves endured the further indignity of having a person or company's brand forever seared into their flesh, a practice that was initiated in at least some locations from the very start. In certain areas, each party with an interest in a given slave, whether their initial owner in Africa, the merchants who subsequently bartered them to ship captains, or the local government, had its own separate brand to be applied to the flesh of the Africans. Thus some slaves were branded multiple times before leaving Africa and often yet again upon arrival in the Americas. The branding process was especially painful. As Robert Harms describes the ordeal, after the irons were heated red hot on a bed of burning charcoal, several stout sailors would hold the African in place while an assistant would rub the spot intended for branding with tallow and then place a piece of greased or oiled paper over it. The branding iron would then be pressed into the piece of paper, marking the bodies of the Africans for the rest of their lives. These marks were variously made on the shoulder, breast, thigh, stomach, or even on the buttocks in the case of small children, and took four to five days to heal.[29] Weak, in pain, possibly ill, certainly homesick, surely frightened, but also perhaps filled with rage and thoughts of vengeance, the Africans were now officially ready for their voyage across the Atlantic.

ON BOARD THE SLAVERS

Having already undergone unfathomable hardships over a period of weeks or months, the Africans now had to embark on what would be perhaps the most difficult aspect of their entire experience with enslavement. This was the Middle Passage. When slave ships anchored off shore, imprisoned men, women, and children on shore would be stripped naked and ferried in small groups to the floating hell that would become their home for the next five to ten weeks or more. Probably never having seen such a huge ship, perhaps never having even seen the ocean before, slaves must have been both frightened and awed as they were slowly paddled out to the menacing slavers. As one survivor of the Middle Passage later remembered, "The ship was lying some distance off. I had never seen a ship before, and my idea of it was, that it was some object of worship of the white man. I imagined that we were all to be slaughtered, and were being led there for that purpose. I felt alarmed for my safety, and despondency had almost taken sole possession of me."[30] Ottobah Cugoano similarly recalled his own experiences with the arrival of a ship, noting that "it was a most horrible scene; there was nothing to be heard but rattling of chains, smacking of whips, and the groans and cries of our fellow men."[31] Many refused to get in the boats and flung themselves on the sand in an effort to stay on land. Specially appointed "captains of the sand" beat, dragged, and otherwise forced these desperate Africans into the canoes and sent them on their way. Some would then take the opportunity to jump overboard. As Captain Thomas Phillips wrote, "[T]he Negroes are so wilful and loth to leave their own country, that they have often leap'd out of the canoos . . . and kept under water till they were drowned, to avoid being taken up and saved by our boats, which pursued them."[32] Tragic accidents at this stage of the slaving process were not unheard of either, as boats would periodically capsize, drowning numerous slaves. So many canoes were capsizing in the heavy surf during the loading of one vessel that the captain organized a group of men whose only job was to swim out and rescue slaves who had fallen into the water.[33] In many locations along the African coast, local Africans expert at maneuvering canoes through the tricky surf were hired to bring both slaves and trade goods back and forth from ship to shore.

Finally on board, the men, who were perceived to be more of a threat than the women, were chained right leg to left leg and sometimes by the hands and even the neck as well, and all were loaded securely below.[34] At this point most were familiar with having their hands bound tightly with rope or some other makeshift bonds, but for many the cold iron manacles now clamped on their limbs were a new and distressing development. These shackles could not be easily loosened or broken, and the sharp edges pressed deeply and painfully into their skin. In this state, the Africans often had to endure weeks or even months of sailing along the coast as the ship's captain gradually completed his complement of slaves. In these first weeks, the slaves made desperate efforts to come to grips with their situation—attempting to figure out what was happening to them and trying to determine from the other Africans on board why they were taken, where they were going, and what was to happen to them when they got there. Identifying fellow captives who shared a common language or with whom a slave had bonded during the long process of enslavement and imprisonment was an important part of the process. But for many, such individuals were absent, and those around them were complete strangers with bizarre customs and indecipherable languages. The inevitable misinformation, confusion, and rumor that surely surrounded this early stage of the journey contributed an incredible amount of fear to an already tense and confusing situation. All alone in a terrifying new world, with sights, sounds, and smells unlike anything their lives had thus far prepared them for, many Africans' first reaction must have been intense loneliness and inconsolable grief.

Contributing in no small way to this situation was the fear among some Africans that they had been captured to be eaten. In March 1737, for instance, more than one hundred slaves aboard the English ship *Prince of Orange* jumped overboard, believing that the Europeans were planning to pluck out their eyes and then make a meal of the Africans. As the captain noted, "[W]e lost 33 of as good Men Slaves as we had on board, who would not endeavour to save themselves, but resolv'd to die, and sunk directly down."[35] Compounded by the hours of agonizing and wondering in the darkness of the ship's hold, such fear of European cannibalism was apparently very common among some Africans and certainly contributed to the high levels of suicide, particularly early in the voyage. Slaves often believed that they were being carried away to be offered as human sacrifices to gods of the white man's religion or to be murdered to provide blood to dye cloth red. Others were convinced that their body fat would be processed into products such as oil or lard or that their brains were to be made into cheese. The black shoe leather of the Europeans was sometimes mistaken for African skin, while gunpowder was similarly considered by some terrified captives to be the burnt and ground bones of previous slaves.[36] On Portuguese ships, owners urged captains to avoid using metal cauldrons, which were often left steaming on deck for the purpose of cooking the slaves' food, because many Africans believed they were to be boiled alive in them, while red wine was commonly avoided on slave ships because captives sometimes suspected that it had been made from the blood of their predecessors.[37] At least one French slave trader ordered doctors on his ship never to perform an autopsy on a dead African because the sight of a partially dissected body might be seen as evidence of the sailors' cannibalistic intentions.[38] As Willem Bosman wrote, "[W]e are sometimes sufficiently plagued with a parcel of Slaves . . . who very innocently persuade one another, that we buy them only to fatten and afterwards eat them as a Delicacy."[39] The former slave Olaudah Equiano expressed precisely such fear in his famous narrative published in 1789:

> I asked [some other slaves] if we were to be eaten by those white men with horrible looks, red faces, and loose hair. They told me I was not. . . . I was soon put down under the decks, and there I received such a salutation in my nostrils as I had never experienced in my life: so that, with the loathsomeness of the stench and crying together, I became so sick and low that I was not able to eat, nor had I the least desire to taste anything. I now wished for the last friend, death, to relieve me.[40]

Sailors were wise to do whatever they could to calm fears of cannibalism, because the terror of being devoured could encourage the Africans to rebel. As one trader noted, "When we are so unhappy as to be pestered with many of this sort, they resolve and agree together (and bring over the rest of their Party) to run away from the ship, kill the *Europeans,* and set the Vessel a-shore; by which means they design to free themselves from being our Food."[41] In spite of these fears, however, in most cases the Africans learned relatively quickly that the sailors had no desire to eat them.

A week or so after leaving, when the African coast was out of sight, the chances for effective escape were gone, and captains felt the motivation for revolt was lessened, slaves would customarily be taken on deck in small groups each morning to have their chains checked for tampering, to use the toilets sometimes constructed on the sides of the ship, and to get a quick inspection by the surgeon for any new signs of disease. Every couple of weeks, their nails would be trimmed and their heads, underarms, beards, and pubic hair shaved to reduce lice.[42] At this time, they would generally be allowed to wash up with a bucket of salt water and stretch their limbs before having breakfast, which usually occurred between 8:00 A.M. and 10:00 A.M. On French ships, this meal often consisted of a quart of soup, composed mostly of beans and rice, and sometimes supplemented by corn meal, hot peppers, or salt.[43] After breakfast, slaves often spent much of the afternoon cleaning the ship, scrubbing the decks, preparing the afternoon meal, cleansing the hold, and emptying the toilets. African women sometimes performed the role of maid, tidying up the crews' quarters. Around 3:00 P.M. or 4:00 P.M., the slaves' other meal of the day was served, consisting of basically the same substance as the first meal. Manioc was a staple on Portuguese vessels, maize and beans on English ships, and barley and dried peas or beans on Dutch ships, although captains would often choose the fare for a given voyage based on their perceptions of what slaves from different areas preferred to eat. Periodically, items such as dried fish, plantains, yams, potatoes, coconuts, dried turtle meat, small livestock meat, palm wine, pepper, limes and oranges might be added. Occasionally, slaves might receive a shot of rum or brandy and were at times even issued pipes or tobacco.[44] In other cases, resourceful slave ship captains took advantage of the fact that sharks regularly followed in the wakes of slavers and caught some of them for food. The sharks were attracted to these ships because of the perpetual specter of death on board and fed off of the discarded bodies of Africans. Sometimes dead slaves would even be dragged behind the vessel as bait.[45] By the late eighteenth century, as one historian writes, "A typical ration per day for a slave might be three pounds, ten ounces of yam, ten ounces of biscuit, three and a half ounces of beans, two ounces of flour, and a portion of salted beef. One plantain and one ear of corn might be added three days out of five. A mouthwash of vinegar or lime juice might be given in the mornings, to avoid scurvy."[46] To save the crew the chore of cooking, and perhaps also because they were thought to know what the slaves wanted to eat most, the African women on board were sometimes involved with the preparation of the food.[47] This was probably a smart move, as food that tasted at least somewhat familiar may have lessened the traumatic experiences of the Middle Passage. However, as will be touched upon later, giving slave women access to the preparation of food also left the door open for potential poisoning attempts against the crew.

In addition to the food rations, each captive would get a half to a full pint of water at each meal. The food would often be served in small tubs or troughs (which had probably been used on the voyage to Africa to feed livestock), around which approximately ten of the slaves would gather to eat. Like all activities aboard a slave ship, security demanded that this be a heavily regulated process. Africans were adept at taking advantage of the smallest cracks in security, and mealtime regularly provided the first opportunities for resistance. Slaves were sometimes provided with wooden spoons but otherwise ate with their hands lest some utensil fall into their possession that might be smuggled into the hold at night and used to pick the locks on their chains. The spoilage of food, and particularly of the water, was a major problem on slave ships and was responsible for countless outbreaks of dysentery throughout the history of the trade. Because of dehydration caused by seasickness and by sweating due to high temperatures in the hold, water was very important for the health of slaves, but because large barrels of water took valuable space that could otherwise be used for carrying slaves, it was invariably in short supply.[48] Furthermore, the large wooden barrels were often leaky and unsanitary, and dozens of them typically spoiled during a given voyage. In the Brazil-Angola trade, for instance, the same barrels that brought the cane brandy over from Brazil were subsequently used to store the water for the Middle Passage. These were rarely sufficiently cleaned, which often contributed to the spoilage of the water carried within.[49] And in the era of the illegal trade, the fear of being captured on the coast caused captains to rush their procedures, often resulting in a vessel's leaving without sufficient supplies of water or food.

Compounding the sickness caused by poor rations, the living conditions for slaves were appalling, with captives chained together in ships specifically designed to hold the maximum number of human beings. The spaces in which the Africans lived usually offered no more than about three or four feet of room between ceiling and floor but were occasionally as little as eighteen inches high. To maximize carrying capacity, a shelf was built inside the slave quarters along each side of the ship. This shelf jutted out towards the center of the vessel so that a second layer of Africans could be loaded on top. Those who occupied the space on and beneath these shelves had to lie down for the entire passage, as there was no room to sit upright. Those in the center of the ship were forced to sit upright, with no room to lie down. As Captain Parrey of the Royal Navy reported in 1788 of the English ship *Brooks,* which he considered typical, each adult male slave was given a space six feet long by sixteen inches wide, while each woman was allowed a space just slightly smaller. As for children, each boy was allotted five feet by fourteen inches, and each girl four and a half feet by twelve inches.[50] Tightly packed into a tiny space, the Africans were forced to sleep on their sides either naked or nearly so with nothing but the uneven, bare wooden floors as a bed. On the nineteenth-century Spanish ship *Panchiata,* "the men on the slave deck sat upright in rows in a space so low that none could stand, legs spread and knees raised so that each occupied the space between the limbs of the man behind."[51] Early in the seventeenth-century French trade, some captives had to stand upright, bound to stakes, throughout the entire voyage. Shackled by the hands and feet, "not as one would chain animals," as one author asserts, "but only as people are chained whose captors live in terror of rebellion," the slaves endured this bondage for the duration of the trip.[52] Throughout the history of the trade, male slaves were shipped at a ratio of roughly 2:1 over females, and the men's and women's quarters on slave ships were virtually always separated, with children often being housed with the women but sometimes in their own separate quarters. As time went on, a greater percentage of women and children were shipped across the Atlantic, but market demands for labor typically dictated a preference for young men. Men were generally more closely watched than women and thus had much more restricted mobility. Women and children were customarily allowed to be unchained and on deck during the day, but when night fell, wise captains demanded that all be locked securely below.

Nighttime in the crowded, dark hold of a slaver must have been truly horrifying. It would have been an experience unlike anything the Africans had ever faced. With nothing but the moonlight creeping through the hatch gratings, darkness enveloped the slaves. As the Africans were unable to see clearly, their other senses became heightened, and the captives sat or lay there listening to the sounds of slavery—chains rattling as the others tried in vain to get comfortable, unfamiliar voices and languages on all sides muttering softly or perhaps angrily plotting escape or rebellion, and quiet sobbing as the slaves thought back on the homes and families they would probably never see again. And if grief, panic, and confusion weren't enough, more immediate biological concerns added further misery to an already overwhelming experience. As Alexander Falconbridge reported of the toilets in the slave quarters,

> In each of the apartments are placed three or four large buckets, of a conical form, being near two feet in diameter at the bottom, and only one foot at the top, and in depth about twenty-eight inches; to which, when necessary, the negroes have recourse . . . those who are placed at a distance from the buckets, in endeavouring to get to them, tumble over their companions, in consequence of their being shackled. . . . In this distressed situation, unable to proceed, and prevented from get-

ting to the tubs, they desist from the attempt; and, as the necessities of nature are not to be repelled, ease themselves as they lie.[53]

As a result of this imprisonment and the bacterially infested conditions caused by the accumulation of human waste, untold numbers of Africans died from disease. Moreover, depending on the perceived temperament of a given shipload of Africans, some captains felt obliged to have the filth in the hold cleaned out only once a week, and "a few even left their slaves to wallow in excrement during the whole Atlantic passage."[54] The resulting stench was often unbearable, and contemporaries of the slave trade report being able to smell the approach of slavers from miles away. As one survivor remembered, "The loathsomeness and filth of that horrible place will never be effaced from my memory; nay, as long as memory holds her seat in this distracted brain, will I remember that. My heart even at this day, sickens at the thought of it."[55] Furthermore the holds of slave ships had very poor ventilation, becoming unbearably hot and stifling. Under normal circumstances, hatches would be left uncovered so that air could get in, but during rough seas or rainstorms, when the hatches and vents had to be closed, the putrid odors made life almost unbearable, and slaves nearly died of suffocation. As Falconbridge noted, "[T]he confined air, rendered noxious by the effluvia exhaled from their bodies, and by being repeatedly breathed, soon produced fevers and fluxes, which generally carries off great numbers of them."[56]

As a result, slaves perpetually suffered from the constant transmission of bacteria and viruses. In addition to seasickness and the inevitable bruises, sores, blisters, and cuts that all slaves received from their shackles, the captives were subject at any time to individual cases or shipwide epidemics of diseases such as smallpox, measles, yellow fever, typhoid, pneumonia, scurvy, gonorrhea, diarrhea, syphilis, malaria, dysentery, elephantiasis, hookworm, tapeworm, and leprosy, among others, and occasionally even went blind from diseases of the eyes such as ophthalmia. As Falconbridge noted of the slave compartments on one voyage, "The deck, that is, the floor of their rooms, was so covered with the blood and mucus which had proceeded from them in consequence of the flux, that it resembled a slaughter-house. It is not in the power of the human imagination, to picture to itself a situation more dreadful or disgusting. Numbers of the slaves having fainted, they were carried upon deck, where several of them died, and the rest were, with great difficulty, restored."[57] The biggest killer of all was dysentery, or the notorious "bloody flux," which may have accounted for a third of all deaths. This disease was an infection of the intestines resulting in frequent bowel movements, vomiting, severe abdominal pain, headaches, and high fevers. The bloody flux got its name from the fact that those who suffered from the disease would often lose blood as a result of ulcerated intestines.[58] This and other diseases took an extraordinarily heavy toll. When the *Indian Queen* reached Buenos Aires in 1716, 140 slaves had died during the passage, 45 others were in advanced stages of smallpox, and another 43 had early symptoms of the disease.[59] In 1731, 150 slaves on the Dutch ship *Beekesteyn* died of scurvy.[60] And in 1789, measles broke out on the Liverpool ship *Brothers,* leaving nearly 60 Africans dead.[61] Indeed, such stories are not uncommon in the history of the slave trade, with disease of one form or another often decimating the African populations on slave ships.

To make matters worse, when surgeons on slave ships finally made their appearance by law, they were totally unequipped to deal with the problems that regularly arose on the vessels. In the seventeenth century, many surgeons on French slave ships started their careers as barbers and essentially learned surgical skills on the job. In 1717, the French government forced shipboard surgeons to take an apprenticeship in a hospital and pass an oral exam before joining the crew of a slave ship, but it was not until 1767 that surgeons had to undertake serious medical studies.[62] Johannes Postma notes that slave ship surgeons in the Dutch trade had been trained "to deal primarily with trauma cases, such as gunshot wounds, ulcers, and amputations, and to apply bleeding procedures. They knew little or nothing about internal medicine, the diseases that were rampant on slave ships." It wasn't until 1769 that a training school for Dutch ship surgeons was finally established—too late to have any meaningful effect on Holland's then declining slave trade.[63] As a result of the poor medical care available, mortality rates at sea were often staggering. As sailors made their daily rounds in the holds, they would unshackle the dead slaves from the living and throw their bodies overboard to the sharks. Mortality was so high in fact that merchants would regularly load more slaves than they were licensed to carry, agreeing to pay extra for any excess "cargo" that managed to survive the Middle Passage. And when slavers were hampered on their Atlantic crossing by storms, poor navigation, or the doldrums, thus prolonging the voyage for several months, sick and healthy slaves alike were sometimes jettisoned in order to save provisions. In the most famous instance of this, the slaver *Zong* left West Africa crammed with more than four hundred slaves. Unpredictable winds and an inexperienced captain's navigational errors doubled the length of the voyage, and by the time the vessel finally pulled into port in Jamaica, the journey had taken nearly four months. Along the way, provisions began to run low and the Africans were dying rapidly. The captain evaluated the situation based on financial concerns and recognized that only live, healthy slaves would net him a profit once he reached the West Indies. To prevent economic failure of his venture, the captain decided to capitalize on the fact that his slaves were insured. Accordingly, over the course of a few days, the crew was ordered to throw the sickest slaves overboard alive. When it was all over, more than 130 Africans had been murdered in this fashion.[64] As on the *Zong*, death and disease seemed to stalk the Africans at every turn, and although most managed to survive the journey, one historian notes that many were "crippled, covered with mange, losing their hair, emaciated in frame, suffering from fevers . . . often barely alive," demonstrating that merely surviving was a remarkable feat in itself.[65]

In addition to illness, slaves suffered terribly from depression and de-spair, many simply losing their will to live. As one crew member aboard the *Zong* wrote of the slaves' first night at sea, "They felt the ship's move-ment. A worse howling I never did hear, like the poor mad souls in Bedlam Hospital. The men shook their fetters which was deafening. . . . One young woman [broke loose] and ran screaming tearing her hair on the deck."[66] As a result of such terror, slaves were commonly subject to madness, and "in their frenzy some killed others in the hope of procuring more room to breathe. Men strangled those next to them, and women drove nails into each other's brains."[67] Fights among Africans in the slave hold were common, as strangers who now found themselves chained to one another struggled for personal space. One entry in the log of the slave ship *San-down* reveals that the ship's doctor had to amputate the infected finger of an African bitten by another slave. Similarly, the log of the Danish ship *Fredensborg* noted that two slaves were whipped for fighting.[68] On the *Lady Mary*, fights among the captives were responsible for several African deaths.[69] So overtaken by madness was a woman on the slaver *Emilia* that she had to be chained to the deck so that she could not harm herself or others. Those showing signs of insanity might be whipped to death or simply clubbed on the head and thrown into the sea.[70] Still others suffered from a sort of lethargy, known as "banzo" by the Portuguese and "fixed melancholy" by the English, which seems to have been caused by dehydration due to the poor nutritional quality and scant quantity of food and water on slave ships. Many captains attempted to remedy such lethargy by forcing their slaves to dance and even sing on deck each day that weather permitted, often to the beat of a drum kept on board for precisely such occasions. As Falconbridge reported, "[E]xercise being deemed necessary for the preservation of their health, they are sometimes obliged to dance. . . . If they go about it reluctantly, or do not move with agility, they are flogged."[71]

No effort to depict the true horrors of the Middle Passage would be complete without acknowledging the abuse of female slaves by captains and crew members. It is possible that a major reason the men's and women's quarters were separate on slave ships was so that the sailors could have easier access to the women without dealing with angry African men. Similarly, the relative freedom of movement that slave women had on board may also be partly attributed to the desire to have these women more accessible for the advances of the crew. While Falconbridge noted that "on board some ships, the common sailors are allowed to have intercourse with such of the black women whose consent they can procure," he went on to infer that "intercourse" without "consent" was not uncommon, for "the officers are permitted to indulge their passions among them at pleasure, and sometimes are guilty of such brutal excesses, as disgrace human nature."[72] As Captain John Newton wrote, "When the women and girls are taken on board a ship, naked, trembling, terrified, perhaps almost exhausted with cold, fatigue, and hunger, they are often exposed to the wanton rudeness of white savages. The poor creatures cannot understand the language they hear, but the looks are sufficiently intelligible. In imagination, the prey is divided, upon the spot, and only reserved till opportunity offers."[73] It is not improbable that the rape of African women occurred on just about every ship that crossed the Atlantic with slave women. The comments of a French captain anchored at Whydah in 1702 are telling. Fearing rebellion from the slaves on board after witnessing a revolt nearby, the captain lamented: "To avoid a similar incident, we put the largest part of our Negroes in irons, and even among the Negresses those who appeared to us the most resolute and the most dangerous . . . although because of their beauty they were very dear to the chief officers and sailors who had each given their names to chosen ones, there was nothing left to do but put them in chains."[74] The relationship between slave ship crew members and the African women was one of severely un-equal power that encouraged the crew to engage freely in sexual abuse. A French captain matter-of-factly wrote in his memoirs that each officer on his ship selected an African woman to serve him "at the table and in bed."[75] Ottobah Cugoano acknowledged the prevalence of sexual abuse in a much different tone, angrily recalling that "it was common for the dirty filthy sailors to take the African women and lie upon their bodies."[76] As will be explored in chapter 4, this abuse periodically came back to haunt sailors, as the same conditions that facilitated close proximity to African women for sexual purposes also gave the women unusual access to sensi-tive areas of the ship and enabled them to gather much-needed informa-tion for slave insurrections.

Sometimes sexual assault was discouraged by the captain, as indicated by a notation in the log of the Rhode Island ship *Mary* in 1796 that "this morning found our women Slave Apartments had been attempted to have been opened by some of the Ships crew, the locks being spoiled and sun-derd." Ten days later, the captain stripped an officer of his rank for sleep-ing in the slave room, commenting that he was "no longer fit Companion for the Cabin."[77] Owners and financiers would similarly include language in their instructions to captains that abuse of slave women was not to be tolerated. The owners of the French ship *La Rochelle,* for instance, in-structed the captain to "prevent encounters of the whites with the women slaves because it often leads to unfortunate results."[78] For fear of retalia-tion by the slaves, or simply out of genuine human decency, some captains frowned upon this abusive behavior on the part of their crews. Usually, however, whether officially prohibited or not, rape was quietly passed over, if not condoned. As one historian writes, "For the attractive woman there was the added ignominy of being fought over by lustful white men. Quarrels erupted, insults and blows were exchanged to win the right to be the first to rape a good-looking Black woman, or the right to make her one's exclusive sexual possession for the duration of the voyage."[79] Other captains would take privately owned African girls or boys on board with them, and it is conceivable that sexual exploitation sometimes played a role in this. With slave ship crews composed of temperamental, violent, and often drunken sailors who had been away from wives and girlfriends for months on end, one can only speculate how widespread sexual assault must have been. The historical record is relatively silent on the issue, al-though in one case it is recorded that a certain Captain Liot "mistreated a very pretty Negress, broke two of her teeth, and put her in such a state of languish that she could only be sold for a very low price at Saint Domingue where she died two weeks later. Not content, the said Philippe Liot pushed his brutality to the point of violating a little Negro girl of eight to ten years, whose mouth he closed to prevent her from screaming. This he did on three nights and put her in a deathly state."[80] A similar tale of abuse is offered by Captain John Newton, whose slaving journal notes that during the afternoon of January 31, 1753, one of the sailors "seduced a woman slave down into the room and lay with her brutelike in view of the whole quarter deck." What makes this account particularly horrifying is the fact that the women was "big with child" at the time she was raped.[81] On Dutch ships, although sexual contact with slaves was forbidden, the female quarters were often referred to as the *hoeregat,* or "whore hole," clearly referring to the sexual exploitation that obviously occurred there.[82] Needless to say, rape was a particularly personal attack, and the African women on slave ships suffered immeasurably. Some may have attempted to reduce the violence of these assaults by at least partially acquiescing and entering into sexual relationships of mutual consent. Others no doubt steadfastly refused to be exploited and resolved to fight, kill, or commit suicide before they would let a sailor touch them. But in either event, and regardless of the level of bodily force or violence, sexual exploitation surely both humiliated and enraged the women who were targeted by sailors, and might well have been the spark for rebellion in some cases.

On top of all of these conditions that typified slave ship voyages, slaves and crew alike could be killed by catastrophic accidents. The wooden ships would frequently be struck by lightning and burn, get blown off course for months, run aground on shallow coastal rocks, or encounter hurricanes in the mid-Atlantic and sink. The Danish *Cron-Prindzen* was lost in a storm in 1705, for example, causing the deaths of some 820 slaves. In January 1738, the Dutch *Leusden* was similarly caught in a storm off the Surinam coast and got caught on the rocks. While the crew and a few of the slaves escaped, more than 700 Africans below deck drowned.[83] Numerous other cases of catastrophic deaths on board slave ships are documented in eighteenth-century newspapers. In 1737, some 200–300 slaves drowned when the ship *Mary* sprang a leak;[84] the Liverpool vessel *Pallas* was slaving on the African coast in 1761 when she mysteriously blew up, taking some 600 slaves down with her;[85] 380 slaves were reported killed when the London ship *Den Keyser* blew up on the African coast in 1783;[86] 420 Africans lost their lives the same year when the Bristol ship *Phoenix* was overset on the Calabar coast;[87] and on its way to Havana in 1787, the *Sisters* capsized in the West Indies, drowning nearly 500 slaves.[88] These represent just a few of the countless disasters that threatened slave ships. Seafaring was a dangerous enterprise, and simply making it safely across the Atlantic was often a struggle. Furthermore, depending on the time period, slavers often faced the threat of attack by interlopers, privateers, or pirates, and warships were always a problem as European nations waged seemingly endless war. When the French *Hercule* found itself in combat with a Dutch warship in 1707 during the War of Spanish Succession, the slaves on board paid a high price. Outfought, the French slaver exploded and burned, killing thirty-eight Africans.[89]

With violence, illness, malnutrition, dehydration, despair, and the ever-present threat of fatal catastrophe, it is no wonder that mortality rates in the Middle Passage were so high. Mortality declined over time, however, thanks to a number of factors. A Portuguese act of 1684, for instance, reduced overcrowding on slave ships by establishing limits on the numbers of slaves that could be carried per ton. The same law also regulated the amount of food and water on board. In the 1720s, the French Company of the Indies offered captains financial rewards for keeping slaves alive. If fewer than 20 percent of the Africans on a ship died, the captain would receive a cash bonus, which increased depending on just how low the mortality rate was.[90] In Dolben's Act of 1788, Britain's first major legal ruling on slave mortality, regulations were introduced limiting the number of slaves that could be carried per ton, and a system of bonuses to motivate captains and surgeons to monitor the health and safety of their slaves was developed. The following year, Dutch officials followed with their own regulations designed to curtail slave mortality.[91] Voyage lengths also decreased with shorter routes and advances in shipping technology, such as the introduction of vessels with copper-sheathed hulls into the trade beginning in the second half of the eighteenth century. Additionally, breakthroughs in medical knowledge, such as smallpox vaccinations around the turn of the nineteenth century, may have resulted in fewer illness-related deaths. All of these factors helped reduce slave mortality on the transatlantic crossing, but death remained one of the primary hallmarks of the slave trade from its beginning to its end. Mortality varied greatly depending on the voyage but was generally at least 20 percent into the early eighteenth century, fell to some 10–15 percent by the end of the century, and finally hit a low of about 5–10 percent during the nineteenth-century slave trade.[92] In the end, the ships of the Middle Passage probably claimed the lives of at least 1.5 million Africans.

Placed in such an overwhelmingly disadvantaged position, Africans found resistance aboard slave ships difficult and opportunities to resist limited. Unlike in the plantation societies of the Americas, where slaves could manipulate the work regime, sabotage tools or equipment, earn money on the side with the hope of eventually purchasing freedom, flee to fugitive slave communities, or tend personal gardens for their own sense of self-esteem, the forms of resistance available to Africans on ships were effectively limited to suicide, the rare opportunity for escape, and insurrection. Slaves were ever watchful for opportunities to escape while ships were still anchored offshore. A number of slave women aboard an English ship, for instance, escaped through the ship's gun port gratings, which had been left unlocked, and thus managed to reach the water and swim toward the beach; they were apparently captured, however, before they reached land.[93] In a more successful attempt, another woman spent two weeks aboard a slaver on the coast of Africa before she finally found means to slip into the water and swim ashore.[94] In spite of cases such as these, however, escape from slave ships seems to have been an extreme rarity. It became obvious to the Africans who found themselves aboard these ships that escape was not a particularly promising means of resistance and that something more drastic had to be done if they were to regain their freedom.

For others, suicide seemed the brightest hope of ending the horror that had become their lives. Many desperate men and women chose this ultimate form of resistance throughout the history of the slave trade. As their final earthly act, these individuals surely weighed their options carefully and ultimately chose death over slavery. Slaves often tried to starve themselves to death, but captains and crew members were quick to observe such attempts and, for fear of losing profits, take measures to prevent it. Those who attempted suicide through starvation were force-fed through a funnel, whipped, or underwent such tortures as having their lips scorched by coals, their teeth broken, or their mouths forced open with the aid of a device known as the *speculum oris,* which was hammered between an African's teeth so that his or her mouth could be opened with a thumbscrew.[95] As Falconbridge wrote, "Upon the negroes refusing to take sustenance, I have seen coals of fire, glowing hot, put on a shovel, and placed so near their lips, as to scorch and burn them. And this has been accompanied with threats, of forcing them to swallow the coals. . . . I have also been credibly informed, that a certain captain in the slave trade poured melted lead on such of the negroes as obstinately refused their food."[96] Occasionally, a monitor was employed during meal times to instruct slaves when to dip their fingers or spoons and when to swallow. Those attempting to starve themselves would be identified by this monitor and severely whipped.[97] Others managed to die by refusing medicine, hanging themselves with bits of clothing, suffocating themselves, or smashing their heads against the walls of ships' holds. An African aboard the slaver *Brookes* even managed to slit his throat twice using his fingernails and, when that failed to work, starved himself by refusing to eat, finally accomplishing his purpose in just over a week's time. Part of the reason behind the practice of periodically trimming slaves' fingernails may have been to guard against such acts of self-destruction. Captain Theophilus Conneau recorded that one of his slaves choked himself to death one night, only some twenty-four hours after another African had "leaped overboard in a fit of passion."[98] An interesting method of suicide was observed by a veteran sailor of three slaving voyages who noted that when a large gust of wind pushed a vessel over on its side, the slaves would sometimes all together rush to the low side with the intent of capsizing the ship.[99]

Even during actual revolts, it was extraordinarily common for slaves to jump into the sea and drown themselves, many believing that death would return them spiritually to their home country. To combat this belief, one captain ordered the decapitation of any Africans who committed suicide, attempting to send a message to the slaves that "if determined to go, they must return without heads."[100] Other captains tried to avoid the suicide of slaves by rigging a special netting around the ship. As the instructions to the captain of the English *Dispatch* in 1725 stated, "so soon as you begin to slave let your knetting be fix'd breast high fore and aft and so keep 'em shackled and hand Bolted fearing their rising or leaping Overboard."[101] However, despite attempts to thwart it, resistance in the form of suicide remained common throughout the history of the slave trade. In some cases, suicide even took on attributes of insurrection, as Africans determined that they would take as many of slave traders to the grave with them as they could. For instance, Ottobah Cugoano wrote of the attitude of the captives when he was placed in the hold of a slaver, "When we found ourselves at last taken away, death was more preferable than life, and a plan was concerted amongst us, that we might burn and blow up the ship, and to perish all together in the flames."[102] As sad as these stories are, they make clear that some truly felt death was preferable to the terror of enslavement.

People from all walks of life, time periods, and cultures have fought back when oppressed. Of course, personality, temperament, and opportunity all affect the frequency and effectiveness of resistance, but remarkably large numbers of people reach deep down and manage to find the courage and will to resist and survive. The Africans who found themselves loaded onto the ships of the slave trade were no exception. Countless numbers of slaves surely did fall into states of depression and shock that disabled them from mounting any significant defense to their enslavement, but tens of thousands of others overcame these tendencies and became part of the long history of shipboard resistance. Enslavement itself and the horrifying conditions that accompanied it were the motivations behind this resistance. While death, rape, disease, and violence might have stifled the spirit of revolt in one slave, it is precisely these factors that encouraged it in another.

"Stabbed one of the Negroes." Africans engaged the crew in fierce combat.
From Arthur Thomas Quiller-Couch, *The Story of the Sea* (London, 1895–96), 2:433. Courtesy Corbis.

2

Conditions Favorable for Revolt

In the spring of 1750, the Bristol ship *King David,* commanded by Captain Edmund Holland, had purchased some 350 slaves and set sail across the ocean. The vessel left the port of Old Calabar in the Bight of Biafra destined for the West Indian island of St. Kitts. Among the Africans confined to the hold was a man who must have had some prior experience with Europeans on the coast, for he spoke English well, which earned him the captain's trust. Captain Holland was so taken with this individual that he often permitted the man to come to his cabin to speak with him. Other Africans on board also received favorable treatment and were allowed many of the same freedoms as the crew. The journey progressed without incident for some time, but when a number of the crew became ill and died, the significant reduction in crew size did not go unnoticed by the Africans. Down on the slave deck, the English-speaking African formulated a scheme for rebellion and managed to win over a core group of about fifteen conspirators. On May 8, these Africans put their plans into action. At 5:00 A.M., the slaves aboard the *King David,* none of whom was in shackles at the time, rose in a sudden revolt. The leader of the uprising quickly directed his fellow rebels to the captain's quarters to confiscate the weapons he had seen there on numerous visits. The revolt was swift and efficient. Within a few minutes, the Africans had secured the arms, killed the captain and five others, and taken control of the vessel. The surviving crew sought refuge in the ship's hold, where they thought they would be safe from the Africans' assault. The leader of the insurrection called down to them and promised to spare their lives if they would surrender. All but one of the sailors quickly complied and were chained on deck. The Africans then turned their attention to the chief mate, who was the only man refusing to surrender. After a brief stalemate, the Africans sent down a white boy to tell the officer that the slaves would descend into the hold and kill him if he refused to give up. Recognizing the futility of his position, the man relented and emerged from the hold voluntarily.

After a relatively short and coordinated attack, the Africans now had complete control of the ship and all of the surviving crew. Not willing to risk the position they had fought for, the insurrectionists decided around eight o'clock that night that there were still too many sailors alive for their comfort. Nine crew members were thrown overboard and the Africans were about to do the same to the chief mate when one of the revolt's leaders intervened, saying that they needed him alive to navigate the ship and threatening death to anyone who defied his order. For the next twenty-four hours, the vessel drifted at sea as the slaves debated where to take the ship. The Gold Coast, Calabar, and Sao Tome were all suggested but ultimately rejected. Since the ship had already entered Caribbean waters, the leaders of the rebellion decided that another month's sail back across the Atlantic offered too many hazards, and they persuaded the rest of the Africans that they should instead look for an isolated destination in the West Indies where they could get ashore without being observed. This proved more difficult than they had hoped, but five days later, on May 14, the *King David* finally arrived at the island of La Desirade off the coast of Guadeloupe. This island appeared safe, and that evening the Africans ordered the chief mate to lower the ship's boat and sent four of their men to the island, accompanied by two sailors. The Africans were instructed to return to the ship immediately if any whites were encountered, at which time the remainder of the crew would be killed. It is unclear exactly what occurred on the island, but apparently the sailors who went ashore were able to alert local French authorities, and the Africans remaining on the ship put back out to sea. After another five days, the *King David* arrived at the eastern point of Grand Terre island in Guadeloupe, where they anchored. But in spite of the Africans' careful planning and the consequent success of their rebellion, finding a safe place to anchor the captured ship was more difficult than they had anticipated. A sloop with one hundred men was sent to retake the *King David* and succeeded in capturing the ship and the rebels on board, carrying her into Port Louis and thus ending the nearly two-week-old insurrection.[1]

As this case illustrates, while the transatlantic voyage was a truly horrifying experience, it did not defeat the spirit of resistance. And while actions such as escape attempts and suicides were important components in the arsenal of resistance, as previously discussed, they are only a relatively small part of the story. Though some felt that suicide was the best way to conquer their enslavement, others demanded a fighting chance at something greater than death. This is not to say that such men and women were not willing to die in their quest for freedom, but they wanted at least a chance to reclaim their liberty. Like the Africans on board the *King David*, they felt that passivity or self-destruction was pointless. If death or perpetual enslavement was to be their destiny, they owed it to themselves to fight it every step of the way. These were the participants in the many slave revolts that exploded whenever Africans could gain the slightest advantage. There were circumstances that made revolt a more or less viable alternative at any given time, and the success of an insurrection depended on the slaves' ability to identify and take advantage of these circumstances. Many opportunities would be fleeting, but that was often all the Africans needed. As John Newton wrote, "One unguarded hour, or minute, is sufficient to give the slaves the opportunity they are always waiting for. An attempt to rise upon the ship's company, brings on instantaneous and horrid war: for, when they are once in motion, they are desperate; and where they do not conquer, they are seldom quelled without much mischief and bloodshed on both sides."[2] This chapter explores some of these unguarded moments that Africans seized upon, enabling a fuller comprehension of the context in which rebelliousness among shipboard Africans brewed. From the physical location of slave ships on the coast to the many shortages of manpower and shipboard crises that regularly occurred aboard slavers to the culture and status of the Africans themselves, this chapter will explore how the men and women who found themselves enslaved on board the ships of the Middle Passage patiently watched and waited for the perfect opportunity to rise.

REDUCTION IN CREW STRENGTH

Perhaps more than any other factor, the physical location of the slave ship seems to have been a key element that slaves used in deciding when to revolt. Without question a large percentage of shipboard uprisings occurred when slaving vessels were still close to the African coast, where the proximity of the shore provided a constant reminder of freedom and a motivation for resistance. In fact, captains were so concerned with this potentiality that they often chose to disembark at night so that the Africans could not watch in agony as the coast receded into the background. Nevertheless, in spite of such tricks, rebellions on the coast broke out continuously.[3] As Francis Moore reported of his experiences in the Gambia River, "All the Time [a slaver] lies there he runs the Hazard of the Sickness and Rebellion of those Slaves he already has, they being apter to rise in a harbour than when out at Sea; since if they once get Masters of a Ship, in the River, their Escape to Shore is almost certain, by running the Ship aground; but at Sea it is otherwise, for if they should surprize a Ship there, as they cannot navigate her, they must have the Assistance of the White men, or perish."[4] Many Africans felt this was their one chance. Although they did not know where they would be taken, it was clear that they were about to venture on a long journey into the vast expanse of the ocean where the likelihood of ever becoming free would certainly dissipate rapidly. This reality alone provided many with the courage to resist. Of course, as Moore's comments indicate, the crews of slave ships were well aware of the dangers that Africans presented when first boarding a ship or during the first few days at sea and thus made an effort to keep the slaves locked securely below during this time. But for every African who was stirred to rebellion by a ship's proximity to the shore, there were others who remained paralyzed with fear and grief. It is plausible that the extreme shock often caused by the process of enslavement created an environment from which some Africans would need "time to recover, time to regain some stability of reflection, to overcome initial reactions. . . . It would take time for the will to resist to revive, and for resistance to approach effectiveness."[5] The first few days or even weeks on board may have been so traumatic for many Africans that they simply couldn't muster the will to resist. At this time, they would have been preoccupied with simply surviving and dealing with their terrifying new fate. Planning a rebellion was surely the farthest thing from the minds of some slaves. Instead, the thoughts of many were focused on getting used to the movement of the ship beneath them, desperately trying to identify other Africans with whom they might be able to communicate, learning the daily routine, and finding some way to tolerate the tiny amount of space into which they were crammed each night. Though both opportunities and cause for hesitation probably existed on any given slaver along the coast, the historical evidence suggests that revolts did commonly occur when ships were still on or near the coast. However, the reason for this probably involved more than simply a vessel's location.

In truth, it was not so much the sight of the nearby shore that sparked rebellion as it was the reduction of crew manpower during this stage of the slaving process. Vessels belonging to government-owned slaving operations like the Royal African Company occasionally had the luxury of completing their cargo and provisioning their ship in one fell swoop at a trade castle and embarking on their journey across the Atlantic almost immediately. But most slave ships were regularly kept in African waters for weeks or even months at a time as sailors made frequent excursions ashore to acquire slaves and provisions, often leaving the slave ships dangerously undermanned. Independent Dutch traders, for example, spent an average of 200 days on the coast, while those ships belonging to the West Indian Company spent 100 days. And in two studies of the British trade at the end of the eighteenth century, the average stay on the coast was found to be somewhere between 100 and 115 days, although some voyages more than doubled this figure.[6] Throughout this time, sailors were continually busy provisioning the ship, making repairs, trading for slaves, and performing any number of other tasks that required them to be away from the ship for extended periods of time. As John Newton wrote after uncovering a plot aboard the *Duke of Argyle,* "I have reason to be thankfull they did not make attempts upon the coast when we had often 7 or 8 of our best men out of the ship at a time and the rest busy."[7] This situation existed throughout a vessel's stay on the coast, and if the Africans on the slave deck were able to suppress their fear and pain enough to strike at such a time, they had an increased likelihood of success. In 1704, two boats with twelve crew members were on shore, leaving not more than ten sailors on board, when slaves on the *Eagle* of London rose up. A number of slaves managed to gain access to the deck and wage battle with the crew before finally being recaptured.[8] Similarly, in January 1759, slaves on the English ship *Perfect* staged a successful insurrection when more than half of the crew was on shore. In this case, the Africans captured the vessel, killed at least five of the sailors, ran the ship ashore, and escaped.[9] And in the case of an insurrection aboard the French slaver *Ville de Basle* in August 1786, the slaves seized the opportunity to rise in rebellion when they realized that a number of sailors were on shore procuring water, leaving only five crew members on board guarding some 270 captives.[10] The Africans were well aware that success was a long shot, but in such situations, they recognized that they might never again see such an opportunity. Before the rigid regime that would be in place once the ship had begun its passage to the Americas had taken hold, Africans were sometimes presented with their best opportunities to seize control.

But whether it was because of the sight of nearby land or the more practical reality that slave ships inevitably had security weaknesses while on the coast, one of the primary hallmarks of shipboard slave revolts is that they were often tied to a vessel's proximity to the shore. Of the shipboard revolts in the transatlantic slave trade for which the location is known or can reasonably be inferred, 75 percent, or upwards of three hundred, took place in sight of the African coast. By contrast, 21 percent broke out during the Middle Passage, while only 4 percent occurred on ships that had arrived in the New World. As there are 110 instances of rebellion for which the location is unknown, the proportion of incidents occurring on the African coast might well be even higher than 75 percent. Indeed, it seems likely that most of the rebellions in unidentified locations occurred on the coast as well. As Behrendt, Eltis, and Richardson note, however, the high proportion of rebellions near the coast is somewhat misleading because ships regularly spent four or five months in African waters, whereas the transatlantic crossing took less than half that time. Furthermore, the substantially greater chances of a revolt on the coast being witnessed by others, and therefore reported, also suggest that the percentage of known revolts taking place near the coast may be artificially high in comparison with all revolts, known and unknown. Allowing for these variables, therefore, the preponderance of revolts on the African coast may not be as great as the numbers suggest.[11] Whereas Africans on ships in coastal waters may have plotted rebellion in part because of the seeming opportunity the nearby shore offered, those who revolted during the Middle Passage probably did so out of a greater sense of desperation and urgency. But regardless of where or why the Africans rebelled, the most significant point is that they never gave up hope.

A reduction in crew size, strength, and surveillance was one of the pivotal circumstances that slaves seized upon, whether on the coast or not, and it was not only shore excursions that brought about such an opportunity. Injury, sickness, and death could also affect the strength of a given crew, for at just about every stage of a slave ship's voyage, the European or American sailors were subjected to disease environments for which their bodies were unprepared. Illness was especially rampant in West Africa during the rainy season from late summer though early fall, and crews who were delayed on the African coast provisioning their ship or acquiring their allotment of slaves during these months often faced deadly consequences. Both slave and crew mortality declined over time as voyage lengths lessened and medical advances were made, but mortality rates for sailors often reached 20 percent or more, rivaling or even surpassing the death rates of Africans in many instances. In 1716, for example, sixteen crew members died aboard the *Indian Queen*. And in 1769, an astonishing thirty-one of the thirty-nine sailors on board the French slaver *Marie-Gabrielle* died.[12] The potential for sickness was a serious problem on the coast, and the observant Africans were quick to act upon any ailments that might strike the crew. In 1686, for instance, as the English ship *Benjamin* was on its way from Gambia to Antigua, the Africans on board rose against the crew and killed one of the officers. Although details in this case are scant, the letter reporting the incident stated that "[t]he Seamen [were] Sick soe as the Negroes were Neglected," strongly suggesting that it was this neglect brought about by the crew's illness that encouraged the slaves to strike.[13] In other cases, illness was more explicitly considered a cause of slave revolt. In the case of the *King David*, described at the beginning of this chapter, the fact that "a great many" of the crew were sick and dying was an important contributing factor to the slave insurrection.[14] The same year, another successful insurrection aboard the *Ann* was widely reported in the American press and attributed to "most of their white men being sick."[15] When multiple revolts struck the voyage of the *Rebecca* in 1759, they too were noted to have occurred in part because of the fact that those sailors who were not dead were "so feeble" as to be ineffective guards.[16] And in the case of yet another successful insurrection, on the Liverpool ship *Nancy* in 1769, the 132 Africans took advantage of an ill crew when they realized that only 5 able-bodied seamen were left on board.[17] As dangerous as it was commonplace, a crew's illness often provided Africans the advantage they were always looking for.

The log of the slaving ship *Sandown*, which voyaged to West Africa and then on to Jamaica, demonstrates the ways in which crew sickness could debilitate a ship's defenses. Arriving in the area of Sierra Leone in April 1793, the crew spent nearly nine months on the coast before beginning the Middle Passage. They had arrived in the middle of an outbreak of yellow fever that was spreading rapidly along the coast. By December, some of the crew had already died, and on December 18 the disheartened captain wrote, "Fevers and Ague rages very much. Begin to be very uneasy, there being no prospect of soon getting away and all Hands very sickly. The Medicines nearly expended." Two days later, the following note appears in the log: "Departed this life after a Lingering illness of 5 months

Dennis McCorty Seaman aged 36 Years." But in spite of this specter of illness and death, the captain kept loading slaves. Two more Africans were brought on board Christmas day and another two the next. Soon, nearly fifty Africans had been brought on board, and they clearly began to sense that their numbers were large enough to overpower the sickly crew. The details are sketchy, but the captain reported on January 17 that eight slaves were killed and two escaped in an insurrection on board three days earlier.[18] As this case vividly demonstrates, crew illness on the African coast was a very serious problem that did not escape the watchful eyes of the Africans. Once slave ships began the Middle Passage, sailors typically began to recover from the ailments they picked up on the African coast. Therefore sailors were most often incapacitated through illness during the weeks spent along the West African coastline, which may further explain the disproportionately high number of insurrections documented to have occurred at this stage of the voyage.

Sailors understood that illness and death within their ranks put them in a precarious position, and accordingly they sometimes attempted to hide their declining numbers. One way this was accomplished was by disposing of crew members' bodies without the slaves' knowledge. Whereas dead slaves would simply be tossed overboard at any time, crew members who had died were often slipped overboard at night or smuggled ashore.[19]

Injury was also an ever-present danger, as sailors could fall from the rigging while adjusting sails, develop hernias from the constant lifting and pulling that a sailor's work demanded, break an arm when caught off guard by shifting cargo, or burn themselves while tarring ropes.[20] Depending on the severity of these injuries, sailors could be laid up for an extended period of time, unable to play their part in guarding the Africans on board.

Whether resulting from death, absence, or injury, it was not uncommon for the crew of a slave ship to be at less than full strength, and slaves often used this to their advantage. In one analysis of seventeen revolts on Rhode Island vessels, eight of the twelve in which the circumstances surrounding the uprising are known were facilitated by sickness, death, or absenteeism among the crew.[21] A fully healthy crew was by far the exception on slave ships, and the Africans were well aware of the crew's relative strength. The number of sick sailors and the seriousness of their ailments were all carefully noted by the slaves, and this information became a key component of their intelligence gathering as they determined the most opportune moment for insurrection.

SHIPBOARD CRISES

A small or weakened crew was only one of the numerous circumstances that slaves could seize upon to stage effective revolts. Other factors increasing the risk of rebellion included unusually harsh conditions, indifference by the crew toward the welfare of the slaves, and sudden shipboard crises. One fairly frequent crisis that slaves sometimes took advantage of was the frenzy provoked by violent storms or their aftermath, when the crew's attention was not on the slaves. Keeping the ship afloat was all that mattered, and the Africans were locked up and largely left unattended. One can imagine hundreds of slaves crammed into a dark hold, perhaps taking in water from the storm, with violent and deafening waves crashing into the sides of the ship and bodies being heaved back and forth, chains digging into wrists and ankles in the process. This situation was far from beneficial to the Africans, yet they were sometimes able to use a storm as their ally in staging an attack on the crew. It was just such circumstances that helped spark a deadly insurrection aboard the French vessel *Flore* in 1787, allowing the Africans to break out of their shackles while the crew was busy.[22] Sometimes, if rough seas endangered the safety of the ship, the Africans would even be brought up on deck to help. This advantage was surely not lost upon the slaves, and insurrections were occasionally the consequence.

In 1762, for example, as the English ship *Phoenix* was bound from the African coast for Maryland with 332 slaves on board, a strong thunderstorm struck. The ship was severely damaged and rapidly taking on water. The crew did the best they could to pump the water out, but six hours later there was seven feet of water in the hold, the masts and sails were carried away, and the cannons had to be thrown overboard to help right the ship. The crew knew it was facing a losing battle with the storm and realized the slaves must be let out of irons to assist in pumping and baling. With their help, the crew was able to save the vessel for the moment, but the slaves remained out of irons for days as all hands continued to be needed to keep the ship afloat. Most of the food had been washed out to sea, and having gone two days without sustenance, the Africans were becoming increasingly restless and the crew was obliged to put half of the most unruly back in irons. Two days later, weak, hungry, and tired, many of the slaves managed to release themselves from their irons and attempted to break through the gratings and capture the ship. However, the crew was able to defend itself quickly and brutally, killing fifty Africans in the process.[23]

Another type of crisis that captives occasionally benefitted from were encounters with pirates, warships, or privateers. In these situations, as during storms, the key element in the Africans' favor was that the crew was distracted. All of the sailors would have been busy attending to the vessel's swift escape, for capture could very possibly result in death. As a result, the slaves suddenly found themselves relatively free of supervision, and a quick-thinking group of Africans could turn this to their advantage. Encounters with pirates may have offered an especially promising motivation for revolt. Pirate ships displayed a racial egalitarianism unmatched in most other spheres of existence at the time. The Africans wouldn't have known this when a ship was first attacked, but once they were brought on deck to help the slave ship escape or fight, it may have become apparent. If the two vessels were close enough, the Africans may have looked out and seen black faces staring back at them. They wouldn't have mistaken these men for slaves like themselves, for the black pirates would have been fully dressed and armed. This baffling situation may have offered hope. There were certainly no assurances that capture by pirates would end their suffering, and the potential of exactly the opposite also loomed, as the pursuing pirates might have intentions to slaughter all on board or resell the slaves to other ships, but the gamble may nevertheless have seemed worth taking. Of course, other slaves would have felt very differently. Finally having come to grips with their predicament and having carved out some semblance of a stable existence on board, the last thing they would have wanted was a further jolt to their fragile identities. The replacement of old masters with new ones, in spite of any possible benefits, was simply too much to bear. But those who no longer feared death and felt that little could be worse than what they were already enduring might well have been encouraged by the sight of a multiracial pirate crew either to rebel against the slave ship's crew or simply to refuse to fight the pirates or aid the slaver in escaping, preferring to cast their lot with the buccaneers instead.[24]

More common than pursuit by pirate ships, however, were encounters with warships and privateers. As early as 1571, for instance, a Spanish slave ship had neared its destination in the West Indies when it was engaged in bloody battle by a French privateer. Although the details are not clear, the Africans on the Spanish slaver took advantage of the commotion to rise and slit the throats of the crew.[25] When the English slaver *Ann* and all of the Africans on board were captured by the French, the ship was apparently then retaken by the slaves, perhaps in part as a result of the confusion and divided attentions of the sailors brought about by the initial capture.[26] And in 1800, two American schooners were bound for Havana when one of them was chased and boarded by a privateer. The sailors on the second ship, the *Flying Fish,* realized that they must escape quickly to avoid the same fate and thus released the slaves from their irons to help trim the ship. These Africans wasted no time in taking the opportunity to rise against the sailors, killing the captain and a number of the crew and forcing the survivors to take refuge in the ship's rigging. At that point, the privateer bore down upon the vessel and briefly engaged the slaves in battle before the sailors on the *Flying Fish* who were in the rigging called out to the privateer "begging for God's sake to fire, even should they sink her." The resulting broadside by the privateer finally ended the revolt, as the vessel and its slaves were ultimately captured and brought into the Bahamas.[27] While neither stormy weather nor encounters with hostile ships were the most promising situation for slaves to take advantage of, considering that both scenarios involved added difficulties that the Africans would have to overcome in order to be successful, they nevertheless provided that slight crack in security for which the Africans were ever watchful. Promising or not, the slaves realized that this might be the only chance they would see for an effective rebellion.

CREW DISUNITY

Mutiny and other aspects of crew disunity also occasionally provided the opportunity for rebellion, as attentions were divided and vigilance inevitably weakened. These situations were perhaps more promising for the Africans than the cases of shipboard crises discussed above because there were no extra hurdles for the slaves to overcome. Instead, the Africans could simply capitalize on the in-fighting among the sailors. As early as 1685, for instance, a successful slave revolt on the *Charlton* was somewhat cryptically attributed to "Jealousies among the Masters w'ch the Negroes make advantage of."[28] In 1725, two sailors on a slave ship loaded with Africans attempted to persuade their fellow crew members to desert the ship. Although they succeeded in convincing four to join them, the rest of the crew remained with the vessel. As the relieved captain perceptively noted, it was fortunate that this mass desertion attempt wasn't more effective, for had the Africans rebelled, "there could not have been sufficient force to suppress them."[29] Although this vessel was spared, desertion often brought about disastrous consequences, as in the case of a slave rebellion aboard the French ship *Heureux* that was prompted in part by the desertion of six sailors.[30] In 1729, an insurrection on board the American ship *Katherine* was precipitated by a crew mutiny. In this case, the sailors felt that they had been shortchanged by the captain of their share of the slaving profits, so they mutinied and threw the captain into the sea. In the commotion, several slaves were able to rise up and escape.[31] And newspapers reported that the rebellion aboard the Liverpool ship *True Blue,* captured by slaves on the African coast in 1769, was partly the result of "the white people being very mutinous."[32] Clearly, the need for a unified crew to monitor and control slaves was often not met.

Perhaps the most dangerous manifestation of crew disunity that might occur on a slave ship was for a sailor to incite the slaves to rebel. Although such cases were rare, one of the best examples may be seen in the events surrounding a revolt on board the New York ship *Wolf* in 1750. In this case, the insurrection was quickly put down, but it was later determined that the ship's second mate had encouraged the Africans to rise. As the vessel's surgeon reported, the officer instigated the revolt "in revenge to the usage he rec'd from the Capt[ain]" and persuaded the slaves to follow him with the promise of freedom. Apparently, the mate's intention was to capture the ship, kill the crew, take possession of the gold dust on board, and then turn pirate.[33] Once again, divisiveness among the crew nearly led to the loss of the entire vessel at the hands of the Africans. Security on slave ships required constant vigilance, yet vigilance, even where it was so fundamentally needed on a slave ship, often broke down. Officers and sailors lived on different social planes, and physical, emotional, and psychological abuse from those of higher ranks was commonplace. Engaging in everything from shipboard squabbles to outright desertion and even mutiny and murder, the crews of slave ships were often far from unified.

In fact, shipboard life was quite hard and brutal for sailors. Just as slaves could be whipped for various infractions, so too did sailors feel the sting of the lash as punishment for any number of shipboard transgressions, including insubordination, laziness, insolence, and drunkenness. If a clear set of rules and punishments were established, then crew members could go about their day with a reasonable understanding of what was expected of them. But when no such rules had been laid down, officers would customarily dole out arbitrary discipline. Alexander Falconbridge noted numerous eyewitness accounts of the brutal treatment of sailors by officers, including instances in which sailors were severely kicked, beaten with sticks of bamboo, or nearly drowned by having their heads forcibly held under water. Others had knives thrown at them or dogs set on them, and one man was even hoisted into the rigging, stripped, and flogged. Disobedient or mutinous sailors could be abandoned on a remote island, imprisoned on board, or tied to the ship's mast. Whippings were commonplace, as sailors were lashed for the most trivial offenses until their backs were torn to shreds. Officers on slave ships ordered their world around notions of hierarchy and deference, while the sailors they lived among desperately clung to the ideals of equality and autonomy. The gap between these competing and contradictory impulses was often impossible to bridge, and friction and hostility were ever present, often simmering just beneath the surface. Of course the captain's authority was only as powerful as the sailors were willing to tolerate, and when pushed too far, crew members pushed back. As Marcus Rediker has noted, common seamen were usually poor, of humble birth, often illiterate, and driven to the sea by economic necessity.[34] Perhaps bitter and angry at their station in life, surely frustrated by their inability to assert themselves on board, and at the same time terrified by the slaves below deck, slave ship crews were frequently divided and weak. Although the risks inherent on slave ships were such that crews found ways to rise above these issues most of the time and assert their authority for the sake of their own safety, it was the breakdown of their unity, if only momentarily, that sometimes enabled the Africans to strike for liberty.

CREW NEGLIGENCE

Whether it was a storm, a sea battle, or a mutiny, Africans enslaved on board the ships of the Middle Passage seized upon anything that might provide them the smallest advantage. More frequent than any of these relatively unusual circumstances, however, one of the most common conditions that made revolt possible for the slaves was crew negligence. Slave ship voyages were extremely long and complex undertakings, and it would have been virtually impossible to complete an entire journey without moments of lax security. If the Africans on board were watchful and patient enough, the opportunity for an effective rebellion would probably present itself at some time on every slave ship which crossed the Atlantic. Of course, negligence could take a variety of forms. In 1716, for instance, when the London ship *Anne & Priscilla* was on the Gambian coast, the crew not only permitted the slaves on deck to help hoist in the vessel's boat—already a potentially deadly mistake—but they had also carelessly left wood lying up and down the ship's deck. The Africans did not fail to seize upon their good fortune, and using the wood as weapons, they rose against the sailors, killed the ship's captain, and took control of the vessel.[35] In 1765, it was sailors on board the *Sally* of Providence, Rhode Island, whose negligence led to a deadly rebellion. In this case, shortly after the ship had left the African coast for Antigua, a number of slaves were brought up on deck to assist in the ship's duties because several members of the crew were sick. Realizing that this might be the best opportunity for revolt that they would see, the Africans seized the moment and staged an uprising. The crew managed to get the upper hand, however, killing ten slaves in the process.[36]

In 1773, another negligent crew sparked a rebellion aboard the English ship *Bristol* in the Bight of Biafra. In this case, not only did the sailors allow the Africans on deck to assist in navigation, but they also dropped their guard to such an extent that some of the slaves were able to steal the key to the arms room and smuggle out weapons while the crew was eating. These mistakes proved fatal for most of the sailors and ultimately allowed the slaves to capture the ship and reach freedom on the nearby Bonny shore.[37] Yet another example is the 1776 insurrection on board the *Thames* as it lay at anchor off Cape Coast. In this case, while the captain and some of the crew were ashore, the sailors on board decided to let the 160 captive Africans on deck and out of their chains to bathe. This decision was predictably a poor one, for the slaves staged a forty-minute rebellion before finally being put down with the assistance of men from the shore. However, more than thirty Africans jumped overboard, some of whom may well have made their way to land and escaped.[38] These represent just a few of the many instances of crew negligence directly precipitating shipboard slave insurrections. Because it can be defined so broadly, from sleeping on the watch to granting slaves unusual access to sensitive areas of the ship, leaving a storeroom door unlocked, or allowing too many Africans on deck at one time, crew negligence is one of the most common factors leading to shipboard slave insurrections.

NUMERICAL ADVANTAGE OF SLAVES

In spite of its general neglect of shipboard insurrections, much of the groundbreaking work that has been written on the issue of slave resistance in recent years from a plantation perspective also sheds some light on the subject of favorable conditions for shipboard revolt. For instance, one factor commonly regarded as increasing the likelihood of plantation slave revolt was the ratio of slaves to whites in a given population.[39] In this regard, Jamaica, second only to Brazil in its high rate of insurrection, is an excellent example. One reason for this (among many others, such as the absentee nature of Jamaican plantation owners, as well as the island's geography), was the fact that the ratio of slaves to whites ranged from approximately 10:1 to 13:1 throughout most of the island's history of slavery, the highest ratio of any British slave society. This numerical superiority inspired slaves to seize upon their apparent advantage by revolting against the oppressive minority.[40] In such a context, as Genovese suggests, slaves could feel their strength at decisive moments, whereas in a slave society such as the United States, where slaves outnumbered whites only in South Carolina and Mississippi, they "could not help feel their weakness," thus accounting in part for the lower incidence of revolt.[41] Aboard slave ships, the ratio of Africans to whites was rarely less than 10:1 and often as high as 16:1 or 20:1. The sailors were acutely aware of this disadvantage and made efforts to ensure that they weren't overwhelmed by the Africans. An agent for the Compagnie du Senegal serving on a French slave ship in 1682, for instance, lamented that the Africans were forced to endure disgusting conditions below deck, but he recognized that safety demanded that the Africans continued to suffer. As the agent noted, "[W]e did not dare . . . give [them] the freedom to come on deck, as we were only seven Whites against close to 250 Blacks."[42] But in spite of the best efforts of the sailors, the Africans recognized that their numbers put them in a potentially advantageous position. Furthermore, as Genovese suggests, revolts were more likely to occur on plantations with slave populations of one hundred to two hundred slaves, as in Brazil and the sugar plantations of the West Indies. Conversely, in areas such as the southern United States where average slaveholdings rarely exceeded twenty or so slaves, revolt was considered a less effective means of resistance and alternate methods of protest were employed more frequently.[43] Once again, the relevance of this tendency to the context of shipboard insurrections is obvious. With slave cargoes commonly consisting of hundreds of slaves, Africans were certainly amassed in sufficient numbers on slave ships to be inspired to insurrection.

The reality of the slaves' sheer numerical superiority undoubtedly provided psychological encouragement. It must have seemed so tantalizing to the Africans, day after day, to see that there were just a few dozen sailors guarding them. Many would have recognized that if they could only find some way of mobilizing even half of the slaves, they could possibly overwhelm the crew through the strength of their numbers alone. Casualties had to be expected in the initial assault, as the sailors would bring the full weight of their weaponry to bear on the rebels, but after the first onslaught and engagement with the crew, hundreds of African reinforcements would soon be rushing up from below, with a promising chance of prevailing in the struggle. A highly efficient and prepared crew might be able to respond quickly enough to reassert control through force of arms, but a weaker crew might not. As a result, some of the most powerful insurrections on record took place on ships that housed especially large numbers of captives. When Africans who revolted on a Liverpool ship in October of 1772 managed to kill all but one of the crew and take possession of the vessel, for instance, they were able to do so in part because there were 350 of them.[44] Similarly, it was again through the strength of 350 slaves that some of the Africans on the French ship *Sainte Hélène* in 1742 were able to free themselves.[45] And in the successful revolt aboard the *Marlborough* in 1752, at least 420 Africans rose in rebellion, ultimately reaching freedom in West Africa.[46] Recognizing that the numbers were on their side, the most ambitious and rebellious spirits aboard slavers must have agonized about the possibility of overpowering their few white jailers, playing out the scenario repeatedly in their minds and desperately trying to figure out if the risks outweighed the potential rewards.

AFRICAN ORIGINS

Another factor commonly cited in the literature on plantation resistance that tended to increase the likelihood of revolt in a given slave community was the ratio of African-born slaves to those born in the Americas. The suggestion is that when the ratio was high, revolt was more likely because most African-born slaves shared the one significant commonality of having been born free and thus had the common experience of what is was like to have freedom forcibly stolen from them. American-born slaves, on the other hand, were raised from infancy in slavery, and it is argued that their lack of personal knowledge of freedom made them less likely to rise up in defense of it.[47] W. E. B. Du Bois argued that the reason Africans were so dangerous rested in "the fierce and turbulent character of the imported Negro. The docility to which long years of bondage and strict discipline gave rise was absent, and acts of violence were of frequent occurrence."[48] And although more recent scholarship has shown that docility certainly did not govern the lives and actions of American-born slaves, it is nevertheless clear that African slaves were more likely to revolt. For example, Orlando Patterson writes that almost every one of the Jamaican slave revolts of the seventeenth and eighteenth centuries was "instigated and carried out by African slaves." African-born slaves were also prominent in such incidents as the St. Domingue Revolution of 1791 as well as the string of Bahian revolts that rocked eastern Brazil between 1807 and 1835.[49] In fact, the scholarly consensus is that a vast majority of the major revolts in the Americas were instigated by African-born slaves.

Since it does seem clear that a high ratio of African-born slaves increased the likelihood of revolt on plantations, the relevance of this tendency to shipboard slave insurrection is also clear. With a captive population that was always 100 percent African, the frequency of shipboard revolts should come as no surprise, despite the extreme measures taken to avoid them. Even those slaves who were born into domestic servitude in Africa still faced a severe shock when transplanted into a chattel form of enslavement. While some, therefore, did not have total freedom stolen from them, these men and women were nevertheless thrown suddenly into a much more rigid, brutal, and ruthless regime than any of their prior experiences with enslavement had prepared them for. Africans on slave ships still maintained an identity of their own. Absent was the extreme marginalization, domination, and debasement that slave owners would attempt to impose in the Americas—an insidious and calculated process that led to what Patterson has called the "social death" of a slave. The Africans were instead able to cling to their honor, culture, and memory in a way that people born into chattel slavery could not.[50] In short, none of the captives on board a slave ship, whether born free and captured or born slave and sold, had ever experienced the level of physical abuse and psychological brainwashing that so many were subjected to in the Americas to break down their will to resist. Instead, slave ships held captive populations of hundreds of Africans who inevitably felt angry and victimized by their new fate. Any docility that might have resulted from having been born into chattel slavery was missing, and acts of resistance and protest were commonplace.

Accordingly, the fact that slaves aboard the ships of the Middle Passage were all African-born was itself a condition favorable for revolt. There remains, however, the question of whether certain Africans, because of their culture and background, were more susceptible than others to rebellion and, if so, why this may have been the case. After all, it is not inconceivable that the makeup of a given shipload of Africans along lines of status or culture may have contributed to the likelihood of resistance. Following local conflicts, for instance, large groups of prisoners of war were sometimes sold to slave traders who may not even have been aware of their status as trained soldiers. In such cases organized revolt would probably have been a more viable and realistic possibility than it would have been among a group of ordinary civilians. An excellent example can be found in the account of slave resistance culminating on board the French vessel *Sultane* in 1750. Following a civil war between two lineages in the Senegambia region, one slave trader on the island of Goree was able to purchase some five hundred captives whom he imprisoned in a barracoon on the coast. The slave trader described these men as warriors who had recently fought on the side of the deposed king. "Because of their high status in African society," as one historian writes, "where slave warriors served the monarchy and were normally exempt from agricultural labor, the prisoners proved to be dangerous captives."[51] Indeed, the French learned from a child who had been placed in the slave pens for petty theft that a well-planned conspiracy had been formulated among the Africans. The prisoners planned on dividing into thirds, one group attacking the guard, another seizing the arsenal, and the last group dispersing themselves on the island and killing all of the whites. Once in control of the island, they planned to seize weapons, trade goods, and boats and flee to the mainland to rejoin their exiled king. Although the conspiracy was never carried out and two leaders were executed the following day, the trouble was not over, for the remaining rebellious slaves were subsequently sold to the slaver *Sultane*. Once on board, the 500 slaves revolted yet again, and only after 230 of the insurrectionists, 6 sailors, and the captain had been killed was the ship retaken and the Africans secured.[52]

In a similar situation on another French ship some forty years later, the leader of a deadly revolt is said to have been a general of a late Muslim leader who had been defeated by one of his rivals in a local power struggle, after which the general was then sold to the French ship. He immediately assumed a leadership position aboard the slaver, where "he behaved with a sullen dignity, and, even in chains, addressed his fellow slaves, in his wonted tone of authority." Although this charismatic man was able to rally other Africans to his cause, the ensuing revolt was unsuccessful.

When the insurrection broke out, the sailors opened fire on the Africans and killed several of them. In the end, the slaves were recaptured and their leader was executed.[53] Since prisoners of war provided one of the largest sources of slaves for the Middle Passage, particularly as time progressed, there would have been many men and women enslaved on the ships who had some sort of military training or experience. Furthermore, as one historian notes, "by the early eighteenth century, guns were becoming more and more common on African battlefields, and skill in their use was being passed on to a larger and larger group of soldiers."[54] Thus prisoners of war, skilled in both the discipline and tactics of warfare and possibly familiar with the use of European weapons that could be found on board, may well have made up a significant proportion of the leadership of shipboard insurrections. It seems likely, therefore, that the slave population on a given ship might be more prone to violence and rebellion than another, similar-sized population of free Africans would have been.

Familiarity with Europeans may also have been an issue, for there were cases where certain slaves' prior status or occupation in African society allowed them to become familiar with Western behavior, ideas, and languages, thus making them potentially valuable assets in planning and carrying out effective shipboard rebellions. In the case of the deadly insurrection aboard the French vessel *Affriquain* in 1738, for instance, there is the brief but intriguing comment that one of the revolt's leaders was a man who "had sailed with the English," perhaps indicating his possession of some specialized knowledge that his fellow slaves on board did not have, which he used to help initiate the revolt.[55] Similarly, as noted earlier, the 1750 insurrection on board the *King David* was led by a slave who had a good command of the English language and often even spoke with the captain in his cabin.[56] The leader of the revolt on a Brazilian ship headed for Bahia in 1823 also benefitted from his language skills, for he is said to have been a *ladino* who already spoke Portuguese and was thus able to place himself in an excellent position on board. With this advantage, he and his fellow Africans were able to rise up and kill the crew, eventually making landfall in Brazil.[57] Yet another example occurred in 1825 when several slaves aboard the small ship *Deux Soeurs* who had been employed as laborers and boatmen in Sierra Leone led a revolt in which the Africans killed at least eight of the French crew, leaving only three men alive to navigate the vessel back to the coast. The likely familiarity with the slave trade that their prior occupational status gave them may well have helped instigate these slaves to rebellion.[58] The slave trade on the African coast employed local labor for many purposes. From carrying bags to cleaning ships and ferrying slaves to board ships, certain Africans became very familiar with the operation of the slave trade as a function of their employment. And it was not uncommon for these individuals to find themselves seized and sold as slaves themselves. While they probably had no greater knowledge about what lay on the other side of the Atlantic than the rest of the slaves on board, these Africans did stand apart. They were familiar with Europeans and wouldn't have been frightened by their appearance or confused by the menacing slavers anchored off shore. They may have been knowledgeable about the daily routine of a ship on the coast and the moments when crew strength was weakened through absence. Perhaps they had been aboard slave ships in the past bartering for goods and had observed security on board. And in certain cases, as has been seen, they even mastered the language of the slave traders. Although none of this necessarily provided these individuals with any specialized ability to stage effective rebellions, their familiarity with the slave trade did enable them to rise to positions of leadership among the Africans and to relate to crew members in a way that might prove beneficial.

Of course, determining which Africans may have been more or less likely to participate in an insurrection is a highly speculative enterprise. One's initial impulse is to believe that enslavement in and of itself was a more-than-sufficient motivating force for resistance, rather than to look for any societal or cultural conditions that may have preconditioned some to resist. However, the possibility is worth considering, and here again we can look to the work that has been done on plantation resistance as a guide. Indeed, records from the plantations are filled with commentary about African slaves. Great efforts were put into determining which groups were aggressive, which were passive, which would work the hardest, which were the strongest and most robust, and the like. Although often contradictory, popular consensus among slave traders held that the Senegalese were particularly intelligent and responsible. Mandingoes, on the other hand, were supposed to be prone to theft and susceptible to fatigue. Slaves from the Gaboon were considered gullible and inclined towards alcoholism, while Congo and Angola slaves were stereotyped as honest yet stupid and lazy. Also noted as being lazy were the Fon, who had the further distinction of being considered easily depressed slaves who ate too much. Slaves from Calabar were often believed to be suicidal, while the Whydahs, Nagoes, and

Pawpaws of the Slave Coast were thought to be cheerful and submissive.[59] Obviously, such gross generalizations say much more about those making the characterizations than about those being stereotyped, and they tell us virtually nothing about any African's actual likelihood to revolt. However, other comments regarding the background of African slaves may in fact shed some light on the issue of shipboard resistance.

Certain groups developed a reputation for their stubbornness, anger, and violence that was noted by a surprisingly large number of observers. The one group that stands out most in this regard is the Coromantees (also known as the Koromantyn, or Elminas) who represented not a single ethnic or linguistic group but derived from any number of distinct groups from the Gold Coast, including Asante, Akan, Ga, Fanti, Akwamu, and Denkyira, many of whom share similar cultural and linguistic traits.[60] These Gold Coast slaves developed a reputation for participating in slave revolts throughout the West Indies, including the massive and nearly successful revolt in Berbice in 1763–64, Cuffy's plot in Barbados in 1675, a revolt on the Danish island of St. John in 1733, the 1736 Antigua conspiracy, Tacky's Rebellion in Jamaica in 1760, and the Demerara revolt in Guyana in 1823, just to name a few. The leading cell of the 1741 slave revolt in New York City was made up of Akan-speaking Coromantees from the Gold Coast as well. As Peter Linebaugh and Marcus Rediker have noted, many of these slaves "had been an *okofokum,* a common soldier trained in firearms and hand-to-hand combat in one of the mass armies of West Africa's militarized, expansionist states."[61] In 1701, the governor of the Leeward Islands wrote of Africans from this region that "there never was a raskal or coward of that nation. Intrepid to the last degree, not a man of them but will stand to be cut to pieces without a sigh or groan . . . [and] implacably revengeful when ill-treated."[62] A West Indian planter wrote that "being habituated from infancy to war," the Coromantees were "by far the most hardy and robust; yet bringing with them into slavery lofty ideas of independence, they are dangerous inmates."[63] As the West Indian planter and historian Bryan Edwards wrote, "The circumstances which distinguish the Koromantyn, or Gold Coast negroes, from all others, are firmness both of body and mind: a ferociousness of disposition; but withal, activity, courage, and a stubbornness . . . which prompts them to enterprizes of difficulty and danger; and enables them to meet death, in its most horrible shape, with fortitude or indifference. . . . It is not wonderful that such men should endeavour, even by means the most desperate, to regain the freedom of which they have been deprived."[64] Once again, each of these characterizations is made by a white observer and must be considered with both care and suspicion. However, the singular reputation that these Africans gained at the time is nevertheless intriguing and worth considering in relation to its impact on shipboard resistance. Thus, in determining the favorable conditions for shipboard slave insurrections, perhaps one should include the cultural makeup of the Africans on board, at least if they included Coromantees.

Captain William Snelgrave offered some supporting evidence for this, writing, "Sometimes we meet with stout stubborn People amongst [the slaves], who are never to be made easy; and these are generally some of the *Cormantines,* a Nation of the *Gold Coast.*" Discussing the Coromantee leadership of a revolt aboard the *Henry,* Snelgrave noted that these Africans were "the stoutest and most sensible Negroes on the Coast" and were very dangerous and despised punishment.[65] Alexander Falconbridge similarly noted that Gold Coast Africans were "very bold and resolute, and insurrections happen more frequently among them, when on shipboard, than amongst the negroes on any other part of the coast."[66] This was perhaps accurate, for a number of cases of shipboard revolt involving slaves from the Gold Coast do appear in the historical record. In 1770, for instance, the leader of a revolt on board the Dutch ship *Guinese Vriendschap,* was an Asante slave named Essjerrie Ettin, who led his fellow slaves in a nearly successful insurrection before they were finally defeated and Ettin was brutally executed.[67] In 1776, Accra slaves were centrally involved in a revolt on board the *Thames,* and in 1786, it was once again a group of Accras who led a deadly insurrection aboard the Danish ship *Christiansborg.*[68] Thus the idea that Coromantee slaves may have been more likely to revolt on board a slave ship is certainly plausible. At the same time, it is important to point out that the large number of revolts attributed to this group may also be due in part to the simple fact that so many people over such a wide geographical area were all thrown together under the broad term of Coromantee, thus making them stand out disproportionately to other smaller or more specifically and accurately defined cultural or language groups.

Coromantee slaves were not the only ones singled out as dangerous and prone to shipboard revolts. In fact, it seems that just about any group could develop such a reputation following even the most moderately successful insurrection. As Jean Barbot wrote of Africans from the Slave

Coast, for instance, "One thing is to be taken notice of by sea-faring men, that these Fida and Ardra slaves are of all the others, the most apt to revolt aboard ships, by a conspiracy carried on amongst themselves. . . . [They] will therefore watch all opportunities to deliver themselves, by assaulting a ship's crew, and murdering them all, if possible."[69] This comment becomes even more interesting in light of Theophilus Conneau's characterization of slaves from this region as "generally humble, docile, and gentle to manage."[70] Another slave ship captain wrote that the slaves most given to revolt are those from the east of the Cape of Good Hope and those to the north of the Gold Coast.[71] Still another writer declared that it was Bonny slaves from the Bight of Biafra who "are kept under a stricter guard, because they are more vicious, and therefore more care is obliged to be taken against insurrections."[72] Robert Harms notes that the French feared those from the kingdom of Oyo, who were thought to frequently organize revolts on slave ships.[73] In East Africa, it was the Makua who developed this reputation. As one French trader wrote, the Makua "are almost always those who instigate shipboard revolts, and it is necessary to watch them carefully."[74] In other words, determining just which Africans were likely to revolt and which were not appears problematic, for while groups such as the Coromantees may well have been culturally more disposed to meeting their enemy with violence, the record is often biased and contradictory.

In fact, the editors of the Transatlantic Slave Trade database have found that it was not Gold Coast Africans who seem to have been the most prone to shipboard insurrections after all, as ships leaving from this region suffered rebellions at a rate that was about average for West Africa as a whole. Instead, the area that stands out for its rebelliousness appears to be the Upper Guinea regions of Sierra Leone, the Windward Coast, and above all, Senegambia, with its major slaving areas at Senegal, Goree, and the Gambia River. In fact, slaves from Sierra Leone and Senegambia seem to have had a rate of rebellion three to five times higher than would be expected from their share in the slave trade. Furthermore, not only were revolts more frequent, but those leaving from Senegambia were more severe as well, with a much higher incidence of death.[75] Although the prevalence of rebellion in this region may seem surprising, slave traders at the time did betray a fear of the Senegambia in their writing, some insisting that it was Africans from the vicinity of the Gambia River who were most likely to rise upon a ship's company. A group of Liverpool merchants warned captains to "keep a watchfull Eye over you[r] Slaves to prevent any insurrections, which has too often been the Case, especially amongst those of Gambia."[76] In the present analysis, the statistics point to a similar conclusion. As illustrated in the map on the following page, of the 216 revolts in which the specific location of an insurrection on the African coast is stated or can be reasonably inferred, the Senegambia region stands out as the most prominent, with more than forty rebellions occurring in the region. Many of these incidents occurred on vessels in or near the Gambia River, an important waterway in the slave trade, as it was navigable for five hundred miles inland.[77] As early as 1686, for example, a vague letter from an agent of the Royal African Company in Gambia noted simply, "Jobsons Boate was cast away. . . . His Negroes rose."[78] Slave traders in the region learned quickly that this was no anomaly. Thirteen years later, the *Dragon*'s passage from the Gambia to Barbados was delayed by a powerful slave insurrection on the coast costing the lives of two sailors and seven slaves.[79] That very same year, the English vessel *Cothrington* was on the Gambia River when it suffered what appears to have been a successful slave rebellion on board. In this case, the Africans took possession of the ship and forced the sailors to flee.[80] The coming century would see little relief for slave ships trading in the Senegambia, as vessels in the region were struck by at least thirty-seven more revolts before 1800. In a span of just four months in 1716, for example, three different ships on the Gambia were hit with slave insurrections.[81] When Sierra Leone and the Windward Coast are added, these three Upper Guinea regions combined account for eighty-seven revolts, or 40 percent of the incidents in which the specific location of a rebellion on the coast is known. Of course, these statistics should not be taken as an exact indicator of where rebellions occurred, for there are sixty-two rebellions that took place on the African coast for which we do not have a specific location and more than one hundred others for which the location of the revolt is a complete mystery, possibly taking place on the coast, possibly at sea. Nevertheless, based on a sample of the evidence and the findings of other historians, the Upper Guinea region does seem to have played an important role in the history of shipboard slave revolts.

But in spite of the seeming predominance of revolts among slaves from Upper Guinea, it is important to recognize that shipboard revolts were prevalent in all regions of the continent where slave trading occurred. Largely because of the fort at Whydah, the Bight of Benin saw a substantial number of rebellions, with thirty-six separate incidents, or 17 percent of the total. With significant slaving at the major trading forts of Elmina,

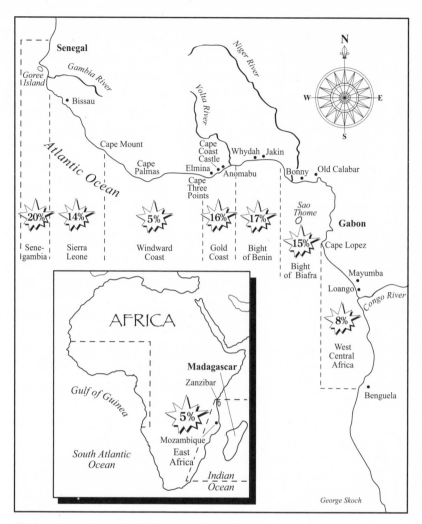

Shipboard revolts on the African coast by region

Cape Coast Castle, and Anomabu, the Gold Coast accounted for a nearly identical proportion of revolts, with thirty-four separate instances taking place there. And with the slaving regions of Bonny and Calabar, the Bight of Biafra accounted for thirty-two separate rebellions. West Central Africa similarly saw substantial slaving and had its share of insurrections as well, accounting for about 8 percent of the total. Thus while some degree of military training or the like may have predisposed certain Africans such as the Coromantee to consider insurrection a viable and realistic means of resistance, the lack of such training in different ethnic or cultural groups does not seem to have discouraged precisely the same reaction, suggesting once again that above all else, it was the simple fact of enslavement that was the true motivation behind revolt. In the more than two hundred cases of revolts occurring on the African coast where the general or specific location is given, over seventy different locales are named. From Senegal to Zanzibar, shipboard slave revolts erupted all along the African coast.

For those Africans aboard slave ships who went to sleep each night dreaming of rebellion, there were a surprisingly large number of shipboard situations that appeared promising and encouraged them in their plans. Sailors could become sick or die, they might fight among themselves, sometimes they would desert a vessel entirely, and they often were absent at times when the ships were still on the coast. Storms or other shipboard crises could provide small lapses in security that the Africans could take advantage of. Negligence was commonplace, and slaves could capitalize on mistakes when sailors permitted too many of them on deck, fell asleep on night watch, or were careless in their supervision of the weapons on board. Even the Africans' numerical advantage over the sailors seemed a potential asset. And if they were lucky, a few of the captives on board might have some familiarity with European languages, customs, or more significantly, firearms. In short, opportunities abounded. However, as the next chapter will illustrate, for all the shipboard conditions the Africans could take advantage of, there were equally as many hurdles placed in their path by the crew. Yet this never completely crushed the spirit of resistance. For the Africans, the decision to rebel did not come about by evaluating the situation completely rationally and selecting the most logical solution, for no option open to them was very favorable. Shipboard insurrection was a matter of acting rashly, risking one's life, and attempting to prevail against overwhelming odds. Though slaves often capitalized on a moment of crew weakness or a temporary breakdown of security to revolt, in the end, rebellions could occur under any circumstances. If an opening failed to present itself, then the Africans would often force an opportunity of their own.

3

Precautions against Revolt

In May of 1704, the English slaver *Postillion* made its way down the Gambia River collecting slaves for the Royal African Company. When the vessel arrived at Joar, the ship's captain, John Tozor, purchased one hundred slaves and was given a drum and a *banisou*[1] by the Royal African Company's local representative, which Captain Tozor was instructed to give the Africans during their journey down the river. Although he protested, arguing that such a move was unsafe while the ship was still in the river, the factor was resolute and ordered that the slaves be given the musical instruments in order to pacify them. The representative believed that distributing authentic local African musical instruments among the slaves might help put them at ease and encourage them to entertain themselves. The captain reluctantly obliged and set sail toward James Island, a fort at the mouth of the river. Down below, the Africans appeared to appreciate the instruments, and before long, loud music drifted up from the slave quarters. On deck, Captain Tozor and his crew went about their normal routine with their ears filled with the sound of African music. No captain or sailor ever felt completely safe with a shipload of Africans on board, but something about this music put them at ease. Little did they know that the melodies they were hearing were in fact a clever camouflage for rebellion. Rather than merely entertaining themselves in an effort to forget their sorrow momentarily, the Africans were in fact using the cover of the music to deftly break free of their shackles. Resting easily on the presumption that the Africans were idly passing away the time, the crew was caught off guard when the slaves rose up and attacked. The element of surprise enabled the slave rebels, armed with staves, to injure seven of the crew, but their momentary advantage was short lived. The remainder of the crew responded quickly and managed to regain control by firing into the crowd of Africans and charging at them with cutlasses. Faced with the reality that victory was not to be theirs, most of the Africans jumped overboard, hoping they could at least make shore and escape, but many of them were captured. Ultimately, thirty-one of the insurrectionists died in battle or by drowning.[2]

As the case of the *Postillion* illustrates, a watchful group of slaves had numerous opportunities, if only momentarily, to stage a potentially successful insurrection. Breakdowns in security, order, and vigilance were commonplace on slave ships. Vessels spent long periods on the coast, where the sight of freedom, just one revolutionary impulse away, could well have stirred thoughts of insurrection. Africans found ways of overcoming traditional barriers and animosities between groups and often forged shipboard relationships that bred a unity of purpose and a determination to resist, making them ticking time bombs throughout the voyage, ready to explode into full-fledged revolt at a moment's notice. However, this is only half of the story, for just as revolt seemed so promising in many ways, captains and sailors made it their constant, and often obsessive, business to crush this spirit of resistance no matter what the cost. This chapter examines some of the methods used on slave ships to extinguish the insurrectionary spark before it had a chance to mature into a real threat. With techniques ranging from perceived kindness to outright brutality, captains and sailors on slave ships spent great amounts of time and money attempting to intimidate, cajole, and manipulate their human cargo into believing resistance was futile, unnecessary, or simply too dangerous. The crew of the *Postillion* believed that the captives could be kept content by offering them the luxury of musical instruments. However, as the rebellion of the slaves on the *Postillion* illustrates, this premise was flawed and could backfire with deadly consequences. Ironically, the very luxuries intended to keep the slaves content were used by the Africans to revolt. Although this insurrection ultimately proved unsuccessful, the captain and crew surely learned that it was never safe to assume that Africans on slave ships were ever content or passive. Thus we see that even measures taken specifically to avoid insurrection often failed to do so. As careful and watchful as a given crew may have been, revolt remained an ever-present possibility.

At the same time, however, the reality is that slave revolts had little chance of succeeding. The reasons for this are obvious. In the first place, the crew, although vastly outnumbered, was well armed, generally well disciplined, and constantly on guard for the smallest signs of disaffection among the slaves. They knew that their very lives were at stake throughout the voyage, and it was in their best interest to be alert and observant. Africans who betrayed the slightest hint of bitterness, hostility, or stubbornness would be singled out and punished, and the slaves soon learned that the sailors took their jobs as prison guards very seriously. One of the few Africans known to have written of his experiences during the Middle Passage noted that "when any one of us became refractory, his flesh was cut with a knife, and pepper or vinegar was rubbed in to make him peaceable."[3] In addition, vessels were well equipped with pistols, muskets, cutlasses, axes, swords, and even cannons. Nearly all sailors constantly had a knife at their side for utilitarian reasons, but obviously a knife also provided some protection and gave the crew an advantage in the event that a revolt broke out. Many ships had guns mounted on swivels so that they could be turned inward and fired into the ship during slave rebellions. These guns could be easily mounted at strategic locations on deck and were extremely efficient in short-range battles, as they were designed to project shot over a wide area.[4] Other ships had loopholes in the bridge covering the hold, through which the crew could fire in case of insurrection. Guards were posted at all times, and ships were carefully searched for hidden weapons such as scissors, hammers, metal bars, and files. Slave ship crews were not unaware of the tradition of shipboard rebellion. They knew well from newspaper accounts, stories recounted by fellow sailors, and their own experiences that the slave trade was a particularly dangerous form of seaborne commerce. Demonstrating this attention to safety, Captain Jean Barbot wrote, "We use [sic] to visit them daily, narrowly searching every corner between decks, to see whether they had not found means, to gather any pieces of iron, or wood, or knives, about the ship, not withstanding the great care we take not to leave any tools or nails, or other things in the way."[5] But as we have seen, the careful attention of the sailors was not foolproof. In one search of the slave quarters aboard an English ship, John Newton reported that his men found two knives and a bag of small stones.[6] Of course, the presence of these items did not necessarily mean that an insurrection was being planned, but it did illustrate that the Africans were able to smuggle items around the ship, and it certainly alerted Newton to the disconcerting reality that he was not aware of everything that occurred aboard his own ship. When the close surveillance of the crew made obtaining weapons impossible, slaves occasionally turned to spiritual measures. Newton wrote of one attempted insurrection,

In the afternoon we were alarmed with a report that some of the men slaves had found means to poyson the water in the scuttle casks upon deck, but upon enquiry found they had only conveyed some of their country fetishes, as they call them, or talismans into one of them, which they had the credulity to suppose must inevitably kill all who drank of it. But if it please God they make no worse attempts than to charm us to death, they will not much harm us, but it shews their intentions are not wanting.[7]

Clearly, one of the most elemental barriers that potential African rebels faced was the crew's fear, which made them eternally vigilant. Sailors may not have cared about the fate of the Africans on board once they reached the Americas, and other than their own salary, they may not have cared about the profitability of the voyage or about how many Africans survived the passage. Some were filled with hatred and self-righteousness, while others surely felt compassion and perhaps even remorse for the obvious brutality of the slave trade. But regardless of how crew members felt about the voyage in particular or the slave trade in general, they all valued their own lives, and this provided the first line of defense against slave revolts.

Furthermore, especially as the journey progressed, the physical differences between slave and crew may have also played an important role, with the better fed, clothed, and cared for crew members able to exert physical control over the comparatively weakened Africans. Of course, this is not to say that crew members on slave ships had an easy time of it by any means. In fact, for the majority of crew members, life on board a slave ship was an extremely grueling and unhealthy experience. Particularly when still on the African coast, death rates for sailors were extraordinarily high, and few slavers left Africa without having some of their crew decimated by disease or death. In many cases, death rates for crew members exceeded those of the slaves. Nevertheless, sailors were not subjected to nearly the same debilitating living conditions that slaves were forced to endure. Once the Atlantic passage began and the unhealthy conditions of the African coast faded into the distance, crews recuperated and began feeling reinvigorated. They knew that the time spent on the African coast was the most dangerous in terms of the potential for slave rebellion, and they recognized that the worst part of the journey was behind them. Sailors now realized that only a few weeks, if all went well, separated them from the end of their long journey and that the payment they had worked so hard for was soon to be theirs. Many drew strength and encouragement from this realization and used it to motivate themselves to become as healthy and strong as possible in order to finish up the voyage without any further trouble.

As the crew gradually regained their sense of vitality and strength, the Africans below deck were going in the opposite direction. Each day that passed found the Africans progressively weakened, dispirited, increasingly sickened by the stench of their quarters, rubbed raw and cut by their chains, and inevitably tired of the horrible routine that had become their lives. They still had no firm understanding of where they were being taken or how long the voyage would last. While some may have developed friendships with strangers enslaved beside them, rivalries would also have ensued because of differences in temperament, age, ethnicity, or a myriad of other factors. Of course, the strongest among the Africans would not be beaten into submission by their fate, and revolts would continue to occur, but as Lorenzo Greene asserts, in general the Africans were "unorganized, undisciplined, and united only in their insatiable desire for liberty. They were unarmed, shackled and weakened by confinement."[8] These conditions alone made revolt appear to be an extraordinarily difficult undertaking, and yet the Africans faced still further impediments. Even beyond the alertness and surveillance of the crew and the harsh physical realties of being imprisoned on board a slave ship, the Africans constantly faced numerous other obstacles to successful insurrection.

BRUTALITY AND VIOLENCE

One of the most important aspects of the power relations between slaves and crew members that helped crush rebellious impulses among the captives was the brutality continually meted out to Africans by sailors on slave ships. Indeed, as C. L. R. James noted, "fear of their cargo bred a savage cruelty in the crew," which served as one of the most effective means of preventing insurrection.[9] As we have seen, the crews of slave ships were not unfamiliar with slave rebelliousness, and many probably tried to learn as much as they could about the hazards before undertaking a voyage to Africa. There is little doubt that virtually every crew member serving aboard a slaver of any nation had either experienced revolt firsthand or had heard tales of the brutal reprisals faced by sailors during shipboard slave insurrections. Such knowledge resulted in a great deal of fear on the part of crew members that, in turn, sometimes led to violence. People often reserve their most brutal tendencies for situations they fear the most. Perhaps in a desperate effort to convince themselves of the docility of the Africans on board their ships—and thus of their own safety, superiority, and righteousness—the crews of slave ships regularly brutalized, beat, raped, and even murdered slaves at all stages of the journey. This brutality served both to reassure the sailors in their feelings of superiority and to terrorize and intimidate the Africans. In some instances, crew brutality could take even more extreme forms, as captains would sometimes cut off the legs and arms of the most willful slaves to terrify the rest into submission.[10] In order to strike fear into the hearts of the Africans, one particularly sadistic captain killed a slave, divided the heart, liver, and entrails into three hundred pieces, and made each of the African captives on board eat one, threatening those who refused with the same savage death.[11]

Because the slave trade was a business, this form of control through violence was normally kept at a relatively benign level. In fact, arbitrary violence of any sort was often frowned upon by ship owners and captains. As the instructions to the captain on a Danish slave trading voyage stated: "It is recommended to the captain that the greatest importance is attached to the conservation of the slaves. He shall personally and frequently see to it that the officers ensure their proper treatment on board the ship, and that no member of the crew strikes or kicks them. The crew shall not mistreat them, but encourage them instead, and be careful when bringing them in and out of the hatches, etc."[12] But these were theoretical instructions written from the safety of the Royal Chartered Danish Guinea Company's offices in Copenhagen. The captain was not transporting crates of merchandise or barrels of alcohol but forcing hundreds of Africans into slavery. The human element on a slave ship—the feelings of fear, hostility, and rage—were such that a daily checklist of activities and a sterile manual on how to treat the Africans was simply insufficient. Each passing day had to be evaluated anew and factors such as sickness, weather, and evidence of slave unrest considered in determining what was safe or unsafe at any given time. Surely Africans were pushed around, given orders at knifepoint, kicked for not responding quickly enough, and generally yelled at, shoved, and tripped by crew members continually asserting their dominance, but this was a delicate process. Scarring, maiming, or killing a slave was bad for business because it would affect his or her value when sold in the Americas. Captains, who bore the brunt of the responsibility for undertaking a profitable voyage, regularly would have stepped in to stop any overt forms of violence that they deemed unnecessary. Furthermore, the sailors had to strike a balance between exerting their authority to intimidate the slaves and pushing their violence to the point of enraging the Africans and prompting them to fight back. Brutality toward slaves was not uniform or constant, but it could be unleashed at any moment, whether arbitrarily or in a calculated effort to intimidate. Many Africans were spared the brutality and violence of sailors, but as the examples above indicate, extreme violence was not unheard of, particularly when used to make an example of an African who had challenged the authority of the ship's crew, and the consequences of this type of extreme violence and brutality should not be underestimated. In moderation, sailors' brutality toward slaves undoubtedly filled the hearts and minds of even the most courageous Africans with a certain level of trepidation.

NEGLECT OF SLAVE HYGIENE

Beyond physical, psychological, and emotional violence, ship captains took still further precautions to ensure a safe journey across the Atlantic. The personal cleanliness of the slaves, for example, was often willingly sacrificed to avoid the risk of allowing Africans on deck to wash. Captains knew well the potential dangers of permitting groups of captives on deck at one time, particularly for bathing, which required them to be at least partially released from their bonds. However, bathing was considered of vital importance for maintaining the health of the slaves, and thus for maximizing the profits of the human cargo, so captains had little choice. Slaves were often brought on deck for bathing once or twice a week, sometimes in small groups, sometimes unchained, but nearly always under the watchful eye of armed sailors. Seawater would be hauled up and the Africans would be given the opportunity to wash. But in spite of the precautions captains employed at these dangerous moments, revolts still occurred, as evidenced by the revolt on board the *Thames* when 160 slaves were on deck and out of chains to bathe.[13] Adequate cleaning of waste from the holds was also abandoned by some ship captains because of the danger inherent in unshackling slaves for that purpose. Once again, this must have been an agonizing choice for the captain and sailors, for they knew that the unclean slave quarters could be a breeding ground for diseases that might devastate both slaves and crew. Thus, finding a way to clean the hold was important, but doing so safely was a challenge. Most captains found ways to clean the filth from the slave quarters periodically, while the slaves were on deck eating or otherwise occupied. In many cases, vinegar would then be sprinkled throughout the area in an effort to disinfect and deodorize it. At times, a red-hot cannon ball would be placed in the bucket of vinegar to give off an especially powerful odor. The instructions to one Danish slave ship captain mandated: "Three times a day the ship must be washed down inside and out, and every morning, while the slaves are eating on deck, the hold where they slept must be cleaned out. . . . Three times a week the quarters are fumigated with juniper . . . occasionally with gunpowder, followed by a sprinkling of vinegar."[14] However, careful cleaning was probably not done as often as health concerns required. Cleaning the slaves' quarters to maintain their health and profitability sometimes led to disaster for the ship and crew. A successful revolt aboard the French ship *Diane* off the Gabon coast in 1774, for example, was sparked when the women's quarters were opened to empty the toilets.[15] Because of such potentially disastrous circumstances, slave ship captains typically attended to the health and hygiene of the Africans on board only so far as they deemed absolutely necessary, contributing in no small way to the severely unsanitary conditions that slaves were forced to endure on board slavers.

SHIP DESIGN

In other cases, the very design of slave ships mediated against revolt. Many vessels were constructed with a raised deck at the stern of the vessel. From this elevated vantage point, a ship's officers and crew could more easily monitor the actions of their slaves and could occupy an excellent defensive position in case of insurrection.[16] In addition to this structural advantage, many slave ships regularly had *barricadoes*, also known as slave bulwarks, built on deck. These were partitions as much as ten feet high that were built near the middle of the ship, stretching across the width of the deck and often projecting a few feet over each side. This wall effectively divided the deck into two halves and was designed to keep the male slaves toward the front of the vessel separated from the crew and the African women and children toward the stern. In some cases, a second, smaller barricado known as the front bulwark would be added to provide additional security for sailors on the forecastle. And in a gesture implicitly acknowledging the danger posed by African women, yet a third barrier was sometimes built near the stern to keep the sailors separated from the women. When a slave ship reached the African coast and began unloading its trade goods, perhaps the two most important jobs facing the carpenter were retrofitting the hold so that it could serve as the slave quarters,

"Insurrection on board a slave ship." Crew members are shown here in a defensive position on the poop deck behind a barricado. From William Fox, *A Brief History of the Wesleyan Missions on the Coast of Africa* (London, 1851), 116. By permission of the British Library.

including the construction of a partition separating the men from the women, and building the barricado. The barricado stayed in place for most of the Middle Passage and regulated the areas that slaves were allowed to occupy at important times such as meals, exercise, and bathing. At the central door, a sentinel was placed to make sure order was maintained. If the slaves became unruly, the barricado had one other useful function, for it was typically pierced with several small holes through which sailors could fire on rebellious Africans or stab at them with half-pikes. Barricadoes often had one or more swivel guns attached that could be quickly turned and aimed at the slaves with deadly consequences. To cut down on slave deaths, these swivel guns would sometimes be loaded with peas, sufficient to cause substantial pain and help quell an insurrection but typically not life-threatening.[17]

As Alexander Falconbridge tellingly noted, barricadoes were "found very convenient for quelling the insurrections that now and then happen."[18] On December 7, 1750, Captain John Newton expressed a similar reliance upon barricadoes when he noted in his journal, "This day fixed 4 swivel blunderbusses in the barricado, which with the 2 carriage guns we put thro' . . . make a formidable appearance upon the main deck, and will, I hope, be sufficient to intimidate the slaves from any thoughts of an insurrection."[19] Of course, some Africans refused to be intimidated by anything. On the day before the British *Tryal* reached Barbados, the slaves on board used a knife they had smuggled below to break out of their chains. Just before daybreak, they revolted suddenly and forced their way through the hatch and on deck. An observant sailor spotted the Africans, however, and immediately raised the alarm. A cannon was quickly loaded, pointed through the barricado, and fired at the rebels. Fourteen Africans were immediately killed in the blast, and the remainder fled below deck.[20] This failed rebellion shows how significant barricadoes were in minimizing the threat of a slave rebellion. Not all ships were equipped with these constructions, but those that were presented yet another formidable obstacle that the slaves on board would have to overcome if they were to have any chance at an effective rebellion.

SPIES AND INFORMANTS

Barricadoes provided an obvious physical device for observing the Africans and limiting their mobility. The slaves could see and feel this wall and could begin to formulate ideas on how to overcome it. However, other impediments to rebellion were not so obvious. One relatively common and particularly devious way of monitoring the actions of slaves was to use other Africans strategically against them. This method, which would be used against slaves and their descendants for centuries to come, left the Africans uncertain of exactly whom they could trust. At times, for example, Dutch ships employed free Africans who could understand a number of different languages to act as spies, while Portuguese ships would customarily hire African healers as nurses and surgeons for the same purpose.[21] Some captains employed Africans in other manipulative ways to guard against insurrection and discontent. Captain William Snelgrave, for instance, made sure that one of the first individuals his slaves met upon boarding the ship was a sympathetic interpreter, who could reassure the captives by informing them of their destination, offer them what was surely an idealized version of their probable fate, and dismiss the ever-present rumors that Europeans were cannibals.[22] Africans were terrified at first by their new surroundings, and hearing a fellow African speak to them in a familiar language surely helped alleviate some of their fears. In the process, captains hoped the slaves would more easily come to grips with their enslavement and be less likely to plot hasty rebellions out of fear and confusion. Furthermore, the Africans hired to calm and reassure the captives simultaneously acted as informants, and kept the crew apprised of any rumblings of rebellion circulating within the slave quarters. These tactics would occasionally pay off. In one case, after an unsuccessful 1721 revolt on board the English ship *Henry,* the slaves began plotting once again. The crew discovered the conspiracy because some of the ringleaders had proposed to one of the ship's African linguists that they would become his servants for life if he would help them revolt. To the slaves' dismay, however, the linguist revealed the plan to the ship's crew, who took the necessary measures to end the conspiracy.[23] In another case, Aye, an African who had signed on as an ordinary seaman and interpreter for the slaving voyage of the Danish ship *Fredensborg,* was instrumental in preventing a rebellion. In his journal, the captain recorded that Aye had informed him that several of the male slaves on board had banded together and were planning a rebellion. Aye was able to find out that the Africans intended to strike when all the crew members were eating, at which time they would seize the sailors' knives and murder them.[24] When the plot was revealed, the insurrection was avoided. Africans like Aye lived in a strange world in between that of sailor and slave. Not trusted by their fellow crew because of their potential for joining the Africans in revolt, and equally distrusted by the slaves, who probably found it difficult to see an ally in these men, Africans like Aye probably lived a lonely and marginalized existence on slave ships.

Of course, men such as Aye were often detested by the slaves on board, who saw them as traitors to the cause of liberty. When slaves on board the *Rainbow* revolted in 1758, for example, one of the sailors they killed was the ship's linguist, who was taken aboard at Benin.[25] Similarly, a revolt aboard the American slaver *Coralline* in 1808 was precipitated in part by the cruelty of the ship's "mulatto" overseer, Shakoe. As the account of this incident reports, "the mulatto was hated by every slave on board," and when he became particularly enraged one day and decided to take it out on the slaves with his whip, the captives decided they had had enough. The slaves "attacked Shakoe, and beat his brains out. . . . His head was all beaten to pieces—a ghastly sight, and the negroes tore his whip into bits not bigger than [one's] finger."[26] The Africans' hatred of this individual was apparently quite intense. His physical appearance may have intensified their rage, for the slaves may have hoped that the kinship they clearly shared with this man would soften the treatment they received at his hand. When exactly the opposite turned out to be the case, the captives may have felt a sense of betrayal and thus singled him out for brutal execution. Despite the potential for such retribution, African crew members often enabled sailors to detect and avoid planned insurrections. But like other efforts to keep the slaves in check, hiring Africans to discover plots or conspiracies did not always have the intended effect. In some cases, the presence of African crew members may have instigated rebelliousness among the slaves.

In one rebellion around May of 1728, for example, an African *grometto,* or ship's hand, on board the English vessel *Queen Caroline* was hired to assist the crew in trading for rice on the Sierra Leone coast but duped the captain and crew into trusting him while secretly organizing the twenty slaves on board in an elaborate and ultimately successful plan for revolt. After going ashore with four sailors on the pretense of trading, the grometto and his accomplices on shore suddenly seized the crewmen and killed two of them. Expecting the sailors to be gone for the evening, those left on the ship had no reason to suspect anything had gone wrong. The next morning, the grometto returned to the *Queen Caroline* with four or five Africans, telling the captain that the boat was loaded with goods and would soon be on its way. Failing to recognize the deception, the captain relaxed and waited for the boat to arrive. However, as soon as he got the chance, the grometto put the second half of his plan into action, going on deck and persuading the slaves on board to join him in a rebellion. In the ensuing revolt, all but one of the crew was killed, the slaves secured their freedom, and the grometto plundered the vessel of its goods.[27] In another case, African members of the crew are reported to have assisted in the revolt on the Portuguese slaver *Feliz Eugenia* in 1812.[28] And after a revolt aboard the *Africa* as it lay at anchor in the New Calabar River, the crew began to suspect it was an African sailor serving as the ship's cook who helped the slaves to revolt. The suspicion was that this man furnished the slaves with the cooper's tools so that they could break out of their irons. As punishment, the cook was chained with a neck collar to the masthead, where he was restrained day and night with nothing but one plantain and one pint of water to sustain him. After five weeks in this state, the cook finally died.[29] In spite of these few examples, however, slaves rarely received assistance from crew members in plotting and executing insurrections. In the vast majority of cases, African members of the crew did as they were told, listening and observing, and sometimes using the information they obtained to crush incipient slave rebellions before the Africans had a chance to strike. Using such individuals against the captives in this way was yet another part of the multifaceted effort of slave traders to insulate themselves as best they could against the potential wrath of the enslaved Africans.

LANGUAGE AND CULTURAL BARRIERS

Some captains also attempted to avert insurrections by mixing Africans of various ethnic backgrounds in order to create the obvious communication problems associated with language barriers and cultural conflicts. There was often a great diversity of people enslaved in the hold of a slave ship that mitigated against the formation of a unified group. The racialized concept of black Africans coming together to fight and defeat white slavers was foreign to Africans, particularly in the early days of the trade. Their ethnic, cultural, and linguistic traditions were the basis of any ties of kinship they may have shared with their fellow slaves, and it was these same traditions that often led to hostility between individuals and groups. If a slave ship were filled with prisoners of war from a local conflict, which was often the case, there may well have been soldiers who had once fought against one another on the battlefield and now found themselves enslaved together, sharing a common fate. Such individuals may well have had little interest in joining a unified cause and may even have taken pleasure in spoiling the insurrectionary plans of one another. On a more benign level, people from different language groups may simply have been unable to communicate effectively with one another, making the planning of a rebellion nearly impossible, even when it was a mutually desired goal. In a revolt on board the French ship *Licorne* in 1788, for example, when the ship was three days out from Mozambique, the ultimate failure of the insurrection was attributable in part to the fact that only a portion of the 446 slaves on board participated. Of the four main ethnic groups comprising the slave cargo, one group had to wage the battle on its own, for the rest of the Africans were, for one reason or another, uninvolved.[30] Such breakdowns in communication and unity probably hindered a great number of conspiracies and revolts throughout the history of the slave trade.

Although these impediments to revolt sometimes emerged naturally, at other times captains made a concerted effort to mix the Africans so as to avoid revolt. Late in the seventeenth century, one captain noted that "the means used by those who trade to Guinea, to keep the Negroes quiet is to choose them from severall parts of ye Country, of different Languages; so that they find they cannot act jointly."[31] Similarly, after noting that "I have known some melancholy Instances of whole Ships Crews being Surpriz'd, and cut off," Captain William Smith stated that "the safest Way is to trade with the different Nations . . . and having some of every Sort on board, there will be no more Likelihood of their succeeding in a Plot, than of finishing the Tower of *Babel*."[32] As a case in point, during the 1721 revolt aboard the *Elizabeth,* Snelgrave noted that "above one hundred of the Negroes then on board . . . did not understand a word of the *Gold Coast* Language, and so had not been in the Plot."[33] And in the case of the English vessel *Brome,* an intriguing report noted simply that when "the Jollofes rose, the Bambaras sided with the Master."[34] Mixing the Africans worked equally well on the *Fredensborg,* on which a planned insurrection failed in part because of ethnic divisions among the slaves. Not only were some of the Africans unwilling to participate in the rebellion, but their hostility toward its leaders was such that they even warned the crew to watch them carefully.[35] Clearly, a culturally and linguistically diverse population of slaves may well have helped to avert slave rebellions, and many captains worked hard to assemble precisely such a divided and incompatible assortment of Africans. When captains failed to follow this rule, however, the results could be devastating, as seen in the revolt aboard the English ship

Ferrers. Even though he was warned by another captain "that as he had on board so many negroes of one Town and Language, it required the utmost care and Management to keep them from mutinying," the captain and his ship nevertheless fell prey to a bloody insurrection that claimed his life as well as that of some eighty slaves.[36] Guarding against such a unified group of Africans was something that sailors definitely took seriously. Even if it was ultimately an underestimation of the Africans' ingenuity and rebellious spirit to assume that they could not find ways of overcoming their differences, captains and sailors felt it was a very good precaution to make sure whenever possible that cultural or language divisions existed among the Africans on board. As Peter Wood has written about slavery in colonial South Carolina, most of those involved in the enslavement of Africans believed that "the whites have no greater security than the diversity of the negroes' languages," and this same philosophy reigned on board ships.[37]

On the other hand, however, Wood goes on to note that the remarkable number of slave rebellions that occurred suggests that the common goal of all slaves to become free may have enabled them to come together despite language differences. As he asserts, slaves "were distinctly aware of inter-relations between African languages, yet whites remained oblivious to these links." Thus, the precaution of mixing a slave ship's captives across linguistic lines may not have been quite as effective as captains intended. In fact, it has been suggested that the "shipmate" relationships forged between strangers in the holds of slave ships stimulated dynamic cooperative efforts at survival and resistance that may be considered "the true beginnings of African-American culture and society."[38] The holds of slave ships were perhaps the sites where the long tradition of African American resistance first developed into a coherent and somewhat unified movement. In this way, apparent language or cultural barriers could have been transcended, and the insurrectionary unity of the Africans may not have suffered nearly as much as has been commonly assumed. It was aboard slave ships that men and women of different backgrounds first forged, by necessity, valuable bonds of solidarity that were to remain strong and fundamentally important for many enslaved Africans and their descendants. As has been argued in regard to slaves in Demerara, Guyana, "it is possible that even those who were from ethnic groups constantly at war in Africa but who spoke the same language would become allies."[39] As Michael Gomez suggests, the Africans who found themselves enslaved on board the ships of the Middle Passage certainly did not fail to notice that "all who were in chains were black, and nearly all who were not were white." Although most Africans were not culturally accustomed to identifying themselves along racial lines, this visual reality may have encouraged some degree of bonding based on race. Africans of various ethnic backgrounds, "who had never considered their blackness a source of relation let alone a principle of unity, became cognizant of this feature perhaps for the first time in their lives" and, on the basis of this revelation, were able to unite otherwise distinct individuals in one common revolutionary body.[40] Thus, while the perceived language and cultural barriers between captives that slave traders relied so heavily upon for their security may well have smothered the insurrectionary spark on some slave ships, it failed to do so on many others. Rather, captive Africans found ways to embrace their new situational racial identities, as perplexing and limiting as they were, and use them to mount powerful and united attacks against their captors.

Interestingly, all of the precautions and regulations taken by ship captains and crew members to avoid revolt also serve to reinforce the fact that insurrection was an integral part of the slave trade and are perhaps the best way to comprehend the true extent to which Africans resisted their enslavement. If revolts were not a constant and dangerous threat to slave traders, the records of those involved in the trade would reflect a much more confident and superior tone. As it is, however, many captains, crews, and observers of the trade continually alluded to the rebellious nature of the Africans and to the threat that their rebelliousness posed to the crew, betraying an underlying fear in the process. Virtually all ship owners and financiers who sponsored slaving voyages gave very detailed instructions to the captain on nearly all aspects of the trade—what goods to carry, how many slaves to buy, how to deal with crew quarrels, where to trade on the African coast, and tellingly, how to avoid slave insurrections. As early as 1522, for instance, a Portuguese captain on a trading voyage to Benin was instructed to "keep good guard and watch upon the arms that are in the ship, so that they do not come in the hands of the negroes; thus no mischance shall befall."[41] Thirteen years later, the slaving contract for the *Sam Christova* stipulated that the captain "have caution and vigilance in that which concerns the slaves . . . so that they do not rebel or produce any trouble like we have seen before."[42] In addition to such examples in instructions to captains, similar fears emerge in the writings of those who had experienced the slave trade firsthand. In 1716, one exasperated captain wrote to his ship's owners that "the Negroes Dayly Threaten Us w'th Cutting Us off, Nay if a Vessel has but Thirty Slaves they are for attempting to rise."[43] Captain John Newton, who experienced the threat of insurrection on his ships on at least four separate occasions, wrote in 1788 that the slaves "were frequently plotting insurrections and were sometimes upon the very brink of mischief, but it was always disclosed in time," adding that "when most quiet they were always watching for opportunity." After one conspiracy was uncovered, Newton perceptively noted that "they still look very gloomy and sullen and have doubtless mischief in their heads if they could find opportunity to vent it."[44] Another example of this apprehension can be seen in the comments of Captain Thomas Phillips, who noted:

> When our slaves are aboard we shackle the men two and two, while we lie in port, and in sight of their own country, for 'tis then they attempt to make their escape, and mutiny; to prevent which we always keep centinels upon the hatchways, and have a chest full of small arms, ready loaden and prim'd, constantly lying at hand . . . together with some . . . [grenades]; and two of our quarter-deck guns, pointing on the deck thence, and two more out of the steerage, the door of which is always kept shut, and well barr'd.[45]

Yet another captain reported, "I put them [the slaves] all in leg-irons; and if these be not enough, why then I hand-cuff them; if hand-cuffs be too little, I put a collar round their neck, with a chain locked to a ring-bolt on the deck; if one chain won't do, I put two, and if two won't do, I put three. . . . These are not cruelties; they are matters of course; there's no carrying on the trade without them."[46] Finally, the writings of Captain Jean Barbot also reveal the fear of slave captains. He cautioned that "it has been observ'd before, that some slaves fancy they are carry'd to be eaten, which makes them desperate; and others are so on account of their captivity so that if care be not taken, they will mutiny and destroy the ship's crew in hopes to get away."[47] It would take many pages to record all the fears and misgivings of slave ship captains and crews in relation to their physical safety at the hands of their potentially mutinous "cargo," but these few examples are enough to suggest that the fear of slave revolt, and thus slave revolt itself, was not at all uncommon throughout the history of the trade.

Both Africans and ships' crews understood, if imperfectly, their relative strengths and weaknesses, and this reality resulted in a fascinating war of deception, manipulation, misperception, and constant observation by both sides that lasted throughout a slaver's long voyage, filling the days and weeks with an uneasy tension. Opportunities continually arose that made revolt seem a viable option to the Africans, while ships' captains and crews simultaneously employed a constant array of precautions to make rebellion seem fruitless and self-destructive. Those who found themselves enslaved weighed their opportunities against the crew's wariness on a daily basis, and the Africans' decision at any given time to revolt or remain peaceful must have been agonizing in either case. If a window of opportunity seemed too small, the anxious and frustrated slaves had to face the possibility that they might never get another chance. They knew that their decision to wait was a gamble that might well end in their perpetual enslavement. However, the choice to seize upon the moment and revolt was an equally distressing one, for while the chance at freedom and the knowledge that they were not submitting passively would have fueled the Africans with courage, they were also fully aware that a poorly timed or ineffectually planned revolt would probably lead to death on a massive scale and increased brutality and restrictions for the duration of the voyage. This agonizing choice between slavery and freedom, between fear and courage, and very often between life and death is what faced the millions of Africans who crossed the Atlantic. Shipboard revolts were not something lightly embarked upon, and when they occurred, it is safe to presume that most were undertaken with great deliberateness and care. Some would succeed while others would fail, but shipboard revolts continued to take place time and time again. In the next three chapters, the revolts themselves are explored in detail, thereby illustrating the ways in which shipboard slave insurrections were carried out by Africans over the many centuries of the slave trade.

4

Revolt

On the night of December 2, 1769, the captain and crew of an English slaver retired to their quarters as they had done so many nights before, unaware that this night was to be like no other. The ship, a Liverpool vessel named the *Delight,* was anchored off the coast of Little Cape Mount on the Windward Coast. As the majority of her crew lay asleep, the Africans below were wide awake, preparing to wage war on the crew who had taken their freedom. Around 3:00 A.M., under the cover of darkness, the slaves turned their plans into action. Somehow, the Africans managed to get out of their chains and on deck, surprising the small group of men who had been assigned to keep watch for the night. Armed with a variety of weapons, including billets of wood, a cutlass, and a broadax, the slaves swiftly engaged these men in battle and killed them. After gaining the upper hand on deck, several of the rebels turned their attention to the rest of the crew sleeping below, who the Africans must have known would soon try to reenslave them once roused. The Africans raced to the crew's quarters where the ship's surgeon, the cook, and the others slept. Awakened by the noise, the surgeon rushed to the captain's quarters to wake him but was pursued by the slaves and managed to escape up the ship's mainstay with great difficulty, having been injured by blows from a billet of wood and a cutlass. As the surgeon fled from the pursuing rebels, it was apparent that the crew was no longer in control of the vessel. Instead, gazing down on the mayhem below he saw a deck littered with dead bodies, many of them his fellow crew members, including a young man who lay bleeding and pleading for mercy, having had his arms and legs cut off. Now in control of the deck, the Africans turned their attention to the rest of the crew, who by this time were rushing up from below. The sailors were no match for the Africans, however, and all of them were killed except for the cook and a boy, both of whom joined the surgeon by fleeing into the maintop for protection. Two others who had avoided the Africans' notice attempted to join their fellow crew members in the rigging about an hour later, but only one made it, as the second was caught trying to climb up the mast.

The Africans now had the few surviving whites cornered but found it difficult to attack the sailors from below, not yet having discovered the cache of muskets on board. Furthermore, the crew members in the maintop and the foretop were able to arm themselves with knives and other weapons. As the sailors moved between the maintop and the foretop looking for additional weapons, the Africans attempted to knock them out of the rigging by throwing wood at them but only managed to injure the cook in the process. High above the chaos below, the few surviving crewmen felt a sense of relative safety, realizing that the Africans' weapons could not reach them and that they could easily defend their position against any of the rebels who climbed up and tried to overtake them. However, this sense of security was tenuous, because the sailors knew that the *Delight* carried muskets and that their safety depended on the Africans inability to locate them. Their hopes of escaping were quickly dashed when an African woman who apparently spent much of her voyage in the crew's quarters led the rebels to the firearms supply. As the standoff continued, now nearly four hours old, the *Delight* was rapidly drifting toward another slaving ship, the *Apollo,* as a result of her cables having been cut by the Africans during the revolt. Rather than forcing the ship toward land as they had intended, setting the ship adrift had instead sent her barreling toward an ally of their enemy. Recognizing this fortuitous turn of events, the sailors in the ship's rigging called out to the crew of the *Apollo* to alert them of the revolt that had crippled their ship. The Africans also recognized the significance of the presence of the *Apollo* and knew that the cries of the sailors would eventually be heard. To prevent this, the Africans let loose a barrage of musket fire, attempting to kill the *Delight*'s surviving sailors before the *Apollo* became aware of the situation.

One of the four crew members, terrified by being fired on by the slaves, decided to try to cut a bargain with the Africans by offering to help them sail to safety in exchange for sparing his life. But the offer was too little and too late from one who had likely shown little mercy or compassion for the slaves' predicament prior to the insurrection. Not needing his assistance and granting him no mercy, the Africans quickly caught him, split his skull with a broadax, and threw his body into the sea. Despite the slaves' efforts to keep the insurrection on board a secret from the nearby *Apollo,* that vessel's captain had either seen or heard the commotion aboard the *Delight* and soon gave chase, firing upon the fugitive ship and her new African masters. Angry at the crew members' success in bringing the unwanted attention of the *Apollo* and frustrated at having come so far only to have this new obstacle placed in their way, the Africans again fired their muskets at the crewmen in the rigging but only managed to wound the cabin boy. When this tactic did not have the desired effect, one of the Africans armed with a pistol and a cutlass attempted to climb up to the three surviving crew members and kill them but fell overboard when the surgeon struck him over the head with a bottle. But at this point the sailors on the *Delight* were the least of the Africans' concerns, and they turned their attention to fighting off the advancing *Apollo.* The two ships engaged in battle for the next four hours, and the Africans succeeded in killing one of the *Apollo*'s men. The insurrectionists showed no sign of backing down until a barrel of powder exploded on the *Delight,* setting it on fire. The *Apollo*'s captain seized the opportunity to have his crew board the *Delight* and retake the burning ship. After controlling the *Delight* for nine hours, the slaves were ultimately defeated by the armed men from the pursuing ship, who doused the flames and reenslaved the rebels. The battle, which claimed the lives of as many as thirty slaves and ten crew members, had come to an end—forty more lives lost to the brutality of the slave trade and the countless rebellions it sparked.[1]

When captured Africans found themselves on slave ships, they were confronted with a profoundly frightening and confusing situation. For the sake of their own mental health, they had to adjust quickly. However, adjustment did not mean acceptance, and the minds of many soon turned to resistance. While still on the coast, slaves knew that they could always try to escape by quietly slipping overboard in the middle of the night or during an unguarded moment when assembled on deck for meals or exercise, but it was obvious that such opportunities were severely limited. They quickly realized that their best chance of making it off of the ship alive and free was to take up arms against their captors. Of course, not all Africans would participate, but for those who did, when the time for rebellion came, the first few moments could be the most important of their lives. For some, the revolt would be over in a matter of minutes and lead to death and suffering on a massive scale. For others, such as those on board the *Delight,* the battle might be fought for hours or even days. But only the most fortunate rebels would beat the odds and regain their freedom. A careful exploration of the pivotal moments in the lives of the African insurgents will help us break down the elements of shipboard slave revolts in order to understand the broader phenomenon more fully. Although shipboard revolts occasionally occurred spontaneously when Africans suddenly recognized that a given situation was favorable to them, such opportunistic revolts were the exception. In general, revolts appear to have been carefully, patiently, and secretly planned by the Africans, who realized that they probably would not get a second chance. Rushing into a rebellion before being adequately prepared was foolhardy. Risks had to be weighed, leaders had to be selected, weapons needed to be obtained, and the plan had to be understood by all who were to participate. In addition, the mobility, gender, age, and status on board of all participants had to be considered in the planning of shipboard rebellions. The rebellion on board the *Delight* was marked by many common features of slave revolts such as the important role of women, the creative use of weapons by the slaves, and the timing of the insurrection. As will be shown, each of these factors played an extremely important role in the drama of shipboard resistance, and it was largely the combination of all of these factors that enabled the rebels on board the *Delight* to achieve the level of success that they did.

MOBILITY AND STATUS ON BOARD

Quite often, the success of a revolt was tied to one or more slaves who had access to the upper decks. Most commonly, this agent was a woman or a child, as women and children were generally granted more mobility on deck and around the ship than were the men. This relative freedom of movement, however, did not go unnoticed by an observant crew. As one captain wrote to another sailing to Africa in 1734, "For your safety as well as mine . . . you'll have the needful guard over your Slaves, and put not too much Confidence in the Women nor Children lest they happen to be Instrumental to your being surprised which may be fatal."[2] Nevertheless, in spite of such warnings, women and children were often pivotal to a plot's chance of maturing into an insurrection. When the ship in which Ottobah Cugoano found himself enslaved finally pulled up anchor and began its Middle Passage, he and the other Africans decided they would rather die than submit to their enslavement. They devised a plot in which the women and children would burn and blow up the ship, killing everyone in the process.[3] Although this conspiracy never came to fruition, it demonstrates that the sailors' overwhelming concern with the adult male slaves was sometimes misplaced. In the case of children in particular, many sailors would have considered their presence to be completely benign. The idea that a small boy or girl could play a key role in the formation of a shipboard rebellion was easily overlooked. However, such an attitude was extremely dangerous on board a slave ship and periodically had disastrous consequences. It was four boys, for instance, who were found to be responsible for supplying weapons such as knives, stones, shot, and a chisel to the slaves below deck after a plot on board the *African* was uncovered in 1752.[4] Similarly, the uprising of more than two hundred slaves aboard the *New Britannia* in January of 1773 was precipitated by the fact that the Africans "had conveyed on Board, by some of the black Boys, some of the Carpenter's Tools, wherewith they ripped up the lower Decks, and got possession of the Guns, Beads, and Powder." In this case, unfortunately, virtually everybody involved on both sides was killed when the slaves apparently decided to blow up the ship.[5] And the captain of the *Fredensborg* discovered that a boy was to play an extremely important role in a planned revolt. Once the women determined when all of the sailors were going to be eating, this boy had the duty of conveying the intelligence to the African men who were waiting below for their signal.[6] Through the efforts of children such as these, numerous revolts were facilitated aboard the ships of the Middle Passage. For every captain who recognized the inherent danger of allowing children the run of the deck, there were others who failed to see that their very lives hung precariously in the balance so long as African boys and girls were allowed significant freedom of movement.

Substantially more significant than the role of children, however, was the highly important role of women in plotting and executing revolts. African men and women on slave ships were regularly separated throughout the voyage. One of the primary reasons for this segregation was to prevent them from devising plans to take over the ship. As a result, slave women were not typically privy to the plotting of rebellion that occurred in the men's quarters and had to find other ways to contribute to the cause. Most notably, since the men were so carefully watched and guarded, African women had to be the ones who observed and gathered information about the crew, the ship, the arms supply, the daily routine, and any other factors that might aid the rebellion when it finally erupted. This would not have been an easy task. In spite of the fact that women had a greater level of mobility on board, sailors were not foolish, and most recognized that they had to keep all Africans, regardless of gender, under careful supervision. The success of these women in contributing to insurrections, therefore, rested in their subtlety and their ability to play the role of harmless captive. Hesitation, fear, and anger all had to be agonizingly subdued, which must have required great patience. Days or weeks may have gone by before a woman would have access to key pieces of information or earn the full trust of the crew and be given access to certain areas of the ship. It would have taken time to determine the roles that each sailor played, to pinpoint the number of men on night watch, to figure out precisely when and where the crew ate or slept, or to discover who the keeper of the key to the arms chest was. In many cases, the voyage would end without the women ever having the opportunity to discover such needed information. At other times, women learned important clues that would have aided an insurrection but never had the opportunity to communicate with the men and coordinate their attack. And in still other cases, they may have been caught by observant crew members. One captain became infuriated, for instance, when he suddenly realized that an African woman who had been serving him his dinner had surreptitiously stolen a knife from the table. To punish her, the captain strung the woman up and whipped her until she nearly died.[7] Clearly, even with their greater mobility, involvement in a rebellion was no easy task for the African women on slave ships. But in spite of the difficulties, they did manage to play key roles in a remarkable number of shipboard rebellions.

Perhaps the most famous instance of women's participation in shipboard slave insurrections occurred on the English ship *Robert* as it was anchored offshore at Sierra Leone in 1721. Although the rebellion was ultimately unsuccessful, it was an unnamed woman who noticed that the number of sailors on watch one night was small enough for a surprise attack. With this information, she found means to inform at least some of the men on board and brought them all the weapons she could find. Sensing that this was probably the best chance they would get, she and two others made their desperate attempt at freedom. Although they got on deck and succeeded in swiftly killing three of the five-man watch, all of whom were asleep at the time, the other sailors were awakened by the commotion and quickly put an end to the rebellion. As punishment for her part in the revolt, the captain decided to make an example of the woman, tying her up by her thumbs, and then whipping and slashing her with knives in front of the other slaves until she was dead.[8] During a revolt on the English slaver

Industry in about April of 1729, another African woman was injured when she was caught smuggling gunpowder and ammunition through a hole in the partition that separated the men's and women's quarters. After the other insurrectionists were disarmed and control was regained by the sailors, a council was called to decide how to punish this woman. Because she had been scarred so badly in the revolt and thus "would not be fit for the Market," the council decided that the woman should be made an example to the rest. Accordingly, "they hoisted her up to the Fore-Yard-Arm, in View of the other Slaves . . . and fired half a Dozen Balls thro' her Body; the last Shot that was fired cut the Rope which she was slung by, [and she] tumbled amain into the sea."[9] In 1764, the London press reported that the captain, doctor, mate, and seventeen crew members of the Liverpool ship *Johnson* were poisoned by the slaves on board.[10] While the details are vague, one can speculate that this was accomplished by contaminating the crew's food or water supply. As slave women were occasionally recruited to assist in food preparation, it is possible that they may have been centrally involved in this incident. While this case is inconclusive, it is highly probable that African women serving as cooks on slave ships periodically used their position to facilitate rebellions in precisely such a manner. If they could find a way to weaken the crew through sickness, even if only temporarily, these women knew that they might be able to diminish the effectiveness of the sailors' care and vigilance enough to help pave the way for an effective insurrection.

Another group of twenty to thirty African women and children appear to have been responsible for a revolt on a ship in the West Indies in February of 1766. The ship had been on a voyage from Antigua to North Carolina but was apparently caught in a storm and lost its rigging. The stricken vessel was left drifting at sea for about four months. Because of their predicament and lack of food, the crew was "put to the necessity of eating one of the dead Negro children, which so exasperated the Negroes on board that they fell on the crew," killing three in the process.[11] Female slaves were also centrally involved in the rebellion aboard the British ship *Wasp* in 1783. Before departing from the African coast, the women seized the captain and attempted to throw him overboard.[12] In a more successful insurrection aboard the *Thomas* in 1797, it was again a group of African women who discovered that the ship's armor chest had been left unlocked and thus managed to steal several weapons and pass them to the men below.[13] And in yet another case, reports note that several women had to be stabbed during a revolt on the *Venus* before it could be recaptured by the crew.[14] As these examples indicate, African women were not mere spectators in shipboard slave rebellions. Instead, they planned and fought alongside the men whenever the opportunity arose and often helped tip the scale in favor of the rebels through their efforts. After a partially successful revolt by the male slaves on board the Rhode Island ship *Thames,* one perceptive crew member wrote to the vessel's owner that "had the women assisted them in all probability your property here at this time would have been but small."[15]

In the case of the *Delight,* which was profiled at the beginning of this chapter, while the woman who sparked the insurrection was never specifically referred to as an African or a slave, she was described as a woman "who lay in the cabbin." That a white woman would be on board a slave ship and willing to help provide weapons to the slaves below seems highly improbable, so it seems very likely that this person was a slave. Furthermore, the description surely suggests that she was being sexually exploited by a member of the crew. The surgeon's phrasing in recounting that "we were all (who lay in the cabbin) alarmed with a most horrid noise of the negros," suggests that the woman "who lay in the cabbin" slept in the crew's quarters. If the woman was indeed a slave, it appears that she took advantage of her status as a woman and the opportunities that came with it to turn the carefully regulated world of the slave ship upside down. Although the account is too vague to positively ascribe such intent to her actions, it is intriguing to wonder whether such women on slave ships were able to use the whims and passions of the white crew against them, sacrificing themselves sexually to move into a position of power on board the ship. Such women may have strategically positioned themselves as spies with privileged access to the inner workings of the ship and then used this position to facilitate rebellions. In the case of the *Delight,* we can only speculate as to the woman's methods of espionage, but by making her way into the cabin and keeping her eyes and ears wide open, she managed to learn where the ship's weapons were kept, one of the pivotal pieces of information in this particular rebellion.

Women and children's success in taking advantage of their greater mobility was related to the very structure of the slave trade. Regardless of how foolish a structure it turned out to be, slave ship captains and crew members commonly devoted the great majority of their efforts to restricting and controlling the seemingly more dangerous men below deck.

Women and children thus existed on the periphery of white surveillance, and their pivotal participation in so many acts of shipboard resistance often resulted not from any conscious effort to place themselves in such a position but rather from a remarkable skill in knowing how and when to exploit their position in order to gain an advantage. By successfully using the very organization and routine of the trade against their captors in this way, women and children firmly established themselves as fundamentally important figures in the history of shipboard revolt, helping to free thousands of captured Africans through their efforts. As their example shows, mobility in one form or another was often the key factor that enabled a small segment of Africans to contribute significantly to shipboard rebellion. Indeed, whether simply enabled by the structure of the slave trade itself or won by clever and opportunistic Africans, the ability to move into positions of access or relative privilege on board provided the greatest opportunity for slaves to gain some advantage in a rebellion.

In some instances, slaves would feign illnesses so that they would be released from their chains and brought up from the ship's hold for treatment in the infirmary. Diseases were so feared aboard slave ships that Africans would regularly be quarantined once they began showing signs of sickness, so that they would not infect the others. By feigning sickness, then, a small group of organizers could be placed together and lay plans for revolt.[16] For example, one revolt was avoided when a sailor saw "a young man . . . who has been the whole voyage out of irons, first on account of a large ulcer, and since for his seeming good behaviour," pass a spike down through the gratings in the deck into the hold.[17] Insurrectionists also commonly relied on those slaves who maneuvered themselves into positions of privilege or authority. These individuals were often in an excellent position to survey the state of affairs on board. Similar to the relative mobility of women and children, such privileged positions were not usually created in any sort of strategic sense on the part of the slaves themselves. Rather, as part of the structural organization of the slave trade, the idea of placing some Africans in privileged positions as sailors, overseers, or the like was a decision made by the captain. The skill of the slaves, therefore, was to turn this structural feature into a weakness. By subtle acts of dissembling, this small segment of slaves was able to take advantage of the trust that had been placed in them by appearing to be industrious and trustworthy workers. This placed them in the perfect position to serve as the eyes and ears of the less-privileged masses, monitoring the state of affairs, collecting valuable information, perhaps securing arms, and often rising to the position of leader when a revolt was ready to break out. As we have seen, the leader of a revolt on board the English ship *King David* in 1750 was an African who spoke English and often conversed with the captain in his cabin, where all the arms were stored. This position of authority made all the difference when the insurrection broke out, as the arms were easily secured, the captain killed, and the vessel quickly captured.[18] Just two years later, it was twenty-eight Gold Coast slaves who had been employed on deck to assist in navigating the *Marlborough* who led the other Africans in revolt. In part because of their efforts, the more than four hundred Africans on board soon captured the ship and reclaimed their freedom.[19]

Whether women or children, sick slaves or Africans who earned some degree of trust, those who managed to obtain positions of access or privilege on board slavers were the ones most able to gather intelligence and instigate slave rebellions. And yet these individuals would have had a difficult time succeeding alone. These leaders needed followers as much as the majority below deck needed leaders. It was only through a coordinated effort between the masses and the relatively privileged few that revolt was ever a realistic possibility, for the success of any attempted rebellion ultimately lay not in the intelligence or cunning of its leaders or facilitators but in the numerical advantage resulting from all or most of the Africans fighting together as one determined body for one common goal. With this in mind, it is truly remarkable to consider the resolve of the Africans during the planning stage of shipboard rebellions. Confined in the darkness of a ship's hold, a leadership had to emerge and convince frightened, weak, and despairing slaves, many of whom could not even communicate with one another, to risk everything in a desperate act of resistance. Confidence had to be instilled, care had to be taken to avoid detection by the crew, and incredible self-control had to be maintained in the face of constant provocation and extreme oppression. It would have taken time for all of the slaves to be made aware of the plan in detail and for nervous tendencies to harden into an insurrectionary spirit. Furthermore, potential spies and informants had to be singled out and effectively intimidated or won over to the cause. Planning a slave rebellion was clearly an incredibly complex undertaking. Convincing hundreds of individuals to come together and lay everything on the line in one insurrectionary impulse must have been a monumental feat. As Clarence Munford has written, "it is a token of the indestructibility of African popular resistance" that so many were able to accomplish this.[20]

WEAPONRY

After having gathered needed information, chosen an effective leadership, and agreed on the circumstances under which they would strike, the next crucial step would be for the captives to get out of their shackles and chains and procure the weapons necessary for battle. Although the tools needed for this were usually provided by the slaves themselves, having smuggled bits of metal into the hold that they could use to pick the locks, occasionally it was the carelessness of the crew that made escape possible. Of course, instructions given to slave ship captains would often anticipate rebellions and offer methods of security to prevent them. In one such missive, the captain was instructed to

> give strict orders to the carpenters, the cooper and the cook, along with the rest of the men who use iron and suchlike implements to keep this equipment under lock and key. When these are needed and used, great care must be taken to keep the slaves from getting hold of them. Likewise, and at all times, as long as the slaves are on deck, the gun lockers in which the muskets and ammunition are stored must remain closed, and kept on the quarterdeck where the male slaves must never be allowed. When these gun lockers are opened, no one—neither male nor female slaves, nor children—must be allowed on deck as long as these remain open.[21]

But in spite of the best efforts of captains and attentive crew members, the Africans found ways to obtain weapons they could use to stage rebellions. Willem Bosman wrote of one of his voyages in the latter seventeenth century that a discarded anchor was recklessly placed in the hold with the male slaves and used by the captives as an anvil. Unbeknownst to the crew, the slaves had stolen a hammer and used it to break out of their chains by hitting them against the anchor. The slaves then revolted and were on the brink of capturing the ship when two nearby ships, one French and one English, arrived on the scene and came to the crew's rescue.[22] Similarly, in a 1787 revolt on board the English ship *Ruby,* some of the slaves managed to arm themselves from a small cask of trade knives that had been stored in the hold with the male slaves.[23] While it is hard to imagine the crew of a slave ship could be so careless, such lapses in judgment demonstrate that constantly maintaining an impenetrable defense was a virtual impossibility on a slaver. There were simply too many things to worry about, too many security risks to monitor, too many people to keep

Table 1. Weapons used by slaves and number of times mentioned

Weaponry		Tools and utensils		Miscellaneous	
Small arms[a]	33	Axes	8	Pieces of wood[b]	19
Swords/cutlasses/sabers	10	Hammers	3	Bars/pieces of iron	11
Knives	11	Carpenter's tools	2	Shackles/chains	7
Ship's guns[c]	4	Cooking utensils	2	Food bowls	2
Lances	1	Files	2	Oars	2
Pikes	1	Hatchets	2	Boiling water	1
Razors	2	Buckets	1		
		Cooper's tools	1		
		Hand spikes	1		
		Scissors	1		
		Shovels	1		
		Sledgehammers	1		
Total	60	Total	26	Total	43

[a]"Small arms" include blunderbusses, guns, muskets, pistols, rifles, ammunition, gun powder, and items referred to simply as "arms."

[b]This category includes billets, firewood, logs, planks, staves, ax handles, blocks, and boards.

[c]"Ship's guns" include carriage guns, swivel guns, and "great guns."

track of, and things periodically slipped through the cracks. It was precisely such momentary breakdowns in crew vigilance that the Africans were ever watchful for.

But regardless of whether it was the carelessness of the crew or the ingenuity of the slaves that facilitated the acquisition of tools or weapons, the Africans' first move was to release themselves from their restraints and then find a way to get out of the locked slave quarters, past the watch, and on deck to attack the crew. In some cases, this would be done slowly and silently over a period of time, so as to take a sleeping watch by surprise. At other times, a sudden and violent surge was called for, leading the slaves to burst through the hatch and engage the crew in battle on deck. Either way, the Africans were inevitably at a disadvantage when it came to weapons and had to be creative. As table 1 indicates, surviving accounts of shipboard rebellions yield quite a bit of detail in regard to the weapons used by slaves in battle. The most common and obvious weapons were, of course, the slaves' own bodies, for hand to hand combat was the principal means of fighting available to the Africans. Firearms and other proper weapons were in relatively short supply, and the adrenaline-fueled Africans typically had to rely on their own strength and determination. And yet it is

"Révolte sur un bâtiment négrier." Rebelling slaves used a variety of weapons, including their own chains.

From Albert Laporte, *Récits de vieux marins* (Paris, 1883), 267.

remarkable how often the insurrectionists did manage to arm themselves with firearms or other potentially deadly weapons.

As the table shows, rebelling slaves used a variety of weapons, depending on what they could get their hands on, ranging from the very chains that had held them in bondage, to the ship's own guns. Firearms head the list, for while the majority of insurrectionists never got their hands on such weapons, the rebels did periodically manage to disarm a few sailors and confiscate their weapons, or even break into the arms room and seize large numbers of pistols and muskets. Furthermore, particularly as time progressed, the Africans on board might have had a familiarity with European firearms after they had become favored trade items on the African coast, and those enslaved as prisoners of war may actually have had experience using them. Clearly, the acquisition of firearms by slave rebels was a key element to success and often made the difference between victory and failure. In addition, the Africans would sometimes manage to break into storerooms, the kitchen, or the carpenter's room, picking up weapons along the way. Through such means, items such as axes, hammers, and hatchets would quite often be found on board, and sometimes the Africans would get their hands on tools such as files or scissors. Indeed, slave ships were loaded with items that could be used as weapons, including sticks, ropes, cables, branding irons, hooks, tar brushers, broomsticks, mops, oars, and any number of other normal seafaring items that would have been on board.[24] In some cases, even the ship's trade items could be used in revolts, as indicated by a number of separate references to the use of iron bars by slave rebels during shipboard insurrections. While these were sometimes simply bits of iron broken off of storeroom gratings or other parts of the vessel, in many cases they were the trade bars that captains would use to barter for slaves on the African coast. Yet another relatively common weapon was the billets or chunks of wood that were sometimes issued to slaves as pillows. As Theophilus Conneau observed, "Billets of wood are sometimes distributed to [the Africans], but as slaves shipped are often of different nations this luxury is not granted till well assured of the good disposition of the Negroes, as in many occasions slaves have been tempted to mutiny only by the opportunity at hand of arming themselves with those native pillows—indeed a very destructive missive in case of revolt."[25] Knowing their advantages were few, slaves seized upon anything they could find. With weapons as deadly as a pistol or sword to those as seemingly harmless as a nail or a broken link of chain, the Africans involved in shipboard revolts scrapped and fought for their lives in these intense and violent confrontations and achieved a remarkable level of success.

TIMING

The time at which a revolt broke out was another key element in the effectiveness of a rebellion, and the available evidence suggests that Africans followed a pattern in this regard. Indeed, the attempt to unloose themselves from their shackles and put their plans into action was very often carried out at night when most sailors were asleep and when panic and confusion could easily spread and be used to the insurrectionists' advantage. The key element was surprise, for once the slaves had gotten out of their irons, they often had only to kill a small watch guarding the entrance to the hold in order to have a good chance at success.[26] Two examples of insurrections aboard English vessels, both occurring in 1721, illustrate this point clearly. In the case of the *Robert,* a woman informed the ringleader of the revolt one night that there were no more than five sailors on deck and that they were all asleep. Seizing upon this good fortune, the slaves were able to slip onto the deck and immediately kill three of these men. In the case of the *Elizabeth,* it is similarly noted that "all the white Men set to watch were asleep" one night, allowing the slaves to stage an insurrection in which one of these sailors was killed.[27] Such carelessness provided a very favorable situation for slaves contemplating an uprising and led to the deaths of many sailors throughout the history of the slave trade. As table 2 shows, of the forty-four cases in which the exact time of the revolt is given, 43 percent occurred between the hours of 6:00 P.M. and 6:00 A.M., when it was dark. However, when nonspecific times are also factored in (e.g. "night," "afternoon," "morning," etc.), there are an additional twelve cases that took place when it was dark. These cases raise the total percentage of revolts occurring while it was dark to nearly 40 percent. Thus daytime and nighttime revolts appear to have occurred at about the same rate. We get a more interesting picture when the nighttime hours are divided in half. Indeed, in the pre-midnight hours, when sailors may well have still been awake, revolt occurred at a modest rate. But as the night wore on, particularly around 2:00 to 3:00 A.M., there was a sharp increase in the Africans' propensity to revolt. These are the hours when the majority of the ship's crew would have been asleep and the slaves on board may have considered a surprise attack a better gamble. Of course, it is important to note that revolts could and did occur at any time of day. In addition to the late-night attacks, mealtime seems to have been a favorite time for rebellion, for at these moments relatively large numbers of slaves were on deck and had an opportunity to use their numbers to rush the crew in a sudden attack. In these instances, the Africans would come on deck for the meal, just as they had done on a daily basis since the voyage began. Although slaves were closely watched by crew members during meals, the routine nature of meals may have lulled the sailors into some degree of complacency, particularly as the voyage wore on. After weeks of daily meals without incident, crew members may have felt comfortable relaxing their guard. Revolts under these circumstances may have been spontaneous and unplanned, as the Africans took advantage of some weakness they observed among the crew, but more commonly these incidents appear to have been carefully

Table 2. Percentage of revolts at known times of day

Time of day	Percentage of revolts
Day	
6:00 A.M.–11:59 A.M.	30%
12:00 P.M.–5:59 P.M.	27%
Night	
6:00 P.M.–11:59 P.M.	16%
12:00 A.M.–5:59 A.M.	27%

planned, and the Africans would sometimes have devised a predetermined signal to be given when the attack was to begin. On the English vessel *Pearl,* for example, the slaves were brought up one morning for breakfast. The Africans came on deck peaceably and made an effort to put the sailors at ease, for they did not want to tip the crew off to the rebellion they had planned. Shortly after all the slaves had assembled on deck, one of them called out an African word that immediately sent the rest of the Africans scattering to various parts of the ship, each surely assigned a specific task. To the slaves' dismay, the crew responded quickly, soon killing or wounding forty of the rebels and ultimately crushing the insurrection.[28] Although this rebellion was unsuccessful, it is clear that mealtime was often a propitious time for revolt, with all or many of the slaves on deck.

Twelve cases in this analysis are specifically identified as having occurred during mealtime. In another five cases in which the exact time is not recorded, the revolts are identified as having occurred in the morning, very possibly during breakfast.[29] As the following description shows, however, captains were aware of this danger and often made sure that security was especially tight during meals: "[T]hey are fed twice a day, at 10 in the morning, and 4 in the evening, which is the time they are aptest to mutiny, being all upon deck; therefore all that time, what of our men are not employ'd in distributing their victuals to them, and settling them, stand to their arms; and some with lighted matches at the great guns that yaun upon them, loaden with partridge, till they have done and gone down to their kennels between decks."[30] Although probably effective in most instances, this kind of vigilance by the crew was not always a sufficient deterrent, as many insurrections nevertheless broke out during meals. On the English ship *Ferrers* in 1722, for instance, the captain imprudently assumed that the slaves on his vessel were content. One day when the African men were eating, the captain found himself on deck among them when they suddenly "laid hold on him, and beat out his Brains with the little Tubs, out of which they eat their boiled Rice."[31] In a similar case in 1806, slaves on the American ship *Nancy* rose during the afternoon meal and "seized the master as he was pouring molasses into his victuals."[32] Such situations appeared promising to slaves, for they knew that their numerical advantage at these moments was strong and that a well-orchestrated attack might catch the sailors by surprise. Similarly, slaves could sometimes even take advantage of their presence on deck for religious indoctrination, a ritual that was not at all infrequent on slave ships. When some eighteen Africans were assembled on the deck of the French ship *Levrette* one morning for prayers in May 1754, they used the opportunity to rise against the crew. Although ultimately unsuccessful, the Africans in this case killed as many as fifteen of the sailors and managed to take possession of the ship temporarily.[33] Though slaves frequently attacked late at night or at mealtime, sailors knew that there was not a moment of the day when they could let their guard down and that strict vigilance had to be maintained at all hours for their own safety.

THE RESPONSE OF THE CREW

It was not uncommon for slave rebellions to reach a certain level of success. If all went well, slaves might free and arm themselves and overwhelm a portion of the crew within minutes. If the Africans were careful and secretive enough in their planning, there was little the sailors could do to avoid this first insurrectionary wave. At this point, however, the tide tended to turn. As one historian of the French trade has written, "It was at this stage that most rebellions ended; the aroused sailors usually managed to capture the supply room and beat the captives into submission. Very rarely, the slaves gained the upper hand, seized the rifles and powder, and forced the whites to abandon ship in utter terror. Most of the time the sailors easily dominated the situation and put a quick end to the revolt."[34] This comes as no surprise, of course, considering the extremely disadvantaged position of the Africans. The odds were clearly against the slaves, who were often nude, mostly unarmed, and perhaps still wearing their shackles. Clarence Munford notes that the Africans had to rely heavily on intangibles such as "surprise, disdain for death, implacable hatred, audacity, and the union born of common adversity."[35] Against such an unconventional arsenal, the sailors usually had little trouble. To bring insurrections to an end as quickly as possible, crews often attempted to corner the slaves in the hold or in a certain part of the ship where they would be unable to resist effectively for long. At times, however, slaves would intentionally retreat to a confined location as a last resort. Indeed, there are a number of cases in which the slaves fled below into the hold or to another part of the vessel with their weapons and began a standoff with the crew. On the *Jane* in 1756, for instance, the slaves took possession of the ship and locked themselves in the cabin, where they fought the sailors for several hours before they ran out of ammunition.[36] Sadly, this tactic was almost always unsuccessful, for the crew had only to wait until the slaves tired or ran out of ammunition. When slaves on the *Ruby* took refuge in the hold during a 1787 revolt, the captain ordered some of the sailors to fire at the slaves through the gratings, while others armed themselves with muskets and blunderbusses, boarded the ship's small boat, and fired through the air ports of the vessel. When these tactics did not succeed, the captain ordered a scalding mixture of water and fat to be thrown down upon the stubborn rebels.[37] Another captain succeeded in quieting rebellious slaves in the hold by sealing up all of the air holes and covering the gratings with sails, after which he ordered the muskets to be filled with powder and cayenne pepper and fired into the hold. "In a few minutes," a report noted, "there was a stench enough from the burnt pepper to almost suffocate them."[38] Through such efforts, most slave revolts were brought to an end shortly after they began.

Shipboard slave revolts did not necessarily follow any pattern but depended heavily upon circumstances the Africans had no control over such as the experience of the crew, the temperament of the captain, the health of the sailors, and the efficiency and duration of the slaving process along the African coast. However, it is noteworthy how frequently revolts did share common characteristics, even though they involved Africans from different regions, aboard vessels of different nations, and took place over a period spanning centuries. Insurrections in the transatlantic slave trade tended to rely on slaves who gained privileged positions or unusual access on board, to involve the creative use of tools and weapons, and to occur at certain times of day, and they most often resulted in a swift and ruthless response from the crew. But whatever circumstances surrounded a given revolt, once the rebels began their attack, there was no turning back. Most revolts were crushed quickly and efficiently, but others managed to get past the initial surge and rage on for hours, days, or weeks. In many cases, even these rebellions were ultimately quelled, often with outside assistance, but occasionally the Africans would win. The following two chapters explore the vastly different circumstances and consequences attending failed and successful insurrections. Issues such as aid from other vessels, the punishment of slave rebels, the ways in which Africans dealt with captured sailors, and the various levels of success that some rebels attained are examined in detail.

5

Unsuccessful Revolts

In the late summer of 1797, Captain Peter McQuay set sail from the West Central African port of Loango after loading his ship, the *Thomas*, with 375 slaves. The Liverpool ship was destined for Barbados, but the captain and many of his crew would never make it that far alive. On the morning of September 2, the Africans on board readied themselves for a rebellion, taking advantage of the fact that all of the crew was eating breakfast at the time and unprepared to deal with a sudden ambush. While the crew ate, two ever-watchful African women noticed that the arms chest had been left unlocked and, seizing the moment, smuggled the weapons down to the African men. In a matter of moments, nearly two hundred rebels had freed themselves and began waging a surprise attack on the unsuspecting crew, killing all who crossed their path. Captain McQuay and his remaining crew took up a defensive posture at the first sign of trouble and attempted to fight the Africans with the small cache of arms that was stored in the crew's quarters. These efforts proved futile, however, as the Africans overpowered the sailors, killing the captain along with many of his crew. Of those who survived, twelve managed to escape in the ship's stern boat, although ten of these men would die from exposure and lack of provisions before reaching safety in Barbados. Another nine sailors evaded death because the Africans needed their assistance in sailing the ship. Four of these men managed to escape later in the longboat and barely reached land in the Bahamas alive, having spent six days and nights at sea without food or water. The hundreds of Africans and five sailors on board the *Thomas* drifted at sea for forty-two days before finally encountering an American ship that was carrying rum. When the American ship pulled alongside the *Thomas,* the slaves succeeded in commandeering the ship. Surely overwhelmed by thirst, when the Africans discovered casks full of liquid on board, they ordered them opened and consumed large amounts of the rum. Of course, this indulgence caught up with the Africans. Soon, many of them had become drunk, and several fell overboard and drowned. Taking advantage of the Africans' drunkenness, the remaining crew of the *Thomas* killed the leader of the revolt, recaptured the American ship, and sailed it to the nearest port. The remaining Africans were left on board the *Thomas* and were later recaptured by the crew of the English ship *Thames*.[1]

As the case of the *Thomas* demonstrates, even powerful revolts in which African slaves took possession of a ship often ended in failure. In spite of the Africans' courage and cunning, the simple reality that they were prisoners on a slave ship usually presented more obstacles than even the most resolute rebels could overcome. And when the Africans did appear to overcome these obstacles, unforeseen forces such as betrayal by fellow slaves or swift assistance from nearby slave ships presented still further impediments to success. An examination of unsuccessful rebellions illuminates the ways in which these various obstacles combined to maintain the severely unequal balance of power and prevent most insurrections before they ever had a chance to reach truly critical proportions.

BETRAYAL

For the crew, the key to minimizing a revolt's effectiveness was to catch it early and take quick and decisive measures against it. As discussed in chapter 3, a very common means of early detection was to hire free Africans to monitor the actions of the slaves, thus forestalling any attempts at rebellion before they ever had a chance to get started. In other cases, captains chose a select group from among the slaves on board to be watchdogs over the others. These slaves performed such duties as settling quarrels among the captives, organizing the Africans into groups for eating, supervising the work parties that cleaned and scrubbed the ship, and most importantly, informing the crew of any plots or conspiracies that they may have detected.[2] As Captain Thomas Phillips reported, "We have some 30 or 40 gold coast negroes, which we buy . . . to make guardians and overseers of the [others], and sleep among them to keep them from quarreling; and in order, as well as to give us notice, if they can discover any caballing or plotting among them. . . . When we constitute a guardian, we give him a cat of nine tails as a badge of his office, which he is not a little proud of, and will exercise with great authority."[3] Lured by promises of small benefits and advantages over their fellow captives, these men and women who were recruited to act as spies were encouraged to betray the plans of their shipmates and surely foiled many insurrectionary plots throughout the history of the slave trade. In other cases, sailors did not have to manipulate their captives but instead could rely upon the diversity and differences among the African population below deck. There is a tendency in African and African American historiography to imagine an idealized version of the past. The struggle against slavery is often painted in stark terms of good versus evil, with all of the white villains filled with raw hatred, self-righteousness, and brutality and all the enslaved men and women standing shoulder to shoulder, presenting an imposing and powerful wall of resistance to their oppression. This is a comforting way to analyze the history of enslavement, but it does so at the expense of truly seeing the people caught up in the slave trade as human beings. After all, people are filled with a complex mix of weakness and strength, cowardice and bravery, hesitation, caution, and a driving goal of self-preservation. While it is certainly true that Africans came together, transcended differences, and staged powerful rebellions, the concept of a unified slave consciousness bent on the revolutionary overthrow of their bondage is largely a fallacy.

When a revolt was being planned, some individuals would have been petrified with fear. They would have felt that such a rash and frightening move could lead to misery and death. Frightened children must have begged for parents or relatives to stay out of the way of danger. Women with infants recognized their children's complete dependence upon them and perhaps sometimes felt the urge to protect themselves from danger if only for the sake of their young. Other Africans would have held out hope that they would somehow return to wives, fathers, and children back home and believed that this hope alone was reason enough to endure suffering. In a desperate effort to come to grips with their predicament, some internalized their enslavement and began to feel as if they deserved their plight. All of these conflicting impulses and crippling fears complicated these little-understood shipboard communities. The reality was such that not all slaves would participate. Some would sit by passively as their shipmates fought and died. Others would sympathize and perhaps help out but not to the point of endangering their own safety. And still others would take more extreme measures in the hope of preserving their safety by betraying their fellow captives and revealing their insurrectionary plots to the sailors. Indeed, it is important not to overstate the unity of Africans on slave ships, for while it is true that remarkably large numbers of people managed to transcend their differences and come together for one common cause, there were always others who were afraid of, uninterested in, or even hostile to the idea of insurrection. Captains and crew members made it a point to identify and manipulate such individuals to better ensure their ship's safety.

Numerous slaving voyages were in fact saved from potentially disastrous slave rebellions by African men and women who chose to reveal the plans of their shipmates. On the Rhode Island ship *Mary* in 1796, a slave who worked on deck as a sailor betrayed the plans of the slaves below and allowed the crew to be prepared when the revolt struck. The crew was able to get their weapons ready, remove items from the slave quarters that could have been used to rebel, and double-check to make sure the slaves were chained securely. Despite these precautions, some of the Africans were able to get out of their chains and on deck. The battle was quick, with four of the insurrectionists losing their lives, but there is no telling what success the rebels may have had were it not for the informant who revealed the plot.[4] In another case aboard an unnamed British vessel late in the eighteenth century, a Jamaican newspaper reported the following:

> The lives of the Captain and Crew of an African ship, which lately arrived safe in this port [Montego Bay], with a large cargo of slaves, were preserved on the passage by the providential attachment of two females: An insurrection had been planned with much art and secrecy, and was on the point of being carried into execution, when the two girls made a disclosure of the plot, and effectual measures were taken for the common security. Since their arrival the Captain has, with much justice and liberality, freed his preservers.[5]

Occasionally, certain slaves would even break ranks and fight on the side of their captors. During a revolt aboard the *Eagle* in 1704, a fierce battle ensued. When the captain observed that the Africans were about to throw the sentry overboard, he intervened and was himself struck by a slave with a billet of wood so hard that he was almost knocked unconscious. As the report of this incident continues, "The Slave was going to repeat the Blow, when a young Lad about seventeen years old, whom we had been kind to, interposed his Arm, and received the Blow, by which his Arm-bone was fractured." After the crew restored order, the young slave who had intervened was attended to by the ship's doctor, and upon the *Eagle*'s arrival in Virginia, he was given his freedom as a reward.[6] In a similar case in 1731, the slaves aboard the *Ruby* staged a successful insurrection in which most of the crew was killed. However, "with the Help of his black Boy" the captain managed to escape through his cabin window.[7] Why certain Africans chose to take such a stand will never be known, but it could have resulted from any number of circumstances. As two of the cases above attest, betraying the plans of other slaves could actually win one his or her freedom, thus ironically achieving for the individual precisely the same goal that the insurrectionists had sought for themselves and others. In other cases, such as those of the two young slaves mentioned above who intervened to protect crew members, perhaps a certain affinity or even friendship may have evolved over the long journey. Sailors came from all walks of life, and even on slave ships there would have been men who had a greater sense of tolerance and a more compassionate nature than others and may have made real efforts to be kind to the Africans. Maybe this kindness was patronizing, perhaps it was illusory, or maybe it was heartfelt, but in such cases it is not surprising that some of the Africans would come to the defense of a crew member with whom they had established some relationship. But regardless of why certain Africans chose to betray their fellow captives, the reality is that such incidents did in fact occur periodically.

Although unity of purpose was a very significant aspect of effective shipboard resistance, the existence of slave informants and spies aboard ships shows that this unity was not universal and that it should not be overstated. The Africans who crossed the Atlantic often came from different locations, had different cultures, spoke different languages, and had different goals and motivations. As a result, this diverse group of people forcibly brought together by the slave trade had its share of disunity, divisiveness, and outright betrayal. However, although the history of shipboard insurrection is occasionally punctuated by such instances of disloyalty, one is nevertheless struck by the remarkable level of cooperation that did seem to exist on board more often than not. In spite of their differences, those who endured the Atlantic crossing together shared the one fundamental commonality of being enslaved. This reality undoubtedly bred a high level of unity that directly influenced the frequency and significance of shipboard resistance.

ASSISTANCE FROM OTHERS

When faced with the threat of insurrection, captains and crews could also usually rely upon other nearby ships, regardless of nationality, to come quickly to their rescue. This presented another crucially significant obstacle to a successful rebellion, for the arrival of other vessels on the scene was not only quite common but also very effective. It was a difficult enough proposition for slaves to rise up and capture their own vessel, without also having to withstand pursuit by others before they could reach freedom. When faced with a serious enough insurrection that help was needed, the first thing a crew would attempt to do was alert others to their predicament, as has been seen in the case of the *Delight* discussed in chapter 4. When a ship was anchored in a busy slaving harbor, trouble on board was often readily apparent by the commotion and the sound of gunfire, and assistance was usually soon forthcoming. When the nearest vessel was some distance away, however, more creative measures had to be taken by the sailors. For example, when the crew of the slaver *Dauphin* was faced with an insurrection in 1724, they fired three cannon shots to signal for assistance. When help soon arrived, the revolt was quickly subdued. When slaves aboard the French ship *Ville de Basle* revolted, the crew lowered the ship's flag to half-mast as a call for assistance.[8] Another, rather ingenious, method of attracting the attention of nearby vessels was used by the crew of the Rhode Island ship *Little George* in 1730. After the slaves surprised the crew, the overwhelmed captain and four others took refuge below deck, where they waged war with the slaves for a number of days. Surviving off of raw rice, the crew remained below for more than a week. In desperation, they decided to bore a number of holes in the bottom of the ship, thus letting in about three feet of water, with the hope that the ship would be forced on her side and serve as a distress signal to nearby vessels. While this did not have the intended effect, it did enable the sailors to bargain with the Africans for their lives. Faced with the threat of a sinking ship, the slaves agreed to sail for shore, where the crew members would be spared.[9] Such negotiations are rare in the historical record, but they show that the fundamental objective of the Africans was simply to get off of the ship as quickly as possible. If sparing the crew or striking a bargain with them was the best means to accomplish their goal, then the Africans were surely willing to do so. As the efforts of sailors to signal their distress demonstrate, when a slave rebellion had reached a certain critical point and there was nothing left the crew could do to save their own vessel, the desperate hope that other ships would speed to their rescue became the dire wish of many a sailor.

These distress signals were very effective, and dozens of insurrections that might otherwise have been successful were put down as a result of nearby vessels' identifying these signals and coming swiftly to the crew's aid. For example, after a fierce battle aboard a Portuguese slave ship in 1733, the Africans succeeded in killing most of the crew and gaining control of the slaver. The rebels held the ship for five days before an English vessel arrived on the scene, ultimately prevailing over the Africans after a grueling battle lasting twenty-four hours.[10] In 1762, Africans on board the English ship *Dove* similarly took possession of their ship and were only defeated with the aid of a schooner and two boats sent from James Fort to crush the rebellion.[11] After a group of Africans on a ship from Virginia rose and killed the crew while the vessel was on the Gambia River in 1766, they made for land and would certainly have succeeded had it not been for several ships in the vicinity that rushed to the scene and recaptured the rebels.[12] And on October 18, 1785, after slaves aboard the Dutch vessel *Neptunis* revolted, not only did an English ship come to the aid of the crew, but canoes from the coast filled with soldiers and armed free Africans were also sent to help put down the insurrection. Sadly, this incident ended with the explosion of the Dutch slaver, either set off intentionally by the Africans on board or caused by a cannon shot from the English ship, resulting in the deaths of anywhere from two hundred to five hundred slaves.[13] Slave ships could regularly rely on help from others, and numerous insurrections were thwarted in this way. Indeed, in more than thirty cases considered in this study, nearby vessels are documented to have come to the aid of ships upon which slaves had revolted, and the actual number of such instances probably far exceeds this number. Of course, as discussed in chapter 2, a reduction in crew size and strength was often the precipitating cause of shipboard insurrection, so captains who mobilized large numbers of sailors to assist a nearby ship suffering a revolt might just be leaving the door open for a rebellion on their own vessel. This was nearly the case in 1790 when a British slave ship anchored at Bonny sent thirteen of her men to help suppress an insurrection on a French vessel. As the British master later recounted, after this rebellion was finally crushed and the sailors returned to their ship, they "were informed that, seeing through the scuttle-holes what was going on in the French ship, our slaves had been endeavouring to force up the gratings to get on deck, but seeing us return desisted."[14] Nevertheless, even though providing assistance sometimes left ships in a precarious position, aid was nearly always quickly on the way when a revolt had occurred in sight of other ships.

At other times, it was assistance from land rather than nearby vessels that saved the crew of a ship upon which the slaves had rebelled. In the case of the *London* in 1703, soldiers from James Fort at the mouth of the Gambia River were sent to help quell a powerful insurrection.[15] In 1761, similarly, it was again only with the aid of the nearby James Fort that a rebellion aboard the English ship *Mary* was put down. The ship was subsequently warned to stay within range of the fort's guns so that such an incident would not be repeated. Recklessly, however, the captain of the *Mary* decided to tempt fate and stray from the security of James Fort. In an effort to secure more favorable trading, he took his vessel into an area of the Gambia River beyond the fort's protection. Perhaps having learned from their earlier failed insurrectionary attempt that the situation was now much more in their favor, the Africans on board revolted a second time, this time killing most of the crew and escaping.[16] And in 1775, the captain of the Danish slaver *Christiansborg* managed to escape from his ship during a slave rebellion just off Fort Fredensborg on the Gold Coast. Racing to shore, the captain sounded the alarm and was soon on his way back with soldiers from the fort who helped end the insurrection.[17] Upon arrival in the Americas, sailors on vessels that had been rocked by slave rebellion could also hope for assistance from land in some cases. When the French *Annibal* anchored at Caye St. Louis in St. Domingue, having already suffered one slave revolt on the passage, the slave women on board attempted a second insurrection. However, the ensuing gunfire alarmed the entire port, and several boatloads of armed men were soon on their way to help end the disturbance.[18] In a similar example, the rebellion aboard the English *King David* that was profiled in chapter 2 finally came to an end only after French authorities in Guadeloupe sent one hundred men in pursuit of the slaver, recapturing the Africans and ending the insurrection in a matter of hours.[19] Whether from the sea or from the shore, time and time again the captains and crews of slave ships were rescued by their compatriots nearby.

Making matters all the more difficult for the Africans, this "brotherhood of people-buyers"[20] established and maintained their alliance in spite of the broader political conflicts that were often going on between them. Vessels from competing slave-trading firms, or even from rival or hostile nations, would not hesitate to come to the aid of ships in distress. Indeed, in the face of slave revolt, all that mattered was its swift and total defeat, partially to end the immediate threat, partially to keep the spirit of freedom from spreading to other Africans on nearby vessels, but also to salvage at any cost the indispensable notions of racial, cultural, and religious superiority that were so fundamental to the slave trade. It was in the psychological best interest of all sailors involved in the slave trade to convince themselves not only that they were justified in enslaving the Africans but that they faced no real danger in doing so. By jumping swiftly to the aid of fellow sailors who were being threatened by their slaves, the crews of both the vessel being assisted and the ship providing the assistance could feel more confident in their personal and professional security. Without this network of mutual assistance, the historical record would be filled with far more examples of successful rebellions.

PUNISHMENT

Along with taking precautions to avoid revolt in the first place and dealing with it as it occurred, slave ship captains and crew members also sought to place severe obstacles in the way of any Africans who participated in a failed revolt, with the intent of crushing their insurrectionary spirit and avoiding future outbreaks. Following a failed uprising, ship captains would very commonly make examples of the ringleaders. After a revolt aboard the Danish *Fridericus Quartus* in 1709, for instance, the reprisals were brutal. The morning after the revolt, all of the ship's captives were forced to watch as the ringleader was executed. First, the man's right hand was cut off and shown to each slave "with the severe warning that the restless heads should see themselves mirrored in this." Then the man's left hand and his head were cut off, and the body was hoisted up and suspended by the ship's mainsail yard, where it remained as a warning for two days. The others who had participated in the revolt were lashed and their wounds rubbed with crushed pepper, salt, and ashes, a punishment that in some variation or another was relatively common throughout the history of shipboard insurrections.[21] While the theory behind treating wounds in this manner originally had to do with preventing infection, slave traders quickly realized that it also served as a form of torture. After a revolt on the French ship *Affriquain,* for instance, the slaves were severely whipped, and one crewman reported that "once [the slaves were] bleeding from the lashes, we rubbed the wounds with cannon powder, lemon juice, and brine of peppers, mixed together with a drug prepared by the surgeon. This mixture prevents gangrene, and also has the advantage of cooking their butts."[22] In another violent variation of this punishment, the surgeon on the English ship *Pearl* actually sliced twelve ringleaders down their backs with a scalpel-like instrument following a rebellion on board. Into the bleeding gashes, the sailors rubbed salt water to add further stinging agony to the already painful open wounds.[23] The pain associated with such punishment must have been excruciating, and the screams of those being so punished probably served as a very effective deterrent for others who were forced to watch.

Others felt that mere executions and whippings were not impressive enough, and that more extreme measures needed to be taken in order to convince the Africans of the folly of insurrection. Following a defeated revolt, Jean Barbot advised captains, "Spare no effort to repress their insolence and, as an example to the others, sacrifice the lives of all the most mutinous. This will terrify the others and keep them obedient. The way of making it clear to them, I mean the form of punishment that scares the Africans most, is by cutting up a live man with an ax and handing out the pieces to the others."[24] A variation of this barbaric practice was used in 1721, when two slaves aboard the British ship *Robert* were forced to eat the heart and liver of a dead crew member before being executed after a failed rebellion.[25] Following an insurrection aboard the *Ruby* in 1787, yet another brutal punishment was meted out to the slave rebels, as the wounded ringleader of the revolt was brought upon deck, fastened with an iron collar around his neck, and chained to the foremast. The surgeon on board was ordered not to provide him with any medical assistance, and the crew was warned not to give him any food. As the incident was reported, "he lived for three days in a state of stupefaction and his body was then thrown overboard in the sight of all the slaves aboard." Two other insurrectionists were decapitated and "the two gory heads were successively handed to the slaves, chained on deck, and they were obliged to kiss the lips of the bloody heads. Some men who refused to obey were unmercifully flogged by the captain and had the bloody part of a head rubbed against their faces." One African boy who had been injured in the revolt had bricks tied to his neck and was thrown overboard.[26] In yet another example, the captain of the French ship *Alexandre* punished his rebellious slaves by setting them on fire. To avoid this fate, many of the slaves were forced to jump into the sea.[27] And in the case of the American ship *Kentucky*, upon which fifty-two Africans were executed for their role in a revolt in 1844, one of the crew later testified,

> They were ironed or chained two together, and when they were hung, a rope was put round their necks and they were drawn up to the yard-arm clear of the sail. This did not kill them, but only choked or strangled

them. They were then shot in the breast and the bodies thrown overboard. If only one of two that were ironed together was to be hung, a rope was put round his neck and he was drawn up clear of the deck, beside of the bulwarks, and his leg laid across the rail and chopped off, to save the irons and release him from his companion, who, at the same time, lifted up his leg till the other's was chopped off as aforesaid, and he released. The bleeding negro was then drawn up, shot in the breast, and thrown overboard as aforesaid. The legs of about one dozen were chopped off in this way. When the feet fell on deck, they were picked up by the Brazilian crew and thrown overboard, and sometimes at the body, while it still hung living; and all kinds of sport was made of the business. When two that were chained together were both to be hung, they were hung up together by their necks, shot, and thrown overboard, irons and all. When [a] woman was hung up and shot, the ball did not take effect, and she was thrown overboard living, and was seen to struggle some time in the water before she sunk.

In addition to this horrific experience, about twenty men and six women on board the *Kentucky* were subsequently tied down to the deck and severely flogged. They were whipped by two men at a time, one with a two-foot-long stick and the other with a four-foot long strip of hide.[28] This measure of violence was totally unnecessary, and fortunately quite infrequent. Despite the crew's desire to make an example of the ringleaders, most instances of execution following shipboard insurrections singled out just a few for torture and death. Slaves were valuable commodities, and death on the scale of that which occurred on board the *Kentucky* resulted not from any logical calculation to intimidate the survivors and avoid future revolts but more likely represented a terrified crew trying to reassert their dominance at any cost.

It is important to remember that the brutal punishments seen here were not created for use in the slave trade. Traditional forms of punishment and torture may have been adapted to the trade, but violence and brutality were part of life. As Jeffrey Bolster reminds us, humanitarianism was not a cultural norm in the era of the slave trade, and punishment, suffering, and exploitation were normal aspects of existence.[29] In much of Western Europe, violence and terror were used to control the peasantry through imprisonment, martial law, capital punishment, banishment, and forced labor. Troublemakers would be brutally executed and have their heads stuck on pikes or be publicly hanged at the gallows.[30] Terror was used to enforce social roles and codify acceptable heavier. During the era of the slave trade, literally hundreds of crimes in England were punishable by death, including treason, forgery, piracy, grand larceny, and any number of violent crimes. The other slave trading nations of Europe similarly relied on torture and punishment to control their populations, a practice that was widespread throughout much of the continent. Those violating the rules established from above were dealt with mercilessly. When execution was not called for, the guilty could be branded, tied to the back of a cart and whipped, have their ears cropped, or be pilloried.[31] Malefactors, whether they were runaway English indentured servants, pirates who dared to challenge the carefully constructed social hierarchy of the Western world, or slaves who refused to recognize the professed superiority of white, Christian, mercantilist dogma were hanged, burned, or broken on the wheel—whatever it took to terrorize the people into accepting their assigned roles. The racial and religious components of the slave trade may well have ensured an especially brutal treatment of Africans, but violence was an accepted form of social control, and slaves were subject to it not only because they were slaves but because they were outsiders who were expected to obey the rules and who had to be savagely corrected when they dared to question them.

Although violence was common, and sailors had little compunction doling it out to Africans in liberal amounts, the desired profitability of the slaving venture helped place limits on this brutality. As table 3 indicates, the overwhelming majority of shipboard revolts in which a numerical slave death toll is known resulted in fewer than fifty Africans losing their lives. The average number of slave deaths in these 170 cases works out to approximately 32 per revolt. While there are certainly a number of cases in which hundreds of slaves died, when rebellions for which the number of slave deaths is not known are taken into account, the average number was probably somewhere below thirty slaves per incident—most likely far below this number. A precise average figure is impossible to determine because captains rarely bothered noting when no slaves died in an insurrection, whereas they almost always reported slaves being killed. Obviously, most captains made an effort to kill as few slaves as possible because, despite the threat they posed, they nevertheless represented a great deal of money. On a French ship in the early nineteenth century, for example, the captain was so concerned about jeopardizing his investment that he ordered his sailors not to fire on rebelling slaves but instead quelled the insurrection by non-

Table 3. Slave deaths resulting from shipboard revolts

Number of slave deaths	Instances	Percentage of all incidents
0–49	143	84%
50–99	13	8%
100–149	4	2%
150–199	2	1%
200–249	5	3%
250 or more	3	2%

lethal means, covering the deck in multipronged nails so that the barefoot Africans could not advance upon them.[32] In other cases, captains would instruct sailors to fire over the heads of the Africans to frighten them. Only when this tactic failed were the shots fired directly at the rebels. In the case of a revolt on the British ship *Golden Age,* the captain ordered a mixture of ashes and pepper to be ground up and instructed his sailors to throw it into the eyes of the Africans as they rushed the crew. Such an odd approach surely represented the captain's desire to end the rebellion without undue loss of his precious human cargo.[33] As a result of captains' tendency to protect their investments, in the hundreds of cases where no specific numerical death toll is provided, it seems likely that few or no slaves died. If these were factored into the equation, the average death toll could easily plummet to fewer than fifteen slaves per revolt.[34]

Regardless of how many slaves were killed in an insurrection, Africans certainly took heed of their companions' deaths. When slaves were brutally punished after shipboard insurrections, it undoubtedly took a massive psychological toll on the survivors and helped considerably in avoiding the repetition of revolt. In some cases, public executions of slaves were meant not only to subdue those slaves left on a given ship, but to teach slaves on neighboring vessels that insurrection was a dangerous and futile enterprise. Following the 1721 revolt aboard the *Elizabeth,* for instance, slaves on nearby ships were forced to watch the execution of the ringleader. As William Snelgrave explained the decision, "this would in all probability prevent future Mischiefs; for by publickly executing this Person at the Ship's Fore-yard Arm, the Negroes on board their Ships would see it; and as they were very much disposed to mutiny, it might prevent them from attempting it."[35] There are indications that this was a smart ploy, for as we have seen, sometimes a revolt on one ship would inspire the slaves on a neighboring vessel to revolt. Upon witnessing a violent insurrection aboard a ship anchored nearby, one captain in the early nineteenth century trade noted that "after this misfortune it became necessary to be more watchful of the blacks . . . who, instigated by the example of their insurgent countrymen, had already begun to exhibit an impatience of restraint."[36] The violence attending unsuccessful insurrections was extremely brutal, and surely any slave witnessing such excessive bloodshed and listening to the shrieks and screams of those being tortured and killed would have to call on every last ounce of courage and determination in order to make another attempt. Beyond discouraging future eruptions of slave resistance, the extreme punishments meted out to slave rebels may also have served an important psychological function for captains and crew members. Indeed, the brutality of the executions illuminates the unwillingness on the part of captains and sailors to acknowledge the fundamental humanity of black men and women. By stripping them of any value associated with human life, the bodies of slaves could thus be freely brutalized, tortured, and sold without guilt. This perception on the part of the crew that the Africans were less than human provided another barrier to insurrection as effective as the crew's weaponry.

Nevertheless, such gruesome reprisals never completely crushed the will of the slaves, as evidenced by the number of cases in which Africans revolted a second and even third time after an unsuccessful initial attempt. Evidence exists of at least fifteen separate voyages in which the slaves on board revolted multiple times. As early as 1693, for instance, two separate revolts occurred on board a Brandenburg vessel as the ship was making its way from Whydah to the island of Sao Tome. During these two revolts, it appears that at least twenty slaves were killed.[37] In May of 1783, slaves aboard the *Wasp* also staged two insurrections. In the first, the African women attacked the captain and tried to throw him overboard while the ship was still on the African coast but were prevented from doing so by the rest of the crew. Twelve days after sailing, a larger insurrection was attempted in which the crew had to shoot and kill a number of slaves before the vessel could be recaptured. In all, at least sixty-seven slaves lost their lives.[38] And in the cases of a London ship in about 1771, another English ship named the *Warwick Castle* around 1777, and the Dutch *Vigilantie* in 1780, three separate revolts were recorded.[39] Although most shipboard insurrections were unsuccessful, it is clear that the Africans who found themselves prisoners on the ships of the Middle Passage never gave up in their efforts to be free. Fighting against weapons, brutality, and racism, the men and women involved in these revolts faced betrayal, assistance from nearby vessels, brutal executions, and innumerable other barriers to success. And yet on hundreds of separate occasions, some of the most resolute, brave, or lucky of these Africans managed to beat the odds and reclaim their liberty.

6

Successful Revolts

In October of 1752, more than four hundred Africans from Bonny and the Gold Coast found themselves on board the Bristol slaver *Marlborough* as it was about to embark on the treacherous journey across the Atlantic. Among them, twenty-eight Gold Coast Africans managed to earn the trust of the *Marlborough's* master, Captain Codd, to such an extent that they were permitted on deck and out of chains to assist in the sailing of the ship. This decision would prove to be a fatal mistake. Three days into the journey, an opportune moment for rebellion arose when the captain decided to bathe the slaves and ordered all of the more than thirty sailors on board except himself and two sentries to go below to prepare the equipment needed for the process. Recognizing that they far outnumbered the crew members left on deck, the Africans seized their opportunity and attacked. Their first move was to disarm the sentries standing post at the ship's barricado and throw them overboard to drown. They next turned their attention toward Captain Codd, now the lone white man on deck, who managed to flee to the foretop despite having been hit in the head with the butt of a blunderbuss. The Africans then had to deal with the remainder of the sailors, who had now come on deck and were determined to defend the ship and reenslave the Africans. Locked in this battle for self-preservation, the crew proved the weaker adversaries, for the revolt had happened so suddenly that they were taken by surprise and were unequipped to deal with the armed slaves. All they had to wage their defense were an empty musket and a few boards. When the Africans quickly killed two men, most of the remaining sailors realized that it was futile to engage them in such a one-sided fight and fled to various points in the ship's rigging in a desperate attempt to distance themselves from the slaves' wrath.

In the confusion of the moment, the unfortunate sailors who had fled to less secure parts of the ship were quickly tracked down and killed. Some of the Africans fired at the crewmen who had taken refuge in the rigging, while others targeted those they could reach. One of these less-fortunate men was the ship's doctor, who was shot in the side and thrown overboard after having been bludgeoned to death with a mallet taken from the ship's kitchen. Others were also shot or stabbed, and soon all but those who remained in the rigging were dead. One of these men attempted to throw himself upon the mercy of the Africans by climbing down and surrendering after being shot in the thigh, but this sailor's poor judgment quickly became apparent when he was swiftly executed. Now in control of the ship, the Africans realized that the number of crew members still alive was so small as not to present a threat, and they convinced the survivors that they would not be killed if they surrendered. However, when twelve crew members came down, the Africans determined that there were still too many alive for their comfort and threw four of the men overboard. The others were soon put to work in turning the *Marlborough* around and sailing it back to land. Two days later, the ship arrived back in the vicinity of the Bonny coast. Unbeknownst to the Africans, the captain, despite being badly injured, was still alive and hiding in the foretop. The crew managed to smuggle him down to the forestay sail netting and hide him under a sail, where they hoped he would be safe until they could be rescued or until the Africans abandoned the ship for shore. However, their hopes were soon dashed when the Africans discovered the captain's coattail exposed underneath the sail. When they realized he was still alive, the rebels quickly killed the captain and threw him overboard.

Eager to end the revolt and secure their freedom back on land, the Africans forced the crew to anchor the ship and lower its longboat and yawl so that they could get to the coast as soon as possible. However, the boats, already heavily loaded with goods and people, both sank when hundreds of Bonny slaves anxious to get back on land attempted to force their way on board. Angered by this, the Gold Coast slaves remaining on board the *Marlborough* refused to let these Africans back on the ship, leaving nearly one hundred of them to drown. This incident sparked two days of violent fighting between the Gold Coast and the Bonny slaves that was halted only momentarily by a truce to dress and eat. No longer having the longboat and yawl at their disposal, the Africans ordered the sailors to sail the ship closer to shore. When the sailors finally found a location to anchor, the Africans realized that they were in view of nearby ships and, fearful of being recaptured, threatened the lives of the crew. Although the discomfort the slaves felt at being so close to other ships was well founded, the sailors somehow managed to persuade the Africans to let them anchor there despite the potential threat. The Africans ordered one of the ship's boats to be lowered so that they could send small groups of slaves ashore. Reluctantly convinced by the ship's cook that a crew member could best navigate the small boat, the Africans allowed one sailor to join the group setting off for the shore. As darkness began to fall, the small group in the punt rowed feverishly for the beach and soon achieved the freedom they had fought so hard for. Other small groups would follow in the hours to come, and in the end, some 270 Africans would land on the Bonny shore as free men and women.

But the journey was not yet over for all of the Africans on board. Not content with stepping foot in a strange land, the Gold Coast Africans were determined to sail the vessel back to their own home. After two or three days anchored off the Bonny coast, however, the Gold Coast Africans found themselves faced with yet another obstacle. The Bristol ship *Hawk* had sighted the *Marlborough* and noticed that the ship appeared to be in distress. Passing by the vessel, the captain of the *Hawk* hailed the *Marlborough,* and the slaves responded that some of the crew had gone ashore and that the rest were sick. Not convinced of this story, the captain of the *Hawk* sent a yawl to the *Marlborough* to investigate further, and upon discovering the truth, the sailors in the yawl quickly retreated. That night, the *Hawk* attempted to retake the captured slaver, but the Africans prevailed in this battle by their skilled use of the ship's cannons and firearms. When daylight broke, the Africans cut the anchor and set back out to sea, bound for the Gold Coast. As the *Marlborough* was making her escape, one of the remaining crew members jumped overboard and swam to the *Hawk*. What became of the Gold Coast slaves and the few surviving sailors on the vessel remains a mystery. Ironically, it was noted in an editorial commentary on the incident that "Captain Codd has left a Widow and four Children, and is much lamented, as he was a worthy, facetious, good-natur'd Commander."[1] Clearly, white readers were capable of understanding the tragedy inherent in a father being prematurely taken away from his family. However, the limits of whites' compassion and empathy are evidenced by the author's complete disregard in his account of the fact that Codd himself had attempted to tear more than four hundred slaves permanently away from their own families.

A slaving voyage was a common business venture that was repeated thousands of times over throughout the history of the slave trade. In the beginning, African rebels might have benefitted from the novelty of such a business as sailors gradually learned how best to manage and control their human cargo. However, as time went on and the business of slaving became more and more entrenched, slave-ship outfitters, owners, captains, and crews learned from their mistakes and developed more efficient methods of minimizing the potential danger faced by the crew. This clearly did not stop Africans from revolting, as the hundreds of rebellions they waged demonstrate, but it did very effectively limit the success of such revolts. Captains learned the strongest chains to use, they filled their ships with the most modern weapons available, they built barricadoes on deck and separated the men from the women, and they mandated a highly regulated and monitored daily routine on board. But in spite of this reality, the slim chance for freedom was all that mattered, and the slaves rebelled in spite of these obstacles. The Africans surely were under no misconception about their chances of success and realized that a revolt was in many ways a reckless and foolhardy venture, but tens of thousands nevertheless decided that the smallest chance of reclaiming their liberty was worth whatever risks or retribution might come with it. Win or lose, live or die, they at least knew that they gave it their best effort and refused to be enslaved without a fight. But while the great majority of attempted uprisings were unsuccessful, there were also a surprisingly large number of cases, such as that of the *Marlborough,* in which the Africans did achieve success in one form or another. This success ranged from temporarily capturing a vessel to securing freedom for a few of the Africans on board to rising up, taking possession of the ship, and reclaiming freedom on shore for the entire shipload of Africans. This chapter deals with these powerful insurrections and analyzes some of the problems that are encountered when attempting to fully and accurately evaluate successful shipboard slave revolts.

THE CAPTURE OF A VESSEL

In spite of all the measures taken to ensure a safe voyage across the Atlantic, numerous insurrections were indeed successful. However, the quantitative analysis of such revolts depends upon how one defines success. While the ultimate goal of any slave revolt was freedom from slavery, the most pressing and immediate goal of a shipboard rebellion was the capture of the vessel. Before true freedom could ever be hoped for, the Africans on board had to stop the progress of the ship. They had to turn their shipboard world upside down, reversing the balance of power on board and forcibly taking command of the slaver, even if only for a brief period. If the vessel had begun its passage, they had to find some way of capturing the helm and turning it around. Once this was accomplished, the revolt can fairly be classified as successful. Indeed, dozens upon dozens of insurrections reached this early stage of success. Although many of the insurrectionists involved in these incidents would find to their dismay that the hardest part still lay ahead of them, it was not that uncommon for slaves to find some way of slipping out of their chains and striking swiftly and without warning. If all went well and the crew was unable to react quickly or decisively enough, the slaves could take control of the ship.

When sailors were faced with such a powerful insurrection, they fought for as long as it was safe to do so. Once defeat seemed inevitable, however, they surrendered to the reality of the situation and typically fled or hid in fear for their lives. Sometimes, as was the case during an insurrection on board the Portuguese vessel *Misericordia* in 1532, some of the crew would escape by fleeing in the ship's launch. As this case demonstrates, this tactic was a smart move on the part of the sailors whenever possible, for the three men who managed to get away were the only three who survived the ordeal.[2] Crew members used the same tactic in 1729 when slaves aboard the *Clare* staged a powerful insurrection off Cape Coast Castle and again ten years later when sailors were forced to flee the *Princess Carolina* following a slave rebellion.[3] When the crew did not have access to such a means of escape or did not have time to coordinate an effective escape, they did whatever they could to avoid the wrath of the slaves. Following a 1757 revolt aboard the English vessel *Black Prince,* a letter written from the African coast criticized one such response on the part of the crew. The authors wrote to the vessel's owners that "There were others of ye Crew on board at the Time, but instead of doing their Duty & acting like Men, basely deserted their Trust, & run up the Tops, where they were infamous Spectators of the whole Transaction."[4] Although it is easy to criticize after the fact, the reality is that the terrified sailors probably had little choice and did the only thing possible to try to save their lives. As has been seen, taking refuge in the ship's masts and sails was a relatively common reaction, for the rigging of the ship, rising as high as seventy-five feet from the deck in some cases, promised a potential escape and shielded the sailors from much of the danger. Since the primary motivation for the Africans was to get back to land as quickly as possible, sailors realized that they might be spared if they could just flee into the rigging and wait out the worst of the revolt. Of course, this did not always work, as evidenced by the cases of the *Marlborough* and the *Delight*, in which crew members who had taken to the rigging in the face of slave insurrection were shot and otherwise wounded by the Africans.[5] Similarly, during an 1800 revolt aboard the *Flying Fish*, the captain, mate, cook, and a sailor were all shot by the Africans after having climbed their way to what they had hoped would be safety.[6] In one unusual case, two crew members chose not to climb the rigging but instead managed to save their lives by hiding until the next morning under chicken coops stored on board.[7] One can imagine the terror that these sailors must have felt in the face of such powerful slave rebellions. Feeling hopelessly outnumbered and having watched their fellow sailors being killed, surely they felt that their own death was imminent. If they couldn't flee from the ship and didn't have access to the rigging, they had to hide wherever they could. Draped under a sail or hidden behind boxes in the darkness of the ship's hold, frightened sailors had to limit their movement and muffle their breathing, praying for their lives and knowing full well that the Africans were hunting them. But regardless of where sailors attempted to hide or how successful they were in doing so, clearly the Africans in these cases were in complete control, and the vessels upon which they revolted were soon under their command.

However, this success was often short lived, for as we saw in the previous chapter, nearby vessels would commonly come to the aid of a captured slave ship, and in numerous cases insurrectionists were reenslaved after an engagement with a pursuing ship. Needless to say, after having come so far and now finding themselves on the brink of reclaiming their liberty, the Africans were not quick to submit, and just as the slaves on board the *Marlborough* successfully thwarted the efforts of the *Hawk* to recapture them, battles of many hours and even days were not uncommon. Slaves who had taken over the New York vessel *Venus*, for instance, engaged a pursuing ship in battle from daybreak until 11:00 that night, when the Africans were finally overpowered.[8] In another case in 1764, the slaves were in control of the ship for ten days before finally being recaptured. The insurrectionists overcame two separate attempts from nearby vessels to board her, and it was only when a third ship with enough firepower went in pursuit of the captured slaver that the revolt was finally brought to an end. Even then, however, a newspaper account of the incident noted that during the ensuing engagement, "the Negroes, with swivels and small-arms, maintained with firmness and vigour, till between 20 and 30 of them were wounded, two of whom died."[9] Occasionally, the slaves fought so well that they even managed to inflict casualties on the pursuing ship's crew. For instance, one sailor was killed on a French ship that went to the aid of the vessel *Debut* in January of 1767 after the slaves on board had revolted.[10] Similarly, as we saw in chapter 4, after slaves captured the English ship *Delight* in December 1769, the nearby *Apollo* gave chase, and during a four hour battle, the Africans on the *Delight* defended themselves so well that they even managed to kill a sailor on the *Apollo*. The battle came to an end only when a barrel of gunpowder on the captured slaver blew up and set the ship on fire.[11] And when an English ship attempted to aid the sailors aboard the French ship *Bienfaisant* in 1777 following a slave insurrection, the vessel was unable to approach the French slaver closely without endangering her own crew because the slaves on the *Bienfaisant* were firing upon the English vessel.[12]

In yet another case around 1793, a slave trader alerted to an insurrection on board an American ship gathered together as many hands as he could and went in pursuit of the ship in an armed schooner. During the battle, three men were killed and four were wounded on the schooner before the slaves on the American ship finally ran out of ammunition and fled to the shore.[13] And in September 1797, it took the efforts of two separate ships over a period of at least forty-two days to successfully recapture the English ship *Thomas* after it had been captured by the slaves on board.[14] Similar examples of slaves successfully capturing and holding a slave ship for a period of hours or days are peppered throughout the historical record. In fact, evidence exists of more than thirty such cases. These moderately successful revolts are remarkable in their own right and constitute an intermediate category between total defeat and freedom. The Africans on these vessels were successful in capturing the ship upon which they were held prisoners, if only temporarily. It can be plausibly argued that they reclaimed their status as free men and women through their efforts, establishing a sort of floating maroon colony of fugitive slaves. The slave regime—defined in this case as the authority of the slave ship captain and crew—had been overturned and the slaves had indeed staged a successful revolution. The fact that they were subsequently reenslaved should not influence one's appreciation of these revolts and the remarkable level of success they attained.

ON BOARD A CAPTURED SLAVE SHIP

Once a slaver was captured, the Africans were immediately faced with a number of pressing questions, the most important of which was how

"La révolte." Though the odds were against them, slaves occasionally took control of a vessel.

From Albert Laporte, *Récits de vieux marins* (Paris, 1883), 268.

to get the ship back to shore as quickly as possible. Depending on the extent of maritime experience in the communities from which they were captured, the Africans would either choose to kill all of the sailors and attempt to turn the ship around by themselves or, as occurred on numerous occasions, keep a few crew members alive for the purpose of navigating back to the African coast. In one such instance, slaves who had captured the French vessel *Necessaire* killed all of the crew except one man who was tied to a post and ordered to guide them back to the place they were taken from.[15] This was a very smart tactic on the part of the Africans, for if all the crew were killed and the slaves had no idea how to sail the ship, then the successful rebels might well have drifted on the ocean until they died of starvation or were captured by another ship. With feelings of power and rage welling up inside of them, it may have been difficult in some cases for Africans to spare the lives of sailors and acknowledge that they needed these men who had been their oppressors to help them succeed. But rational and calm leaders knew not to act impulsively and recognized that the job was not yet finished. In some cases, the Africans may have felt competent enough to handle the ship on their own. Indeed, sub-Saharan Africans had developed extensive trading networks that utilized local rivers and coastal routes. From small and swift canoes to much larger vessels capable of carrying one hundred or more people, many coastal communities thrived on the expert boatmen that conducted trade. These skills were translated for use in the slave trade as crews of slave ships regularly hired African boatmen to ferry slaves out to their ships or to serve as temporary deckhands while on the coast.[16] However, most Africans had little or no experience with navigating or sailing a vessel the size of a slave ship, and while lessons learned as free men and women on the African coast may have equipped certain captives with knowledge of the sea, currents, and winds, applying these skills to the massive slavers that they now found themselves on was a real challenge. The Africans knew that overconfidence in their ability to maneuver the ships or blind revenge against the sailors who had held them in bondage on board might leave them with nobody to sail the ship, thus dooming the insurrection to failure. As John Atkins observed, "When we are slaved and out at Sea, it is commonly imagined, the *Negroes* Ignorance of Navigation, will always be a Safeguard." In spite of this, Atkins conceded that sometimes slaves did revolt on the high sea, proving that "a Master's Care and Diligence should never be over till the Delivery of them."[17]

Nevertheless, a slave rebellion during the Middle Passage did indeed carry with it the potential for disaster from the Africans' perspective, for if all the crew were killed and none of the Africans was able to maneuver the ship, then the slaves were doomed. After keeping the rebellion a secret, coordinating themselves, and ultimately beating overwhelming odds and actually capturing the slave ship, the Africans in these instances must have felt incredibly frustrated. They could now only wait for weeks on end, slowly running out of food and water and completely open to attacks by other vessels or the ravages of mid-Atlantic storms. If not captured and reenslaved by another ship, the insurrectionists would ultimately die. Three cases illustrate this unfortunate reality. In 1771, a newspaper reported the following: "They write from Barbadoes that a French Guineaman, in her Passage between Goree and Martinico, had been cut off by an Insurrection of the Slaves, who murdered all the Crew; and that the Ship, after being tossed about for several Weeks, was found at Sea lately, with only nine Negroes alive on Board."[18] A second report in 1785 noted that "A schooner, which sailed about 12 months since from New-Port, for the coast of Africa . . . was lately met with at sea, by a vessel bound to Bristol, in England. She was without sails, had only 15 negroes on board and those in a very emaciated and wretched condition, having doubtless been long at sea. The negroes it is supposed, had rose and murdered the Captain and crew; after which many of the blacks must have died."[19] And in 1808, finally, there is the case of the American ship *Leander,* found drifting on the ocean some 250 miles off the coast of Charleston, South Carolina. Aboard the vessel were fifty-six Africans and no crew. "From her manner of steering, and from a piece of a torn sail which looked like a white flag," according to reports, the ship appeared to be in distress. When the *Leander* was finally encountered by another vessel, the slaves told the crew that all of the whites had died, but after their arrival in port, part of a journal was apparently found that suggested the slaves had risen and the crew had been thrown overboard, after which the Africans found themselves unable to steer the ship.[20] As these cases show, keeping at least one crew member alive on board for navigation was an important part of most slave insurrections. There is no telling how many ships during the Atlantic crossing were captured by slaves, only to end up crippled and helpless, drifting on a vast sea with nowhere to go.

In other cases, presumably valuing freedom over retribution, the insurrectionists made no attempt to kill their captors but merely locked them up, set them adrift, or sent them ashore. In 1742, when slaves on board the *Mary* of London rose up, they simply locked the captain and mate in the cabin, where they remained for twenty-seven days.[21] On an English ship that slaves had captured in 1764, one of the surviving crew members was placed at the vessel's helm and commanded to steer the ship every morning toward the rising of the sun. As for the other captured sailors, it is noted that the leader of the revolt "maintained the strictest order, in particular with respect to the allowance of provisions, distributing the same quantity to the white men and boys, as was allowed to the rest."[22] And in about 1793, rather than needlessly butchering injured sailors, the slaves who captured an American vessel near Sierra Leone permitted the crew to take the wounded ashore in a boat.[23] Another instance of slave rebels showing mercy can be seen in the case of the *Regina Coeli* in 1858 when the slaves spared the life of the ship's surgeon, who had apparently been kind to the Africans during the voyage.[24] Although large numbers of sailors were in fact killed in the many revolts that occurred, on the whole unnecessary violence, cruelty, and vengeance do not seem to be typical of the slaves' actions. Indeed, reports of large-scale crew massacres at the hands of revolting slaves are not a common occurrence in the historical record.

Support for this is found in the fact that accounts of shipboard revolts often noted that insurrectionists spared the lives of the "boys" who commonly shipped out with the crews of slave ships. Although the term *boy* on a ship often referred not to a child but to the lowest-ranking member of a ship's company, regardless of age, this individual was often a young man, sometimes only fourteen or fifteen years old. New to the sea, and without the hardened spirit of a sailor, boys were probably the least likely of the crew members to present a threat to the Africans' intentions to free themselves. Shipboard communities were rigidly hierarchical, and slave ships were at least theoretically even more so, considering the discipline and authority that had to be maintained on board to control the slaves. As the lowest-ranking members of the crew, "boys" were forced to do menial and undesirable tasks such as coiling and tarring ropes, swabbing the deck, oiling gear, and mending sail canvas and were traditionally mistreated and abused by more experienced sailors.[25] The cabin boy on one English slave ship, for example, was so viciously targeted for harassment by the vessel's chief mate that he ended up committing suicide to escape the officer's sadistic behavior.[26] Paid nearly nothing, boys performed a servile role, and it is conceivable that the Africans may have felt some affinity with such young men, particularly if they had shown no indication of any overt hostility to the Africans. Of course, this was not always reciprocated. In fact, some boys, precisely because of their mistreatment at the hands of the sailors, surely brutalized and persecuted the Africans in an effort to exert some degree of power on board and thus feel better about themselves in the process. Conversely, however, the boys themselves may have noted similarities between their status and that of the slaves, and while this would probably not have led them to respect or admire the Africans in any meaningful way, it may have encouraged them to acknowledge a bond that the other crew members were blind to, perhaps leading to kinder treatment on their part. New to the business of slaving, all that most boys would have known about the trade was what they gathered from the adventurous tales of those who had gone before them. Coming face to face with the harsh reality of a slave ship may have elicited some sort of empathy or pity.

Regardless of why "boys" were often spared, the reality is that they were not typically targeted by slave rebels. After the *William* suffered a slave revolt on the Gold Coast in 1730, for example, the Africans killed the entire crew except for three boys.[27] In the case of the English *Exeter,* accounts reported that the slaves "rose upon the white People, killed the Captain, Mate, and all the Crew, except a Boy."[28] In 1764, the more than one hundred Africans who revolted on an English ship "killed the Captain, Mate, and some others, leaving only two men and two boys alive."[29] And after a Liverpool ship was retaken and brought into port in 1772, it was discovered that the 250 slaves on board had killed the entire crew "but one little Boy."[30] Particularly when the "boys" who shipped out on slavers were in fact children, such as the "little Boy" mentioned here, the Africans may have felt some moral obligation not to harm them, especially if their age and position carried no threat to the rebels. Similarly, slaves who revolted on a French ship on the Senegal coast in 1774 "murdered all the crew, except a white woman and a passenger on board."[31] Once again, it can be reasonably inferred that the objective of the slaves was not irrational and random vengeance but success in gaining their freedom. Presumably innocent bystanders without weapons or training, individuals such as these young boys and passengers would have appeared to pose little or no threat to the slaves' goal of freedom and thus were not targeted for death.

Whether crew members lived or died, the pressing issue for the Africans was how to get the captured ship close enough to land to escape. Rebelling slaves commonly cut the cables that anchored a vessel offshore, which they hoped would allow the ship to drift back toward the beach and eventually run aground, allowing the slaves to escape. Many accounts of successful revolts conclude by noting that the slaves ran the ship ashore. If this occurred in a busy trading harbor or within site of a European fort, chances were that an armed contingent of slave traders or local Africans would be there as soon as the ship ran aground, but if the ship were anchored in a more remote area, cutting the anchor lines and beaching the ship was a very effective method of escaping. Slaves escaping from a Dutch ship that was run aground in 1701, for example, "saved themselves by jumping into the Mud."[32] Even when the Africans were unable to get the upper hand in an insurrection, they might still be able to escape. If they acted quickly, slaves might steal the ship's small boat and make their way to shore, as a few rebels did to escape a French ship in 1695.[33] In November of 1754, twelve slaves similarly managed to escape in a dinghy after they revolted on the French vessel *Finette*.[34] In another case, the Africans actually built a raft upon which they succeeded in getting to shore.[35] However, even in these instances, often only some of the slaves managed to free themselves, while the rest were reenslaved.

There are also a number of cases in which slaves escaped to the water or to the beach temporarily, only to be recaptured by either the ship's crew, the crew of a vessel providing assistance, or even people on the shore. When ninety-three slaves on the French ship *Don de Dieu* rose up in November of 1719, for example, twenty-six of the Africans who managed to reach land were tracked down and reenslaved before they had a chance to flee inland.[36] In 1775, four slaves attempted to swim to shore after a shipboard revolt just off the Senegal coast, but before they could reach the beach, crew members caught up with the Africans and returned them to the ship.[37] Complete and permanent success for an entire shipload of Africans was by far the exception; indeed for many reasons the exact number of cases in which this was achieved cannot be determined. As crew members, sailors on nearby ships, or officials on shore are the ones upon whom historians must depend for the surviving documentation of shipboard insurrections, one cannot expect their narratives to go much beyond the point at which the slaves made their way to shore. The last thing observers would have noted was the Africans jumping overboard, swimming to shore, or racing up the beach and rapidly dispersing in all directions, disappearing inland as fast as they could. What happened to these men and women and whether they were recaptured was beyond the knowledge of the witness. However, there are dozens of examples of revolts in which the Africans appear to have succeeded in getting to shore and for which there is no evidence to suggest that they did not escape. In these truly successful insurrections, the Africans did in fact prevail in securing their freedom, at least for the short-term. These will be discussed momentarily, after a discussion of one other major impediment to our ability to assess accurately the degree to which Africans on slave ships succeeded in their insurrectionary efforts.

SHIPS "CUT OFF" ON THE AFRICAN COAST

Perhaps the greatest obstacle to a full understanding of successful ship-board slave insurrections is the phenomenon of slave ships being "cut off" or "cut out" on the African coast. The use of such phrases presents a problem of identification, for they could refer to both slave insurrections and cases of resistance from free Africans. In fact, the term *cut off* seems to have been applied at one time or another to the attack and capture of a ship under just about any conceivable circumstances, regardless of who was involved. A letter written in 1719 from one of the Royal African Company's agents in West Africa refers to a sailor being discharged because of his implication in a plot to "cut off" his own ship because he and his fellow crewmen were dissatisfied with their pay.[38] In another case in 1748, a vessel named the *Londonderry* was described as being "cut out" by a Spanish privateer, whose crew plundered and burned the ship.[39] With yet another meaning, the same term is used to describe prisoners on board the Liverpool ship *King's Fisher* rising up, killing the captain and crew and running the vessel ashore on the Virginia coast.[40] Clearly, occurrences of these terms are difficult to classify, as they signified different things in different circumstances.

When these terms are used to refer to events on the African coast, their ambiguity becomes particularly frustrating for those interested in the magnitude and frequency of successful shipboard slave insurrections. Since ships that were "cut off" were by definition complete losses, those so described may be relevant to our understanding of the frequency of successful slave revolts. But because of the broad use of the term, only those accounts of slavers being "cut off" in which the attackers are specifically identified as slaves can truly be documented as shipboard rebellions. For instance, the following brief account of a ship being "cut off" clearly refers to a slave insurrection: "Capt. Nicoll, in a Brig belonging to New-York, had been cut off on the Coast of Guinea, by the Slaves."[41] Similarly, it was reported in another paper that the "*Cadiz Dispatch,* [Captain] Baldy, from London, with 132 Slaves on board, was cut off by the Slaves in May last—the Crew (except the Chief Mate) saved."[42] While such cases are refreshingly easy to identify, others are far more nebulous. The difficulty lies in the terminology, for the word *Negroes* or *Blacks* could easily be used to refer to slaves, whereas *Africans* or *Natives* might be more likely to refer to free Africans. Consider, for example, the following ambiguous accounts:

> The *Robert,* Capt. Hamilton, was lately blown up by the Negroes on the Coast of Guiney.[43]
>
> The *Three Friends,* Trigs, of and from London, is cut off by the Negroes on the Coast of Africa.[44]
>
> A Schooner belonging to this Port, Lewis, Master, we hear, was lately cut off by the Negroes, on the Coast of Africa.[45]
>
> The *Hero,* captain Bunce, belonging to Carolina, is cut off by the negroes at Domel, near Goree, on the coast of Africa.[46]
>
> The *Sally,* [Captain] Draper and the *Fly,* [Captain] Jones of Liverpool are both Cut Off on the Coast of Africa.[47]

All of these cases, or none of them, could in fact be instances of shipboard slave insurrections. The term *Negro* referred to any African, whether slave or free, and is thus a very difficult term to deal with when attempting to classify such incidents as slave revolts or not. The term *native,* however, is less ambiguous and usually applied to free men and women, as in the following accounts:

> The last letters from Senegal mention, that a Portuguese vessel has been cut off by a conspiracy of the natives, on the coast of Angola, and that they had murdered the Captain and all the crew.[48]
>
> Capt. Sharp . . . says that he saw some persons who had been on board a vessel just arrived from Africa, and that they told him there were three vessels belonging to London cut off by the natives.[49]
>
> Captain Gideon, in a brig belonging to Liverpool, had arrived on the coast, and went into the river Pungoes, in order to slave off, and had not been there but a few days before he was cut off by the natives.[50]

These cases seem far less likely to have been cases of shipboard slave revolts but are, again, extremely difficult to classify correctly. Indeed, even here, where the term *native* seems to refer to free Africans, one can be fooled. In 1731, for instance, it was reported that the vessel *Ruby* and its men "had the Misfortune to be cut off by the Natives," with one of the ship's captains and most of the sailors killed. If this were all we knew, this case would appear to be one of local Africans attacking a slave ship on the coast, a frequent occurrence throughout the history of the slave trade, but newspaper accounts provide a clearer picture of this incident, noting that the ship was anchored on the Guinea coast purchasing slaves when the fifty Africans on board suddenly rose, killed the sailors, ran the ship ashore, and made their escape.[51] Once again, the terminology is deceptive, and the incident turns out to be something different than what it would appear to be based only on the initial account.

Determining whether these and other similar cases were shipboard slave revolts is often impossible. As in the case of the *Ruby*, it is sometimes possible to make this determination only when complementary pieces of evidence exist. A reference in 1765 to the English ship *Jolly Prince,* for instance, says only that the ship "was cut off on the Windward Coast of Africa" and that the captain and crew were killed. Only based on a second reference to this incident in a different newspaper stating that the vessel "was cut off by the *slaves*" can it finally and accurately be classified as a revolt.[52] Similarly, in spite of long and descriptive pieces in numerous colonial American newspapers clearly describing a powerful slave insurrection on board the *Ann,* when *Lloyd's List* of London picked the story up, it reported simply that the *Ann* was "cut off by the Negroes on the Coast of Guiney. The Captain kill'd on the spot, and all the Crew murdered."[53] In a more subtle bit of clarification, two of the four primary sources of an incident that occurred on the *Restoration* in 1729 note that the ship was simply "cut off by the Negroes." This would have to be considered another ambiguous case of resistance on the African coast were it not for the changing of a single word in the two additional sources regarding this event, but the other accounts state that the vessel was "cut off by *her* Negroes" and that the captain was attacked by "*his* Negroes."[54] The ownership implied by these words allows this otherwise ambiguous incident to be classified as a true case of shipboard slave rebellion.

Since many of these cases of vessels being "cut off" on the African coast appear just as likely to be outbreaks of shipboard insurrections as not, they need to be considered in any comprehensive analysis of shipboard resistance. However, since they cannot be determined for certain to be cases of revolts, these incidents are excluded from the chronology of revolts in the appendix. These ambiguous cases are particularly important to any full understanding of successful shipboard insurrections because the term "cut off" implies the complete loss of a ship or the sudden and often tragic end to its voyage. Thus any of these incidents that were actual revolts are additional cases not just of insurrection but of *successful* insurrection. If only half of the dozens of references to a ship being "cut off" did in fact refer to actual shipboard revolts, then we would have to substantially reconsider our understanding of the rates of success that slave rebels enjoyed. It may well turn out that Africans were able to rise up, capture a ship, and regain their freedom on shore much more often than previously thought. Nevertheless, since it cannot be determined for certain that the ambiguous cases are in fact cases of shipboard slave insurrections, they have been excluded from consideration here.

FREEDOM

Even when rigidly defining a successful shipboard revolt as an incident in which some or all of the slaves actually managed to free themselves in the process, the figures are quite remarkable. If the cases where slaves captured a ship temporarily are thrown out and incidents in which slavers were "cut off" by unknown assailants are excluded, there still remain dozens of examples of shipboard slave revolts in which true freedom was attained by the rebels. Of the 493 cases of shipboard revolts listed in the appendix, it appears that slave insurrections led to the freedom of at least some of the slaves on board in 120 cases. These are the revolts in which all of the pieces managed to fall in the right places for the Africans. They were not necessarily the best planned, the best led, or the best executed examples of shipboard rebellion, but they worked. The result of a complex mixture of courage, luck, determination on the part of the Africans, and perhaps overconfidence or inattention on the part of the crew, these incidents stand as true testaments to the ability of severely oppressed people to find the will to capably stage highly effective rebellions against those attempting to keep them in bondage. Furthermore, they stand in powerful contrast to conventional wisdom regarding slave resistance, for the scholarship completed in recent decades on American plantation slave societies has necessarily had to conclude that virtually all efforts at slave rebellion have been failures. With the exception of St. Domingue and perhaps the impressive fugitive slave communities in such places as Brazil, Jamaica, and Surinam, our definition of slave resistance has heretofore been unable to include the notion of complete success as one of its components. Instead, it is the effort that we celebrate rather than the result. However, when shipboard insurrections take their place alongside this powerful tradition of resistance in the Americas, historians will have a more nuanced view of the ways in which slaves resisted their status and of the degree to which they achieved their goal of escaping bondage. The concepts of not only limited success but outright freedom may now be interwoven into the history of African and African American resistance to slavery, enabling a fuller understanding of slave resistance as a whole.

A number of successful revolts have been profiled throughout this book and are notable for the substantial level of detail of their stories that has survived. However, we know very little about most successful insurrections because the sailors were killed, the revolts were denied or covered up by embarrassed captains, or they occurred in areas where there were no witnesses to tell the tales. Perhaps historians must give the Africans the benefit of the doubt in many of these cases and presume that the rebels succeeded in freeing themselves even when precise evidence of such an outcome doesn't exist. In 1730, for instance, newspaper accounts and a letter written by a Royal African Company agent at Cape Coast Castle all reported that the Africans rose and killed all but three of the sailors on board the Boston ship *William*. No mention was made of the fate of the Africans, and although the vessel was later reported to have run aground at Anomabu, there is no reason to believe the victorious Africans did not either jump overboard or take the *William*'s boats, ultimately getting ashore and reclaiming their freedom.[55] In January of 1747, a Rhode Island ship underwent a revolt off of Cape Coast Castle, and the entire crew was killed except for two mates who jumped overboard and swam ashore. Taking its information about this revolt from a letter, one Boston newspaper wrote that "what became of the Vessel and Negroes afterwards the Letter does not mention." Even though this incident occurred in a busy slaving region, this powerful revolt happened within swimming distance of the shore, and it is not at all unreasonable to presume that at least some of the Africans succeeded in escaping inland.[56] As these two examples indicate, any analysis of successful shipboard insurrections necessarily involves a bit of speculation. Once the narrative of the official, sailor, or observer ends, the historian is left to ponder the fate of the insurrectionists without any hard evidence. And while it is unreasonable to simply assume that the slaves necessarily freed themselves simply because there is no documentation to the contrary, it is perhaps even more unreasonable to conclude that they did not. The cases in question were powerful revolts. The sailors had been killed or fled and the Africans had taken control. The vessels were near land and the slaves had gained an advantage, if only momentarily. Success beckoned from the nearby shore, and surely a great many of the Africans involved attained it. When such cases are combined with revolts where factual evidence explicitly states that the Africans escaped, it becomes clear that shipboard rebels did indeed achieve freedom in quite a few cases.

For centuries, Africans waged well-planned and highly effective insurrections aboard the ships of the transatlantic slave trade. Despite the trauma of capture and enslavement, the brutality of the crew, the inhuman living conditions on the ships, the lack of adequate weaponry, the hesitancy and betrayal of some of the captives, and the swift aid provided to the sailors by nearby ships, the Africans found ways to prevail, and countless slaves succeeded in regaining their freedom in the process. Evidence exists of 120 insurrections that were either partially or completely successful in reclaiming freedom for those Africans involved. If the 32 marginally successful cases in which the Africans captured the vessel upon which they were enslaved only to be subsequently recaptured are added to the mix, the number rises to more than 150. And if one added the ambiguous cases of slavers being "cut off" on the African coast, the number would rise higher still. Furthermore, these numbers are only part of the story, for the influence of successful shipboard insurrections undoubtedly surpassed their frequency. The thousands of Africans involved in these successful revolts convinced captains and sailors alike through their actions that the destruction of an entire ship and its crew was a very real possibility on any vessel undertaking the Atlantic crossing laden with slaves. While the most obvious result of this knowledge was the imposition of ever more repressive and restrictive security measures on slave ships, perhaps the possibility of revolt also helped earn Africans a grudging respect from those whose business it was to enslave them. As one sailor was compelled to write of a revolt in 1790, after more than one hundred slaves had taken possession of a French slaver as it was at anchor off the African coast, "I could not but admire the courage of a fine young black, who, though his partner in irons lay dead at his feet, would not surrender, but fought with his billet of wood until a ball finished his existence. The others fought as well as they could, but what could they do against firearms?"[57]

Those engaged in the slave trade did not have the luxury of relaxing. The legacy of shipboard rebellion caused them great fear and anxiety. Fortunes were ruined, ships were destroyed, and sailors were executed. Most whites may well have felt that slaves were inferior and ignorant, but the long tradition of shipboard resistance certainly kept them from believing the Africans were harmless or weak. Fearless, organized, and desperate, the actions of slave insurrectionists confronted even the most hateful of slave traders with the reality that Africans were human beings, forced to do what any other group in their position would do. By fighting, and sometimes winning, these Africans proved their humanity in a way that later abolitionists could never do. They stood toe to toe with their oppressors, challenging them at every turn, and in so doing, powerfully dismantling the argument that they were meant to be slaves.

7

Shipboard Revolts in the Americas: a New Wave

One fascinating case of resistance aboard a ship engaged in the international American slave trade can be seen in the incidents surrounding a revolt that occurred off the coast of Chile on the Spanish ship *Tryal* in the early morning hours of December 27, 1804. Of the 493 cases of insurrection identified in this study, this marks the only case of shipboard insurrection occurring in Pacific waters. However, what makes this insurrection particularly compelling is not the location but the incredible amount of surviving information about it[1] as well as the fact that the story was seized upon by Herman Melville as the basis for his story "Benito Cereno."[2] The *Tryal*[3] was seven days out from Valparaiso, Chile, with a "cargo" of about seventy slaves to be delivered to Lima, Peru, when an eighteen-year-old slave named Jose communicated to Mure,[4] the leader of the revolt, that the moment was right for rebellion. The captives wasted no time and struck quickly and boldly, capturing the crew by surprise. In the ensuing revolt, the slaves killed eighteen of the Spanish sailors outright, seriously wounded the boatswain and carpenter, and threw an additional seven crew members overboard in the days to follow. The insurrectionists then ordered the *Tryal*'s captain, Benito Cereno, to take them to Senegal. This was a smart ploy on the part of the rebels, for there was no turning back at this point, and making it to the African coast was the best chance they had to secure their freedom. But West Africa was weeks away, and the likelihood of making it there safely on a vessel inadequately supplied for such a voyage was extremely small. Nevertheless, the *Tryal* apparently changed course to sail around Cape Horn, headed for Senegal, while the surviving sailors maintained a constant hope that they would encounter a friendly vessel that would help them recapture the ship. The slaves held daily conferences to discuss the best way to successfully carry out their bid for freedom, but after more than fifty days at sea, the acute shortage of provisions forced them to turn the ship toward shore to procure water. Fearing recapture, the slaves warned the sailors that they would be killed the moment any city, town, or settlement was observed. But in spite of the rebels' efforts to remain undetected, their excursion ashore near the island of Santa Maria, just to the southwest of Concepcion, signaled the beginning of the end for the insurrectionists. On the morning of February 20, the *Tryal* was sighted by the U.S. ship *Perseverance,* commanded by Captain Amasa Delano.[5]

Believing the *Tryal* to be in some sort of distress, Captain Delano ordered provisions to be offered to the crew of the Spanish ship, and upon boarding the vessel, Delano at first sensed nothing to suggest anything out of the ordinary. Benito Cereno and his crew were so terrified by the slaves that they did exactly as they were instructed, telling Delano that the ship was from Buenos Aires and that everything was under control. Mure kept Benito Cereno in check by remaining constantly at his side, ensuring that he gave no indication of the true state of affairs aboard the *Tryal.* As Delano subsequently noted,

> The Spanish captain had evidently lost much of his authority over the slaves, whom he appeared to fear, and whom he was unwilling in any case to oppose. . . . Several . . . instances of unruly conduct, which, agreeably to my manner of thinking, demanded immediate resistance and punishment, were thus easily winked at, and passed over. . . . The act of the negro [Mure], who kept constantly at the elbows of Don Benito and myself, I should, at any other time, have immediately resented; and although it excited my wonder, that his commander should allow this extraordinary liberty, I did not remonstrate against it, until it became troublesome to myself.[6]

Additionally, Delano's attempts to speak to Benito Cereno in Spanish were futile, for Mure and his companions were also Spanish speakers, and the captain was thus forced to tell Delano that Mure was simply his trusted servant. Cereno introduced Mure as the "captain of the slaves," who kept his fellow captives in good order, and he informed Delano that he had made Mure his confidant and companion following the death of a number of his crew. In his later testimony, Benito Cereno described Mure as "a man of capacity and talents, performing the office of an officious servant, with all the appearance of submission of the humble slave," while all the while maintaining total command of the situation.[7] Having detected no evidence that anything was amiss, Captain Delano got ready to leave the ship. Upon bidding farewell to Delano, Benito Cereno attempted to give him subtle hints that something was wrong, first acting coldly toward him and then giving him a telling squeeze as he shook the captain's hand, but to no avail. Unwilling to let what could be his last chance at survival slip through his fingers, Benito Cereno waited until Delano's boat had shoved off from the side of the *Tryal* and then suddenly leaped overboard, calling out in Spanish that the slaves had risen and murdered the crew, and imploring his surviving men to either jump overboard or take to the ship's rigging. The slaves quickly ordered the chief officer to sail out of the bay, and they would certainly have escaped the pursuit of two of the *Perseverance*'s boats had it not been for the Spaniards left aboard the *Tryal*, who cut the ropes holding the ship's sails in place. About twenty men from the *Perseverance* soon boarded the *Tryal*, killing one of the Spanish crew members as well as seven slaves. The rebels attempted to fight the advance of the sailors by constructing a makeshift six-foot-high barricade across the deck using water casks and other materials, but they were overmatched by the weaponry of the sailors and were soon captured.

After order was restored, Captain Delano returned to his own ship for the night. The following morning, Delano boarded the *Tryal* and found that the Spanish crew had chained the male slaves to the ship's deck by their hands and feet and were abusing them mercilessly. He reported that "some of them had part of their bowels hanging out, and some . . . half their backs and thighs shaved off." Delano quickly realized he had to watch the *Tryal*'s crew very carefully, as they were intent on severely torturing the insurrectionists. As he wrote, "I observed one of the Spanish sailors had found a razor . . . and had made a cut upon [a] Negro's head. He seemed to aim at his throat, and it bled shockingly." Shortly thereafter, Benito Cereno himself was seen attempting to stab one of the slaves.[8] In the days following the revolt, it was determined that the principal participants in the insurrection were twelve or thirteen slaves between the ages of twenty-five and fifty and that approximately twenty others between the ages of twelve and sixteen, while aware of the plot, were not actively involved. The degree of participation by female slaves is not specifically stated, although it is said that they sang a melancholy song during the revolt "to excite the courage" of the men. Of the slaves who were still alive after the *Perseverance* had retaken the *Tryal*, the surviving record provides us with a valuable and unusual list of names, including Mure, as well as Matinqui, Alathano, Yau, Luis, Mapenda, Yola, Yambaio, Jose, Joaquin, and Francisco.

The record of the names of slave rebels such as these is an interesting aspect of this new wave of shipboard resistance in the Americas. Very rarely in the long history of insurrection during the transatlantic trade is there ever any record of the names of the African participants. Generally, such men and women are simply known by a number branded in their flesh. With the exception of a very few individuals such as Captain Tomba[9] and Essjerrie Ettin,[10] the identities of rebel leaders during the Atlantic crossing are absent from the record, and the whole history tends to take on a very anonymous character. This anonymity encourages the confluence of the thousands upon thousands of individuals who participated in these insurrections into one homogeneous set of slave rebels. History can still celebrate their actions, but it becomes difficult to appreciate these men and women as people. However, it is not at all unusual for the names of slave rebels to survive in the historical record of shipboard resistance in the Americas. Many of the participants in these insurrections had been born in the Americas, and others had spent a considerable amount of time there. These individuals now typically had names, whether given or adopted, that have survived in the historical record. Names allow us to better identify with these men and women and appreciate more fully the attributes that made them valuable as insurrectionists. And while knowing the names of slave insurrectionists is not necessary for an understanding or appreciation of shipboard resistance, it does add an additional level of meaning to the story. When we can name the participants, they are able to rise to the forefront of history as courageous individuals. Rebels such as those who rose up aboard the *Tryal* become historical actors with all of the attributes of humanity that come with being seen as distinct from the anonymous group of which they are a part.

As final punishment for their efforts to free themselves from bondage, at least nine of the *Tryal* insurrectionists were sentenced to death on March 2, 1805, in the city of Concepcion, Chile. As the sentence handed down read,

> [The slaves] shall be executed, by taking them out and dragging them from the prison, at the tail of a beast of burden, as far as the gibbet, where they shall be hung until they are dead, and [are sentenced] to the forfeiture of all their property, if they should have any, to be applied to the Royal Treasury; that the heads of the [first five?] be cut off

after they are dead, and be fixed on a pole, in the square of the port of Talcahuano, and the corpses of all be burnt to ashes. The negresses and young negroes of the same gang shall be present at the execution . . . [and] the negro Jose . . . and Yambaio, Francisco, [and] Rodriguez [shall also be condemned] to ten years confinement in the place of Valdivia, to work chained, on allowance and without pay, in the work of the King, and also to attend the execution of the other criminals.[11]

Much like the excessive violence routinely committed against rebel leaders during the Middle Passage, this punishment was formally intended to make an example of the insurrectionists. However, the degree of cruelty in this case goes beyond any calculated effort to intimidate the surviving captives from further acts of resistance and once again hints at the obsession of those involved in the slave trade with convincing themselves of their own superiority and of the benign and harmless nature of trading in human chattel.

Although shipboard slave insurrection is traditionally conceived of as a phenomenon that struck the vessels of the Middle Passage, such a view is somewhat limited, for it tends to obscure the fact that slaves continued the tradition of shipboard resistance long after the Middle Passage was over. In much the same way that captives rebelled while being transported down local African rivers prior to boarding the ships that would carry them across the Atlantic, Africans and African Americans alike throughout the Americas had their own opportunities for shipboard resistance. And while the recorded number and frequency of these events pale in comparison to those that took place during the transatlantic voyage, there were nevertheless numerous incidents that occurred. An investigation of these cases illuminates the ways in which the legacy of shipboard resistance during the Middle Passage was carried on within the domestic and international slave trades of the Americas. Like that aboard the *Tryal,* much of this shipboard resistance took place on larger, oceangoing ships in the Americas. In other cases, insurrections broke out on smaller, river-going craft engaged in the local domestic slave trade of regions such as the American South. Together, these incidents illuminate a little-known second wave of shipboard slave resistance with both similarities to and differences from that which preceded it during the Middle Passage. Inextricably linked, these two distinct histories of insurrection hint at a larger continuum of slave resistance that spanned continents, generations, and centuries.

SHIPBOARD REVOLTS ON OCEANGOING VESSELS
IN THE AMERICAS

Once slaves had endured the weeks upon weeks of suffering during their Atlantic passage from Africa to the Americas, their experiences with and opportunity for shipboard resistance were not necessarily over. When a slave
ship pulled into port in the Americas, people from far around came to inspect
and purchase the slaves. In the West Indies, it was not uncommon for slave
traders to sail over from nearby islands to inspect a lot of newly arrived
Africans. Thus, although many of the Africans would be sold to planters
in the immediate vicinity, others found that their ultimate destination was
still quite some distance away. Whether being transported to a different
colony, to the other side of a large West Indian island, or just a few miles
down a local river, slaves in the Americas often remained on the move
after their arrival in the New World. Some would continue their journey by
foot, recalling the still fresh memories of their initial capture and march to
the African coast. If the distance to be traveled was greater than could be
reasonably accomplished on foot, however, these African men and women
might find themselves loaded onto ships in what must have seemed like a
terrifying extension of the Middle Passage. Many slaves surely feared that
they were embarking not on a comparatively uneventful voyage of a few
days' sail but on yet another long and violent journey filled with death,
disease, and near starvation. Not surprisingly, the thoughts of many turned
once again to insurrection. Others being transported in the Americas had
never known the experience of the Middle Passage personally, having been
born slaves on the plantations of the Americas. In either case, shipboard
revolt was an ever-present possibility that countless Africans and African
Americans seized upon in an effort to free themselves.

In some cases, revolt in this situation may well have been easier than it
was during the Middle Passage. The initial fear and uncertainty surrounding being captured and sold was now months behind the Africans, and
they would have had time to make at least tentative conclusions about the
intentions of their captors and about their own ultimate fate in this strange
new world. In addition, the men and women who had survived the passage
from Africa had often been encouraged to bathe regularly and thoroughly,
had exercised more often, had been issued new clothes in some cases and
given alcohol or tobacco in an attempt to lift their spirits, may have been
seen and treated by a doctor, and generally found themselves regaining
some strength and vitality during a period of imprisonment prior to their

embarking on this second voyage. In fact, throughout the time a slave ship lay in port, and even a few days before its arrival, captains typically ordered an increase in rations and probably attempted to minimize brutality against the slaves by sailors. And while such actions were simply a calculated effort by the slave traders to prepare the slaves for sale at the highest prices, this brief period of recuperation following the Middle Passage may well have reinvigorated slaves with thoughts of rebellion.

In other cases, the slaves caught up in this second wave of shipboard movement were not Africans journeying to their final destination but African Americans being transferred from one location to another. This may have been the first sea voyage for many of these slaves, and the experience may have conjured feelings of confusion, despair, and fear similar to those their ancestors felt on the African coast before boarding the ships of the Middle Passage. However, these American-born captives were nevertheless better equipped than their African-born counterparts to deal with their voyage. They knew why they were being sold, they understood their role as laborers within the slave system, they generally spoke the same language as their captors, and they were not subject to such terrifying thoughts as whether they were going to be eaten by the ship's crew. Surely, slaves who found themselves being sold in the domestic or international slave trades of the Americas faced their own set of fears, frustrations, and terror, but unlike those of African rebels aboard the ships of the Middle Passage, their plans for resistance could unfold in a context of relative familiarity and psychological well-being. The usually short duration of the voyage, furthermore, did not lead to the same levels of disease, filth, and starvation that prevailed during the transatlantic voyage. In short, a substantial proportion of these African American men, women, and children would have been physically and psychologically strong and well prepared for the planning and execution of an insurrection. Thus, whether they were Africans enduring an extension of their initial transportation into slavery or African Americans being shipped from one location to another, the slaves who found themselves on ships in the Americas would have seen insurrection as a real and potentially effective means of resistance.

Regardless of whether the insurgents were African or American-born, however, shipboard revolt in the Americas was doomed to nearly inevitable failure. Unlike on the African coast, where a reasonable prospect of reaching freedom beckoned to any enslaved Africans who were able to rise up and successfully capture a ship, the situation was vastly different on the other side of the Atlantic. Even if a group of slaves were able to take a ship by force, their freedom would have been short lived, for as soon as the vessel made land and the rebels set foot on American shores, whether in Brazil, Martinique, or Virginia, reenslavement stared them coldly in the face. The Americas were essentially one vast slave regime, and any slaves who managed to make it to shore would almost invariably have been swept back into slavery by local slave patrols or police authorities. The language and cultural differences probably would have prevented native Africans from quietly melding into a community of freed men and women, and the chances of escaping inland and establishing or joining a maroon community in the interior of some colony were extremely small. For African Americans, the possibility of capturing a vessel, running it ashore, and escaping by joining a free community were greater because of their language skills and cultural norms but still very slim. The only real chance for true freedom was to capture a ship and its crew and force them to sail the vessel back across the Atlantic, a nearly impossible goal that was unsuccessfully attempted by Africans on board both the *Tryal* in 1804 and the *Amistad* in 1839. Thus while shipboard revolt itself may have seemed very enticing to slaves being moved from place to place in the Americas, the possibility of reclaiming their freedom in the process was far more remote than it was for slaves held on ships that were still in African waters.

The typical conditions on large, oceangoing ships in the Americas did not make the situation any easier. In many cases, the circumstances were much like those of the Middle Passage. The vessels often held from 100 to 150 slaves, and longer voyages could last for three weeks or more. The slaves on some vessels were allowed to remain on deck and unchained, although closely guarded. They were usually fed twice a day, once in the morning and once in the evening much as they were on the Middle Passage. Also as on the Atlantic passage, the slaves greatly outnumbered the crew, with perhaps a dozen sailors and a few overseers on board to guard them. After the evening meal, all of the slaves were driven into the hold and locked securely in place. As one writer described the conditions on these coastal slavers, "The hold was appropriated to the slaves, and is divided into two apartments. The after-hold will carry about eighty women, and the other about one hundred men. On either side were two platforms running the whole length; one raised a few inches, and the other half way up the deck. They were about five or six feet deep. On these the slaves lie, as close as they can be stowed."[12]

As the experiences of slaves during the Middle Passage have shown, however, such obstacles were far from impossible to overcome, and Africans
and African Americans alike continued to find ways to revolt. Many of the
tactics for rebellion were the same as those employed during the transatlantic slave trade, and slaves seized upon the same weaknesses of the crew
and flaws in security. In the case of one planned insurrection, for example,
a group of African American slaves being shipped to New Orleans staked
their hopes on the watchful eyes of a privileged slave in much the same
way that countless Africans did on their voyage to the Americas. In this
case, the man was a waiter who regularly visited the captain to serve him,
and was able to determine exactly where the various crew members slept,
as well as where the captain kept a small cache of weapons.[13] One can see
how the conditions on board, the fear of rebellion, and the actual strategies used by slaves in shipboard revolts were strikingly similar to slave
rebellions during the Middle Passage. And even though a bout of smallpox
kept this revolt from getting off the ground, others did, and slave traders
were reminded yet again that Africans and African Americans would not
submit to their enslavement without a fight.

The Case of the *Decatur*

The insurrection aboard the *Tryal* is an example of slave resistance in the
international slave trade in the Americas. Slaves also staged rebellions on
domestic slave ships, as they did on the U.S. ship *Decatur* in 1826. The insurrection began with the resistance of a man named William Bowser. While
the slave of a planter, Bowser had already made one unsuccessful attempt
to regain his liberty. When captured, he was sent to a Baltimore prison
and later purchased by a well-known slave dealer named Austin Woolfolk, who was one of the earliest slave traders to actively ship his slaves
using the coastal route.[14] Bowser was then shackled and placed in Woolfolk's own prison for some four weeks while Woolfolk bought a sufficient
number of additional slaves to warrant a trip south. During his imprisonment there, one of Bowser's fellow captives became so overcome with
despair that she cut the throat of her child and then took her own life to
avoid being sold into the Deep South. By late April, Woolfolk had finally
purchased a large enough complement of slaves. He led thirty-one men
and women to the wharf and boarded them for what he hoped would be
an uneventful trip to New Orleans, and thus the fateful voyage of the
Decatur began.[15]

As the vessel set sail from Baltimore, Bowser and the others began plotting a rebellion. After four days of planning, the twenty-four-year-old Bowser led the way as at least fifteen men, four boys, seven women, and three girls rose against the crew at mid-morning on April 25. The captain, who was scraping mud from the anchor stock at the time, was seized by the leg and thrown overboard by two slaves named Thomas Harrod and Manuel Wilson. Below deck, the ship's mate heard the commotion and approached to investigate, but he too was seized and thrown into the water, as he leaned over the rail to see if the captain was all right. A third sailor was roused from his sleep and attempted to help his fellow crewmen, but he was restrained by the slaves. The rebels apparently then ordered another crew member to sail the ship to Haiti. After ransacking the cabin and taking new clothes for themselves from boxes stored in the hold, the slaves retained command of the *Decatur* for a number of days, taking care to avoid all vessels they saw.[16] However, the slaves had unwittingly doomed their rebellion to eventual failure by killing the two men with the most sailing knowledge.

The end finally neared when the ship fell in with the whaler *Constitution,* whose captain requested to board the *Decatur* seeking supplies. Attempting to use the same tactic that the rebels on the *Tryal* had used twenty years earlier, the slaves instructed the *Decatur*'s crew to state that the officers had been lost overboard. In spite of their efforts, the whaler's captain was ultimately able to discern what had happened and sent an armed boarding party to retake the ship from the slaves. However, the captain soon realized that he was unequipped to recapture the stricken slaver from its new masters, for "having no hand cuffs to confine the men, most of whom were young, and powerful, he was fearful of an attempt to regain their liberty." Instead, the *Constitution* set sail, taking one sailor from the *Decatur* and, curiously, about half of the slaves. Then on May 5, yet another ship fell in with the *Decatur*. This time, the vessel was the *Rookes,* commanded by Captain Atwood, who took fourteen of the remaining slaves onto his ship and placed an officer on board to conduct the vessel into port. Although the details are unclear, once the ship arrived in New York, the rest of the slaves somehow escaped. No mention was made of the fate of these men and women, with the single exception of Bowser, who was soon apprehended and brought back to New York City for trial.[17]

The formal sentencing that was handed down in the case of the *Decatur* marks one of the most distinctive elements of shipboard revolts in the

Americas. Indeed, in every case presented in this chapter, the insurrection-ists faced a court of law at one time or another to answer for their actions. This stands in absolute contrast to the history of shipboard resistance on the transatlantic voyage. Whereas captives who revolted on the African coast or during the Middle Passage were dealt with on the spot, typically in an extremely violent way, captains of vessels in the Americas apparently felt the need to turn their insurrectionists over to the authorities. Issues of ownership, property rights, and insurance were rigidly set in the Americas, and it was much more difficult to punish or execute a slave without legal consequences. Just as the *Tryal* rebels faced a Chilean judge to answer for their actions, Bowser's participation in the revolt aboard the *Decatur* would be dealt with by the New York judicial system. On December 15, more than seven months after being captured, Bowser was convicted of the murder the *Decatur*'s captain and mate and sent to Ellis Island, escorted by a U.S. marshal and a contingent of marines, to be hanged. Bowser was re-ported to have given a short speech to the spectators at his execution, but it was particularly directed toward Austin Woolfolk, who was said to be present. Bowser apparently expressed his willingness to forgive the slave trader for the injuries he had done to him, but Woolfolk did not share his compassion. As one newspaper reported, Woolfolk "with a brutality which becomes his business, told him with an oath (not to be named,) 'that he was now going to have what he deserved, and he was glad of it.'"[18] This display of hatred and lack of remorse, along with the particulars of the revolt itself, inspired Benjamin Lundy, the editor of Baltimore's *Genius of Universal Emancipation,* to publicly condemn Woolfolk in his paper. As a member of the preeminent slave-trading firm in Maryland at the time, Woolfolk was a logical target of Lundy's antislavery sentiment. To Lundy, Woolfolk personified all of the atrocities of the trade, an associa-tion Woolfolk made a concerted effort to distance himself from.[19] Lundy reprinted an article from a New York paper that referred to Woolfolk as an "unfeeling 'soul-seller'" and a "demon in human form" and added that the slave trader was a "monster in human shape" and an "adamantine-hearted creature." He wrote that Woolfolk himself was responsible for the deaths of the *Decatur*'s crew and concluded by saying, "Hereafter, let no man speak of the humanity of Woolfolk."[20]

Angered by such derogatory remarks, denying that he was even present at the execution, and perhaps further instigated by the uproar surrounding a recently published memorial by Lundy urging the gradual abolition of slavery in the District of Columbia, Austin Woolfolk confronted Lundy on the street in front of the Baltimore post office on the afternoon of January 9, 1827. The enraged Woolfolk verbally accosted Lundy as a crowd gathered around the two men. Suddenly, Woolfolk removed his coat, handed it to an acquaintance, and as Lundy later wrote, "With a brutal ferocity, that is perfect [illegible word] character with his business, he choked me until my breath was nearly gone, and *stamped* me on the head and in the face, with the fury of a very demon! One of the blows from his heel, was given about the middle of the forehead, with such violence that it stunned me exceedingly; and, I was confident that, had it not been a glancing stroke, it must inevitably have fractured the scull, if it had not caused immediate death."[21] It was only the quick intervention of a few bystanders that saved Lundy's life. Incapacitated for a number of days, Lundy eventually recovered, and on February 20, Woolfolk was brought to trial for the attack in Baltimore. After pleading guilty to assault, but declaring that his actions were justified because of the extreme provocation of Lundy's articles, Woolfolk was sentenced to pay a fine of one dollar, along with court costs. Clearly agreeing with Woolfolk's sentiments, the judge stated that he "had never seen a case in which the provocation for a battery was greater" and that "if abusive language could ever be a justification for a battery, this was that case." The judge also noted that Lundy was wrong for condemning the domestic slave trade because it was economically beneficial to Maryland and "removed a great many rogues and vagabonds who were a nuisance in the state." "But for the strict letter of the law," the judge wrote in his order, "the Court would not fine Woolfolk any thing," making clear the adversity that both slaves and abolitionists faced in the struggle for freedom, even from those sworn to administer justice.[22]

The Case of the *Lafayette*

Almost exactly three years after William Bowser was hanged for his role in the insurrection aboard the *Decatur,* the schooner *Lafayette* was making its way from Norfolk to New Orleans with 197 slaves. On December 17, 1829, as many as one hundred of the captives rose in rebellion. Apparently inspired by the not-too-distant events of the Haitian Revolution, the insurrectionists intended to take the ship to Haiti, where they hoped to make their escape. One report suggested that the ringleaders of the insurrection convinced the rest of the slaves that the 150 kegs of oysters on board were actually filled with money that could be theirs if the revolt was successful. During the ensuing insurrection, several of the slaves were severely wounded, and the ship's captain was saved from death only by the intervention of a passenger who came to his rescue. After considerable difficulty, the crew finally recaptured the ship. Twenty-five of the slaves were bolted down to the deck, and others were confined to the hold until the vessel's arrival at New Orleans, where all involved in the uprising were arrested by local authorities. Many of the slaves involved in this revolt had been taken from the *Ajax* in Norfolk, upon which the rebellion was originally planned. In addition, the slaves stated that a similar effort was to be made on another Norfolk ship, the *Transport,* but the fate of this revolt is not recorded. Of those deemed responsible for the revolt aboard the *Lafayette,* four were sentenced to ten years' imprisonment at hard labor, while three others were sentenced to five years.[23]

The cases of the *Tryal, Decatur,* and *Lafayette* are each examples of powerful insurrections occurring on large vessels, but none of them is very well known. In 1839, however, shipboard slave rebellion would become the talk of the nation.

The Case of the *Amistad*

The most famous of all shipboard slave revolts occurred on the Spanish slaver *Amistad* in the summer of 1839. Although this incident took place within the domestic Cuban slave trade, the insurrectionists were African-born and had just been illegally imported from West Africa. Only a few months prior to the revolt, the *Amistad* rebels had embarked on a two-month journey across the Atlantic aboard the Portuguese vessel *Tecora.* Among the rebels was a young man named Sengbe Pieh, known to history as Joseph Cinque. Of the five hundred Africans on the *Tecora,* more than a third had died by the time the ship arrived in the West Indies. Since the slaving voyage of the *Tecora* was in violation of an Anglo-Spanish treaty of 1817, the surviving slaves had to be smuggled ashore under the cover of darkness, eventually reaching the city of Havana, where they were all imprisoned in a barracoon. In June, two Spaniards by the name of Jose Ruiz and Pedro Montes arrived in the Havana slave market looking for slaves to take to plantations at Puerto Principe, Cuba. Montes purchased three girls and a boy, and Ruiz bought forty-nine men, including Sengbe.[24]

A couple of nights later, Ruiz and Montes led their newly purchased slaves through Havana to a small, Baltimore-built schooner they had chartered named the *Amistad.* At midnight on June 28, the ship departed for the three-hundred-mile journey to Puerto Principe under the command of Captain Ramon Ferrer. In addition to Ruiz, Montes, and Ferrer, the ship also carried two sailors, a cabin boy named Antonio, and a cook named Celestino. The fifty-three Africans were confined to the vessel's hold. For all the slaves knew, this second voyage was going to be as bad as the first, and they remained uncertain where they were being taken or what would await them when they finally arrived. Provisions were low, with each captive allotted only one plantain, two potatoes, and half a cup of water each day. To make matters worse, Celestino cruelly suggested to the Africans that they were going to be killed, processed, and eaten by the Spaniards. As has been seen, this was a relatively common fear among African slaves and only served to heighten the tension and fear on board. The Africans also later reported that they had been repeatedly flogged and that the Spaniards would then rub vinegar and gunpowder into their wounds. Fearing for their lives, and anxious for their freedom, Sengbe and his fellow Africans realized that something had to be done.[25]

On July 1, the slaves' third night at sea, Sengbe and a captive named Grabeau managed to free themselves from their fetters using a nail that Sengbe had found. These men soon freed their companions and then made the fortunate discovery that some of the boxes stored below contained sugarcane knives. This sort of negligence had led to the deaths of countless sailors throughout the long history of the Middle Passage, and it was once again to prove pivotal. Armed and unchained, the Africans prepared to strike. Around 4:00 A.M., Sengbe and the others made their way up on deck and caught the crew completely by surprise. The captain was the first to die. Sengbe struck him with his blade, and others joined in and soon strangled Ferrer to death. The two sailors apparently either jumped overboard and probably drowned or escaped in the *Amistad*'s boat. Celestino was also killed by the Africans, who were by now almost in complete control. Montes put up a struggle but was soon struck to the deck. He managed to make his way to the hold, where he hid behind a barrel and under an old sail. Sensing the hopelessness of the situation, Ruiz and Antonio sensibly surrendered. With the exception of losing two of the Africans in the battle, the revolt had been a complete success and was over very quickly. At dawn, Montes was discovered in his hiding place and brought on deck. Remembering that the *Tecora* had sailed away from the rising sun, the rebels ordered Montes and Ruiz to sail in the opposite direction. Soon, the Africans hoped, they would arrive back home.[26]

"Death of Capt. Ferrer, the Captain of the Amistad, July, 1839." Slaves being transported from Havana to Principe, Cuba, rose up and killed the captain and the cook and imprisoned their new owners. The slaves were eventually freed by U.S. courts. From John W. Barber, *A History of the Amistad Captives* (New Haven, 1840). Courtesy Library of Congress (LC-USZ62–52577).

Unknown to the Africans, Ruiz and Montes devised a plan to sail the *Amistad* as ordered during the day but turn northward at night with the hope of being spotted by a British ship on patrol for illegal slavers. Montes also kept the sails of the ship very loose during the day so that the ship would make little headway. For two months the *Amistad* sailed gradually along the North American coast. During this time, the vessel passed many ships, but Ruiz and Montes did not have an opportunity to signal them safely. Some ships had in fact spotted the *Amistad* but retreated when their crews noticed the armed Africans on board. Meanwhile, provisions were running dangerously low, the ship's sails were tattered, and some of the insurrectionists had become sick and died from drinking medicines stored in the hold. Ten of the Africans were now dead. Finally, Sengbe and the others realized that they had no choice but to sail for the closest land to find fresh food and water. On August 25, the *Amistad* anchored off of Long Island, New York. Sengbe and some of his companions went ashore, where they managed to purchase two dogs, a bottle of gin, and some sweet potatoes using Spanish gold doubloons that they had found on the ship.[27]

As it did for the insurrectionists on the *Tryal,* going ashore proved costly to the *Amistad* rebels, for it was at this point that the ship was sighted by the USS *Washington* under the command of Thomas Gedney. Upon investigation, the *Washington*'s men boarded the *Amistad,* where they encountered the dozens of hungry, half-clothed Africans, some of whom were armed. Sengbe and the others who had gone ashore were soon located and brought to the ship. Not having any idea who these men were or what their intentions were, and fearing yet another horrifying chapter in their lives as slaves, Sengbe leaped overboard in an effort to escape. Pursued by men from the *Washington,* Sengbe eventually tired and was brought on board yet again. In a last-ditch effort, Sengbe apparently attempted to stir his fellow Africans to a new revolt, but nothing was to come of this. Instead, Gedney took control of the slaver and towed it into New London, Connecticut. The Africans were imprisoned in the New Haven jail and waited to find out if they would be tried in a court of law for mutiny and murder.[28]

Immediately, northern abolitionists rallied around the case of the *Amistad* and arranged for attorneys to represent the Africans in court. Popular sentiment for these Africans was so high that the New Haven jailer began charging an entrance fee for well-wishers and other visitors who came to see the captives.[29] The issue of the captives' guilt or innocence was complicated by claims of salvage and charges of piracy and murder, but in the end, the major issues to be decided essentially boiled down to the terms of two international treaties. The first of these was the 1795 agreement between the United States and Spain in which each nation pledged to return any ships or goods belonging to the other that might be encountered on the high seas. Secondly, an 1817 treaty between Great Britain and Spain declared that Spain had outlawed the importation of slaves into her colonies after December 30, 1820.[30] The prosecution, supported by Spanish officials, argued that the United States had no right to question the validity of the *Amistad*'s papers, which were drawn up to indicate that the Africans on board were in fact legally slaves. It was well known that falsified papers were commonplace in Cuba after the legal abolition of the trade, but the prosecution argued that the 1795 agreement did not permit the United States to presume that fraud played any role in this particular incident. Therefore, the prosecution demanded that the Africans be returned to Cuba. The defense and the antislavery vanguard on the other hand argued that the documents were fraudulent and that the Africans had in fact been illegally kidnapped from Africa and thus were never actually slaves by law. As a result, they had the same right as any free men or women to take up arms and defend themselves against illegal imprisonment. As William Jay wrote, the *Amistad* Africans were being penalized "for an act which but for the color of their skin, would be generally regarded as most heroic and praiseworthy."[31] An editorial in the *New-York Commercial Advertiser* similarly stressed the Africans' right to rebellion: "They were prisoners of war, and had an undoubted right to take up arms against their captors. The whites who seized them in Africa had virtually declared war against their nation. They were made captives, no matter whether in battle or by surprise, and being retained in duress of captivity, they retained all the rights of belligerents. One of these rights is that of making rescue, whenever opportunity presents itself, and by any available means."[32] Since the Africans had been kidnapped and were thus not actually merchandise, it therefore followed that the Treaty of 1795 did not apply to them.

When the case went to trial in the U.S. District Court in New Haven in 1840, the position of the defense won out, the Africans were declared to be free, and it was ordered that they be sent back to their homeland in West Africa. However, the U.S. Attorney immediately appealed, taking the case to the Supreme Court. Realizing the need for a powerful and charismatic figure to help argue their case, the abolitionists persuaded former president John Quincy Adams to lead the defense. On February 24, Adams delivered his historic four-and-a-half-hour address to the Supreme Court. Finally, on March 9, 1841, the justices upheld the initial ruling. Once again the Africans were declared free, and in November of 1841, they found themselves crossing the Atlantic once more, but now on their way home.[33] Interestingly, the return to Sierra Leone was not an entirely positive experience for many of the *Amistad* Africans. The *Gentleman,* which had been chartered with funds raised by abolitionist sympathizers, arrived in Freetown in January of 1842, nearly three years after the Africans had originally been captured and sold. While many of the Africans did manage to find family and friends and rejoin their old circles upon arrival, Sengbe was greeted with the tragic news that his village had been decimated by warfare and that much of his family had been killed.[34]

The Case of the *Creole*

Just two years after the celebrated case of the *Amistad,* a similar incident occurred aboard the American brig *Creole* that would once again thrust the issue of shipboard revolt onto the international stage. The voyage began at midnight on Monday, October 25, 1841, when the ship, under the command of captain Robert Ensor, left port in Richmond bound for New Orleans with a cargo of slaves and tobacco. The Chesapeake-to–New Orleans route that the *Creole* was taking was by far the most important domestic sea route for slavers at this time in the United States. It was on this same route just twelve years earlier that the slaves aboard the *Lafayette* had staged their insurrection. Slave transportation along this route was highly organized and regulated, and there were a number of ships specially designed and fitted out for slaving that were regularly engaged in this traffic. A typical voyage lasted approximately nineteen days.[35] On board the *Creole* were 135 slaves, a crew of 10, 4 passengers, 8 servants, and the Captain's wife, daughter, and niece. By all appearances, the trip was progressing normally, with no signs of any discontent from the slaves. However, this all changed on the evening of November 7. Just after 9:00 P.M., a slave named Elijah Morris informed crewman Zephaniah Gifford, who was on watch at the time, that a male slave had improperly entered the women's quarters. Gifford called for assistance from his fellow sailor William Merritt, and the two went to investigate. When Merritt released the grating to the hatch and climbed below, he was met by a slave named Madison Washington. Washington immediately leaped for the ladder and made his way onto the deck. At the same time, Morris, who had somehow armed himself with a pistol, fired at Gifford, wounding him. Washington, by now having clearly emerged as the leader of the revolt, reportedly called to his fellow captives to join him on deck, saying, "[W]e have commenced, and must go through; rush boys, rush aft; we have got them now!"[36]

The insurrection was now in full swing. Both Gifford and Merritt managed to escape, and Gifford roused Captain Ensor and four others to join the fight. Another sailor named Hewell tried to hold the slaves at bay with his gun, but he and the others were soon overwhelmed by the rebels, who themselves were armed with pistols, bowie knives, handspikes, knives, and clubs. Hewell was mortally wounded when a slave named Ben Blacksmith stabbed him in the chest with the captain's bowie knife. It was the only white fatality, and Hewell's body was thrown overboard. Captain Ensor was also stabbed several times, but just as countless sailors on the ships of the Middle Passage had done before him, he escaped into the ship's rigging, where he hid out until the battle ended. Merritt attempted to hide in the cabin by concealing himself beneath the bedding, where he was soon discovered, but he was spared by Madison Washington so that he could navigate the *Creole*. Other sailors had taken to the ship's rigging in desperation, including Gifford, who encountered the wounded captain and tied him in place so that he would not fall.

By 1:00 A.M. the slaves were in control of the ship. That accomplished, nobody else was injured. The sailors in the rigging were brought down and their injuries tended to, and the slaves established their own order on board. Apparently only nineteen slaves, led by Washington, were principally involved, and it was these individuals who made the rules. One of them was constantly at the helm, and the sailors were forbidden from communicating with one another unless observed by the slaves. Furthermore, perhaps familiar with the trick used by the sailors aboard the *Amistad* two years earlier, the insurrectionists made sure to watch the compass so that the navigator did not alter the vessel's course. Merritt and the rebel leaders sat down in the cabin to discuss the next course of action. While Washington wanted the ship to be taken to Liberia, Merritt pointed out that there was not nearly enough food or water for such a voyage. Ben Blacksmith suggested going to a British island, apparently basing his proposal on the recent case in which slaves aboard the shipwrecked vessel *Hermosa* were taken off by English sailors and brought into the Bahamas, where they were set free based on the British Emancipation Act of 1833.[37] Believing this to be their best option, Washington and the others agreed, and the *Creole* was steered toward the Bahamas and landed at Nassau on the morning of November 9.

As in the case of the *Amistad,* much of the interest of the *Creole* case to historians is in what occurred after the revolt. Once the vessel arrived in Nassau, it set off a chain of events that enraged and frightened slave owners in the South, gave hope to northern abolitionists, and briefly put a serious strain on Anglo-American relations. As soon as the *Creole* entered the harbor in Nassau, the local quarantine officer met the ship as it was being led in, and Gifford jumped into his boat, informed the officer of what had occurred, and sought immediate consultation with the colonial governor, Francis Cockburn. Gifford wanted to make sure that the slaves remained aboard the ship so that there would be no chance of their being declared free on British soil. Cockburn hesitated but nevertheless agreed to station a military attachment aboard the *Creole* until the situation could be resolved. Sensing that the British government was not going to rule in their favor, Gifford along with American consul John Bacon and Captain Woodside of the nearby *Louisa* which was in port, attempted to retake the ship and liberate it from British authorities. They concealed whatever arms they were able to acquire in an American flag and rowed out to the *Creole* intent on recapturing the ship. However, the slaves saw them coming, and the alarm was sounded. When the men approached the slaver, they were met by an armed force and ordered to retreat. This signaled the end for American hopes that the slaves would be returned. Instead, Attorney General George Anderson soon boarded the ship, informed the nineteen slaves deemed to be the leaders that they were to be taken ashore as prisoners until their case had been pled before officials in London, and told the rest that the British authorities had no further interest in detaining them. By this time, some fifty or more boats full of locals had surrounded the ship and were quick to offer their services, ferrying the newly freed slaves to shore and freedom.[38]

From the perspective of the slaves, this insurrection was a successful one, but abolitionists who had hoped the case would set an important precedent were soon to be disappointed. In 1855, an Anglo-American claims commission awarded more than $110,000 in damages to the owners of the liberated slaves. Unlike the *Amistad,* the *Creole* was on a legal slaving voyage, and it was determined that when the vessel entered Nassau, it had the right to expect assistance from a friendly nation. Furthermore, the British Emancipation Act was ruled irrelevant because it did not allow for the boarding of an American ship by British authorities. Thus it was determined that officials in Nassau had violated international law, and therefore the British government was responsible for the losses incurred by the owners of the slaves aboard the *Creole*.[39]

In 1843, the great African American nationalist Henry Highland Garnet, urging U.S. slaves to strike for their liberty, declared Madison Washington a "bright star of freedom" who "took his station in the constellation of true heroism." In the early 1850s, Frederick Douglass paid similar tribute in his short story "The Heroic Slave" by naming his protagonist after Washington.[40] Madison Washington was indeed a remarkable man. Prior to leading the revolt, he had escaped from a Virginia plantation and lived for a while as a fugitive slave in the North. His subsequent reenslavement (and thus his presence on the *Creole*) was apparently the result of his courageously returning to the South to rescue his wife from slavery.[41]

Although they faced some of the same obstacles that those crossing the Atlantic had faced, the individuals caught up in this second wave of slave trading also faced new and different conditions. Some of the differing circumstances made insurrection seem promising, while others made it appear useless or even suicidal. As the examples highlighted in this chapter indicate, opportunities for resistance did periodically occur in American coastal slave trafficking, and both Africans and African Americans took advantage of such opportunities when given the chance, staging a number of effective rebellions.

SHIPBOARD REVOLTS IN THE RIVERINE SLAVE TRADES OF THE AMERICAS

We have seen the ways in which those who found themselves loaded onto oceangoing slave ships in the Americas took a cue from their own or their ancestors' experiences during the Middle Passage and seized opportunities to stage powerful insurrections. However, cases of revolt on these large vessels are only a part of the story of shipboard slave rebellion in the Americas. While hundreds of thousands of slaves were indeed transported from one location to another within the Americas in large sailing vessels, hundreds of thousands of others experienced transport in smaller, slower, and less grandiose craft. These were the men, women, and children who found themselves loaded onto flatboats, steamboats, or barges when their owners sold them "down the river."

River transport was a common method of moving slaves throughout the Americas. Perhaps the best-known wave of domestic riverine slave trading is that which followed in the wake of the Chesapeake Bay area's decline as a major region of slave labor in the antebellum South. When tobacco and rice farming began to exhaust the land in colonies such as Virginia, Maryland, and South Carolina in the late eighteenth century, the slaves who worked the plantations there became less needed. Some were manumitted, and large communities of free African Americans began to crop up in the Chesapeake area. Other planters, however, took a decidedly different approach and got every last dollar they could out of their slaves by selling them. By the end of the eighteenth century, an organized domestic American slave trade was in operation, and by the time of the Civil War, more than a million slaves were relocated farther south.[42] Particularly after the invention of the cotton gin in 1793, which caused a reinvigoration of the southern slave system as slaving frontiers expanded westward into areas such as Mississippi and Alabama where cotton flourished, the destination for these former Chesapeake laborers increasingly became the Deep South. Some slaves were sent via the coastal route around Florida to slave markets in places such as New Orleans, as has been seen in the cases of the *Decatur*, the *Lafayette*, and the *Creole*, while others were shipped down local rivers on small boats. As cotton continued to flourish and slavery kept progressing westward, more and more rivers became part of this system, and more and more slaves found themselves on small craft floating down rivers such as the Ohio and the Mississippi.

Many of the individuals packed into these smaller boats did not simply submit passively to their predicament but sought to seize upon opportunities for resistance when they presented themselves. Whereas the Africans who boarded slave ships in West Africa were physically weakened, terrified by their lack of knowledge concerning where they were being taken, and hampered somewhat by language barriers with their fellow slaves, those being transported in the domestic trades of the Americas did not have such obstacles to overcome. While it is true that American-born slaves had their own set of barriers that Africans did not generally face, such as the potential for self-hatred and accommodation with the slave regime borne from a lifetime of living within it, American slaves did share a level of bonding with one another that helped them resist and survive very effectively. The weeks these individuals spent together in the jails of slave traders and aboard the vessels they soon boarded helped to forge alliances between them. Common experiences shared through storytelling and simple acquaintanceship built from everyday interaction often helped to create a relatively cohesive slave community.[43] There was a deep level of shared experience, beyond anything that Africans on the Middle Passage would have initially had with one another, that provided the foundation from which rebellion could begin to coalesce. Compared with slaves on ocean-going vessels, those in transport on riverine vessels had greater freedom of movement and greater opportunity to observe the activities of their captors. Many of the river vessels were too small to have a hold in which the slaves could be securely locked, and slaves were customarily kept bound on deck. In some cases, they were free to roam the deck during the trip and would only be chained when the boat needed to dock. In other cases, traders would grant slaves full freedom of movement only after the vessel had passed far enough into the South that slavery loomed on both sides of the river and the captives would become discouraged by their prospects.[44] Being on deck provided both an advantage and a disadvantage for potential insurrectionists, for while riverine slave rebels did not face the obstacle of getting on deck to wage battle, they were also under constant observation by the sailors. The segregation of the hold where so many shipboard insurrections during the Middle Passage initially formulated and matured was absent, and revolts probably tended to take a more opportunistic character. However, this certainly did not prevent them from happening and even from achieving a surprisingly large measure of success in certain cases.

One such incident involved the Kentuckian Edward Stone, who had been in the slave-trading business for some ten years before announcing that he was going to retire from the business. However, having a few unsold slaves on hand, Stone decided to purchase enough additional slaves to make one final trading trip South.[45] Fate was not on his side, though, for on the morning of September 17, 1826, as his flatboat was slowly working its way down the Ohio River, seventy-seven slaves armed with clubs, axes, hatchets, brickbats, billets of wood, and knives suddenly revolted when the vessel neared Stephensport in Breckinridge County, Kentucky, approximately ninety miles down the river from Louisville. It is unclear what the crew was doing when the revolt broke out. Some newspaper reports suggested that four of the five crew members—Edward and Howard Stone, David Cobb, and James M. Gray—were below eating breakfast and were easily surprised and killed by the slaves. After accomplishing this part of their plan, the slaves then reportedly went up on deck, where they encountered the fifth man, Humphrey Davis, who was acting as steersman. Davis immediately leaped overboard and attempted to swim for shore but was pursued by some of the insurrectionists in a skiff and killed. This seems like a perfectly probable scenario, but other press accounts of the event tell a different tale.[46]

In these accounts, while it is agreed that Davis was acting as steersman, it is said that at the time of the revolt, Gray was sitting near the bow reading a newspaper, while the Stones and Cobb were at the other end of the vessel conducting business. In this version of the story, the slaves killed Gray first and threw him overboard. When the men at the other end of the boat heard the commotion, they ran toward the slaves and met them in a brief engagement in the middle of the vessel. Edward Stone attempted to shoot one of the slaves, but his pistol was knocked out of his hand when he fired, and the bullet dislodged his own eye. The other two men were promptly killed. Only after the slaves landed the boat on the Indiana side of the river was Davis finally killed.[47] At this point, press coverage of the events converges. The slaves apparently affixed weights around the necks of the white men's bodies and threw them overboard. They also took some money, sank the boat, and then made their escape into Indiana. Almost immediately, however, fifty-six of the escapees were apprehended and brought back into Breckinridge County, where they were held in the Hardinsburg jail.[48] On November 29, five slaves named Jo, Duke, Resin, Stephen, and Wesley were publicly executed, while most of the remainder were resold into the Deep South.[49]

In late 1829, another group of slaves being transported down the Ohio River to the New Orleans market rose and killed their owner. After being recaptured, four slaves were subsequently executed at Greenupsburg, Kentucky. At their execution, a number of these men are said to have addressed the crowd in an effort to explain why they had revolted. As one newspaper reported, "They died with astonishing firmness, without shewing the least compunction for the crime committed, and one of them, the instant before he was launched from the cart, exclaimed—'death—death at any time, in preference to slavery.'"[50] While the evidence of insurrection in the slave trades of the Americas pales in comparison with the hundreds of known incidents that took place in the Atlantic trade, the few cases profiled in this chapter illustrate that revolt aboard ships and boats was still a viable means of resistance for both Africans and African Americans.

Shipboard resistance did not end once the Middle Passage was over. Indeed, whether during transshipment in large oceangoing vessels or during slow trips down American rivers in flatboats, Africans and African Americans alike continued to stage bold and sometimes successful bids for their freedom. The setting of these incidents was similar to that of the Middle Passage in many ways but in other respects was sufficiently distinct to mark this rebelliousness as a separate and unique manifestation of shipboard resistance. Perhaps most significantly in this regard, many of the individuals who participated in these revolts were American-born and were without personal memories of an African past or of the Middle Passage. Nevertheless, resistance continued to be discussed, plotted, and executed by slaves on ships or boats throughout the era of slavery in the Americas. Whether the insurgents were African or African American, whether the captives were locked below in the hold of a large ship or left sitting on the deck of a small flatboat, whether the human cargo consisted of hundreds of individuals or just a dozen or so, resistance on the seas and rivers of the Americas did occur. And while freedom was extremely difficult to achieve aboard ships and boats in the Americas, the slaves who attempted to attain it never yielded to the idea that the effort itself was fruitless. Instead, they picked up where shipboard resistance during the Middle Passage left off and continued to wage an unrelenting battle for freedom in the waterways, rivers, and oceans of the Americas.

Conclusion

The poem that inspired the title of this book captures the very essence of shipboard revolt. Although written many decades after slavery and the slave trade had been abolished in the Americas, Harlem Renaissance poet Claude McKay's "If We Must Die" conjures up images of heroic resistance in the face of overwhelming racial hatred and violence that perfectly convey the spirit of shipboard rebellion. McKay advocates coming together in a united front to "meet the common foe," and urges those faced with the prospect of an indignant death to rise up against their oppressors so that if they must die, they will at least have died nobly, fighting to the very end. Indeed, while the Africans who found themselves hunted on the coast and penned on board the ships of the Middle Passage could very easily have given up hope and succumbed quietly to their captivity, they did not. Instead, these men, women, and children fought back time and time again. The history of the slave trade is filled with hundreds upon hundreds of incidents in which slaves rose up on board the ships that confined them and let loose with all the fury and determination they could muster. As we have seen, many of these efforts did not win back freedom for the insurrectionists, but others did. Thousands of slaves, both African and African American, surprised their oppressors, mastered their ship, and reclaimed their freedom by force. This was no easy task, and countless individuals lost their lives in the struggle, but the slaves continued to rebel. In the words of McKay, they faced the "murderous, cowardly pack, / Pressed to the wall, dying, but fighting back!"[1]

As a result of this continual rebelliousness, these shipboard insurrectionists contributed in a significant way to limiting the effectiveness, and thus the profitability, of the slave trade as a whole. Because of the revolts that so often struck slave ships, large amounts of money were spent to ensure the safest voyage possible. A broad array of both weapons and methods of restraint had to be purchased, medical treatment had to be constantly available, and large crews had to be paid, fed, and maintained in order to deal with the perpetual threat of insurrection.[2] David Richardson estimates, for example, that in the eighteenth-century British slave trade perhaps one-third of all crew members were hired primarily to help manage the slaves in one way or another.[3] As a result, operational costs were greatly inflated, limiting profits. In addition, fear of insurrection caused some captains to spend a longer time on the African coast so as to mix their "cargo" of Africans in hopes of minimizing the chance of rebellion. The provisioning costs associated with these extended stays were yet another expenditure that the traders had to absorb. Furthermore, as David Eltis has argued, regions of Africa such as the Senegambia, which developed a reputation for slave rebelliousness, effectively redirected the slave trade, forcing slavers to sail further south to acquire what they hoped would be more acquiescent slaves, spending larger amounts of money on longer, less efficient, and less profitable voyages in the process.[4]

Insurance was yet another cost that slave traders had to take into consideration. Many insurance contracts for slaving voyages had specific insurrection clauses. Full insurance against slave rebellion regularly increased insurance expenditures by 25–50 percent, and sometimes the costs nearly tripled the expense of ordinary transatlantic voyages. However, knowing the propensity of Africans to revolt, insurance companies often built a loophole into the contract language to protect themselves from having to pay a multitude of claims. Insurance policies at the time covered certain unnatural deaths, such as when Africans were drowned in storms or were killed during naval battles, but they often did not cover deaths resulting from slave insurrections, which were argued to be the result of negligence by ship captains. Furthermore, when insurance companies did agree to pay for slaves who were killed in rebellions, the policies almost always included language such as "warranted free from average by insurrection under 5 percent," meaning that the insurers' liability was limited to those cases in which 5 percent or more of the Africans died. Insurers knew that captains made an effort to kill only a few Africans as deterrents to future rebellions following shipboard revolts, and felt it was a safe gamble to offer insurance coverage with the 5 percent clause.[5] As we have seen, however, some revolts did in fact lead to the deaths of a great number of slaves. Unless the insurance companies could make a plausible claim that negligence brought about the insurrection, they were legally obliged to pay.

One legal case of insurance liability resulting from slave insurrection involved the English slaver *Wasp,* which was struck by two rebellions during its 1783 voyage. In this case, the underwriters had inserted a clause into the policy providing that deaths due to rebellion would only be covered if they surpassed 10 percent. The captain vividly described the revolts, giving evidence that some slaves were shot, some threw themselves down the hatchway and later died of their injuries, and others died afterward of injuries received during the battle, of starvation, and from "chagrin at their disappointment." The insurance company did not argue some of the facts, and it paid for those who died in battle or from wounds sustained in the revolt. However, the plaintiff also argued that payment should be made for all of the other slaves who died of "disappointment" or starvation in the days that followed. Even though these people did not die during the revolt, the argument was made that they nevertheless died *because* of the revolt, for had there been no insurrection, they would still be alive. The case went to the jury, which decided in favor of the insurance company, because the slave revolt clause of the contract did not cover any deaths except those immediately due to the revolt itself. Thus, they concluded that those Africans who jumped into the sea uninjured but later died from swallowing seawater, those who died afterwards of despair and disappointment, and those who starved themselves to death did not in fact die as a direct result of the revolt and thus were not covered.[6] Although underwriters clearly went to great lengths to avoid paying for losses by insurrection, a number of companies did offer the coverage at a hefty price, thus entailing yet another expense as a result of the rebellious nature of the Africans.

These costs incurred by slavers as the result of shipboard revolts, and in their efforts to avoid them, had important consequences for the slave trade itself. Longer stays on the coast meant fewer total slaving voyages, which led in turn to fewer slaves being purchased and fewer slaves being available for sale in the Americas. Higher expenses for risky slaving ventures led to fewer merchants engaging in the slave trade. And both successful revolts and slave deaths resulting from shipboard insurrections led to a smaller number of slaves arriving in the Americas. In the insurance case of the *Wasp,* the captain also argued that, because of the insurrection, the value of the surviving slaves had been substantially lessened in the eyes of the planters, and therefore the insurance company should cover the losses he was forced to accept when the Africans were sold. Although his claim was thrown out, it does demonstrate another way in which slave insurrections affected the profitability of slaving. All of these losses were, of course, factored into the prices of slaves and helped to keep the price of slave labor too high for many plantation owners.[7] High prices meant a smaller demand and thus a smaller supply. All of these added costs and the effect they had on the profitability of the slave trade were due directly to the rebelliousness of the Africans on slave ships, and the slave trade became an uncertain business. It has been suggested that between 1680 and 1800, shipboard revolts, along with coastal resistance by free Africans, lessened the volume of slaves shipped across the Atlantic by 9 percent. This resistance thus saved as many as 600,000 Africans from being enslaved during the eighteenth century alone and perhaps as many as a million throughout the history of the trade.[8] Slave resistance, whether successful or not, directly influenced the rise and evolution of slavery, eventually combining with a number of other forces to destroy it altogether. Without this threat of rebellion and the terror that it caused those involved in the trade, there is no telling what additional depths slavery may have reached. The thousands of men and women who participated in the many shipboard revolts of the slave trade placed their lives on the line for the cause of freedom and are largely unknown and unsung heroes of African and African American history.

Africans also affected the evolution of the slave trade and helped to hasten its abolition through their rebelliousness when their powerful and frequent revolts caught the attention of abolitionist writers and thinkers. Shipboard revolts were seized upon by abolitionists to point out the horrors of slavery, helping in this way to lead to the ultimate abolition of the slave traffic. For centuries, the African slave trade was an accepted and normal part of the Western world that was thought by most to be a progressive form of labor and economic advancement. Only the slaves themselves seemed opposed to slavery. However, as time passed, economic and political revolution, religious enlightenment, and moral reform swept the Atlantic world, casting slavery in a different light. As historian David Brion Davis has so effectively argued, by the end of the eighteenth century slavery had come to be considered unseemly and unnecessary, the vestige of a less civilized past and an embodiment of capitalist excess.[9] The climate was right for the whole system of enslavement to collapse under the weight of new ideas, and slavery opponents began to voice their objections in increasingly boisterous ways. However, the arguments of those activists would have been shallow and unpersuasive without the actions and experiences of the slaves themselves. In order to argue their position effectively, abolitionists had to be able to point to the destruction of slave families. They had to be able to document the sexual abuse of African American women. They needed the scarred flesh of the field hand to show to the world. They also relied on the constant rebelliousness of slaves to make the simple but highly effective point that Africans and African Americans did not submit willingly to their enslavement.

In the last quarter of the eighteenth century, as antislavery sentiment was spreading, many authors who published books in support of the abolitionist cause included accounts of shipboard revolts. In 1771, for example, America's leading Quaker abolitionist, Anthony Benezet, published *Some Historical Account of Guinea,* which provided the antislavery moment with powerful evidence of the barbarity of the slave trade. Benezet was known for chronicling slave uprisings around the world in an effort to help launch new attacks against the slave trade, and in this book he provided a long and detailed account of a revolt aboard the English slave ship *Expedition* in 1740. Benezet's account is sympathetic to the Africans and intended to point out the inhumanity that would spark such a revolt. Referring to the "bloody piece of business" and "horrid scene" of the executions, Benezet encouraged his reader to recognize that no enterprise that inspired such violence and bloodshed could possibly have a place in a modern world based on principles of progress and equality.[10] A similar effort to educate the public about the horrors of slavery was made by Alexander Falconbridge, a former surgeon in the slave trade. Gradually becoming disgusted with the traffic, Falconbridge let his antislavery sentiment inform his writing, which was widely circulated as propaganda for the abolitionist movement. His *Account of the Slave Trade* was published in 1788 by a member of the Committee for the Abolition of the Slave Trade.[11] In this book, Falconbridge did not refer to any specific revolt but commented on the terrible state of life aboard a slave ship and how those conditions might inspire the Africans to revolt, noting that slaves were "always ready to seize every opportunity for committing some act of desperation to free themselves from their miserable state."[12] After confronting readers with vivid depictions of suicide, kidnapping, disease, and rape, Falconbridge hoped his audience would better understand the motivations behind revolt and sympathize with the Africans as victims. That same year, former slave-trader John Newton published an effective antislavery pamphlet entitled *Thoughts Upon the African Slave Trade.* He laid out the justification for revolt in no uncertain terms:

When a hundred and fifty or two hundred stout men, torn from their native land, many of whom never saw the sea, much less a ship, till a short space before they had embarked; who have, probably, the same natural prejudice against a white man, as we have against a black; and who often bring with them an apprehension they are bought to be eaten: I say, when thus circumstanced, it is not to be expected that they will tamely resign themselves to their situation. It is always taken for granted, that they will attempt to gain their liberty if possible.[13]

In this case, rebellion is presented as the virtual responsibility of every African captured and sold into slavery. Newton refers to slaves who betray the plans of the other Africans as "traitor[s] to the cause of liberty," while the rebels themselves are labeled "patriots." Clearly seizing upon revolutionary rhetoric, Newton challenged his audience to see insurrection not as the violent embodiment of savage and uncivilized Africans but as a fundamental assertion of humanity.

And when Thomas Clarkson's effective antislavery work *The Substance of the Evidence* appeared in 1789, he too used rebellion to highlight the horrors of the trade. Although the primary themes running through this work are the kidnapping of Africans for sale into the slave trade, the brutal treatment of sailors by captains and officers on slave ships, and the horrifyingly cramped and unhealthy conditions under which slaves were forced to endure their journey, shipboard rebellion also emerges as a significant theme. In fact, no less than fourteen separate revolts are mentioned throughout this text, intended to show the reader how wrong and unnatural enslaving another human being was and how any effort to do so would inevitably spark violence caused by fear or anger. In presenting the evidence of one sailor, Clarkson noted that "the wretched situation, in which the slaves feel themselves to be, when torn from their country, and under the dominion of the Europeans, is discernible from their actions," including suicide and insurrection.[14] In explaining one revolt, Clarkson wrote that "many of [the slaves] are unable to bear the loss of liberty, and try every means to regain it," thus humanizing the Africans and encouraging his readers to imagine what they would do under similar circumstances.[15] Such authors could have written about theoretical issues of freedom and equality and how Africans deserved better treatment than they received on slave ships, but there was something about rebellion that helped to accentuate the point. If slavery was not patently wrong and against human nature, then the Africans would not be continually staging bloody insurrections to secure their freedom.

Newspapers also took their place in the antislavery movement, although they tended to take no particular stance on the slave trade throughout most of the eighteenth century. Antislavery sentiment had not yet taken hold in any meaningful way, and the trade was treated simply as a normal part of the Western economy and the modern world. However, as the century went on and abolitionist efforts of powerful and eloquent orators, as well as writers such as Benezet, Falconbridge, and Newton, to bring the horrors of slavery to light increased, newspapers began taking sides. When shipboard insurrections occurred, those papers with antislavery leanings often took the opportunity to editorialize on their significance. In an impassioned essay referring to a shipboard revolt that had just taken place on the Rhode Island vessel *Nancy,* one writer noted that during the Middle Passage the Africans

> [m]ade an attempt to recover that liberty with which they were endowed by the common Parent of the Universe, and of which they could not have been deprived without the most outrageous violation of every Principle of Religion, Justice, and Humanity; [b]ut in consequence of this laudable attempt to assert their natural and unalienable right, several of their number were destroyed by the captain and crew of the Brig. It may perhaps be alledged, in extenuation of the crime, that the white people only acted in self-defence; but the reply is obvious. Who were the aggressors? Who forced the wretched Africans from their native country; from all the tender and endearing attachments of Husband, Parent and Child? Who crowded them in the hold of the vessel? . . . Who by such base and barbarous means, provoked them to a natural and just resistance?[16]

In this way, slavery opponents seized upon shipboard slave revolts as the embodiment of all that was unjust about the slave trade. Africans were human beings and did not deserve to be enslaved any more than anyone else. As a consequence, abolitionists argued, not only was rebellion to be expected, but it should be condoned and praised.

In 1825, similarly, several slaves aboard the small French ship *Deux Soeurs* led a revolt in which the Africans killed at least eight of the French crew, leaving only three men alive to navigate the vessel back to the coast. Once there, the ship was seized by authorities in Sierra Leone, and the 132 slaves ultimately regained their liberty. As a local Freetown paper subsequently wrote of the slaves involved, "These poor wretches, degraded as they were conceived to be by their tyrants when they designated them 'logs of ebony wood,' have, however, taught [the whites] a lesson which, for the sake of humanity, we regret is not more often shewn them."[17] A year later, when William Bowser was hanged for his participation in the revolt aboard the *Decatur,* a newspaper commented on his execution:

> This man was taken from his former residence and sold to be carried, he knew not to what place, without his consent, and rather than submit to this he engaged in this fatal experiment to obtain his liberty. Who, we may ask, placed in similar circumstances, would not have been disposed to do the same thing? Liberty is the birthright of every one, for high authority has declared, that "ALL MEN ARE BORN FREE AND EQUAL," and therefore all have a natural right to obtain and enjoy freedom and equality. Had [Bowser] been a freeman, the verdict would have been *justifiable homicide,* but being a slave he was convicted of *murder.* Hence there is one law for a *freeman,* and another for a *slave;* and yet we hypocritically proclaim to the world that "*all* men are born *free* and *equal!*" . . . This man was first made a slave by us, without his consent, and then we hang him because he *is* a slave. Will not his blood be required at our hands?[18]

Similarly, after Madison Washington and his fellow rebels captured the *Creole* and took the vessel into the Bahamas, another abolitionist paper justified the revolt as follows: "Before [the slaves] there was no prospect in patient waiting, but that of worse bondage. Before them there was a splendid prospect, by valorous resistance, of immediate and perpetual liberty! . . . [A]nd both law and gospel justified their rising."[19] As sentiment was changing and slavery was no longer considered progressive, papers such as these reached a wide audience. In accounts written in stark terms of good versus evil, shipboard rebels appeared as freedom fighters, and the brutal captains and crews of slave ships that sought to keep the Africans under lock and key were villains who deserved whatever the slave rebels had in store for them. If theoretical arguments carried little sway with some readers, the fact that shipboard revolts were actually occurring, and occurring often, helped drive the abolitionist papers' point home. In this way, shipboard rebellions contributed to antislavery sentiment by periodically thrusting the harsh reality of the slave trade on the world. If the system were just, if the treatment of slaves were kind, if the Africans were suited by nature to be slaves, then shipboard revolts would not have been exploding across the Atlantic month after month. Sympathetic readers could see the waste of human life—on the part of both the Africans and the sailors. How could anything that would provoke such anger, violence, and death on so many occasions possibly be something that the modern world could condone? Revolts led to publicity, publicity led to sympathy, and sympathy led to legislative action. Before long, the slave trade would finally be abolished, and although not often credited for their role, the slaves themselves played a crucial part in accomplishing this feat.

The 493 shipboard slave insurrections identified in the appendix no doubt pale in comparison to the number that actually took place. Captains knew that their days at the helm of slave ships were numbered if they developed a reputation for not being able to control their slaves, and they were quick to cover up any negligence or laxity in security on their part that may have helped facilitate an insurrection, and as a result, there were probably hundreds of revolts that were never recorded. Beyond this intentional underreporting of revolts, one historian of the French trade has suggested that revolts were so common that they "scarcely merited mentioning."[20] In many cases, particularly those in which insurrections were quickly suppressed, this assertion is very likely an accurate one. Indeed, shipboard rebellions seem to have been an epidemic that plagued slave ships from the very start and never subsided so long as ships were still plying the waves with captives on board. The price paid by Africans in these revolts, however, was not inconsequential, with more than 5,500 of them losing their lives in only 170 revolts in which a numerical death toll is known or estimated. As discussed in chapter 5, however, because so many revolts were minor and went unreported, the average of some thirty slave deaths per insurrection among those for which an approximate number of deaths is known is certainly inflated and should not be applied to shipboard revolt as a whole.[21]

From other statistical information uncovered in this investigation, much can be learned about shipboard revolts. The location for most of these revolts, for instance, was the coast of Africa and its vicinity, with 75 percent of cases in which location is known occurring there. As has been stated, the frequency of revolts on the coast is attributable to both the sight of the nearby shore and the reduction in crew size that often accompanied a ship's presence on the coast. However, another important factor is the simple fact that busy harbors provided lots of witnesses, and a captain attempting to hide the outbreak of an insurrection would have had a much harder time doing so around other vessels. The accounts of many slave revolts come from sailors aboard neighboring ships or from agents based at the coast. By contrast, when a ship was at sea, there were generally no witnesses beyond the slaves and crew. The eighty cases in which insurrections happened during the Middle Passage should therefore be considered a conservative figure. While revolts very likely did occur more often on the coast than anywhere else, the huge statistical gap between incidents on the coast and those during the Middle Passage is probably somewhat exaggerated. In only thirteen cases uncovered in the research for this book were revolts known to have occurred after a slaver had reached the Americas. As on the African coast, the presence of witnesses once slave ships arrived in the New World may have affected the probability of revolts being recorded.

As many as 40 percent of all revolts took place during the nighttime hours, when slaves could use the cover of darkness to their advantage. The next most common time for revolt was mealtime, when large numbers of Africans were on deck to eat. At these times, some resourceful slaves would even use the bowls they ate their food out of as weapons against the sailors. More commonly used weapons included small arms, swords of varying types stolen from the crew, pieces of wood, and carpentry and kitchen utensils. Some slaves even used the very shackles that bound them to attack the crew. Such creative use of the limited means at their disposal allowed many Africans to stage very effective rebellions. Indeed, of the 493 known revolts, some 25 percent appear to have succeeded in reclaiming freedom for at least some of the insurrectionists involved, while in an additional 32 cases the slaves managed to temporarily capture the ship they were on. These last statistics are perhaps the most impressive of all, for they dramatically illustrate the remarkable degree of success that shipboard rebels achieved. As much as the odds were stacked against them, not only did slaves find the will to rise up and lay their lives on the line, but they did so with remarkable effectiveness. In the eighteenth century alone, this investigation has found that revolts in which at least some of the slaves freed themselves occurred at a rate of more than one per year. Seen in this light, shipboard rebellion becomes a very important part of the history of the African diaspora, for it shows a level of success otherwise unheard of in the annals of slave resistance. For this reason, it is vital that the history of shipboard slave insurrections be considered in any general assessment of the ways in which Africans and African Americans resisted their enslavement.

Shipboard revolts influenced the lives of thousands of people, both slave and crew alike, and in the process raised the stakes of the transatlantic trade. Revolts made people such as captains, sailors, underwriters, and ship owners fearful of both the economic and human losses they might face at the hands of a rebellious African cargo. This, in turn, compelled them to impose tight restrictions and severe punishments on the Africans on board. Simultaneously, the nature of seafaring meant that the crews of slave ships were often at least partially made up of men whose personalities and temperaments did not suit them for the role of prison guard. Angry, dispossessed, and troublesome, many of the men who signed onto a slaving voyage despised their lot in life and refused to submit themselves to the rigid order required to keep the slaves below in check. As a result, Africans found ways to exploit these human weaknesses and take advantage of the frailties and divisions among the sailors on board. The contradictory forces of constraint and opportunity were continually at play on slave ships, sometimes favoring the Africans, more often favoring the crews. This drama was the history of shipboard slave revolts, a drama that frustrated the smooth operation of the transatlantic trade for hundreds of years. But while there is no question of the significance of these revolts to those who fought and died, it is intriguing to wonder how these shipboard events may have influenced the slave societies of the Americas, bridging the gap between the long traditions of shipboard and plantation resistance.

Taking a conservative average of 200 slaves on board each of the 493 ships that are documented to have suffered slave revolts, it is conceivable that as many as 100,000 slaves may have been aboard those ships. Even after subtracting the losses from escape and death during these revolts, one is still left with 75,000 or more slaves who were landed in the Americas and distributed throughout the slave communities of the New World. These men, women, and children had personally planned, witnessed, or fought in revolts attempting to regain their freedom. Some had stolen weapons, others had stood on deck and fought eye to eye with sailors. Some had suffered injuries, others had inflicted them on crew members. Some had actually captured their ship, taking control temporarily before being retaken by other vessels. Some had drawn white blood or perhaps even taken the lives of sailors. Some had been mercilessly tortured, while others were spared such injuries so that they would be better fit for the slave market. But whatever the case, these individuals, whether actively involved in the revolt or not, undoubtedly found themselves still frustrated, still frightened, still enslaved, making them prime candidates for participation in future revolts. While the historical record is relatively silent on the subject of such a connection between individuals who had revolted on ship later revolting on land, surely the case of Samba, an African who had participated in an insurrection aboard a French ship, only to strike yet again for his liberty while a slave on a Louisiana plantation, was not an isolated incident.[22] Bonds between Africans who crossed the Atlantic on the same ship could be strong and may well have been even stronger among slaves from a ship on which an insurrection had occurred, perhaps stimulating further acts of resistance. It seems reasonable to presume that Africans who had already attempted or experienced rebellion did not suddenly give up hope once arriving on land. Individuals like Samba, having already once fought for their freedom, would probably have been among the first to join in when a plantation revolt was being formulated.

But regardless of the degree to which the Africans used their experiences to launch new revolts against their bondage, these experiences inevitably became woven into the fabric of their new identities as plantation slaves. And the rebellions they fought in or observed would have been meaningful not only to the individual but to the community of which he or she was now a part. African and African American slaves used an oral culture to help mitigate the oppression of slavery. They built their own system of communication through storytelling—an oral culture separate from, and often hostile to, the world of the overseers, drivers, and masters that surrounded them. For those Africans who had come across the Atlantic without ever experiencing the opportunity or the motivation for revolt, and for the American-born slaves who had never known anything but slavery, stories of shipboard insurrection would have confronted them with the reality that slavery was something that could be effectively challenged with a fight. Tales such as these would have contradicted the assertions so carefully and constantly made by the white power structure that slaves were born to be slaves. Frederick Douglass wrote in his autobiography that he descended into the darkest part of his enslavement only after he was finally made to feel like a slave. As Douglass wrote, "I was broken in body, soul, and spirit. . . . The cheerful spark that lingered about my eye died; the dark night of slavery closed in upon me; and behold a man transformed into a brute!"[23] In other words, slavery was only truly effective once those held in bondage felt that they were intended to be slaves, which was only possible through a lifetime of negative social indoctrination and brainwashing. This is precisely the pitfall that the slave community fought so hard against. Tales told late at night in the cabins, or in fields away from white ears, were the slave community's way of resisting the pressures and manipulation of the slaveholding regime. And in tens of thousands of slave communities throughout the Americas, tales told by survivors of shipboard revolts would have been among the inspiring stories that fueled this powerful underground slave culture.

Of course, the context had dramatically changed. The hold of a slave ship was nothing like a plantation. Methods of resistance effectively employed in the former would not necessarily work in the latter. And even if some tactics of rebellion did carry over, insurrectionary violence did not hold the same promise in the Americas. On a ship, the possibility of freedom beckoned. Particularly near the African coast, a well-executed rebellion might actually lead to freedom for those involved. In the Americas, outright insurrection was much less viable, and slaves resorted to other forms of resistance. Nevertheless, the tales of shipboard rebellion would have filled the slave communities of the Americas with hope—not so much the hope that they could escape their enslavement, for such an outcome was nearly impossible, but hope that they too could effectively survive and maintain their dignity as human beings. At its core, shipboard revolt was an assertion of humanity. It was the embodiment of that part within each participant that absolutely refused to be enslaved without a fight. Regardless of success or failure, life or death, humiliation or triumph, shipboard revolts put the world on notice that Africans and African Americans were not going to submit passively to enslavement. When backed into a corner, human beings do not give up. They fight. And this resistance—exhibited by hundreds of thousands of captives hundreds of times over centuries—contradicted everything that slavery stood for. Revolt is the assertion of humanity, and humanity is the antithesis of slavery. With the powerful tales of these Africans' courage and refusal to submit to bondage weaving their way into the slave communities of the Americas, enslaved men and women found inspiration and encouragement that would have helped to lessen the psychological impact of slavery and may well influenced the continued development of slave resistance.

The African slave trade was obviously a violent, savage, and terrifying chapter of human history, and its toll upon the region of West Africa and its people, including those who were distributed throughout the New World, can never be fully measured. For this reason, perhaps the most important lesson to take from the study of slave resistance is that the tragedy of enslavement did not occur without a long, bloody, and bitter fight that continued until slavery was finally abolished in the late nineteenth century. The ships of the Atlantic trade were perhaps the first great stage for this dramatic struggle, and the countless instances of resistance and outright insurrection that took place provided a powerful prelude to the tradition of revolt that followed among the plantation societies of the Americas. The courage, determination, and defiance of the enslaved men and women stand as testaments to the human spirit. The Africans fought back and fought hard, refusing to go quietly into bondage.

Appendix:
Chronology of Shipboard Slave Revolts, 1509–1865

Available information on identified shipboard slave rebellions is presented in this appendix in the following sequence:

Date: *Vessel* (Place of Origin). Ship's captain(s). Location of rebellion (Region). Casualties. Outcome. Source(s).

African regions in parentheses following location of rebellion correspond to the regions identified on the map on p. 65. Rebellions in the Americas on voyages not involved in transatlantic slave trade are also identified in parentheses following the location.

Rebellions in which slaves took control of a ship, however briefly, are designated successful, regardless of casualties. Some rebellions in which slaves gained their freedom do not meet this criterion. Incidents that may not have been attempts to take control of the ship are noted.

Sources are listed in the bibliography. The following abbreviations are used:

PD	*Virginia Gazette* publishers Alexander Purdie and John Dixon
PRO	Public Records Office, Kew, England
	C 103 Chancery: Master Blunt's Exhibits, ca. 1250–1859
	C 107 Chancery: Master Senior's Exhibits, ca. 1250–1851
	FO 84 Records of the Foreign Office, Correspondence of the Slave Trade and African Departments, 1816–1892
	T 70 Records of the Treasury, Correspondence of the Company of Royal Adventurers of England Trading with Africa, 1660–1833
TST CD	*The Trans-Atlantic Slave Trade: A Database on CD-ROM* (Eltis et al., eds.) [followed by voyage ID no.]
WR	*Virginia Gazette* publisher William Rind

1509: *Nau Fieis de Deus* (Portugal). Unsuccessful. Saunders, 14–15.

1532: *Misericordia* (Portugal). Capt. Estevao Carreiro. Between Sao Tome Island and Elimina. All but 3 crew members killed. Successful–freedom? Vogt, *Portuguese Rule,* 58; Vogt, *Sao Tome–Principe,* 461.

1571: (Spain?). West Indies. The slaves "slit the throats of the crew." Successful–freedom? De la Roncière, 4:82.

Ca. 1641: (Netherlands). Van den Boogaart and Emmer, 366.

Ca. 1642: (Netherlands). Van den Boogaart and Emmer, 366.

Ca. Sep. 1651: (England). Gambia River (Senegambia). All slaves and crewmen killed. Successful. Recognizing the ship was lost, the captain committed suicide by blowing up the ship with all aboard. Ligon, 57; Linebaugh and Rediker, 128–29.

1654: (England). Capt. Thomas Hiway. Middle Passage. 40 slaves killed. Unsuccessful. Paige, 108.

1678: (France). Capt. Ducasse. Middle Passage. All slaves killed. Unsuccessful. Munford, 2:342.

Sep. 1681: (England). Capt. Branfill. Cape Coast (Gold Coast). PRO, T 70, 10:49.

July 1683: *Trompeuse* (France). Capt. Jean Hamlin. West Indies. 3 slaves killed. Unsuccessful. Fortescue 11:519–21; TST CD, 21557.

Ca. Jan. 1685: *Expedition* (London, England). Capts. John Lambert and Hastings. Middle Passage. Unsuccessful. PRO, T 70, 12:15; TST CD, 9844.

Ca. Nov. 1685: *John & Sarah* (England). Capt. Pinke. Gambia (Senegambia). Unsuccessful. PRO, T 70, 11:57, 61.

Ca. Dec. 1685: *Charlton* (England). Capts. Paine and Browse. Whydah (Bight of Benin). 8 crewmen killed. Successful–freedom? PRO, T 70, 11:22, 102, 103.

1685: *Koninck Salomon* (Netherlands). Capt. Willem Jansen Goes. 1 slave killed. Unsuccessful. Postma, *Dutch in the Atlantic Slave Trade,* 166, 314, 379.

Ca. Sep. 1686: *Ann* (England). Capt. Jobson. Gambia (Senegambia). Some crewmen killed. Successful–freedom? PRO, T 70, 11:60; TST CD, 21027.

Ca. Sep. 1686: *Benjamin* (England). Middle Passage. 1 crewman killed. Unsuccessful. PRO, T 70, 12:163.

Ca. 1686: *Chaldron* (England). Capt. Latton. Accra? (Gold Coast). All crewmen killed. Successful–freedom? Eltis, *Rise of African Slavery,* 226.

Ca. Mar./Apr. 1687: *Lomax* (England). Middle Passage. Several slaves killed. Unsuccessful. PRO, T 70, 12:130.

1689: (England). Capt. Osney. Successful–freedom? PRO, T 70, 12:33.

1689: (France). Bijagos Islands (Sierra Leone). No one killed. Unsuccessful. Brue, 106.

Ca. 1690–1700: (Netherlands). At least 1 slave killed. Unsuccessful. Bosman, 365.

Ca. 1690–1700: (Netherlands). African coast? 20 slaves killed. Unsuccessful. Bosman, 365–66.

Ca. June 1691: *Charles* (England). Gambia (Senegambia). 17 slaves killed. Unsuccessful. PRO, T 70, 11:69.

Apr. 1693: *Friedrich Wilhelm* (Emden, Brandenburg). Capt. Jean le Sage. Between Whydah and Sao Tome Island. About 20 slaves killed in two revolts. Unsuccessful. A. Jones, "Brandenburg-Prussia," 288–89; A. Jones, *Brandenburg Sources*, 180–97; TST CD, 21950.

1693: *Brome* (England). Gambia (Senegambia). Unsuccessful. Eltis, *Rise of African Slavery*, 229; TST CD, 9706.

Feb. 1695: (France). Jakin (Bight of Benin). "A number" of slaves killed; some slaves seized a longboat and escaped. Unsuccessful–freedom for some. Munford, 2:344.

Ca. 1696: *Adventure* (London, England). Capt. Sherring. TST CD, 20127.

Ca. Sep. 1698: *Kobenhavns Bors* (Denmark). Middle Passage? Many slaves killed. Unsuccessful. Westergaard, 146; Highfield, 19.

Ca. Aug. 1699: *Albion-Frigate* (London, England). Capts. Edwards and Stephen Dupont. Middle Passage. 28 slaves and 1 crewman killed. Unsuccessful. Dow, 79–84; TST CD, 20173.

Ca. Aug. 1699: *Dragon* (Topsham, England). Capt. Henry Taylor. Gambia (Senegambia). 7 slaves and 2 crewmen killed. Unsuccessful. Tattersfield, 282–84.

1699: *Cothrington* (England). Capt. Brewser? Gambia River (Senegambia). Successful–freedom? PRO, T 70, vol. 1434.

1699: *Rachel* (Netherlands). 12 slaves and 1 crewman killed. Postma, *Dutch in the Atlantic Slave Trade*, 166.

Late 17th century: (France). 25 slaves killed. Unsuccessful. Gueye, 61.

Ca. 1700–1725: *Marie Anne* (France). Cape Mesurado (Sierra Leone). 1 crewman killed. Unsuccessful. Munford, 2:343.

Jan. 5, 1701: *Don Carlos* (London, England). Capt. William Esterson. Middle Passage. 27–28 slaves and at least 2 crewmen killed. Unsuccessful. Barbot, 5:513; Astley, 3:210–11; TST CD, 20207.

Mar. 1701: *Anna* (Netherlands). Bijagos Islands (Sierra Leone). No crewmen killed. Some slaves jumped overboard and escaped. Successful—freedom for some. Munford, 2:187–88, 286–87, 343.

May 23, 1702: *Tyger/Tiger* (England). Capt. Ralph Ash. Cape Coast Castle (Gold Coast). About 40 slaves and 6 crewmen killed. Unsuccessful. PRO, T 70, 1463:30–31.

1702: (Netherlands). Whydah (Bight of Benin). Munford, 2:344.

May 14, 1703: *Urban* (England). Capts. Bornisher/Bannister and Edward Bond. Middle Passage? 23 slaves and 2 crewmen killed. Unsuccessful. PRO, T 70, 13:21; TST CD, 21139.

Ca. May/June 1703: *Martha* (London, England). Capt. Richard Marsh. Middle Passage. 2 slaves killed. Unsuccessful. PRO, T 70, 13:23, 31; TST CD, 14988.

Nov. 1703: *London* (Bristol, England). Capt. Harris. Between Cape Coast Castle and Accra (Gold Coast). 30 slaves and 3 crewmen killed. Unsuccessful. PRO, T 70, 1463:66.

1703: *Zon/Son* (Netherlands). Capts. Jacob Cortse Visser and Samuel Bleeker. African coast. 36 slaves killed. Postma, *Dutch in the Atlantic Slave Trade,* 166, 317, 378, 381; Postma, "Mortality," 248; Postma, "Dutch Participation," 208.

1703/04: *Mairmaid* (London, England). Capt. Roger Carnaby. TST CD, 21165.

May 28, 1704: *Postillion* (England). Capt. John Tozor. Gambia River (Senegambia). 31 slaves killed. Unsuccessful. PRO, T 70, 14:66–67, 74, and vol. 1434.

1704: *Badine* (La Rochelle, France). Capt. Defroudas. TST CD, 33801.

1704: *Dorothy* (England). Middle Passage. Unsuccessful. Palmer, *Human Cargoes,* 55.

1704: *Eagle* (London, England). Capt. William Snelgrave Sr. Old Calabar River (Bight of Biafra). 2 slaves and no crewmen killed. Unsuccessful. Snelgrave, 164–68.

1705: *Malbrough/Marlborough* (England). Capts. Lawrence Prince and William Freake. Cape Coast (Gold Coast). 30–40 slaves killed. Unsuccessful. PRO, T 70, 14:109; TST CD, 21180.

Ca. Apr. 1706: (England). Capt. Richard Willis. Whydah (Bight of Benin). Unsuccessful. PRO, T 70, 5:27.

1706: (La Rochelle, France). Middle Passage. Unsuccessful. Munford, 2:344.

Ca. Aug. 1707: *Pindar* (London, England). Capt. John Taylor. Cape Coast (Gold Coast). Unsuccessful. PRO, T 70, 5:33, 26:18; TST CD, 9755.

Ca. Oct. 1707: *Sherbrow* (England). Capt. William Gill. Middle Passage. 3 slaves killed. Unsuccessful. PRO, T 70, 8:30, 31.

Mar. 20, 1708: *Mary* (England). Capt. Henry Hooper. Cape Coast (Gold Coast). 36 slaves killed. Unsuccessful. PRO, T 70, 2:4–5, 5:45, 18:20, 26:24.

Ca. Mar 1708: *Dorothy* (England). Capt. Thomas Ashby. Middle Passage. Unsuccessful. PRO, T 70, 8:35.

1708: *Whidah Merchant* (England). Capt. Owen. TST CD, 20905.

Sep. 14, 1709: *Fridericus Quartus* (Denmark). Capt. Phief. Slave Coast (Bight of Benin). 1 slave killed. Unsuccessful. Rask, 75–76; TST CD, 35158.

1710/11: *Joseph* (London, England). Capt. J. Foster/Forster. TST CD, 15215; Uring, 90.

Ca. May 1713: *Victorious Anne* (England). Cape Coast (Gold Coast). All but 7 crewmen killed. The ship was blown up in the insurrection. Successful–freedom? PRO, T 70, 5:90.

May 4, 1714: *Affriquain* (Saint-Malo, France). Capt. Yacinte Lodoye. Middle Passage. 10 slaves killed. Unsuccessful. Mettas, 2:683.

1714: *Duke of Cambridge* (England). 80 slaves killed. Unsuccessful. Palmer, "Slave Trade," 33.

Ca. Jan. 1715: (South Carolina). Barra (Senegambia). Sucessful–freedom? PRO, T 70, 6:2.

Feb. 15, 1715: *Société* (Nantes, France). Capt. Joseph Cavarau. Sao Tome (Bight of Biafra). 14 slaves and 3 crewmen killed. Unsuccessful. Mettas, 1:35.

June 2, 1715: *Affriquain* (Nantes, France). Capt. Rene Budan. Jakin (Bight of Benin). 10–11 slaves and 3 crewmen killed. Unsuccessful. Mettas, 1:31–32.

July 19, 1715: *Affriquaine* (Nantes, France). Capt. Claude Gontard. Senegal (Senegambia). 20 slaves killed. Unsuccessful. Mettas, 1:38.

July 30, 1715: *Prudent* (Nantes, France). Capt. Alexis Gamot. Jakin (Bight of Benin). 39 slaves killed. Unsuccessful. Mettas, 1:39.

Dec. 1715: *Gracieuse* (Nantes, France). Capt. Jean-Bernard Cazalis. St. Thomas, West Indies. 10 slaves killed. Unsuccessful. Mettas, 1:39–40.

1715: *Sonnesteyn* (Netherlands). Capt. Hans Pronk. Postma, *Dutch in the Atlantic Slave Trade,* 166, 317, 380.

June 1716: *Selby/Sylvia* (Dartmouth, England). Capt. John Vennard/Vernard. Gambia River (Senegambia). 1 crewman killed. Unsuccessful. PRO, T 70, 6:43; Tattersfield, 292–93.

Sep. 1716: *Anne & Priscilla* (London, England). Capt. Richard Sayers. Gambia (Senegambia). At least 1 crewman killed; Tattersfield suggests "virtually all" of the sailors were killed. Successful–freedom? PRO, T 70, 6:43, 26:54; Tattersfield, 300.

Oct. 1716: *Sophia* (Dublin, Ireland). Capt. Spring. Gambia (Senegambia). All but 2 crewmen killed. Successful—freedom? PRO, T 70, 6:44.

Mar. 18, 1717: *Union* (Nantes, France). Capt. Jean Viau. Guinea Coast. Unsuccessful. Mettas, 1:54.

July 1717: *Ann/Anne* (England). Capts. Benjamin Clarke and Nicholas Kidgell. Gambia River (Senegambia). 2–8 slaves killed; 6 jumped overboard and may have swum to shore. Unsuccessful—freedom for some? Donnan, 2:231–33.

1717: *Agatha* (Netherlands). African coast. 9 slaves killed; some tried to get ashore, at least 1 successfully. Unsuccessful—freedom for some? Postma, *Dutch in the Atlantic Slave Trade,* 166; Postma, "Dutch Participation," 208–10.

Sep. 26, 1718: *Société* (Nantes, France). Capt. David Henricheman. 2 days from Annobon Island. 12 slaves and 1 crewman killed. Unsuccessful. Mettas, 1:63.

Nov. 1719: *Don de Dieu* (Saint-Malo, France). Capt. Guillaume Masson du Bocage. Revolt 1: Formosa River (Bight of Benin). 59 slaves and 1 crewman killed. Unsuccessful—freedom for some? Revolt 2: Middle Passage. 1 crewman killed. Unsuccessful. Mettas, 2:686.

Apr. 26, 1720: *Aimable Renaute* (Nantes, France). Capt. Robert Joubert. Mesura (Windward Coast?). 3 slaves and 1 crewman killed. Unsuccessful. Mettas, 1:77–78.

Sep. 6, 1721: (England). Capt. Willson. Anomabu (Gold Coast). 2 crewmen killed. Successful—freedom for some. 10 of 17 slaves who escaped were subsequently recaptured. PRO, T 70, 4:22, 7:30.

1721: *Elizabeth* (England). Capt. Thompson. Anomabu (Gold Coast). 3 slaves and 1 crewman killed. Unsuccessful. Snelgrave, 174–85.

1721: *Henry* (London, England). Capt. William Snelgrave. Mumfort (Gold Coast). No one killed. Unsuccessful. Snelgrave, 168–73.

1721: *Robert* (Bristol, England). Capt. Richard Harding/Arding. Sierra Leone. 4 slaves and 3 crewmen killed. Unsuccessful. Atkins, 71–73; D. Richardson, *Bristol,* 1:98.

Ca. Feb. 1722: *Ferrers/Farres* (London, England). Capt. Francis Messervy/Messerve. Middle Passage. 80 slaves and 1 crewman killed. Unsuccessful. Slaves attempted to revolt twice, once landed in Jamaica. Snelgrave, 185–91; TST CD, 75484.

Ca. Feb. 1722: *Marie Galere* (Saint-Malo, France). Capt. De La Ville Durant, de Jegu. Benin (Bight of Benin). 30 slaves and 1 crewman killed. Unsuccessful. Mettas, 2:692–93.

Ca. Mar. 1722: *Excellent* (Nantes, France). Capt. Jean Denier. Whydah (Bight of Benin). 74 slaves killed. Unsuccessful. Mettas, 1:100–101.

Mar.–May 1722: *Marie* (Nantes, France). Capt. Jean Guesneau. Middle Passage. Many slaves killed. Unsuccessful. Mettas, 1:97.

Ca. July/Aug. 1722: (England). Gambia (Senegambia). 1 crewman killed. Successful–freedom? PRO, T 70, 7:49, 76.

July 26, 1723: *Ameriquain* (Nantes, France). Capt. H. Piednoir. Whydah (Bight of Benin). Unsuccessful. Mettas, 1:109, 110.

Mar. 14, 1724: *Dauphin* (Lorient, France). Capt. Filouze. Whydah (Bight of Benin). Unsuccessful. Mettas, 2:560–61. *See also* subsequent rebellion on the same voyage, Mar. 15, 1724.

Mar. 15, 1724: *Dauphin* (Lorient, France). Capt. Filouze. First day at sea. 1 slave killed. Unsuccessful. On Mar. 21, 1 slave wounded during this revolt jumped overboard. On March 23, another slave was killed "attempting to initiate a new revolt." Mettas, 2:560–61. *See also* earlier rebellion on the same voyage, Mar. 14, 1724.

Mar. 1724: *Ruby* (London, England). Capt. Craigue. Joar (Senegambia). 17 slaves killed. Unsuccessful. Moore, 296.

1724: *Haabets Galley* (Denmark). Highfield, 19.

1725: *Vautour* (France). Successful–freedom? Desport, 34.

Ca. May 1727: *Cezar* (Nantes, France). Capt. Barthelemy Joubert. Whydah (Bight of Benin). 30 slaves killed. Unsuccessful. Mettas, 1:118–19; Harms, 153.

Ca. May 1728: *Queen Caroline* (Bristol, England). Capt. Anselm Holliday/Halladay. Cape Mount (Windward Coast). All but 1 crewman killed. Successful–freedom. PRO, T 70, 1465:39, 40–41; *Weekly Journal; or, The British Gazetteer*, Jan. 25, 1729.

July 1, 1728: *Saint Nicholas* (Nantes, France). Capt. Jacques Martin. Whydah (Bight of Benin). 2 slaves killed. Unsuccessful. Mettas, 1:127.

Summer 1728: *Union* (Nantes, France). Capt. Fr. Ernaud de la Rochandiere. Whydah (Bight of Benin). Unsuccessful. Mettas, 1:126–27.

Oct. 4, 1728: *Marie Magdelaine* (Nantes, France). Capt. Gregoire Terrien. Whydah (Bight of Benin). Unsuccessful. Mettas, 1:128–29.

Ca. 1728: *Aurore* (La Rochelle, France). Capt. Bonfils. 32 slaves killed. Unsuccessful. Mettas, 2:242.

1728/29: *Amitie* (Nantes, France). Capt. Pierre Ricard. Unsuccessful. Mettas, 1:130.

Ca. Apr. 1729: *Clare* (England). Capt. Murrell/Morrell/Murrel/Murel/Morrell. Cape Coast Castle (Gold Coast). Successful–freedom. *Fog's Weekly Journal*, Aug. 2, Sep. 6, 1729, Feb. 28, June 20, 1730; *Weekly Journal; or, The British Gazetteer*, Aug.

2, Sep. 6, 1729, Feb. 28, June 20, 1730; *Boston Weekly News-Letter,* Sep. 18–25, 1729; *Pennsylvania Gazette,* Oct. 9–16, 1729, Jan. 6–13, 1730.

Ca. Apr. 1729: *Industry* (Liverpool, England). Capt. James Williamson. Middle Passage. 1 slave killed. Unsuccessful. *Weekly Journal; or, The British Gazetteer,* July 5, 1729.

Ca. Apr. 1729: *Restoration* (Liverpool, England). Capt. Boogs/Boage. Guinea Coast. All crewmen killed. Successful–freedom? *Fog's Weekly Journal,* Aug. 2, Sep. 6, 1729; *Weekly Journal; or, The British Gazetteer,* Sep. 6, 1729; *Pennsylvania Gazette,* Jan. 6–13, 1730.

May 26, 1729: *Annibal* (Lorient, France). Capt. Ch. de Kerguenel. Gambia River (Senegambia). 50 (?) slaves and 4 crewmen killed. Unsuccessful–freedom for some? 1 slave took a lifeboat and several jumped into the river, but it is unknown whether any gained their freedom. Mettas, 2:580–81; Hall, 87–91. *See also* subsequent rebellion on the same voyage, July 13, 1729.

July 13, 1729: *Annibal* (Lorient, France). Capt. Ch. de Keeguenel. Caye St. Louis, St. Domingue, West Indies. Unsuccessful? Mettas, 2:580–81; Hall, 87–91. *See also* earlier rebellion on the same voyage, May 26, 1729.

1729: *Katherine* (Boston, MA). Capt. William Atkinson. Guinea Coast. Unsuccessful–freedom for some. May have been an escape attempt. Halasz, 8.

Ca. 1729: *Ann* (Liverpool, England). Capt. Cadden. Guinea Coast. Successful–freedom? *Fog's Weekly Journal,* Aug. 2, 1729.

Jan. 1, 1730: *Neptune* (Nantes, France). Capt. Pierre Cadou. Between Principe and Sao Thome (Bight of Biafra). 3 slaves killed. Unsuccessful. Mettas, 1:136.

Jan. 19, 1730: *Angelique* (La Rochelle, France). Capt. Louis Herault. Whydah (Bight of Benin). 2 slaves killed. Unsuccessful. Mettas, 2:244.

Apr. 16, 1730: *Aimable Renotte* (Nantes, France). Capt. Jean-Baptiste de Coueteus. African coast. 33 slaves killed. Unsuccessful. Mettas, 1:139–40.

Ca. May 1730: *William* (Boston, MA). Capt. Peter Jump. Anomabu (Gold Coast). The press reported that the captain and all the crew were "murther'd by the Negro's they had on Board," but a letter written from Cape Coast Castle suggests there were 3 survivors. Successful–freedom? PRO, T 70, 7:164–65; *Pennsylvania Gazette,* Nov. 19–26, Dec. 22–29, 1730; *Read's Weekly Journal; or, British-Gazetteer,* Jan. 23, 1731; *London Evening Post,* Jan. 19–21, 1731.

June 6, 1730: *Little George* (Newport, RI). Capt. George Scott. Middle Passage. At least 1 slave and at least 3 crewmen killed. Successful–freedom. Some accounts suggest the slaves were reenslaved by other Africans on shore. *Boston Weekly*

News-Letter, Apr. 22–29, Apr. 29–May 6, 1731; *New York Gazette,* May 3–10, 1731; *Pennsylvania Gazette,* May 6–13, 1731.

July 20, 1730: *Hare* (Liverpool, England). Capt. J. Sacheverel. Cape Coast (Gold Coast). 14 slaves killed. Unsuccessful. *Universal Spectator, and Weekly Journal,* Jan. 16, 1731.

Dec. 7, 1730: (Glasgow, Scotland). Anomabu (Gold Coast). Most crewmen killed. Successful–freedom? *Boston Weekly News-Letter,* Sep. 2–9, 1731.

1730: *Antonia* (Liverpool, England). Capt. Hugh Crawford. Successful? TST CD, 94504.

1730: *Charming Lydia* (London, England). Capt. Peter Poey. TST CD, 76736.

Feb. 28, 1731: *Ruby* (London, England). Capts. Colwell and Craigia/Creague. Junk (Windward Coast). Several/most of the crewmen killed. Successful–freedom. *London Evening Post,* Nov. 13–16, 1731; *Country Journal; or, The Craftsman,* Nov. 20, Dec. 18, 1731; Moore, 64–65.

1731: *Katherine* (England). 2 slaves killed. Unsuccessful. D. Richardson, "Shipboard Revolts," 74.

1731: *Leusden* (Netherlands). Capt. Bruyn Harmensz. Unsuccessful. Postma, *Dutch in the Atlantic Slave Trade,* 166, 315, 379.

Apr. 7, 1732: (Newport, RI). Capt. Perkins. Guinea Coast. Several slaves and 1 crewman killed. 22 slaves escaped in boats but were apparently recaptured. Unsuccessful. *Rhode Island Gazette,* Oct. 25, 1732; *Boston Weekly News-Letter,* Oct. 19–27, Oct. 27–Nov. 2, 1732; *Weekly Rehearsal,* Oct. 30, 1732; *Pennsylvania Gazette,* Nov. 2–9, 1732; *South-Carolina Gazette,* Dec. 2–9, 1732.

1732: *Concorde* (Vannes, France). Guinea Coast. 196 slaves killed. Unsuccessful. Harms, 403.

1732: *Parfaite* (La Rochelle, France). Capt. Elie Seignette. Grand Popo (Bight of Benin). 1 crewman killed. Successful–freedom? Mettas, 2:246.

Ca. 1732: (Bristol, RI). All crewmen killed. Successful–freedom? *Rhode Island Gazette,* Oct. 25, 1732; *Boston Weekly News-Letter,* Oct. 27–Nov. 2, 1732; *Weekly Rehearsal,* Oct. 30, 1732; *Pennsylvania Gazette,* Nov. 2–9, 1732; *South-Carolina Gazette,* Dec. 2–9, 1732.

1732/33: *Vryheyt/Vreyheid* (Netherlands). Capt. Jan Pietrsz Gewelt. Postma, *Dutch in the Atlantic Slave Trade,* 319, 379; Postma, "Mortality," 248.

Ca. Feb. 1733: (England). Capt. Williams. Joar (Senegambia). A "great part" of the crewmen killed. Successful–freedom? Moore, 156.

Ca. Feb. 1733: (Portugal). Oncha. Most of the crewmen were killed. Successful. Slaves held the ship for 5 days before being recaptured after a 24-hour engagement with an English vessel. *Boston Weekly News-Letter,* Apr. 12–19, 1733.

Sep. 10, 1733: *Saint Dominique* (Nantes, France). Capt. Gosmant. African coast. 3 slaves killed. Unsuccessful. Mettas, 1:165.

Sep. 13, 1733: *Diane* (Ile de Bourbon, France). Capt. Dhermitte. Madagascar (East Africa). 5 slaves and 1 crewman killed. Unsuccessful. Mettas, 2:223.

Nov. 5, 1733: *Reine de France* (Nantes, France). Capt. Guillaume Thomas. Whydah (Bight of Benin). Unsuccessful. Mettas, 1:164, 2:591–92.

Dec. 7, 1733: *Renommee* (Nantes, France). Capt. Jean Guesneau. Jakin (Bight of Benin). Several slaves killed. Unsuccessful. Mettas, 1:165–66; 2:591–92.

Apr. 7, 1734: *Aventurier* (Nantes, France). Capt. J. Shaghnessy. Whydah (Bight of Benin). At least 40 slaves and 5 crewmen killed. Unsuccessful. Mettas, 1:166–67.

Ca. Aug. 1734: *Juba* (Bristol, England). Capt. Christopher Allen. (Bight of Benin). 4 crewmen killed. Unsuccessful. *Read's Weekly Journal; or, British-Gazetteer,* Nov. 9, 1734.

Ca. Aug. 1734: (Bordeaux, France). Middle Passage? Some crewmen killed. Successful–freedom? Pluchon, 187–88.

Aug. 1735: *Princess Caroline* (England). Middle Passage. McGowan, "Origins of Slave Rebellions," 84.

1735: *De Hoop* (Netherlands). Capt. Huybrecht Eversen. Postma, *Dutch in the Atlantic Slave Trade,* 166, 330, 383.

1735: *Dolphin* (London, England). African coast. All slaves and crewmen killed. The slaves apparently committed suicide by breaking into the powder magazine and blowing up the ship with all aboard. Unsuccessful. Coffin, 14; Brawley, 43.

1735/36: *Badine* (Lorient, France). Capt. J. Bart. 6 crewmen killed. Unsuccessful. May not have been an insurrection. Mettas, 2:594.

Ca. Feb. 1737: *Phenix* (Nantes, France). Capt. Joseph Negre. Little Popo (Bight of Benin). 1 crewman killed. Unsuccessful. Mettas, 1:183.

Ca. Apr. 1737: *Mary* (England). Capt. John Dunning. Middle Passage. 1 slave killed. Unsuccessful. PRO, C 103, vol. 130, Apr. 20, 1737; Behrendt, letter.

Dec. 1737: *Phenix* (Le Havre, France). Capt. Martin Foache. African coast. 20 slaves killed. Unsuccessful. Mettas, 2:410.

Ca. 1737: *Lively* (Liverpool, England). Guinea Coast. 12 slaves killed. Unsuccessful. Wadsworth and Mann, 228–29.

May 11, 1738: *Galatee* (La Rochelle, France). Capt. Jean Robin. Cape Sainte Apolonnie (Gold Coast). Several slaves and 4 crewmen killed. Successful—freedom? Mettas, 2:257.

June 16, 1738: *Henriette* (Lorient, France). Capt. Richard de Lamarre. Whydah (Bight of Benin). 42 slaves unaccounted for and 1 crewman killed. While some slaves were killed or drowned, others may have escaped to shore. Unsuccessful—freedom for some? Mettas, 2:599–600.

Nov. 27, 1738: *Affriquain* (Nantes, France). Capt. Nicolas Foure. Banana Islands (Sierra Leone). 11 slaves and 2 crewmen killed. Unsuccessful. Mettas, 1:205–6; Stein, *French Slave Trade*, 105–6; Mousnier, 35–44.

1738/39: *Jeune Christophe* (Nantes, France). Capt. Antoine Ducoudray. Guinea Coast. Up to 50 slaves may have freed themselves. Unsuccessful—freedom for some. Mettas, 1:202.

Aug. 26, 1739: *Gloire* (Lorient, France). Capt. Roquet. Middle Passage. 22 slaves and 7 crewmen killed. Unsuccessful. Mettas, 2:601.

Aug. 30, 1739: *Princess Carolina* (Charleston, SC). Capt. John Fumcan. Middle Passage. 3 crewmen killed. Successful—freedom? *Boston Weekly News-Letter,* Nov. 15–22, 1739.

July 13, 1740: *Nereide* (Nantes, France). Capt. Luc Moyen. Middle Passage. 5 slaves killed. Unsuccessful. Mettas, 1:221.

1740: *Expedition* (London, England). Capt. James/John Bruce. Gambia (Senegambia). Many slaves killed. Unsuccessful. Benezet, 126–29.

Mar. 12, 1741: *Marie* (Lorient, France). Capt. Bigot de La Cante. Bissau (Sierra Leone). 24 slaves killed. Some slaves escaped in a dinghy but were recaptured or killed. Unsuccessful. Mettas, 2:604–5.

1741: *Afrikaanse Galey* (Netherlands). Capt. P. de Veyle. Unsuccessful. Postma, *Dutch in the Atlantic Slave Trade,* 166, 321, 387.

Ca. June 1742: *Grand Chasseur* (Saint-Malo, France). Capt. Julien Auffray Du Gue Lambert. Middle Passage. About 40 slaves killed. Unsuccessful. Mettas, 2:704.

Aug. 13, 1742: *Sainte Helene* (Nantes, France). Capt. Germain Blanchard. Epe (Bight of Benin). Some slaves and 7 crewmen killed. Successful—freedom for some. Mettas, 1:260, 2:608.

Sep. 2, 1742: *Badine* (Nantes, France). Capt. Martin Lissarague. Epe (Bight of Benin). 7 slaves killed. Unsuccessful. Mettas, 1:261.

Sep. 4, 1742: *Mary* (London, England). Capt. Nathaniel Roberts? Gambia River (Senegambia). All but 2 crewmen killed. Successful—freedom for some. *South-*

Carolina Gazette, Oct. 24, 1743; *Boston Gazette,* Dec. 20, 1743; *Boston News-Letter,* Dec. 22, 1743.

Dec. 24, 1742: *Maure* (Nantes, France). Capt. Georges Richard. Whydah (Bight of Benin). 17 slaves and 1 crewman killed. Unsuccessful. Mettas, 1:268.

Mar. 1, 1743: *Notre-Dame de Bonne Garde* (Nantes, France). Capt. Etienne Fessard. Middle Passage. 9–11 slaves and 3 crewmen killed. Unsuccessful. Mettas, 1:266–67.

Apr. 8, 1743: *Père de Famille* (Nantes, France). Capt. J.-B. Guyot. Middle Passage. Some slaves and 1 crewman killed. Unsuccessful. Mettas, 1:273.

Oct. 5, 1743: *Jeannette* (Nantes, France). Capt. Julien Hiron. Epe (Bight of Benin). 2 crewmen killed. Unsuccessful. Mettas, 1:280.

Ca. Jan.–June 1744: *Mercure* (Nantes, France). Capt. Yves Armes. Whydah (Bight of Benin). Unsuccessful. Mettas, 1:290.

Oct. 6, 1744: *Duc de Bretagne* (Bordeaux?, France). Capt. Chevalier de la Bretonniere. Annobon Island (Bight of Biafra). 4 crewmen killed. Unsuccessful. Mettas, 2:22.

Jan. 14, 1745: *Favorite* (Lorient, France). Capt. Trublet. Middle Passage. 6–7 slaves killed. Unsuccessful. Mettas, 2:611–12.

Jan. 1747: (Rhode Island). Capt. Bear. Cape Coast Castle (Gold Coast). All but two crewmen killed. Successful–freedom? *Boston Weekly News-Letter,* May 7, 1747; *Pennsylvania Gazette,* May 21, 1747.

1748: *Scipio* (Liverpool, England). Capt. James Stewart. African coast. Freedom? Ship blown up. *Lloyd's List,* Jan. 5, 1749; TST CD, 90227.

1748: *Thomas and Ellinor* (Liverpool, England). Capt. Thomas Rawlinson. Successful? TST CD, 90233.

Ca. Jan. 1749: *Polly* (New York, NY). Capt. William Johnson. West Indies (intra-American slave transport). All crewmen killed. Successful. Slaves subsequently recaptured and jailed. *Pennsylvania Gazette,* Jan. 31, 1749, July 27, 1749.

May 14, 1749: *Auguste* (Saint-Malo, France). Capt. Noel Pinou des Praires. Melimba (West Central Africa). 7 slaves killed. Unsuccessful. Mettas, 2:710–11.

May 27, 1749: *Prince d'Orange* (Nantes, France). Capt. Jaques Broban. Sao Tome Island (Bight of Biafra). 36 slaves and 3 crewmen killed. Unsuccessful. Mettas, 1:301.

July 20, 1749: *Noe* (La Rochelle, France). Capt. Thomas Palmier. Fernando Po Island (Bight of Biafra). 63 slaves killed. Unsuccessful. Mettas, 2:287.

Ca. Sep. 1749: *Lamb* (England). Capt. Timothy Anyon. Middle Passage. 14 slaves killed. Unsuccessful. *Lloyd's List,* Dec. 12, 1749; TST CD, 90118.

1749: *Brownlow* (England). Capt. Richard Jackson. 3–4 slaves and 1 crewman killed. Unsuccessful. Newton, 22; TST CD, 90226.

1749: *Cheval Marin* (Nantes, France). Capt. Bernard Desaas. Unsuccessful. Mettas, 1:304.

Ca. Mar. 1750: *Willingmind* (England). Capt. Appleton. Sherbro River (Sierra Leone). Successful–freedom? May have been either an insurrection or an attack by free Africans. *Lloyd's List,* Mar. 26, 1750.

Apr. 14, 1750: *Ann* (Liverpool, England). Capt. Benjamin Clark. Cape Lopez (Bight of Biafra). At least 3 crewmen killed. Successful–freedom. *Pennsylvania Gazette,* Aug. 9, 1750; *Boston Post-Boy,* Aug. 13, 1750; *Lloyd's List,* Aug. 28, 1750; *Maryland Gazette,* Sep. 5, 1750.

May 8, 1750: *King David* (Bristol, England). Capt. Edmund Holland. Near Guadeloupe, West Indies. 15–17 crewmen killed. Successful. Slaves recaptured by a ship sent in pursuit. *Boston News-Letter,* June 21, Sep. 6, 1750; *Boston Post-Boy,* June 25, 1750; *Pennsylvania Gazette,* July 5, 1750; *Lloyd's List,* July 13, 1750; *Maryland Gazette,* Nov. 14, 1750; TST CD, 17243.

May 15, 1750: *Diligente* (Nantes, France). Capt. Charles Le Breton. Unsuccessful. Mettas, 1:324–25.

June 20, 1750: *Louise Marguerite* (Nantes, France). Capt. Etienne Fessard. Whydah (Bight of Benin). Unsuccessful. Mettas, 1:328.

Sep. 17, 1750: *Samuel-Marie* (Dunquerque, France). Capt. J.-B. Maginel. Cerbera River (Sierra Leone). 13 slaves and 4 crewmen killed. Unsuccessful. Mettas, 2:149–50.

Oct. 5–10, 1750: *Wolf* (New York, NY). Capt. Gurnay Wall. Near Anomabu (Gold Coast). 1 slave killed. Unsuccesful. A group of slaves who apparently escaped aboard a yawl were soon recaptured. Wax, "Philadelphia Surgeon," 465–68, 484–86.

Nov. 7, 1750: *Jamaica Packet* (Bristol, England). Capt. George Merrick. Several crewmen killed. Unsuccessful. May not have been an insurrection. D. Richardson, *Bristol,* 3:39.

Nov. 11, 1750: *Henriette* (Nantes, France). Capt. Antoine Rouille. Whydah (Bight of Benin). 14 slaves and 1 crewman killed. Unsuccessful. Mettas, 1:334.

Dec. 1, 1750: *Sultane* (La Rochelle, France). Capt. Avrillon. Goree Island (Senegambia). 230 slaves and 6–7 crewmen killed. Unsuccessful. Pruneau de Pommegorge, 113–17; Searing, 147–48; Mettas, 2:295.

1750: *Esperance* (Saint-Malo, France). Capt. Ph. Hamon Du Courchamp. Some slaves killed. Unsuccessful. Mettas, 2:712–13.

Ca. 1750: (France). African coast. All but 2 crewmen killed. Successful–freedom? E. Martin, 24.

Jan. 16, 1751: *Hector* (Nantes, France). Capt. Jean Honoraty. Goree Island (Senegambia). 3 slaves killed. Unsuccessful. Mettas, 1:342–43.

Mar. 30, 1751: *Cerf* (Nantes, France). Capt. Luc Lory. African coast. Successful–freedom? Mettas, 1:319.

Oct. 12, 1751: *Parfaite* (Saint-Malo, France). Capt. Pierre Harson. Guinea Coast. 3 crewmen killed. Unsuccessful. Mettas, 2:716–17.

Ca. Oct.–Dec. 1751: *Sirene* (Nantes, France). Capt. Jacques Souchay. African coast. 199 slaves killed. Unsuccessful. Mettas, 1:349.

Nov. 7, 1751: *Sauveur* (Saint-Malo, France). Capt. Joseph Gardon Du Bournay. African coast. 1 crewman killed. Unsuccessful. Mettas, 2:715.

1751: *Grenadier* (Netherlands). Capt. Jan van Kerkhoven. African coast. No one killed. Postma, *Dutch in the Atlantic Slave Trade,* 166; TST CD, 10621.

1751: *Middelburgs Welvaren* (Netherlands). Capt. Jacob Gerritsen. Guinea Coast. 213 slaves and no crewmen killed. Unsuccessful. Postma, *Dutch in the Atlantic Slave Trade,* 167–68, 337, 383.

Feb.–May 1752: *Heureux* (Nantes, France). Capt. Toby Clarc. Principe Island (Bight of Biafra). Unsuccessful. Mettas, 1:348.

Oct. 14, 1752: *Marlborough* (Bristol, England). Capt. Robert Codd. African coast. 100 (?) slaves and at least 27 crewmen killed. One report suggests "upwards of a hundred" slaves were drowned in a dispute between Bonny and Gold Coast slaves arising from the revolt. Successful–freedom. *Lloyd's List,* Feb. 6, 1753; *Felix Farley's Bristol Journal,* Feb. 3–10, 1753, Mar. 24–31, 1753; *Maryland Gazette,* Oct. 5, 1753.

Ca. Nov. 1752: *Addlington* (England). Capt. John Perkins. Bassa (Windward Coast). 19 slaves and 4–5 crewmen killed. Unsuccessful. Newton, 66, 69–70.

1752: (England). Capt. Belson. Sierra Leone. Successful–freedom. This may be the Dec. 5, 1753, revolt aboard the *Adventure.* Rathbone, 17.

Ca. 1752: *Benjamin* (London, England). African coast. 1 slave killed. Unsuccessful. Clarkson, 311.

Mar. 14, 1753: *Saint Philippe* (Nantes, France). Capt. Guillaume Denis Hamon. Middle Passage, 1 crewman killed. Unsuccessful. Mettas, 1:374–75.

June 21, 1753: *Marechal de Saxe* (La Rochelle, France). Capt. Midy. Whydah (Bight of Benin). 47 slaves and 1 crewman killed. Unsuccessful. Mettas, 2:298–99.

Aug. 5, 1753: *Patientia* (Denmark). Capt. Ole Eriksen. Between Elmina and Cape Coast Castle (Gold Coast). 3 crewmen killed. Successful–freedom for some? The ship and at least some of the slaves were recaptured with the aid of a nearby English vessel. Nørregård, *Danish Settlements*, 89–90; Nørregård, "Slaveoproret," 23–44.

Nov. 1, 1753: *Elizabeth* (Rhode Island). Capt. Thomas Carpenter. Apam Road (Gold Coast). Some slaves killed. 11 jumped overboard and swam for land, but at least some appear to have been recaptured by local Africans. Unsuccessful–freedom for some? Rhode Island State Archives, Public Notary Records, vol. 6 (1753–58), 64–65.

Dec. 5, 1753: *Adventure* (London, England). Capt. Beatson. Shebar (Sierra Leone). 1 crewman killed. Successful–freedom. Newton, 88.

1753: *Two Friends* (Rhode Island). Capt. Abraham Hammett/Hamlet/Hamblet. Cape Coast (Gold Coast). The slave traders "lost the best of what they had." Unsuccessful. Mason, 339; Jensen, 491; Donnan, 3:144, 4:310; TST CD, 36156.

1753/54: *York* (London, England). Capt. William Mercier. TST CD, 25021.

May 12, 1754: *Levrette* (Nantes, France). Capt. Julien Marchais. 2 days out from Principe Island (Bight of Biafra). 3–4 slaves and 14–15 crewmen killed. Successful–recaptured. After 5 days in control of the ship and bitter fighting among the slaves, the Africans apparently surrendered the ship to the surviving crew. Mettas, 1:380–81, 382; Eltis, *Rise of African Slavery*, 233.

Ca. Sep. 1754: *Swallow* (Lancaster, England). Capt. Robert Dobson/Dodson. Gambia (Senegambia). 22 slaves and 5 crewmen killed. Unsuccessful. PRO, T 70, 30:81; TST CD, 24016.

Nov. 17, 1754: *Finette* (Nantes, France). Capt. Michel Bauge. Bissau (Sierra Leone). 1 crewman killed. Unsuccessful. Mettas, 1:395–96.

1754: *Jubilee* (England). Capt. Smith. Anomabu (Gold Coast). All but 4 crewmen killed. Successful–freedom? *Gentleman's Magazine,* Mar. 1754.

July 20, 1755: *Saint Joseph* (Saint-Malo, France). Capt. Fr. Josselin Loisement. Guinea Coast. 3 crewmen killed. Successful–freedom? Mettas, 2:725–26.

Sep. 7, 1755: *Printemps* (La Rochelle, France). Capt. Jean Elie Giraudeau. 1 crewman killed. Unsuccessful. Mettas, 2:303.

Oct. 11, 1755: *Jeune Mars* (Nantes, France). Capt. Jean Laurent Robart. Middle Passage. 3 crewmen killed. Unsuccessful. Mettas, 1:411.

1755: *Belle Judith* (Nantes, France). Pluchon, 187.

1755: *Charming Jenny / Charming Elizabeth* (London, England). Capt. John Allman. Successful–recaptured? TST CD, 27240.

July 6, 1756: (England). Capt. Stirling. Gambia River (Senegambia). At least 1 crewman killed. Successful–freedom? PRO, T 70, 30:163, 166; PRO, T 70, vol. 1694, letters dated July 24, 1756, and Sep. 16, 1756.

Ca. July 1756: *Jane* (New York, NY?). Capt. Alexander Hope. Middle Passage. 1 slave and 1 crewman killed. Unsuccessful. *Pennsylvania Gazette,* Sep. 30, 1756; Williams, 480; TST CD, 25030.

1756: *Philadelphia* (Netherlands). Capt. Jan Menkenveld. African coast. No one killed. Postma, *Dutch in the Atlantic Slave Trade,* 166, 339, 385.

1756: *Vliegende Faam* (Netherlands). Capt. Pieter de Moor. African coast. 11 slaves killed. Unsuccessful–freedom for some? 22 of the Africans on board were reported missing following the revolt. Postma, *Dutch in the Atlantic Slave Trade,* 166, 344, 385.

1756/57: *Penelope* (Liverpool, England). Capt. William Wiatt. TST CD, 90490.

1756/57: *Thomas* (Liverpool, England). Capt. John Whiteside. Successful–recaptured? TST CD, 90660.

Feb. 1757: *Black Prince* (England). Capt. Peter Bostock. Gambia River (Senegambia). Unsuccessful–freedom for some? PRO, T 70, 30:179–80; PRO, T 70, vol. 1694, letter dated Feb. 14, 1757.

1757: *Drie Gezusters* (Netherlands). Capt. Maartin Stam. Postma, *Dutch in the Atlantic Slave Trade,* 166, 325, 386.

1757: *Philadelphia* (Netherlands). Capt. Jan Menkenveld. African coast. No one killed. Postma, *Dutch in the Atlantic Slave Trade,* 166, 339, 385.

1757/58: *Mears* (Liverpool, England). Capt. Chris Berrill. TST CD, 90556.

Jan. 14, 1758: *Two Sisters* (Bristol, England). Capt. Robert Cowie. African coast. 3 crewmen killed. Unsuccessful. D. Richardson, *Bristol,* 3:111.

Jan./Feb. 1758: *Rainbow* (Liverpool, England). Capt. Joseph Harrison. Middle Passage. 1 crewman killed. Unsuccessful. Williams, 488–89.

1758/59: *William* (Liverpool, England). Capt. Blackburn Wilcock/Willocks. TST CD, 90587.

Jan. 12, 1759: *Perfect* (Liverpool, England). Capt. William Potter. Mana (Sierra Leone). At least 5 crewmen killed. Successful–freedom for some? At least some slaves apparently recaptured on shore by local Africans. Williams, 492–93, 666; E. Martin, 106; TST CD, 90744.

Ca. Sep. 1759: *Rebecca* (England). Capt. Ross. Gambia (Senegambia). Two revolts. Unsuccessful. PRO, T 70, 30:315, 321.

1759: *Middelburgs Welvaren* (Netherlands). African coast. No one killed. Postma, *Dutch in the Atlantic Slave Trade,* 166.

1759: *Shark* (Liverpool, England). Capt. James Lowe. TST CD, 90727.

1759/60: *Nanny* (Liverpool, England). Capt. James McDougall. TST CD, 90741.

Ca. Oct. 12, 1760: *Ross* (England). Capt. Lear. Gambia River (Senegambia). Unsuccessful. PRO, T 70, 30:386.

1760: *Nanny* (Liverpool, England). Capt. James McDougall. Successful? TST CD, 90742.

Ca. June 1761: *Agnes* (New York, NY). Capt. Nicoll/Nicholls. Guinea Coast. 40 slaves killed. Unsuccessful. *New York Gazette,* June 15, 1761; *Boston News-Letter,* June 25, Aug. 20, 1761; TST CD, 25327.

Ca. Nov. 1761: *Mary* (Lancaster, England). Capt. Samuel Sandys/Sands. Gambia River (Senegambia). Unsuccessful. PRO, T 70, 30:436. *See also* subsequent rebellion on the same voyage, Dec. 1761.

Dec. 1761: *Mary* (Lancaster, England). Capt. Samuel Sandys/Sands. Gambia River (Senegambia). Most crewmen killed. Successful—freedom? PRO, T 70, 30:436; Merseyside Maritime Museum Transatlantic Slave Trade Exhibit; *Lloyd's Evening Post and British Chronicle,* Jan. 4–6, 1762; *Lloyd's List,* Jan. 5, 1762; Elder, 53, 55, 175. *See also* earlier rebellion on the same voyage, ca. Nov. 1761.

1761: *Thomas* (Massachusetts?). Capt. Day. African coast. 1 slave killed. Unsuccessful. *Boston News-Letter,* Sep. 24, 1761; *New York Gazette,* Sep. 28, 1761.

Oct. 25, 1762: *Phoenix* (London, England). Capt. William Macgachan/M'Gacher/M'Gacken/M'Gakin/M'Gachery/McGachen/McGackin. Middle Passage. 50 slaves and no crewmen killed. Unsuccessful. *Pennsylvania Gazette,* Nov. 11, 1762; *New York Gazette,* Nov. 15, 1762; *Boston News-Letter and New England Chronicle,* Nov. 18, 1762; *Newport Mercury,* Nov. 22, 1762; *Lloyd's Evening Post and British Chronicle,* Dec. 29–31, 1762; *Lloyd's List,* Dec. 31, 1762; *Annual Register,* 1762, 117–18.

Nov. 1762: (Newport, RI). Capt. George Frost. Gabon River (Bight of Biafra). 30 slaves and 2 crewmen killed. Successful—recaptured. *Newport Mercury,* June 6, 1763; *Providence Gazette and Country Journal,* June 11, 1763; *New York Gazette,* June 13, 1763; *Pennsylvania Gazette,* June 16, 1763.

1762: *Dove* (Liverpool, England). Capt. Brown. Gambia River (Senegambia). Some slaves and 2 crewmen killed. Successful—freedom for some. PRO, T 70, 31:32; *Lloyd's List,* Apr. 1, 1763.

1762: *Vr. Johanna Cores* (Netherlands). Capt. Willem de Molder. African coast. 24 slaves killed. Postma, *Dutch in the Atlantic Slave Trade,* 166, 345, 385.

Ca. 1762: *Pearl* (Liverpool, England). Capt. Pollet. At least 20 slaves killed. Unsuccessful. Clarkson, 206–8.

Jan. 20, 1763: *Nossa Senhoa de Agoa de Lupe e Bom Jesuz dos Navegantes* (Portugal). Miller, *Way of Death,* 410.

Feb. 22, 1763: *Black Prince* (Bristol, England). Capt. William Miller. Cape Coast (Gold Coast). No one killed. Unsuccessful. *Journal of an Intended Voyage,* entry dated Feb. 22, 1763. *See also* subsequent rebellion on the same voyage, Mar. 4, 1763.

Ca. Feb. 1763: *Ann* (London, England). Capt. David Adam. Pittagarry (Gold Coast). Successful–freedom? PRO, T 70, vol. 1263, entry 179.

Ca. Feb. 1763: (Liverpool, England). African coast. Successful–freedom? *Newport Mercury,* June 6, 1763; *Providence Gazette and Country Journal,* June 11, 1763; *New York Gazette,* June 13, 1763; *Philadelphia Gazette,* June 16, 1763.

Mar. 4, 1763: *Black Prince* (Bristol, England). Capt. William Miller. Middle Passage. No one killed. Unsuccessful. *Journal of an Intended Voyage,* entry dated Mar. 4, 1763. *See also* earlier rebellion on the same voyage, Feb. 22, 1763.

July 16, 1763: *Frere et la Souer* (Dunquerque, France). Capt. Du Colombier. African coast. 2 crewmen killed. Unsuccessful. Mettas, 2:151.

Ca. Dec. 4, 1763: *Africa* (Amsterdam, Netherlands). Gold Coast. At least 1 crewman killed. Successful–freedom? Mettas, 1:436.

Winter 1763–64: *Croissant* (Nantes, France). Capt. Devigues. African coast. 14 slaves killed. Unsuccessful. Mettas, 1:431.

Winter 1763–64: *Entreprenant* (Nantes, France). Capt. Lecerf. Little Popo (Bight of Benin). Some slaves killed. Unsuccessful. Mettas, 1:428.

Feb. 17, 1764: *Fontelle* (Saint-Malo, France). Capt. J. Esturmy. Loango (West Central Africa). 3 slaves killed. Unsuccessful. Mettas, 2:727–28.

Mar. 1764: (England). Barbados. 2 slaves and all but 4 crewmen killed. Successful. After 10 days in control of the vessel and attempts by two ships to recapture them, the slaves were recaptured with the aid of a third vessel. *Newport Mercury,* May 21, 1764; *Pennsylvania Gazette,* May 31, 1764.

Apr. 24, 1764: *Phoenix* (Nantes, France). Capt. Joseph Mary. Bissau (Sierra Leone). 2–4 slaves and 1 crewman killed. Unsuccessful. Mettas, 1:440–41.

Ca. May 1764: *Gallem* (England). Capts. Pye and Mackey. West Indies. Successful–recaptured? *Lloyd's List,* June 5, 1764; TST CD, 24557.

Ca. May 1764: *Hope* (New London, CT). Capt. George Taggart/Taggot/Faggot. Middle Passage. 7–8 slaves and 1–2 crewmen killed. Unsuccessful. *New York Gazette,* Aug. 13, 1764, Mar. 11, 1765; *Massachusetts Gazette Extraordinary,* Aug. 16, 1764; *Pennsylvania Gazette,* Aug. 16, 1764, Mar. 21, 1765; *New London Gazette,* Aug. 17, 1764; *Newport Mercury,* Aug. 20, 1764, Apr. 8, 1765; *Boston Post-Boy and Advertiser,* Aug. 20, 1764, Mar. 4, Apr. 1, 1765; *Massachusetts Gazette and Boston News-Letter,* Aug. 30, 1764, Mar. 7, Mar. 28, 1765.

Aug. 1764: (England). Gambia River (Senegambia). Successful—freedom. Littlefield, 21.

Nov. 5, 1764: *Comte d'Azemar* (Nantes, France). Capt. Mathurin David. African coast. 1 slave killed. Unsuccessful. Mettas, 1:439–40. *See also* subsequent rebellion on the same voyage, Nov. 30, 1764.

Nov. 30, 1764: *Comte d'Azemar* (Nantes, France). Capt. Mathurin David. Middle Passage. 1 slave killed. Unsuccessful. Mettas, 1:439–40. *See also* earlier rebellion on the same voyage, Nov. 5, 1764.

Dec. 23, 1764: *Coueda* (Nantes, France). Capt. Jean Honnoraty. Middle Passage. 51 slaves and 1 crewman killed. Mettas, 1:441–42.

Dec. 27, 1764: *Jolly Prince* (Bristol, England). Capt. Patrick Halloran/Holleran. Windward Coast. All crewmen killed. Successful—freedom? *Lloyd's List,* June 21, 1765; *Felix Farley's Bristol Journal,* June 22, 1765.

Winter 1764: (Bristol, RI). Sierra Leone? All but one crewman killed. Successful—freedom? *Boston Post-Boy and Advertiser,* Aug. 19, 1765; *Massachusetts Gazette and Boston News-Letter,* Aug. 22, 1765.

1764: *Eenigheid* (Netherlands). Capt. Daniel Pruymelaar. African coast. No one killed. Postma, *Dutch in the Atlantic Slave Trade,* 166, 325, 386.

1764: *Johnson* (Liverpool, England). Capt. Robinson. Loango (West Central Africa). "Capt. Robinson, the Doctor and his Mates, together with 17 of the Crew, were poisoned by the Negroes." Unsuccessful. *Lloyd's List,* June 29, 1764.

1764: *Sisters* (Liverpool, England). Capt. Richard Jackson. African coast? Several slaves and crewmen killed. Unsuccessful. *Lloyd's List,* Jan. 29, 1765; TST CD, 91052.

1764: *Vr. Johanna Cores* (Netherlands). Capt. Jan Sap. African coast. 2 slaves killed. Postma, *Dutch in the Atlantic Slave Trade,* 166, 345, 386.

1764/65: *Galam* (Liverpool, England). Capts. John Hill and Shetland. Successful—recaptured? TST CD, 92309.

1764/65: *Haast u Langzaam* (Netherlands). Capt. Jan Menkenveld. TST CD, 10659; Postma, *Dutch in the Atlantic Slave Trade,* 329.

Aug. 28, 1765: *Sally* (Providence, RI). Capt. Esek Hopkins. Middle Passage. 10 slaves and no crewmen killed. Unsuccessful. John Carter Brown Library, Brown Family Business Records, box 536, folder 9; box 643, folder 7 (entries dated Aug. 28, Sep. 19, Oct. 14, 1765); Rhode Island State Archives, Moses Brown Papers, series 2, folder 5; *Newport Mercury,* Nov. 18, 1765; *Boston Post-Boy and Advertiser,* Nov. 25, 1765; *Massachusetts Gazette,* Nov. 28, 1765.

Oct. 1, 1765: *Othello* (Newport, RI). Capt. Thomas Rogers. Désirade Island, Guadeloupe, West Indies. 1 slave killed. 13 slaves jumped overboard and swam for shore; 1 of these was killed, 3 others wounded. Unsuccessful—freedom for some? Rhode Island State Archives, Petitions to the Rhode Island General Assembly, vol. 12, doc. 141; *Pennsylvania Gazette,* Nov. 14, 1765; *Newport Mercury,* Nov. 18, Nov. 25, 1765; *Boston Post-Boy and Advertiser,* Nov. 25, 1765; *Massachusetts Gazette,* Nov. 28, 1765.

Nov. 1765: *Mary* (England). Capt. Davis. Gambia River (Senegambia). All but 2 crewmen killed. Successful—freedom? *Lloyd's List,* Feb. 14, 1766; TST CD, 25384.

1765/66: *Adelaide de Puisegor* (Nantes, France). Capt. Massey de Breban. Angola? (West Central Africa). Unsuccessful. Multiple revolts may have occurred during this voyage. Mettas, 1:464.

Feb. 26, 1766: *Henriette* (Nantes, France). Capt. Durocher Sorin. African coast. All but 4 crewmen killed. Successful—freedom for some? In spite of the assistance of three nearby vessels, a group of Africans succeeded in taking the ship's dingy and rowing for land; some were recaptured, some apparently escaped. Mettas, 1:458, 473.

Feb. 1766: (British North America). Capt. Jones. Bermuda (intra-American slave transport). 3 crewmen killed. Successful—recaptured. *New York Gazette,* May 12, 1766; *Virginia Gazette,* May 23, 1766.

Ca. June 1766: (Virginia). Capt. Watson. Gambia River (Senegambia). All crewmen killed. Successful—freedom for some. Several vessels nearby helped recapture the ship, but 30 Africans escaped. *New York Gazette,* Aug. 18, 1766; *New London Gazette,* Aug. 22, 1766; *Massachusetts Gazette and Boston News-Letter,* Aug. 28, 1766.

1766: *Jeune Catherine* (Nantes, France). Capt. G. Duval. Several slaves killed. Unsuccessful. Mettas, 1:473.

Jan. 21, 1767: *Debut* (La Rochelle, France). Capt. Th. Latouche. Loango (West Central Africa). 8 slaves and 1 crewman killed, the latter apparently on another French ship coming to the aid of the *Debut.* Unsuccessful. Mettas, 2:309.

Mar. 8, 1767: *Badine* (Nantes, France). Capt. J. J. Poisson. Angola (West Central Africa). 14 slaves and 2 crewmen killed. Unsuccessful. Mettas, 1:486.

1767: *Industry* (Liverpool, England). Capt. John Erskine/Erskin. Denby River (Sierra Leone?). Successful–freedom? *Lloyd's List,* July 17, 1767; TST CD, 91098.

1767: *Marie* (Nantes, France). Capt. J. Cheneau. Some slaves killed. Unsuccessful. Mettas, 1:487–88.

Ca. 1767/69: *Tryal* (Liverpool, England). Capt. Price. West Indies. 14 slaves killed. Unsuccessful. Clarkson, 202–4.

Ca. Jan. 1768: *Saint-Pierre* (Nantes, France). Capt. J. Ollivier. Biafra Coast (Bight of Biafra). Unsuccessful. Mettas, 1:494–95.

July 19, 1768: *Saint Nicolas* (France). Capt. Balai de l'Isle. Windward Coast. 43 slaves and 1 crewman killed. Unsuccessful. Mettas, 2:46.

Fall 1768: *Marie Anne* (Nantes, France). Capt. Henry Lemarie Delasalle. Gabon River (Bight of Biafra). 3 slaves killed. Unsuccessful. Mettas, 1:511.

1768: *Esther* (London, England). Capt. Robert Dann. TST CD, 77953.

Ca. 1768: *Africa* (Bristol, England). Capt. John Morgan. New Calabar River (Bight of Biafra). 3 slaves and no crewmen killed. Unsuccessful. Clarkson, 221–22, 224; TST CD, 17661.

1768/69: *Jenny* (Liverpool, England). Capt. Richard Webster. TST CD, 91474.

Jan. 11, 1769: *Nancy* (Liverpool, England). Capt. Roger Williams. New Calabar (Bight of Biafra). 6 slaves killed. Successful–freedom? Williams, 549; Clarkson, 199; TST CD, 91480; Inikori, "Measuring," 67.

Sep. 27, 1769: *Concorde* (Nantes, France). Capt. Carre. Scassery (Sierra Leone?). 2 crewmen killed. Successful–freedom for some? 3 of the 48 slaves were later recaptured. Mettas, 1:516–17, 519, 2:797.

Oct. 28, 1769: *Roy Morba* (Nantes, France). Capt. Adrien Doutrau. Middle Passage. Unsuccessful. Mettas, 1:518–19.

Dec. 3, 1769: *Delight* (Liverpool, England). Capt. William Millroy/Milroy. Little Cape Mount (Windward Coast). 18–30 slaves and 9 crewmen killed. Successful. The slaves were overcome after a 4-hour battle with a nearby ship in which the Africans killed 1 member of the pursuing ship's crew. *Virginia Gazette* (PD), May 24, 1770; *New York Journal, or General Advertiser,* June 7, June 21, 1770; TST CD, 91564.

1769: *True Blue* (Liverpool, England). Capt. Joshua Hutton/Hatton. Bight of Benin. 4 crewmen killed. Successful–freedom? One source suggests the slaves were retaken by another vessel. Clarkson, 204, 221; Inikori, "Measuring," 67; TST CD, 91088.

1769: *Zanggodin* (Netherlands). Capt. Jan van Sprang. African coast. 21 slaves who got ashore were recaptured by local Africans. Unsuccessful. Postma, *Dutch in the Atlantic Slave Trade*, 166, 347, 386.

Winter 1769–70: *Saint-Nicolas* (Bordeaux, France). Capt. De Bellouan. Goree Island (Senegambia). 40 slaves killed. Unsuccessful. Mettas, 2:50.

1769/70: *Unity* (Liverpool, England). Capt. Robert Norris. TST CD, 91567.

Jan. 1770: *Union* (Nantes, France). Capt. J. L. Ruellau. Windward Coast. 1 slave killed. Unsuccessful. Mettas, 1:517.

Apr. 19, 1770: *Brocanteur* (Saint-Malo, France). Capt. Basmeule de Liesse. Gabon River (Bight of Biafra). 19 slaves killed. Unsuccessful. Mettas, 2:747.

1770: *Duke of Bridgewater* (Liverpool, England). Capt. Thomas Adamson. African coast. Successful–freedom? TST CD, 91671; Inikori, "Measuring," 68.

1770: *Guinese Vriendschap* (Netherlands). Capt. Jan Grim. 5 slaves killed. Successful. Ship recaptured with the aid of a Dutch warship. Postma, *Dutch in the Atlantic Slave Trade,* 166, 168, 329, 383.

1770/71: *African Queen* (Liverpool, England). Capt. Thomas North. Kissey River (Sierra Leone). 10 crewmen killed. Successful–freedom for some? TST CD, 91687; Inikori, "Measuring," 68.

1770/71: *True Blue* (Liverpool, England). Capts. Richard Griffith and William Goad. TST CD, 91643.

Spring 1771: *Saint Rene* (Saint-Malo, France). Capt. Chateau-briand, sieur du Plessis. Middle Passage. Some slaves and 1 crewman killed. Unsuccessful. Mettas, 2:750–51.

July 1771: *Pacifique* (La Havre, France). Capt. J. P. Bonfils. Guinea Coast. 4 slaves killed. Unsuccessful. Mettas, 2:441.

Ca. Oct. 1771: *Nécessaire* (Rochefort, France). Capt. Badiaux. Quila (Sierra Leone). Some slaves and all but 4 crewmen killed. Slaves who would not participate were killed by the insurrectionists. Successful–freedom for most. 2 Africans subsequently recaptured. Mettas, 2:318–19.

Dec. 30, 1771: *Cupidon* (Nantes, France). Capt. Jean Arnout. African coast. 1 crewman killed. Unsuccessful. Mettas, 1:546.

1771: *Intelligente* (La Rochelle, France). Capt. Fr. Hubert. 18 slaves killed. Unsuccessful. Mettas, 2:315–16.

1771: *Two Brothers* (Liverpool, England). Capt. Hugh Glenn. TST CD, 91735.

1771: (France). Middle Passage. Some slaves and all crewmen killed. Successful—recaptured. The ship was subsequently found drifting with only 9 Africans alive on board. *Virginia Gazette* (PD), Apr. 18, 1771.

1771: (France). Middle Passage / West Indies. 300 slaves and all but 6 crewmen killed. Unsuccessful. Pluchon, 188.

Ca. 1771: *Warwick Castle* (London, England). Three revolts. All unsuccessful. Clarkson, 214–16.

Ca. Mar. 1772: *Exeter* (London, England). Capt. Savery/Savory. Camaranco (Sierra Leone). All but 1 crewman killed. Successful—freedom for most. About 20 slaves apparently recaptured. *Pennsylvania Gazette*, June 25, 1772; *Virginia Gazette* (PD), July 16, 1772, Aug. 27, 1772.

Ca. Oct. 1772: (Liverpool, England). Middle Passage. All but 1 crewman killed. Successful. Slaves recaptured after a 4-hour battle with a nearby ship. *Pennsylvania Gazette*, Dec. 9, 1772; *Virginia Gazette* (PD), Dec. 24, 1772.

Ca. Oct. 1772: (Martinique/France). Middle Passage. All crewmen killed. Successful—freedom? *Pennsylvania Gazette*, Dec. 9, 1772; *Virginia Gazette* (PD), Dec. 24, 1772.

Ca. Nov. 1772: (New York, NY?). West Indies. All crewmen killed. Successful—freedom? *Virginia Gazette* (PD), Nov. 26, 1772.

1772/73: *Robert* (Liverpool, England). Capt. Ireland Grace. TST CD, 91815.

Jan. 24, 1773: *New Britannia* (England). Capt. Stephen Deane. Gambia River (Senegambia). 222 slaves and 13 crewmen killed. The slaves broke into the powder magazine and, when defeat seemed imminent, blew up the ship, killing all aboard. Unsuccessful. *Gentleman's Magazine*, Oct. 1773; *Virginia Gazette*, Dec. 23, 1773, Jan. 6, 1774; Searing, 156; Inikori, "Measuring," 69.

June 7, 1773: *Jeune Louis* (La Rochelle, France). Capt. David Saint Pe. Cape Mount (Windward Coast). Unsuccessful. Mettas, 2:317–18.

1773: *Bristol* (England). Bonny (Bight of Biafra). Most of the crew killed, a few left alive to navigate the vessel. Successful—freedom? Deschamps, 128.

1773: *Industry* (London, England). Capt. Goguet/Gougwet. Middle Passage. All but 2 crewmen killed. Successful—freedom for some. Inikori, "Measuring," 69; TST CD, 24700.

Ca. 1773: (France). Guinea Coast. About 200 slaves and most of the crewmen killed. Successful. All on board were killed when the mate decided to blow up the ship. *Virginia Gazette* (PD), June 17, 1773; *Virginia Gazette* (WR), June 17, 1773.

July 7, 1774: *Aimable Claire* (Nantes, France). Capt. Thomas Butler. 2 crewmen killed. Unsuccessful. Mettas, 1:572.

Ca. Aug. 1774: *John* (New York, NY). Capt. Daniel Darby. Isles de Los (Sierra Leone). "A number" of slaves and 1 crewman killed. Unsuccessful. *Pennsylvania Gazette,* Nov. 16, 1774; *Massachusetts Gazette and Boston News-Letter,* Dec. 1, 1774; TST CD, 25091.

Sep. 15, 1774: *Diane/Diamant* (Nantes, France). Capt. Jean Arnoult. Corisco Island (Bight of Biafra). Successful–freedom? Mettas, 1:576–77; Stein, *French Slave Trade,* 104–5.

Ca. Oct. 1774: (France). Senegal? (Senegambia). All crewmen killed. The slaves spared the lives of a white woman and a passenger on board. Successful. All but 3 slaves were later killed when the ship foundered. *Virginia Gazette* (DH), Jan. 7, 1775.

Ca. Nov. 1774: *King Herod* (British North America). Capt. Steel. Benin (Bight of Benin). Unsuccessful. *Virginia Gazette* (DH), Feb. 25, 1775.

1774: *Sally II* (England). African coast. Successful–freedom? Elder, 175.

1774: *Zanggodin* (Netherlands). Capt. J. H. Hof. Postma, *Dutch in the Atlantic Slave Trade,* 166, 347, 384.

1774/75: *Lively* (Liverpool, England). Capts. Thomas Beynon and Davies. TST CD, 91716.

1774–76: *Tryal* (Liverpool, England). Capt. William Postlethwaite. TST CD, 92568.

Mar. 10–11, 1775: *Esperance* (France). Zanzibar (East Africa). No crewmen killed. Unsuccessful. Scarr, 33.

Mar. 15, 1775: *Brune* (Honfleur, France). Capt. Louis Thibault Caillot. Off Goree Island (Senegambia). 3 slaves killed. Unsuccessful. Mettas, 2:185–86.

Ca. June 1775: Senegal (Senegambia). All but 4 slaves and all crewmen killed. Successful. The slaves broke into the powder magazine and, when defeat seemed imminent, blew up the ship, killing all aboard. *Virginia Gazette* (DH), July 1, 1775.

1775: *Armina Elisabeth* (Netherlands). Capts. A. de Boer and R. Barendse. 11 slaves and 11 crewmen killed. Postma, *Dutch in the Atlantic Slave Trade,* 166, 322, 382.

1775: *Christiansborg* (Denmark). Capt. Johan Frantzen Ferentz. Approximately 85 slaves died on the voyage, but the number killed in the revolt is not specified. Unsuccessful. Svalesen, 223; Green-Pedersen, 172; TST CD, 35185.

1775: *Geertruyda & Christina* (Netherlands). Capt. Joh. Noordhoek. Postma, *Dutch in the Atlantic Slave Trade,* 166, 327, 385.

1775/76: *Falstaff* (Liverpool, England). Capt. Roger Leatham. TST CD, 92527.

1775–77: *Polly* (London, England). Capt. John Reilly. TST CD, 77165.

Feb. 15, 1776: *Pacifique* (Le Havre, France). Mayumba (West Central Africa). Revolt occurred on a shallop transporting slaves to the ship before they were boarded. Successful–freedom? Mettas, 2:459–60.

Ca. June 1776: *True Briton* (Liverpool, England). Capt. James/John Dawson. Bonny (Bight of Biafra). 1 crewman killed. Unsuccessful. Williams, 560; TST CD, 92566.

Nov./Dec. 8 1776: *Thames* (Rhode Island). Capt. Peleg Clarke. Cape Coast (Gold Coast). 31–33 slaves killed. Unsuccessful–freedom for some? Newport Historical Society, Peleg Clarke Letters, letter book 76, letters dated Dec. 1, 1776, Dec. 15, 1776, Dec. 27, 1776, Jan. 8, 1777; "Protest," "Accounts."

1776: *Phoenix* (Bristol, RI). Capt. Charles Taylor. Cape Coast (Gold Coast). 1 crewman killed. Successful–freedom? Newport Historical Society, Peleg Clarke Letters, letter book 76, letter dated May 6, 1776; D. Richardson, *Bristol*, 4:67.

Ca. 1776: *Comte d'Estaing* (France). Capt. Cesar Gasqui. West Indies? M. Robinson, 142–43.

Jan. 21, 1777: *Bienfaisant* (Nantes, France). Capt. Luc Joly. Melimba (West Central Africa). 6 crewmen killed. Successful–freedom for most. Mettas, 1:603–4; Stein, *French Slave Trade*, 88.

June 6, 1777: *Amphitrite* (Nantes, France). Capt. Jean Guyot. Bonny (Bight of Biafra). 5 slaves killed. Unsuccessful. Mettas, 1:610–11.

Aug. 14, 1777: *Juliet* (England). Capt. King. Cape Coast Castle (Gold Coast). 2 slaves killed. Unsuccessful. PRO, T 70, 1468:4.

Ca. 1777: (London, England). Revolt 1: Gold Coast. 5 slaves and no crewmen killed. Unsuccessful. Revolt 2: Gold Coast. 42 slaves and 1 crewman killed. Unsuccessful. Revolt 3: Middle Passage. No slaves or crewmen killed. Unsuccessful. Clarkson, 314.

1779: (England). Unsuccessful. Piersen, 150–51.

May 14, 1780: *Saint-Antoine d'Almas* (Portugal). Capt. Joseph Caetane Rodriguez. Between the Zambezi River and Mauritius (East Africa). Unsuccessful. Asgarally, 179–80; Alpers, 4.

1780: *Vigilantie* (Netherlands). Capt. Claas Boswijk. Revolt 1: Middle Passage? Unsuccessful. Revolt 2: Middle Passage? Unsuccessful. Revolt 3: Marowin River, French Guiana. 21 slaves killed. Successful–freedom? Postma, *Dutch in the Atlantic Slave Trade*, 166–67, 344, 382.

Ca. 1781: (Liverpool, England). Bonny River (Bight of Biafra). No one killed. Unsuccessful. Clarkson, 315.

Jan. 28, 1782: *Fleury* (Nantes, France). Capt. Joachim Gillard. Middle Passage. 1 crewman killed. Unsuccessful. Mettas, 1:622–23.

May 3, 1783: *Wasp* (England). Capt. Richard Bowen. African coast. 13 slaves killed. Unsuccessful. *Felix Farley's Bristol Journal,* Sep. 13, 1783; *Universal Daily Register,* July 1, 1785; Durnford and East, 1:130–31; M. Robinson, 9:144, 155. *See also* subsequent rebellion on the same voyage, May 22, 1783.

May 22, 1783: *Wasp* (England). Capt. Richard Bowen. Middle Passage. 74 slaves and 1 crewman killed. Unsuccessful. *Felix Farley's Bristol Journal,* Sep. 13, 1783; *Universal Daily Register,* July 1, 1785; Durnford and East, 1:130–31; M. Robinson, 9:144, 155. *See also* earlier rebellion on the same voyage, May 3, 1783.

Ca. 1783: *Cato* (England). *Universal Daily Register,* July 1, 1785.

Ca. 1783: *Oiseau* (France). Capt. Ganachaud. Middle Passage. Unsuccessful. Mettas, 2:636.

Ca. 1783/84: *Bonne Société* (La Rochelle, England). Capt. Gabriel David. Unsuccessful. Mettas, 2:346.

Ca. Feb.–June 1784: *Jeune Aimée* (Nantes, France). Capt. Lazare Perroty. Mayumba (West Central Africa). 7 slaves killed. Unsuccessful. Mettas, 1:638–39.

May 27, 1784: *Creole* (La Rochelle, France). Capt. Crassous. Ceylon. Unsuccessful. Deveau, 266.

1784: *Christiansborg* (Denmark). Capt. Cock. TST CD, 35028.

1784/85: (Newport, RI). Middle Passage. Many slaves and all crewmen killed. Successful–recaptured. A ship was found drifting on the ocean 12 months after its departure with only 15 slaves "in a very emaciated and wretched condition" on board. A report of the incident states that "the negroes it is supposed, had rose and murdered the Captain and crew." *Providence Gazette and Country Journal,* Jan. 29, 1785; *Loudon's New York Packet,* Feb. 14, 1785.

May 23, 1785: *Alexandre* (Honfleur, France). Capt. Ch. Herblin. Gabon River (Bight of Biafra). Unsuccessful. Mettas, 2:193.

Oct. 18, 1785: *Neptunis* (Netherlands). Mouri (Gold Coast). 200–500 slaves and 17 crewmen killed. Successful. This ship was blown up either by the slaves in a suicide attempt or by a cannon from a nearby vessel attempting to recapture them. Postma, *Dutch in the Atlantic Slave Trade,* 166–67; Paiewonsky, 21–23; Curtin, *Africa Remembered,* 133.

1785: (England). Gold Coast. All crewmen killed. Successful. Slaves recaptured on shore by soldiers and local Africans. Paiewonsky, 23.

Ca. 1785: *Kammerherre Schack* (Denmark). Highfield, 19.

Mar. 2, 1786: *Reverseau* (La Rochelle, France). Capt. J. Bargeau. Senegal (Senegambia). 7 slaves killed. Unsuccessful. Mettas, 2:362.

May 7, 1786: *Fleury* (Nantes, France). Capt. J. Fr. Lesourd. Senegal (Senegambia). 3 crewmen killed. Unsuccessful. Mettas, 1:666.

Aug. 30, 1786: *Ville de Basle* (La Rochelle, France). Capt. Villeneau. Porto Novo (Bight of Benin). 36 slaves killed. Unsuccessful. Mettas, 2:364–65.

Oct. 9, 1786: *Christiansborg* (Denmark). Capt. Jens Jensen Berg. Middle Passage. 34 slaves and 2 crewmen killed. Unsuccessful. Paiewonsky, 20, 28; Hansen, 132–37.

1786: *Vigilant* (England). Capt. Duncan. Anomabu (Gold Coast). 2 crewmen killed. Successful–freedom? Inikori, "Measuring," 71.

Winter 1786–87: *Roy d'Ambris* (Le Havre, France). Capt. Guillaume Constantin. Multiple revolts may have occurred on this voyage. Unsuccessful. Mettas, 2:501.

1786/87: *Hudibras* (Liverpool, England). Capt. Jenkin Evans. TST CD, 81890.

Jan. 1787: *Alexandre* (Honfleur, France). Capt. Charles Herblin. Gabon (Bight of Biafra). Some crewmen killed. Unsuccessful. Mettas, 2:199–200.

Ca. July–Oct. 1787: *Breton* (Lorient, France). Capt. Guesdon. Mozambique (East Africa). Some slaves killed. Unsuccessful. Mettas, 2:92–93, 621.

Ca. Oct. 1787: *Ruby* (Bristol, England). Capt. Joseph Williams. Bimbe (Bight of Biafra?). 4 slaves and no crewmen killed. Unsuccessful. Dow, 173–77.

Nov. 26, 1787: *Tigre* (France). Capt. Mathurin Bregeon. Madagascar (East Africa). 15 slaves and 2 crewmen killed. Successful–recaptured. Asgarally, 180–81.

Dec. 17, 1787: *Flore* (Honfleur, France). Capt. Giffard. Gabon River (Bight of Biafra). 1 slave and 3 crewmen killed. Unsuccessful. Mettas, 2:197–98, 202–3.

1787: *Avanture* (Bordeaux, France). Capt. Danberique. Successful–freedom? *New Lloyd's List,* Sep. 28, 1787.

Jan. 23, 1788: *Licorne* (Bordeaux, France). Capt. Brugevin. Between Mozambique and Cape of Good Hope (East Africa). 1 slave killed. Unsuccessful. Mettas, 2:92–93; Brugevin, 152.

Jan. 1788: *Franc Macon / Franmacon* (Le Havre, France). Capt. Le Grand/Jusselin. Gabon River (Bight of Biafra). 5–6 crewmen killed. Successful–freedom? *New Lloyd's List,* July 4, 1788; Mettas, 2:510–11, 512.

Mar. 14, 1788: *Epanronidas* (Flushing, Netherlands). Capt. Isaac Din Baas. Cape Sierra Leone (Sierra Leone). All but 2 crewmen killed. Successful–freedom? *New Lloyd's List,* May 13, 1788.

Oct. 1, 1788: *Antoinette* (Honfleur, France). Capt. J.-P. Varnier. Middle Passage. 1 crewman killed. Unsuccessful. Mettas, 2:204.

Dec. 26, 1788: *Augustine* (Nantes, France). Capt. La Gree. Mayumba (West Central Africa). 2 crewmen killed. Successful–freedom? Mettas, 1:710, 2:800.

Dec. 31, 1788: *Georgette* (Nantes, France). Capt. Le Breton. Middle Passage. Unsuccessful. Mettas, 1:712.

1788: *Aimable Louise* (France). Gambia River (Senegambia). Successful–freedom for some? Deveau, 263–64.

Ca. 1788: *Claire B. Williams / Clara B. Williams* (Denmark). Rokel Estuary (Sierra Leone). Successful–freedom. Wadström, 2:79; Butt-Thompson, 44–45; Rathbone, 19; Rashid, 138.

Ca. 1788: *Golden Age* (Liverpool, England). Bonny River (Bight of Biafra). 5 slaves killed. Unsuccessful. Clarkson, 319–20.

Ca. 1788/89: *Veronique* (Nantes, France). Capt. Mauguen. Loango (West Central Africa). Successful–freedom for some? Mettas, 1:714.

Mar. 26, 1789: *Felicity* (Salem, MA). Capt. William Fairfield. Middle Passage. 3 slaves and 1 crewman killed. Unsuccessful. Bentley, 123; Fairfield.

Ca. Mar. 1789: *Mercer* (Liverpool, England). Capt. John Bellis. Middle Passage. Successful. Slaves recaptured with the aid of another ship. *Lloyd's List*, Apr. 7, 1789; TST CD, 82688.

Nov. 14, 1789: *Phenix* (Nantes, France). Capt. J. Fr. Dupuis. Middle Passage. 14 slaves killed. Unsuccessful. Mettas, 1:728.

1789: *Bons Freres* (Nantes, France). Capt. P. Foucher. Angola? (West Central Africa). 3 slaves killed. Unsuccessful. Mettas, 1:729.

July 1790: *Auguste* (Honfleur, France). Capt. Valentin. Revolt 1: Gabon River? (Bight of Biafra). No slaves killed. Unsuccessful. Revolt 2: Middle Passage. 1 slave killed. Unsuccessful. Mettas, 2:210–11.

Nov. 9, 1790: *Jeremie* (Le Havre, France). Capt. Pierre Girette. Isles de Los (Sierra Leone). 2 crewmen killed. Unsuccessful. Mettas, 2:532–33.

Ca. Dec. 1790: *Pearl* (Bristol, England). Capt. William Blake. Old Calabar (Bight of Biafra). 3 slaves killed. Unsuccessful. PRO, C 107, vol. 12, letter dated Jan. 11, 1791.

1790: *Antoinette* (Honfleur, France). Capt. André Barthelemy de Haussy de La Verpillere. 3 slaves killed. Unsuccessful. Mettas, 2:209–10.

Ca. 1790: (France). Sierra Leone. Some slaves killed. Unsuccessful. Wadström, 2:86–87.

Ca. 1790: (Nantes, France). Bonny (Bight of Biafra). Up to 100 slaves shot or drowned, 2 crewmen killed. Unsuccessful. Childers, 57–59.

1790/91: *Vulture* (Liverpool, England). Capt. Samuel Clough. TST CD, 83982.

Jan. 1791: *Albion* (Bristol, England). Capt. John Robinson Wade. Cape Mount (Windward Coast). Unsuccessful. D. Richardson, *Bristol*, 4:160.

May 16, 1791: *Favourite* (Bristol, England). Capt. John Fitzhenry. African coast. 32 slaves killed. Unsuccessful. D. Richardson, *Bristol*, 4:184.

Dec. 8, 1791: *Friendship* (England). Capt. Thomas Brown. 1 crewman killed. Unsuccessful. Behrendt, "Crew Mortality," 133.

1791: *Coureur* (Bordeaux, France). Capt. J. J. Ducros. Gambia (Senegambia). All but 9 crewmen killed. Some slaves who jumped overboard when the ship caught fire may have freed themselves. Unsuccessful—freedom for some? Mettas, 2:121.

1791: *Victorieux* (Honfleur, France). Capt. Armand Dunepveu. 3 slaves killed. Unsucessful. Mettas, 2:214.

Aug. 27, 1792: *Mermaid* (Bristol, England). Capts. James Mulling and Edward Taylor. African coast? 19 slaves killed. Unsuccessful. D. Richardson, *Bristol*, 4:219.

Ca. Dec. 1792: *Calvados* (Portugal). Indian Ocean. 50 slaves killed. Unsuccessful. *Lloyd's List*, Feb. 19, 1793.

1792: *Christopher* (Liverpool, England). Capt. Charles Molyneux/Mollyneux. TST CD, 80835; *Lloyd's List*, Dec. 28, 1792.

1792: *Sally* (Providence, RI). Capt. Jeremiah Taber. African coast. All but 2 crewmen killed. Successful—freedom—ship destroyed. *Providence Gazette and Country Journal*, Oct. 20, 1792.

1792/93: *Eagle* (England). Capts. Patrick Campbell and David McElheran/McElcheran. TST CD, 81097; *Lloyd's List*, Mar. 22, 1793.

1792/93: *Governor Parry* (Liverpool, England). Capt. John Powell. TST CD, 81646.

1792/93: *Peggy* (Bordeaux, France). Capt. P. Nazereau. African coast. 3 slaves killed. Unsuccessful. Mettas, 2:127–28.

1792–94: *Alice* (Liverpool, England). Capt. Bryan Smith. TST CD, 80190.

1792–94: *Lumbie*. Capt. Richard Rogers. TST CD, 98852.

May 1793: *Cadiz Dispatch* (London, England). Capt. Baldy. 1 crewman killed. Unsuccessful. *Lloyd's List,* Sep. 13, 1793; Durnford and East, 7:186–94.

Sep. 23, 1793: *Pearl* (New York, NY). Capt. Howard. Matacong Island (Sierra Leone). 2 slaves and 1 crewman killed. Successful. Slaves recaptured with the aid of an English ship. Mouser, 93–94; Hamm, 398.

Fall 1793: *Nancy* (Providence, RI). Capt. Joseph B. Cook. Middle Passage. 4 slaves and no crewmen killed. Unsuccessful. *Salem Gazette,* Jan. 28, 1794; *General Advertiser,* Feb. 11, 1794; Sharafi, 71–100.

Ca. 1793: (Boston, MA). Sierra Leone. Several slaves and 7 crewmen killed. 3 of the crewmen killed were on another vessel that had come to the ship's aid. Successful. Slaves recaptured with the aid of another ship. Those who got ashore were retaken by local Africans. Wadström, 2:87.

Ca. 1793: (United States). Sierra Leone. Some slaves and 1 crewman killed. Successful. Slaves recaptured with the aid of an English ship. This may be the Sep. 23, 1793, revolt on the *Pearl.* Wadström, 2:86.

Jan. 14, 1794: *Sandown* (London, England). Capt. Samuel Gamble. Isles de Los (Sierra Leone). 8 slaves killed. Unsuccessful—freedom for some. Mouser, 97.

Ca. Mar. 1794: *Venus* (New York, NY). Capt. Hammond. Sierra Leone. 9 slaves killed. Successful. After a daylong battle with a nearby ship, the slaves reached land but were apparently recaptured by local Africans. Mouser, 99.

Ca. Apr. 1794: Charleston (Charleston, SC). Capt. J. Connelly. Niger River delta (Bight of Biafra). Revolt occurred on a shallop transporting slaves to the ship before they were boarded. 1 slave and no crewmen killed. Unsuccessful—freedom for 1. Hawkins, 140–49.

Spring 1794: *Jemmy/Jemmie/Jimmy* (Liverpool, England). Capt. Richard Pearson. Middle Passage. 4 slaves killed. Unsuccessful. Mouser, 114; TST CD, 82007; *Lloyd's List,* Aug. 5, 1794.

Nov. 1795: *Liberty* (Providence, RI). Capt. Abijah Potter. Between Goree Island and Sierra Leone. 1–2 slaves and 2 crewmen killed. Unsuccessful. Rhode Island Historical Society, log of the *Dolphin,* MS 828; Rhode Island State Archives, Moses Brown Papers, series 2, folder 6.

1795: *Ann* (Liverpool, England). Capt. John Mill/Mills. TST CD, 80246; *Lloyd's List,* Apr. 7, 1795.

1795: (Boston, MA). Goree Island (Senegambia). 4 crewmen killed. Successful. Slaves recaptured with the aid of another vessel after a 6- or 7-hour battle. Donnan, 3:99–101.

June 10, 1796: *Mary* (Providence, RI). Capt. Nathan Sterry. Cape Coast Castle (Gold Coast). 4 slaves killed. Unsuccessful. Donnan, 3:374–75; Coughtry, 151.

Ca. June 1796: *Isabella* (Bristol, England). Capt. Thomas Given. Angola (West Central Africa). Successful–freedom? *Lloyd's List,* June 21, 1796; Powell, 306.

Ca. June 1796: *William* (Liverpool, England). Capt. Bent. Angola (West Central Africa). Successful–freedom? *Lloyd's List,* June 21, 1796; Powell, 306.

1796: *Espera Dinheiro* (Portugal). Miller, *Way of Death,* 410.

Ca. 1796: *Bell* (Liverpool, England). Capt. David Thompson. TST CD, 80472; *Lloyd's List,* June 7, 1796.

Summer 1797: *Ann* (England). Capt. Muir. Middle Passage. Successful–freedom? *Lloyd's List,* July 7, 1797.

Sep. 2, 1797: *Thomas* (Liverpool, England). Capt. Peter McQuay/McQuie. Middle Passage. Several slaves and many crewmen killed. Successful. After about 50 days, the slaves were recaptured by a ship sent in pursuit of them. *Lloyd's List,* Dec. 15, 1797; C. Robinson, 1:322–23; Williams, 592–93; Brooke, 236–37; TST CD, 83783.

Nov. 7, 1797: *Ascension* (Rhode Island). Capt. Samuel Chase. Mozambique (East Africa). No crewmen killed. Unsuccessful. Newport Historical Society, box 43A, folder 26, "Slaves, 1731–1820," letter dated Dec. 11, 1797.

1798: *Diana* (Liverpool, England). Capt. Robert Hume. Windward Coast. Unsuccessful. Behrendt, letter; TST CD, 81015.

Aug. 2, 1799: *Trelawney* (England). Capt. James Lake. Cabinda (West Central Africa). Successful. Slaves recaptured with the aid of a nearby ship after a 90-minute battle. C. Robinson, 4:184–88; TST CD, 83836.

1799: *Lightning* (Liverpool, England). Miller, *Way of Death,* 410.

1799/1800: *Willy Tom Robin* (Liverpool, England). Capt. Edward Kain. TST CD, 84072.

1800: *Flying Fish* (Providence, RI). Capt. Nathaniel Packard/Packwood. West Indies. 10–15 slaves and 4–5 crewmen killed. Unsuccessful. *Providence Gazette,* Aug. 2, 1800; *Newport Mercury,* Aug. 5, 1800; Coughtry, 151, 158.

June 24, 1801: *Lucy* (England). Capt. John Olderman. 1 crewman killed. Behrendt, *Captains,* 137; TST CD, 82404.

Mar. 13, 1801/02: *Doris* (France). Capt. Liard. Zanzibar (East Africa). 110 slaves and 1 crewman killed. Unsuccessful. Garneray, 155–69.

Dec. 27, 1804: *Tryal* (Spain). Capt. Benito Cereno. Chilean coast (intra-American slave transport). 16 slaves and 25 crewmen killed. 9 of the slaves killed were executed in Concepcion, Chile, Mar. 2, 1805. Successful. Slaves recaptured with the aid of a nearby ship. Delano, 318–53.

Ca. 1804: *Anne* (England). Capt. Bicknell? African coast. Unsuccessful. C. Robinson, 5:92–93.

Ca. July 1806: *Bolton* (Liverpool, England). Capt. Patrick Burleigh. Bonny River (Bight of Biafra). About 12 slaves killed when the ship blew up. Successful—most recaptured. Crow, 98–99; TST CD, 80609.

Ca. Oct. 4, 1806: *Nancy* (Rhode Island). Capt. Joshua Viall. Middle Passage. 4 slaves killed. Multiple revolts may have occurred. Unsuccessful. Dow, 271–72; Donnan, 3:395–96, 400–401.

1806: *Eleanor* (Charleston, SC). Capt. Davidson. TST CD, 25504.

1806: *Jane* (Liverpool, England). Capt. John McGinnis/McInnis. Congo River (West Central Africa). All but 4 crewmen killed. Successful—freedom for some. *Royal Gazette and Bahama Advertiser,* Apr. 25, 1806; Inikori, "Measuring," 74.

July 17, 1807: *Independence* (Charleston, SC). Capt. Churchill. Loango (West Central Africa). Unsuccessful. Brevard, 3:522–25; Treadway, 2:707–12.

1807/08: *Hibernia* (Liverpool, England). Capt. Thomas Pratt. TST CD, 81835.

Ca. Feb. 1808: *Leander* (Charleston, SC). Middle Passage. All crewmen killed. Successful—recaptured. Ship found drifting some 250 miles off the South Carolina coast with only 56 slaves on board. Bee, 260–62; *Federal Cases,* vol. 9 (1895), 275–76.

May 20, 1808: *Coralline* (United States). Capt. Richard Willing. Middle Passage. 21 slaves and 3 crewmen killed. Unsuccessful. P. Drake, 44–45.

1810: *Zargozano* (Spain). Capt. Juan Norbeto Dolz. TST CD, 7551

1811: *Amelia/Agent* (Charleston, SC). Capts. Alexander Campbell and Joze Carlos de Almeida. TST CD, 7659.

Ca. Apr. 1812: *Feliz Eugenia* (Portugal). Miller, *Way of Death,* 410.

Ca. Jan. 1813: *Aguia do Douro* (Portugal). Miller, *Way of Death,* 410.

1814/15: *Belle* (Bordeaux, France). Capt. Brian. Daget, *Répertoire,* 1–6.

Ca. Aug. 1819: *Sao Pedro Aguia* (Portugal). Miller, *Way of Death,* 410.

Ca. Sep. 1819: (Portugal). Miller, *Way of Death,* 410.

1819: *Amitie* (Bordeaux, France). Capt. Louis Christiaens. 1 crewman killed. Unsuccessful. Daget, *Répertoire,* 61.

1819: *Rodeur* (Le Havre, France). Capt. Boucher. Middle Passage. Some slaves killed. May not have been an insurrection. Unsuccessful. *Niles' Weekly Register,* Apr. 21, 1821, 118; Rawley, 293; Daget, *Répertoire,* 88–90; *De l'état actuel de la traite des noirs,* 89.

Ca. Mar. 1820: *Industrie* (Nantes, France). Bay of Sainte-Suzanne, Reunion Island (East Africa). Successful–freedom? Lacroix, 205; Daget, *Répertoire,* 133.

1820: *Ceres* (Nantes, France). Capt. Pierre Jean Lemerle. Zimbie (Bight of Biafra). 1 crewman killed. Unsuccessful. Daget, *Répertoire,* 116–18.

1823: (Brazil). Middle Passage. All crewmen killed. Successful–freedom? Reis, 61; Mattoso, 40.

1824/25: *Eleonore* (Nantes, France). Capt. Mourailleur. TST CD, 2817.

Jan. 1825: *Deux Soeurs* (Martinique/France). Capt. Henri Mornet/Mornai. Sierra Leone. 6–8 crewmen killed. Successful. Slaves recaptured with the aid of another vessel; the ship was taken to Sierra Leone, where the slaves were freed. *Royal Gazette and Sierra Leone Advertiser,* Apr. 9, 1825; *Genius of Universal Emancipation and Baltimore Courier,* Sep. 24, 1825; *Niles' Weekly Register,* Oct. 1, 1825; *Irish University Press,* vol. 10, Class A, 9–10.

Apr. 25, 1826: *Decatur* (Boston, MA). Capt. Walter Galloway. Between South Carolina and Bermuda (domestic U.S. slave trade). 1 slave and 2 crewmen killed. The slave killed, William Bowser, was convicted of killing the captain and executed in New York on Dec. 15. Successful–freedom for most. Though the recaptured *Decatur* was taken into New York, all but 1 of the slaves inexplicably escaped. *New York Evening Post,* May 18, May 20, May 23, May 26, Dec. 14, Dec. 15, 1826; *Niles' Weekly Register,* May 20, 1826; *National Gazette and Literary Register,* May 20, May 23, 1826; *Christian Inquirer,* Dec. 23, 1826; *Genius of Universal Emancipation,* Jan. 2, Jan. 8, Jan. 20, Feb. 24, Mar. 31, 1827.

Sep. 17, 1826: (Bourbon, KY). Ohio River (domestic U.S. slave trade). 5 slaves and 5 crewmen killed. The 5 slaves killed were executed Nov. 29 in Kentucky. Successful–freedom for some. The slaves sank the boat and made their way to Indiana, but all but a few were eventually recaptured. Breckinridge County Archives, Circuit Court, book 7, pp. 182–83, 194, 207–8, 219; *Kentucky Reporter,* Sep. 25, Oct. 2, Oct. 9, 1826; *Western Luminary,* Sep. 27, Oct. 4, Oct. 11, Nov. 1, 1826; *Genius of Universal Emancipation,* Oct. 14, Oct. 21, Dec. 16, 1826; *Niles' Weekly Register,* Oct. 14, Nov. 18, 1826; *Connecticut Courant,* Oct. 16, 1826.

1827: *Augusta* (France). All crewmen killed. Successful–freedom? McGowan, "Origins," 83, 88–89.

Ca. 1827: *Gloria* (Brazil). Capt. Ruiz. African coast. 40 slaves "killed and wounded"; no crewmen killed. Unsuccessful. P. Drake, 89.

1828: *Intrepido* (Cuba?). Middle Passage? Some slaves killed in two revolts. Unsuccessful. Buxton, 149.

Dec. 17, 1829: *Lafayette* (United States). Capt. Bisset/Bissell. 3 days out from Norfolk, VA (domestic U.S. slave trade). No slaves or crewmen killed. Unsuccessful. *New York Evening Post,* Dec. 29, 1829; *Genius of Universal Emancipation,* Jan. 1, 1830; *Richmond Enquirer,* Jan. 5, Jan. 28, 1830; *Niles' Weekly Register,* Jan. 9, 1830.

1829: (United States). Ohio River (domestic U.S. slave trade). 1 crewman killed. Unsuccessful. 4 slaves were later executed in Kentucky. *Niles' Weekly Register,* Dec. 26, 1829; *Richmond Enquirer,* Jan. 28, 1830.

Mar. 13, 1831: *Virginie* (Nantes, France). Capt. Aubin. Sherbro (Sierra Leone). 11 crewmen killed. Successful–freedom? Daget, *Répertoire,* 537–38.

Ca. May 1831: *Venus* (Matanzas, Cuba). Capt. Theophilus Conneau. Middle Passage. 6 slaves and no crewmen killed. Unsuccessful. Conneau, 202–10.

July 2, 1839: *Amistad* (Cuba?). Capt. Ramon Ferrer. Cuban coast (domestic Cuban slave trade). 2 slaves and 2 crewmen killed. Successful. Slaves recaptured with the aid of a U.S. warship. U.S. Supreme Court found that these individuals were illegally enslaved, and they were freed. See chapter 7.

Nov. 7, 1841: *Creole* (United States). Capt. Robert Ensor. U.S. coast (domestic U.S. slave trade). 1 slave and 1 crewman killed. Successful–freedom. M. Robinson, 9:111–84.

Ca. Apr. 12, 1843: *Progresso* (Brazil). Off Fogo, Mozambique (East Africa). Successful–freedom? Ship was captured by anti–slave trade cruiser, and the slaves were presumably freed. P. Hill, 19–22.

Sep. 1844: *Kentucky* (New York, NY). Capt. Manoel Pinto da Fonseca. Inhambane (East Africa). 53 slaves killed. Unsuccessful. PRO, FO 84, 563:172–89; Senate Executive Documents, 28-30-1 (1847), 4:71–77; House Executive Documents, 61-30-2 (Mar. 2, 1849), 148, 220–21; *Irish University Press,* vol. 29, Class A, 513–23; Conrad, 39–42.

1846: *Andonovi* (Bahia, Brazil). Capt. Antonio Lopez Guimaraes. Middle Passage. 60 slaves killed. Unsuccessful. *Irish University Press,* vol. 35, Class B, 270.

1847: (Baltimore, MD). Middle Passage? Successful. Slaves recaptured with the aid of another vessel after a long period adrift. Lacroix, 206.

Ca. 1847: *Curioso* (Brazil/Portugal?). 67 slaves killed or wounded, 1 crewman killed. Unsuccessful. Forbes, 97–98.

Feb. 2, 1850: *Aventuera/Ventura* (Brazil). Capt. Joao Moreira da Camara. Middle Passage. 5 slaves killed. Unsuccessful. *Irish University Press,* vol. 38, Class A, 176, 245–46.

Winter 1853: (Matanzas, Cuba). Capt. Antonio Capo. Middle Passage. 200 slaves killed in two revolts. Unsuccessful. PRO, FO 84, 905:115; *Irish University Press,* vol. 40, Class B, 644, 658.

Apr. 1858: *Regina Coeli* (France). Capt. Simon. Cape Palmas (Windward Coast). About 250 slaves and 11 crewmen killed. The slaves were apparently killed as they attempted to swim ashore. Successful–recaptured? Eltis suggests that the slaves escaped in the Monrovia area. *London Times,* June 18, 1858; *New York Times,* June 21, 1858; *Class A Correspondence,* 225, 245; Eltis, *Rise of African Slavery,* 232.

1859: (Cardenas, Cuba). Middle Passage? Unsuccessful. *Irish University Press,* vol. 46, Class A, 14; ibid., Class B, 166; TST CD, 4313.

Ca. Aug. 1865: (Cuba?). Middle Passage. 6–7 slaves and 3 crewmen killed. Unsuccessful. PRO, FO 84, 1241:196; *Irish University Press,* vol. 50, Class B, 137.

Notes

ABBREVIATIONS USED IN NOTES

PRO   Public Record Office, Kew, England

    FO 84   Records of the Foreign Office, Correspondence of the Slave Trade and African Departments, 1816–1892

    T 70   Records of the Treasury, Correspondence of the Company of Royal Adventurers of England Trading with Africa, 1660–1833

    ZHC 1   Publications of the House of Commons, Sessional Papers

NOTES TO INTRODUCTION

1. *New-York Gazette,* August 13, 1764; *Massachusetts Gazette Extraordinary* (Boston), August 16, 1764; *Pennsylvania Gazette* (Philadelphia), August 16, 1764; *New-London Gazette,* August 17, 1764; *Newport Mercury,* August 20, 1764; *Boston Post-Boy and Advertiser,* August 20, 1764; *Massachusetts Gazette and Boston News-Letter,* August 30, 1764.

2. *Boston Post-Boy and Advertiser,* March 4, 1765; *Massachusetts Gazette and Boston News-Letter,* March 7, 1765; *New-York Gazette,* March 11, 1765; *Pennsylvania Gazette* (Philadelphia), March 21, 1765. Shortly thereafter, it was reported that Preest had contracted a fever and died in prison. See *Massachusetts Gazette and Boston News-Letter,* March 28, 1765; *Boston Post-Boy and Advertiser,* April 1, 1765; *Newport Mercury,* April 8, 1765.

3. For instance, in his examination of the Dutch trade, Johannes Postma theorized that there may have been as many as three hundred revolts on Dutch ships alone. See Postma, *The Dutch in the Atlantic Slave Trade, 1600–1815* (New York: Cambridge University Press, 1992), 167. Stephen D. Behrendt, David Eltis, and David Richardson have suggested that revolts may have occurred on 10 percent of all slaving voyages. See Behrendt, Eltis, and Richardson, "The Costs of Coercion: African Agency in the Pre-Modern Atlantic World," *Economic History Review* 54, no. 3 (2001): 456; David Richardson, "Shipboard Revolts, African Authority, and the Atlantic Slave Trade," *William and Mary Quarterly* 58, no. 1 (January 2001): 72.

4. Clarence J. Munford, *The Black Ordeal of Slavery and Slave Trading in the French West Indies, 1625–1715* (Lewiston, NY: Mellen, 1991), 2:337.

5. Messrs. Phipps, Dodson, and Boye, Cape Coast Castle, October 28, 1721, in *Abstract of Letters Received by the Royal African Company of England from the Coast of Africa, No. 3, From January the 12th, 1719 to August the 26th, 1732,* PRO, T 70, 7:32. See also letter dated Cape Corso Castle, September 30, 1721, ibid., 7:30; Messrs. Phipps, Dodson, and Boye, Cape Coast Castle, September 30, 1721, PRO, T 70, 4:22.

6. Herbert Aptheker, *American Negro Slave Revolts* (1943; reprint, New York: International, 1993), 162.

7. Eugene D. Genovese, *From Rebellion to Revolution: Afro-American Slave Revolts in the Making of the Modern World* (Baton Rouge: Louisiana State University Press, 1979), xxiii.

8. Michael Craton, *Testing the Chains: Resistance to Slavery in the British West Indies* (Ithaca, NY: Cornell University Press, 1982), 24.

9. Dennis Wepman, *The Struggle for Freedom: African-American Slave Resistance* (New York: Facts On File, 1996), 12.

10. George Francis Dow, *Slave Ships and Slaving* (Salem, MA: Marine Research Society, 1927), 113-31.

11. Elizabeth Donnan, *Documents Illustrative of the History of the Slave Trade to America*, 4 vols. (Washington DC: Carnegie Institution of Washington, 1930-1935).

12. Gaston Martin, *Nantes au XVIIIe siècle: l'ère des négriers*, cited in Okon Edet Uya, "The Middle Passage and Personality Change," in *Global Dimensions of the African Diaspora*, 2nd ed., ed. Joseph Harris (Washington, DC: Howard University Press, 1993), 85.

13. Harvey Wish, "American Slave Insurrections before 1861," *Journal of Negro History* 22, no. 3 (July 1937), 299-320.

14. Lorenzo J. Greene, "Mutiny on the Slave Ships," *Phylon* 5, no. 4 (1944): 346-55.

15. Darold Wax, "Negro Resistance to the Early American Slave Trade," *Journal of Negro History* 51, no. 1 (January 1966): 1-15; Okon E. Uya, "Slave Revolts of the Middle Passage: A Neglected Theme," *Calabar Historical Journal* 1, no. 1 (June 1976): 65-88; Uya, "Middle Passage and Personality Change," 83-97; Daniel P. Mannix and Malcolm Cowley, *Black Cargoes: A History of the Atlantic Slave Trade 1518-1865* (New York: Penguin Books, 1978), 104-30; Munford, *Black Ordeal*, 2:337-58.

16. Winston McGowan, "African Resistance to the Atlantic Slave Trade in West Africa," *Slavery and Abolition* 11, no. 1 (May 1990): 5-29; Winston McGowan, "The Origins of Slave Rebellions in the Middle Passage," in *In the Shadow of the Plantation: Caribbean History and Legacy,* ed. Alvin O. Thompson (Kingston, Jamaica: Randle, 2002), 74-99; Richard Rathbone, "Some Thoughts on Resistance to Enslavement in West Africa," *Slavery and Abolition* 6, no. 3 (December 1985): 11-22; Joseph Inikori, "Measuring the Unmeasured Hazards of the Atlantic Slave Trade: Documents Relating to the British Trade," *Revue Française d'Histoire d'Outre-Mer* 83, no. 312 (1996), 53-92; Vincent Bakpetu Thompson, *The Making of the African Diaspora in the Americas, 1441-1900* (Essex, England: Longman, 1987), 107-30.

17. Postma, *Dutch in the Atlantic Slave Trade,* 165-68; Jay Coughtry, *The Notorious Triangle: Rhode Island and the African Slave Trade, 1700-1807* (Philadelphia: Temple University Press, 1981), 151-58; Joseph C. Miller, *Way of Death: Merchant Capitalism and the Angolan Slave Trade* (Madison: University of Wisconsin Press, 1988), 410-11; David Richardson, ed., *Bristol, Africa, and the Eighteenth-Century Slave Trade to America*, 4 vols. (Bristol, England: Bristol Record Society, 1986-1996); Serge Daget, *Répertoire des expéditions négrières françaises à la traite illégale (1814-1850)* (Nantes: Centre de recherche sur l'histoire du monde atlantique, 1988).

18. Jean Mettas, *Répertoire des expéditions négrières françaises au XVIIIe siècle*, 2 vols., ed. Serge Daget (Paris: Société française d'histoire d'outre-mer, 1978-1984).

19. David Eltis et al., eds., *The Trans-Atlantic Slave Trade: A Database on CD-ROM* (Cambridge: Cambridge University Press, 1999). The CD-ROM's final total of 338 shipboard insurrections, like the total identified in the present study, does not include cases of slavers being "cut off" on the African coast. For a discussion of this often confusing and ambiguous terminology, see chapter 6.

20. Behrendt, Eltis, and Richardson, "Costs of Coercion," 455. David Richardson also gives the number of 388 revolts in "Shipboard Revolts, African Authority, and the Transatlantic

Slave Trade," in *Fighting the Slave Trade: West African Strategies,* ed. Sylviane A. Diouf (Athens: Ohio University Press, 2003), 201. Note that this is an abridged and slightly revised version of the same essay as it appeared in *William and Mary Quarterly* 58, no. 1 (January 2001), which gave a marginally higher total of 392 revolts. See p. 72 of the journal article.

21. Georg Nørregård, "Slaveoproret pa 'Patientia' 1753," *Årbog (Handels-og søfartmuseet på Kronborg)* (Denmark) (1950): 23–44; Darold Wax, "The Browns of Providence and the Slaving Voyage of the Brig Sally, 1764–65," *American Neptune* 32, no. 3 (July 1972): 171–79; Mitra Sharafi, "The Slave Ship Manuscripts of Captain Joseph B. Cook: A Narrative Reconstruction of the Brig *Nancy*'s Voyage of 1793," *Slavery and Abolition* 24, no. 1 (April 2003): 71–100.

22. Henry Greenhill, Henry Spurway, and Walter Stapleton, Cape Coast Castle, September 28, 1681, in *Abstracts of Letters Rece'd by the Royal African Company of England so far as relate to the Committee of Correspondence, No. 1, From March the 15th, 1677 to February the 8th, 1682,* PRO, T 70, 10:49.

23. *Lloyd's List* (London), January 5, 1749.

24. *Lloyd's List* (London), January 29, 1765.

25. *Weekly Journal; or, The British-Gazetteer* (London), August 2, September 6, 1729, February 28, June 20, 1730; *Fog's Weekly Journal* (London), August 2, September 6, 1729, February 28, June 20, 1730; *Boston Weekly News-Letter,* September 18–25, 1729; *Pennsylvania Gazette* (Philadelphia), October 9–16, 1729, January 6–13, 1730.

26. Quobna Ottobah Cugoano, *Thoughts and Sentiments on the Evil of Slavery and Other Writings* (1787), ed. Vincent Caretta (New York: Penguin, 1999); Robin Law and Paul E. Lovejoy, eds., *The Biography of Mahommah Gardo Baquaqua: His Passage from Slavery to Freedom in Africa and America* (1854; reprint, Princeton, NJ: Wiener, 2001); Olaudah Equiano, *Equiano's Travels: The Interesting Narrative of the Life of Olaudah Equiano or Gustavus Vassa the African,* ed. Paul Edwards (1789; reprint, Oxford: Heinemann, 1996). Some scholars have challenged whether Equiano was in fact born in Africa. See Vincent Carretta, "Olaudah Equiano or Gustavus Vassa? New Light on an Eighteenth-century Question of Identity," *Slavery and Abolition* 20, no. 3 (December 1999): 96–105.

27. William Snelgrave, *A New Account of Some Parts of Guinea, and the Slave Trade* (1734; reprint, London: Cass, 1971), 167.

28. *Boston Weekly News-Letter,* September 8–15, 1737; *Virginia Gazette* (Williamsburg), October 21–28, 1737. Note that the editors of *The Trans-Atlantic Slave Trade CD-ROM* apparently have a broader definition of shipboard revolt, which includes the case of the *Prince of Orange.* See Eltis et al., *Trans-Atlantic Slave Trade,* voyage ID 16873.

29. Francis Moore, *Travels into the Inland Parts of Africa* (London: E. Cave, 1738), 49.

30. Robert Harms, *The Diligent: A Voyage through the Worlds of the Slave Trade* (New York: Basic Books, 2002), 269–70. In another case of individual resistance, a slave attempted to snatch a knife from a crew member on a voyage to Brazil sometime in the 1840s. See Law and Lovejoy, *Biography of Mahommah Gardo Baquaqua,* 154.

31. Gwendolyn Midlo Hall, *Africans in Colonial Louisiana: The Development of Afro-Creole Culture in the Eighteenth Century* (Baton Rouge: Louisiana State University Press, 1992), 69–70.

32. Stanley Elkins, *Slavery: A Problem in American Institutional and Intellectual Life,* 3rd ed., rev. (Chicago: University of Chicago Press, 1976), 100–102.

NOTES TO CHAPTER 1

1. Joseph Hawkins, *A History of a Voyage to the Coast of Africa, and Travels into the Interior of that Country; Containing Particular Descriptions of the Climate and Inhabitants, and Interesting Particulars Concerning the Slave Trade* (Philadelphia, 1797), 140–49.

2. Alexander Falconbridge, *An Account of the Slave Trade on the Coast of Africa* (London: J. Philips, 1788), 19. For similar accounts, see Thomas Clarkson, *The Substance of the Evidence,* in *The British Transatlantic Slave Trade,* ed. John Oldfield (London: Pickering and Chatto, 2003), 3:197, 247.

3. Mungo Park, *Travels in the Interior Districts of Africa,* ed. Kate Ferguston Marsters (Durham, NC: Duke University Press), 276–302. See also Hugh Thomas, *The Slave Trade: The Story of the Atlantic Slave Trade, 1440–1870* (New York: Simon and Schuster, 1997), 384; Miller, *Way of Death,* 191.

4. Miller, *Way of Death,* 192; Thomas Cooper, *Letters on the Slave Trade,* in Oldfield, *British Transatlantic Slave Trade,* 3:32–33.

5. Testimony of Richard Miles in *Minutes of the Evidence Taken Before a Committee of the House of Commons, Being a Committee of the Whole House, to Whom it was Referred to Consider of the Circumstances of the Slave Trade, Complained of in the several Petitions which were presented to the House in the last Session of Parliament, relative to the State of the African Slave Trade* (1789), PRO, ZHC 1, 82:58; W. O. Blake, *The History of Slavery and the Slave Trade, Ancient and Modern. The Forms of Slavery That Prevailed in Ancient Nations, Particularly in Greece and Rome. The African Slave Trade and the Political History of Slavery in the United States* (Columbus, OH: H. Miller, 1860), 101; Miller, *Way of Death,* 194, 385–87.

6. Quoted from a lecture by a Portuguese doctor in 1793, in Robert Edgar Conrad, *Children of God's Fire: A Documentary History of Black Slavery in Brazil* (University Park: Pennsylvania State University Press, 1994), 19.

7. Hawkins, *History of a Voyage,* 141.

8. Phyllis M. Martin, *The External Trade of the Loango Coast, 1576–1870: The Effects of Changing Commercial Relations on the Vili Kingdom of Loango* (Oxford: Clarendon, 1972), 119; Mettas, *Répertoire,* 1:419.

9. Miller, *Way of Death,* 194, 384–85.

10. Thomas, *Slave Trade,* 713.

11. Miller, *Way of Death,* 390.

12. *Observations of the Slave Trade and a Description of some Part of the Coast of Guinea, During a Voyage Made in 1787, and 1788, in Company with Doctor A. Sparrman and Captain Arrehenius* (London, 1787).

13. Miller, *Way of Death,* 391, 401.

14. Colin Palmer, *Human Cargoes: The British Slave Trade in Spanish America, 1700–1739* (Urbana: University of Illinois Press, 1981), 42–43; Nigel Tattersfield, *The Forgotten Trade: Comprising the Log of the Daniel and Henry of 1700 and Accounts of the Slave Trade from the Minor Ports of England, 1698–1725* (London: Cape, 1991), 78–79.

15. William Mutter, Cape Coast Castle, October 25, 1765, PRO, T 70, 31:148.

16. Postma, *Dutch in the Atlantic Slave Trade,* 237–38.

17. Miller, *Way of Death,* 391.

18. Douglas Grant, *The Fortunate Slave: An Illustration of African Slavery in the Early Nineteenth Century* (London: Oxford University Press, 1968), 55.

19. Georg Nørregård, *Danish Settlements in West Africa, 1658–1850* (Boston: Boston University Press, 1966), 86. In addition to this insurrection, this source also briefly mentions two other barracoon revolts.

20. McGowan, "African Resistance," 18.

21. Commodore Collier's second annual report on the settlements on the coast of Africa, September 11, 1820, quoted in Rathbone, "Some Thoughts on Resistance," 13–14.

22. Theophilus Conneau, *A Slaver's Log Book; or, 20 Years' Residence in Africa* (London: Hale, 1977), 254. For a similar abortive effort by a group of slaves to break out of Cape Coast Castle in 1730, see McGowan, "African Resistance," 24.

23. John Atkins, *A Voyage to Guinea, Brasil, and the West-Indies* (London, 1735), 41–42.

24. William Bosman, *A New and Accurate Description of the Coast of Guinea, Divided into The Gold, The Slave, and The Ivory Coasts* (1704; reprint, London: Cass, 1967), 364. See also Clarkson, *Substance of the Evidence,* in Oldfield, *British Transatlantic Slave Trade,* 3:236, 258.

25. Falconbridge, *Account of the Slave Trade,* 17.

26. Postma, *Dutch in the Atlantic Slave Trade,* 236.

27. Leif Svalesen, *The Slave Ship* Fredensborg, trans. Pat Shaw and Selena Winsnes (Bloomington: Indiana University Press, 2000), 94.

28. Conneau, *Slaver's Log Book,* 71.

29. Harms, *The* Diligent, 250. For descriptions of the branding process, see Miller, *Way of Death,* 404–5; James A. Rawley, *The Transatlantic Slave Trade: A History* (New York: Norton, 1981), 59; Thomas, *Slave Trade,* 396–97; Postma, *Dutch in the Atlantic Slave Trade,* 237; "Instructions for a slave-ship captain of the MCC," in Postma, *Dutch in the Atlantic Slave Trade,* 368.

30. Law and Lovejoy, *Biography of Mahommah Gardo Baquaqua,* 150–51.

31. Cugoano, *Thoughts and Sentiments,* 15.

32. Thomas Phillips, *Abstract of a Voyage along the Coast of Guinea to Whidaw, the Island of St. Thomas, and thence to Barbadoes, in 1693,* in *A New General Collection of Voyages and Travels Consisting of the Most Esteemed Relations which have been hitherto Published in any Language Comprehending Everything Remarkable in its Kind in Europe, Asia, Africa, and America,* ed. Thomas Astley (1745–47; reprint, London: Cass, 1968), 2:407.

33. Conneau, *Slaver's Log Book,* 256. Mahommah Baquaqua recollected witnessing about thirty Africans die when the boat taking them to the slave ship capsized in heavy surf. See Law and Lovejoy, *Biography of Mahommah Gardo Baquaqua,* 152.

34. See Clarkson, *Substance of the Evidence,* in Oldfield, *British Transatlantic Slave Trade,* 3:220, 248, 258.

35. *Boston Weekly News-Letter,* September 8–15, 1737; *Virginia Gazette* (Williamsburg), October 21–28, 1737.

36. McGowan, "African Resistance," 21; John Kelly Thornton, *Africa and Africans in the Making of the Atlantic World, 1400–1680* (Cambridge: Cambridge University Press, 1992), 161; John Iliffe, *Africans: The History of a Continent* (Cambridge: Cambridge University Press, 1995), 136.

37. Miller, *Way of Death,* 413. See also William D. Piersen, "White Cannibals, Black Martyrs: Fear, Depression, and Religious Faith as Causes of Suicide among New Slaves," *Journal of Negro History* 62, no. 2 (April 1977): 147–59. These fears began with the first encounters. When a group of Africans attacked a Portuguese ship on the Gambia River in 1455, their explanation was that they believed Christians ate human flesh and only bought Africans to eat them. See G. R. Crone, ed. and trans., *The Voyages of Cadamosto and Other Documents on Western Africa in the Second Half of the Fifteenth Century,* works issued by the Hakluyt Society, 2nd ser., no. 80 (London: Hakluyt Society, 1937), 58–60.

38. Harms, *The* Diligent, 271.

39. Bosman, *New and Accurate Description,* 365.

40. Equiano, *Equiano's Travels,* 22–23. Although the veracity of Equiano's account is questionable, the Africans' fear of cannibalism was a commonly cited concern among new slaves first boarding slave ships. Even if this is not Equiano's personal memory of the slave

trade, it is probably a composite of stories he heard from fellow slaves who had experienced such terrifying thoughts.

41. Bosman, *New and Accurate Description,* 365. See also John Kelly Thornton, "Cannibals, Witches, and Slave Traders in the Atlantic World," *William and Mary Quarterly* 60, no. 2 (April 2003): 273–74.

42. Harms, *The* Diligent, 311.

43. Robert Louis Stein, *The French Slave Trade in the Eighteenth Century: An Old Regime Business* (Madison: University of Wisconsin Press, 1979), 101–2.

44. Miller, *Way of Death,* 413–18; Postma, *Dutch in the Atlantic Slave Trade,* 158, 233–34; Tattersfield, *Forgotten Trade,* 150; Stein, *French Slave Trade,* 101–2; Rawley, *Transatlantic Slave Trade,* 297–98; Thomas, *Slave Trade,* 419–20. See also Clarkson, *Substance of the Evidence,* in Oldfield, *British Transatlantic Slave Trade,* 3:198, 211, 215, 237.

45. Tattersfield, *Forgotten Trade,* 121.

46. Thomas, *Slave Trade,* 419.

47. Palmer, *Human Cargoes,* 51; Miller, *Way of Death,* 415; Postma, *Dutch in the Atlantic Slave Trade,* 258.

48. Miller, *Way of Death,* 419. See also Kenneth F. Kiple and Brian T. Higgins, "Mortality Caused by Dehydration During the Middle Passage," in *The Atlantic Slave Trade: Effects on Economies, Societies, and Peoples in Africa, the Americas, and Europe,* ed. Joseph E. Inikori and Stanley L. Engerman (Durham, NC: Duke University Press, 1992), 321–37.

49. Thomas, *Slave Trade,* 422; Munford, *Black Ordeal,* 2:301.

50. Mannix and Cowley, *Black Cargoes,* 107. See also Harms, *The* Diligent, 263–64; Clarkson, *Substance of the Evidence,* in Oldfield, *British Transatlantic Slave Trade,* 3:198, 259.

51. Miller, *Way of Death,* 412.

52. Munford, *Black Ordeal,* 2:296.

53. Falconbridge, *Account of the Slave Trade,* 20.

54. Mannix and Cowley, *Black Cargoes,* 115. For a further description of the filth aboard slave ships, see also extract from Thomas Nelson, *Remarks on the Slavery and Slave Trade of the Brazils,* in Conrad, *Children of God's Fire,* 44–47.

55. Law and Lovejoy, *Biography of Mahommah Gardo Baquaqua,* 153. See also Clarkson, *Substance of the Evidence,* in Oldfield, *British Transatlantic Slave Trade,* 3:229, 259.

56. Falconbridge, *Account of the Slave Trade,* 24.

57. Ibid., 25.

58. Thomas, *Slave Trade,* 423; Postma, *Dutch in the Atlantic Slave Trade,* 245.

59. Palmer, *Human Cargoes,* 49.

60. Harms, *The* Diligent, 317.

61. David L. Chandler, *Health and Slavery in Colonial Colombia* (New York: Arno, 1981), 32.

62. Harms, *The* Diligent, 274.

63. Postma, *Dutch in the Atlantic Slave Trade,* 244.

64. Thomas, *Slave Trade,* 489; *Felix Farley's Bristol Journal* (Bristol, England), March 16, 1782. See also Robert Weisbord, "The Case of the Slave-Ship 'Zong,' 1783," *History Today* 19, no. 8 (1969): 561–67.

65. Miller, *Way of Death,* 437.

66. Adam Starr, journal entry, August 21, 1781, quoted in McGowan, "African Resistance," 20–21.

67. Lerone Bennett Jr., *Before the Mayflower: A History of Black America,* 5th rev. ed. (Chicago: Johnson, 1982; reprint, New York: Penguin Books, 1984), 49.

68. Bruce L. Mouser, ed., *A Slaving Voyage to Africa and Jamaica: The Log of the* Sandown, *1793–1794* (Bloomington: Indiana University Press, 2002), 103; Svalesen, *Slave Ship* Fredensborg, 108.

69. David Eltis, *The Rise of African Slavery in the Americas* (Cambridge: Cambridge University Press, 2000), 230.

70. Blake, *History of Slavery*, 129; Mannix and Cowley, *Black Cargoes*, 117. See also Falconbridge, *Account of the Slave Trade*, 32.

71. Kiple and Higgins, "Mortality," 327; Falconbridge, *Account of the Slave Trade*, 23. See also Clarkson, *Substance of the Evidence*, in Oldfield, *British Transatlantic Slave Trade*, 3:198, 204, 237. On a number of French ships, an accordion player was brought along to help liven up these exercise sessions. See Harms, *The* Diligent, 295–96.

72. Falconbridge, *Account of the Slave Trade*, 24–25.

73. John Newton, *Thoughts Upon the African Slave Trade*, in *The Journal of a Slave Trader (John Newton), 1750–54, With Newton's "Thoughts Upon the African Slave Trade,"* ed. Bernard Martin and Mark Spurrell (London: Epworth, 1962), 105.

74. Quoted in Munford, *Black Ordeal*, 2:344.

75. Harms, *The* Diligent, 312.

76. Cugoano, *Thoughts and Sentiments*, 15.

77. Log of the *Mary*, in Donnan, *Documents*, 3:374–76. See also Coughtry, *Notorious Triangle*, 160.

78. Harms, *The* Diligent, 312.

79. Munford, *Black Ordeal*, 2:306.

80. Quoted in Stein, *French Slave Trade*, 101.

81. Newton, *Journal of a Slave Trader*, 75.

82. Postma, *Dutch in the Atlantic Slave Trade*, 243.

83. Ibid., 164, 242. Svalesen suggests the *Cron-Prindzen* exploded when anchored off of the island of Principe, possibly resulting from a slave insurrection on board. See Svalesen, *Slave Ship* Fredensborg, 116.

84. *Boston Weekly News-Letter*, September 1–8, 1737.

85. *Lloyd's Evening Post and British Chronicle* (London), January 1–4, 1762; *Lloyd's List* (London), January 5, 1762.

86. *New Lloyd's List* (London), August 12, 1783.

87. Ibid., September 12, 1783.

88. Ibid., July 31, 1787.

89. Munford, *Black Ordeal*, 2:287.

90. Stein, *French Slave Trade*, 226, n. 6.

91. Herbert S. Klein and Stanley L. Engerman, "Long-Term Trends in African Mortality in the Transatlantic Slave Trade," in David Eltis and David Richardson, *Routes to Slavery: Direction, Ethnicity, and Mortality in the Atlantic Slave Trade* (London: Cass, 1997), 37; Herbert S. Klein, *The Atlantic Slave Trade* (Cambridge: Cambridge University Press, 1999), 148, 186; Richard H. Steckel and Richard A. Jensen, "New Evidence on the Causes of Slave and Crew Mortality in the Atlantic Slave Trade," *Journal of Economic History* 46, no. 1 (March 1986): 57; Herbert S. Klein, *The Middle Passage: Comparative Studies in the Atlantic Slave Trade* (Princeton, NJ: Princeton University Press, 1978), 29–31. See also F. E. Sanderson, "The Liverpool Delegates and Sir William Dolben's Bill," *Transactions of the Historic Society of Lancashire and Cheshire* 124 (1973): 57–84. For the text of Dolben's Act, see Donnan, *Documents*, 2:582–89.

92. The question of slave mortality has received much attention in recent years. For some of the main contributions to the debate, see Raymond L. Cohn, "Deaths of Slaves in the Middle Passage," *Journal of Economic History* 45, no. 3 (September 1985): 687; Joseph C. Miller, "Mortality in the Atlantic Slave Trade: Statistical Evidence on Causality," *Journal*

of Interdisciplinary History 11, no. 3 (Winter 1981): 385–423; Robert Stein, "Mortality in the Eighteenth-Century French Slave Trade," *Journal of African History* 21, no. 1 (1980): 35–41; Herbert S. Klein and Stanley L. Engerman, "Slave Mortality on British Ships, 1791–1797," in *Liverpool, the African Slave Trade, and Abolition,* ed. Roger T. Anstey and P. E. H. Hair (Liverpool: Historic Society of Lancashire and Cheshire, 1977), 117–22; Herbert S. Klein and Stanley L. Engerman, "Shipping Patterns and Mortality in the African Slave Trade to Rio de Janeiro, 1825–1830," *Cahiers d'Etudes Africaines* 15, no. 3 (1975): 381–98; Klein and Engerman, "Long-Term Trends," 43; Miller, *Way of Death,* 436; Postma, *Dutch in the Atlantic Slave Trade,* 248–58; Klein, *Atlantic Slave Trade,* 136–42; David Eltis, "Mortality and Voyage Length in the Middle Passage: New Evidence from the Nineteenth Century," *Journal of Economic History* 44, no. 2 (June 1984): 301–8; Robin Haines, John McDonald, and Ralph Shlomowitz, "Mortality and Voyage Length in the Middle Passage Revisited," *Explorations in Economic History* 38, no. 4 (October 2001): 503–33.

93. Testimony of James Fraser, February 3, 1790, in *Minutes of the Evidence taken Before a committee of the House of Commons, Being a Select Committee, Appointed on the 29th Day of January 1790, for the Purpose of taking the Examination of such Witnesses as shall be produced on the Part of the several Petitioners who have petitioned the House of Commons against the Abolition of the Slave Trade,* PRO, ZHC 1, 85:46.

94. *Niles' Weekly Register* (Baltimore), June 3, 1826.

95. Mannix and Cowley, *Black Cargoes,* 119; Edward Reynolds, *Stand the Storm: A History of the Atlantic Slave Trade* (London: Allison and Busby, 1989), 49; Tattersfield, *Forgotten Trade,* 142; Clarkson, *Substance of the Evidence,* in Oldfield, *British Transatlantic Slave Trade,* 3:207, 237, 249.

96. Falconbridge, *Account of the Slave Trade,* 23.

97. Conneau, *Slaver's Log Book,* 82–83.

98. Blake, *History of Slavery and the Slave Trade,* 130; Mannix and Cowley, *Black Cargoes,* 118; Munford, *Black Ordeal,* 2:349; Conneau, *Slaver's Log Book,* 208.

99. Clarkson, *Substance of the Evidence,* in Oldfield, *British Transatlantic Slave Trade,* 3:207.

100. Tattersfield, *Forgotten Trade,* 142; Blake, *History of Slavery and the Slave Trade,* 131.

101. Piersen, "White Cannibals, Black Martyrs," 155; Donnan, *Documents,* 2:327–28; instructions from the firm of Isaac Hobhouse & Co. to William Barry, commander of the *Dispatch,* in Peter Fryer, *Staying Power: The History of Black People in Britain* (London: Pluto, 1992), 53. See also Tattersfield, *Forgotten Trade,* 112, 156.

102. Cugoano, *Thoughts and Sentiments,* 15.

NOTES TO CHAPTER 2

1. Early reports of this incident got the facts slightly wrong, reporting that the *King David* was from London and that the revolt had taken place on May 28. See *Boston News-Letter,* June 21, 1750; *Boston Post-Boy,* June 25, 1750; *Pennsylvania Gazette* (Philadelphia), July 5, 1750. See also *Lloyd's List* (London), July 13, 1750. Later, an account offered by one of the *King David*'s sailors was printed in the press, offering further details and correcting previous errors. See *Boston News-Letter,* September 6, 1750; *Maryland Gazette* (Annapolis), November 14, 1750. See also Eltis et al., *Trans-Atlantic Slave Trade,* voyage ID 17243.

2. Newton, *Thoughts Upon the African Slave Trade,* in *Journal of a Slave Trader,* 103.

3. Miller, *Way of Death,* 409; Postma, *Dutch in the Atlantic Slave Trade,* 167; Uya, "Slave Revolts of the Middle Passage," 75; Wish, "American Slave Insurrections," 300; Clarkson, *Substance of the Evidence,* in Oldfield, *British Transatlantic Slave Trade,* 3:203, 228.

4. Moore, *Travels into the Inland,* 80.

5. Munford, *Black Ordeal,* 2:338.

6. Uya, "Slave Revolts of the Middle Passage," 75; Munford, *Black Ordeal,* 2:282. For the length of time ships spent on the African coast, see Postma, *Dutch in the Atlantic Slave Trade,* 249; B. K. Drake, "The Liverpool-African Voyage, c. 1790–1807: Commercial Problems," in Anstey and Hair, *Liverpool, the African Slave Trade, and Abolition,* 145–50; Klein and Engerman, "Slave Mortality," 116. Interestingly, the fact that larger ships had to spend a greater period of time collecting their slaves on the African coast also explains why revolts appear to be more common on large ships than small ones. See Behrendt, Eltis, and Richardson "Costs of Coercion," 458–59.

7. Newton, *Journal of a Slave Trader,* 55.

8. Snelgrave, *New Account,* 164–68.

9. Gomer Williams, *History of the Liverpool Privateers and Letters of Marque with an Account of the Liverpool Slave Trade* (1897; reprint, New York: Kelley, 1966), 492–93, 666; Eveline Christiana Martin, ed., *Journal of a Slave Dealer: A View of Some Remarkable Ax-cedents in the Life of Nics. Owen on the Coast of Africa and America from the Year 1746 to the Year 1757* (Boston: Houghton Mifflin, 1930), 106.

10. Mettas, *Répertoire,* 2:364–65.

11. Nine cases of rebellion taking place on vessels involved in the domestic or international slave trades within the Americas are not included in these statistics. For more on these incidents, see chapter 7. Behrendt, Eltis, and Richardson have suggested that about two-thirds of revolts occurred on ships the coast and about one-third during the Atlantic crossing. A negligible 3 percent were found to have occurred in American waters. Notably, these historians suggest, "From the perspective of European carriers, the risk of uprising was fairly constant as long as slaves were on board," regardless of the physical location of the vessel. See Behrendt, Eltis, and Richardson "Costs of Coercion," 464–65; David Richardson, "Shipboard Revolts," 75.

12. Palmer, *Human Cargoes,* 54; Thomas, *Slave Trade,* 311. For more on crew mortality, see Rawley, *Transatlantic Slave Trade,* 285–86; Stein, *French Slave Trade,* 98–100; Coughtry, *Notorious Triangle,* 154–55; Postma, *Dutch in the Atlantic Slave Trade,* 156–57; Steckel and Jensen, "New Evidence," 57–77; Stephen D. Behrendt, "Crew Mortality in the Transatlantic Slave Trade in the Eighteenth Century," in Eltis and Richardson, *Routes to Slavery,* 49–71.

13. Clement Tudway and Edward Parsons, Antigua, October 15, 1686, in *Abstract of Letters Received by the Royal African Company of England from the West Indies so far as relate to the Committee of Correspondence, No. 3, From July the 28th, 1683 to April the 28th, 1698.* PRO, T 70, 12:163.

14. *Boston News-Letter,* June 21, September 6, 1750; *Boston Post-Boy,* June 25, 1750; *Pennsylvania Gazette* (Philadelphia), July 5, 1750. See also *Lloyd's List* (London), July 13, 1750; *Maryland Gazette* (Annapolis), November 14, 1750.

15. *Pennsylvania Gazette* (Philadelphia), August 9, 1750; *Boston Post-Boy,* August 13, 1750; *Lloyds List* (London), August 28, 1750; *Maryland Gazette* (Annapolis), September 5, 1750.

16. Joseph Debat and Samuel Randal, James Fort, September 15, 1759, and October 9, 1759, PRO, T 70, 30:315, 321.

17. Williams, *Liverpool Privateers,* 549; Clarkson, *Substance of the Evidence,* in Oldfield, *British Transatlantic Slave Trade,* 3:199; Inikori, "Measuring the Unmeasured Hazards," 67.

18. Mouser, *Slaving Voyage,* xii–xiii, 91, 97.

19. Tattersfield, *Forgotten Trade,* 146; Marcus Rediker, *Between the Devil and the Deep Blue Sea: Merchant Seamen, Pirates, and the Anglo-American Maritime World, 1700–1750* (Cambridge: Cambridge University Press, 1999), 48; Harms, *The* Diligent, 274. Behrendt, Eltis,

and Richardson quote one sailor as saying, "We concealed the death of the sailors from ye Negros by throwing them overboard in the night lest it might give them a temptation to rise upon us seeing us so much weakened" ("Costs of Coercion," 461–62).

20. Rediker, *Devil and the Deep Blue Sea*, 93.

21. Coughtry, *Notorious Triangle*, 156.

22. Mettas, *Répertoire*, 2:197–98, 202–3.

23. *Pennsylvania Gazette* (Philadelphia), November 11, 1762; *New-York Gazette*, November 15, 1762; *Boston News-Letter and New-England Chronicle*, November 18, 1762; *Newport Mercury*, November 22, 1762; *Lloyd's Evening Post and British Chronicle* (London), December 29–31, 1762, 627; *Annual Register* (London), 1762, 117–18. See also *Lloyd's List* (London), December 31, 1762.

24. Rediker, *Devil and the Deep Blue Sea*, 261–63; Peter Linebaugh and Marcus Rediker, *The Many-Headed Hydra: Sailors, Slaves, Commoners, and the Hidden History of the Revolutionary Atlantic* (Boston: Beacon, 2000), 162; W. Jeffrey Bolster, *Black Jacks: African American Seamen in the Age of Sail* (Cambridge, MA: Harvard University Press, 1997), 15–16.

25. Charles de la Roncière, *Histoire de la marine française* (Paris: Plon, 1910), 4:82.

26. *Lloyd's List* (London), July 7, 1797.

27. *Providence Gazette*, August 2, 1800; *Newport Mercury*, August 5, 1800.

28. John Carter, Whydah, December 28, 1685, and January 9, 1686, in *Abstract of Letters Received by the Royal African Company of England From the Coast of Africa so far as relate to the Committee of Correspondence, No. 2, From March the 20th, 1682 to January the 6th, 1698*, PRO, T 70, 11:102–3; Henry Nurse et al., Cape Coast Castle, March 19, 1686, ibid., 11:22.

29. Rediker, *Devil and the Deep Blue Sea*, 102.

30. Mettas, *Répertoire*, 1:348.

31. Nicholas Halasz, *The Rattling Chains: Slave Unrest and Revolt in the Antebellum South* (New York: McKay, 1966), 8.

32. Clarkson, *Substance of the Evidence*, in Oldfield, *British Transatlantic Slave Trade*, 3:204, 221; Inikori, "Measuring the Unmeasured Hazards," 67.

33. Darold D. Wax, "A Philadelphia Surgeon on a Slaving Voyage to Africa, 1749–1751," *Pennsylvania Magazine of History and Biography* 92, no. 4 (October 1968): 485–86.

34. Bolster, *Black Jacks*, 72; Rediker, *Devil and the Deep Blue Sea*, 155–58, 200–201, 208–10, 217, 225; Falconbridge, *Account of the Slave Trade*, 39–44. Abolitionists seized upon the harsh treatment of sailors on slaving voyages as further evidence of the barbarity of the trade. This was a running theme throughout Thomas Clarkson's 1789 *The Substance of the Evidence of Sundry Persons on the Slave-Trade*. See the text of this report in Oldfield, *British Transatlantic Slave Trade*, 3:200, 205, 223, 240–41, 263, 270, 314–15, 317, 320.

35. Extract of letter dated James Fort, Gambia River, December 21, 1716, in *Abstract of Letters Received by the Royal African Company of England from the Coast of Africa, No. 2, From October the 20th, 1714 to December the 5th, 1719*, PRO, T 70, 6:43; David Francis, James Fort, December 21, 1716, in *Extracts of Letters Received by the Royal African Company of England so far as relate to the Committee of Shipping From October the 22d, 1705 to February the 3'd, 1719*, PRO, T 70, 26:54. See also Tattersfield, *Forgotten Trade*, 300.

36. Nicolas Brown & Co. to Captains [Abraham] Whipple, [George] Hopkins, and [Nicholas] Power, Providence, November 15, 1765, Brown Family Business Records, John Carter Brown Library, box 536, folder 9, "Vessels, sloop *Four Brothers* (May 22, 1765–May 3, 1766)"; Nicolas Brown to Abraham Whipple, Providence, December 3, 1765, ibid.; "Brige Saley Trade Book," August 28, September 19, October 14, 1765, ibid., box 643, folder 7, "Vessels, Brigantine *Sally*, Account Book 1764–66, Trade Book 1764–65"; undated, unsigned

manuscript, Moses Brown Papers, Rhode Island State Archives, Providence, series 2, folder 5, "Anti-Slavery"; *Newport Mercury,* November 18, 1765; *Boston Post-Boy and Advertiser,* November 25, 1765; *Massachusetts Gazette* (Boston), November 28, 1765. The newspapers seem to have gotten the information on slave mortality wrong, perhaps either transcribing 8 deaths as 80, or including those who died throughout the entire voyage as opposed to those who lost their lives during the revolt specifically. See also James B. Hedges, *The Browns of Providence Plantations: Colonial Years* (Cambridge, MA: Harvard University Press, 1952), vol. 1, *Colonial Years,* 79–80; Wax, "Browns of Providence," 177–78.

37. Hubert Deschamps, *Histoire de la traite des noirs de l'antiquité à nos jours* (Paris: Fayard, 1972), 128.

38. Peleg Clarke to John Fletcher, Christenborg Castle, Accra, December 1, 1776, Peleg Clarke Letters, 1774–1782, letter book 76, Newport Historical Society, Newport, RI; John Bell to John Fletcher, Cape Coast Road, December 15, 1776, ibid.; "The Danish Government of Coast of Guina To [illegible] Ship Thames," December 27, 1776, ibid.; Peleg Clarke to John Fletcher, Cape Coast, January 8, 1777, ibid.; "Coppy of the Minutes of the Protest Taken onboard 'Thames,'" ibid.; "A Coppy of Account, of ther Monthly Exspence of Ship 'Thames' and Damages sent the Deans Company at Accra," ibid. See also Donnan, *Documents,* 3:323–24, 325, 331.

39. See, for example, Genovese, *From Rebellion to Revolution,* 12, 14–16; Orlando Patterson, *The Sociology of Slavery: An Analysis of the Origins, Development, and Structure of Negro Slave Society in Jamaica* (London: MacGibbon and Kee, 1967), 274–75.

40. Patterson, *Sociology of Slavery,* 274.

41. Genovese, *From Rebellion to Revolution,* 15.

42. François de Paris, *Voyage to the Coast of Africa, Named Guinea, and to the Isles of America, Made in the Years 1682 and 1683,* trans. Aimery Caron (Madison: University of Wisconsin Press, 2001), 27.

43. Genovese, *From Rebellion to Revolution,* 11, 13. Alternative methods of resistance took many forms, including strikes and work stoppages, sabotage, feigned illness or pregnancy, lying, avoiding productivity, stealing with the hope of eventually buying one's freedom, self-mutilation and suicide, flight, infanticide, poisoning, and arson.

44. *Pennsylvania Gazette* (Philadelphia), December 9, 1772; *Virginia Gazette* (Williamsburg), December 24, 1772.

45. Mettas, *Répertoire,* 1:260, 2:608.

46. *Lloyd's List* (London), February 6, 1753; *Felix Farley's Bristol Journal* (England), February 3–10, 1753, March 24–31, 1753; *Maryland Gazette* (Annapolis), May 10, 1753.

47. See, for example, Genovese, *From Rebellion to Revolution,* 12, 18–19; Patterson, *Sociology of Slavery,* 275–76; Carl N. Degler, *Neither Black nor White: Slavery and Race Relations in Brazil and the United States* (Madison: University of Wisconsin Press, 1971), 53–58.

48. W. E. B. Du Bois, *The Suppression of the African Slave-Trade to the United States of America, 1638–1870* (1896; reprint, Baton Rouge: Louisiana State University Press, 1969), 6.

49. Patterson, *Sociology of Slavery,* 275; Joao Jose Reis, *Slave Rebellion in Brazil: The Muslim Uprising of 1835 in Bahia* (Baltimore: Johns Hopkins University Press, 1993), 69, 146–53; Degler, *Neither Black nor White,* 55–58; Genovese, *From Rebellion to Revolution,* 19.

50. Patterson, *Slavery and Social Death: A Comparative Study* (Cambridge, MA: Harvard University Press, 1982), 7, 13, 26, 36–46, 95–101, 337–39.

51. Antoine Edme Pruneau de Pommegorge, *Description de la Nigritie* (Amsterdam and Paris: Chez Maradan, 1789), 112–19; James F. Searing, *West African Slavery and Atlantic Commerce: The Senegal River Valley, 1700–1860* (Cambridge: Cambridge University Press, 1993), 147–48. See also Mettas, *Répertoire,* 2:295.

52. Searing, *West African Slavery*, 147–48. Searing mistakenly refers to the ship as the *Avrillon*, which was the captain's name. See Pruneau de Pommegorge, *Description de la Nigritie*, 113–19; Mettas, *Répertoire*, 2:295.

53. Carl Bernhard Wadström, *An Essay on Colonization, Particularly Applied to the Western Coast of Africa, With Some Free Thoughts on Cultivation and Commerce; Also Brief Descriptions of the Colonies Already Formed, or Attempted in Africa, Including Those of Sierra Leona and Bulama* (1794; reprint, New York: Kelley, 1968), 2:86–87.

54. John Kelly Thornton, "African Dimensions of the Stono Rebellion," *American Historical Review* 96, no. 4 (October 1991): 1109. See also Thornton, *Africa and Africans*, 293–97.

55. Stein, *French Slave Trade*, 105–6; Mettas, *Répertoire*, 1:205–6. See also Thomas, *Slave Trade*, 392.

56. *Boston News-Letter*, June 21, September 6, 1750; *Boston Post-Boy*, June 25, 1750; *Pennsylvania Gazette* (Philadelphia), July 5, 1750. See also *Lloyd's List* (London), July 13, 1750; *Maryland Gazette* (Annapolis), November 14, 1750.

57. Katia M. De Queiros Mattoso, *To Be a Slave in Brazil, 1550–1888* (New Brunswick, NJ: Rutgers University Press, 1986), 40; Reis, *Slave Rebellion in Brazil*, 61. Joseph Miller defines a ladino slave as one "acculturated to Portuguese, or Luso-African, colonial life; usually skilled and valuable" (*Way of Death*, 711).

58. *The Royal Gazette and Sierra Leone Advertiser* (Freetown), April 2, April 9, 1825; *Genius of Universal Emancipation and Baltimore Courier*, September 24, 1825; *Niles' Weekly Register* (Baltimore), October 1, 1825; His Majesty's Commissioners to Mr. Secretary Canning, Sierra Leone, April 10, 1825, in *Irish University Press Series of British Parliamentary Papers: Correspondence with British Commissioners and with Foreign Powers Relative to the Slave Trade*, vol. 10, Class A (Shannon, Ireland: Irish University Press, 1968), 9–10.

59. Ulrich Bonnell Phillips, *American Negro Slavery: A Survey of the Supply, Employment, and Control of Negro Labor as Determined by the Plantation Regime* (1918; reprint, Baton Rouge: Louisiana State University Press, 1966), 42–44; Piersen, "White Cannibals, Black Martyrs," 152; Darold D. Wax, "Preferences for Slaves in Colonial America," *Journal of Negro History* 58, no. 4 (October 1973): 391–99; Rawley, *Transatlantic Slave Trade*, 272–73; Harms, *The* Diligent, 160–61.

60. Monica Schuler, "Akan Slave Rebellions in the British Caribbean," in *Caribbean Slave Society and Economy: A Student Reader*, ed. Hilary Beckles and Verene Shepherd (Kingston, Jamaica: Randle, 1991), 374; Richard Hart, *Slaves Who Abolished Slavery*, vol. 2, *Blacks in Rebellion* (Kingston, Jamaica: Institute of Social and Economic Research, 1985), 8–10; Orlando Patterson, "Slavery and Slave Revolts: A Sociohistorical Analysis of the First Maroon War, 1665–1740," in *Maroon Societies: Rebel Slave Communities in the Americas*, 2nd ed., ed. Richard Price (Baltimore: Johns Hopkins University Press, 1993), 256; Linebaugh and Rediker, *Many-Headed Hydra*, 184–85.

61. Linebaugh and Rediker, *Many-Headed Hydra*, 184–85.

62. Governor Christopher Codrington, quoted in U. B. Phillips, *American Negro Slavery*, 43.

63. Dr. Collins, *Practical Rules for the Management of Negro Slaves, in the Sugar Colonies* (London: J. Barfield for Vernor and Hood, 1803), 39–40.

64. Quoted in Schuler, "Akan Slave Rebellions," 375. See also Bryan Edwards, *The History, Civil and Commercial, of the British Colonies in the West Indies* (Philadelphia: James Humphreys, 1806), 2:267–68.

65. Snelgrave, *New Account*, 168, 172–73.

66. Falconbridge, *Account of the Slave Trade*, 54.

67. Postma, *Dutch in the Atlantic Slave Trade*, 166, 168.

68. For the case of the *Thames,* see Peleg Clarke to John Fletcher, Christenborg Castle, Accra, December 1, 1776; John Bell to John Fletcher, Cape Coast Road, December 15, 1776; "The Danish Government of Coast of Guina To [illegible] Ship Thames," December 27, 1776; Peleg Clarke to John Fletcher, Cape Coast, January 8, 1777; "Coppy of the Minutes of the Protest Taken onboard 'Thames'"; "A Coppy of Account, of ther Monthly Exspence of Ship 'Thames' and Damages sent the Deans Company at Accra," all in Peleg Clarke Letters, 1774–1782, letter book 76, Newport Historical Society, Newport, RI. See also Donnan, *Documents,* 3:323–24, 325, 331. For the *Christiansborg,* see Paul Erdmann Isert, *Reise nach Guinea und den Caribäischen Inseln in Columbien* (Copenhagen, 1788), cited in Isidor Paiewonsky, *Eye-witness Accounts of Slavery in the Danish West Indies; also Graphic Tales of Other Slave Happenings on Ships and Plantations* (St. Thomas, Virgin Islands: Isidor Paiewonsky, 1987), 20–29; Thorkild Hansen, *Coast of Slaves,* trans. Kari Dako (Accra, Ghana: Sub-Saharan, 2002), 132–37.

69. Jean Barbot, *A Description of the Coasts of North and South Guinea,* in Donnan, *Documents,* 1:295.

70. Conneau, *Slaver's Log Book,* 210.

71. Ibid., 85.

72. Testimony of James Fraser, February 3, 1790, in *Minutes of the Evidence taken Before a committee of the House of Commons, Being a Select Committee, Appointed on the 29th Day of January 1790, for the Purpose of taking the Examination of such Witnesses as shall be produced on the Part of the several Petitioners who have petitioned the House of Commons against the Abolition of the Slave Trade,* PRO, ZHC 1, 85:49. See also Rawley, *Transatlantic Slave Trade,* 298. Another trader noted that it was the Ibibios or "Quaws" shipped from Bonny who were the ringleaders of insurrections. See David Richardson, "Shipboard Revolts," 80.

73. Harms, *The* Diligent, 160.

74. Epidariste Colin, "Notice Sur Mozambique," quoted in Edward A. Alpers, "Becoming 'Mozambique': Diaspora and Identity in Mauritius," paper presented at the Harriet Tubman Seminar, Department of History, York University, Toronto, November 15, 1999, 4.

75. These historians further find that even shore-based attacks by free Africans were substantially more likely in the Senegambia area than elsewhere. See David Richardson, "Shipboard Revolts," 76–77, 86, 89; Eltis, *Rise of African Slavery,* 171–72, 180–81 (Table 7.4); Behrendt, Eltis, and Richardson, "Costs of Coercion," 457.

76. Quoted in David Richardson, "Shipboard Revolts," 80. For further evidence of the rebellious reputation of Africans from Senegambia, see testimony of Thomas King, June 19, 1789, in *Minutes of the Evidence Taken Before a Committee of the House of Commons, Being a Committee of the Whole House, to Whom it Was Referred to Consider of the Circumstances of the Slave Trade, Complained of in the several Petitions which were Presented to the House in the last Session of Parliament, relative to the State of the African Slave Trade,* PRO, ZHC 1, 82:253–55.

77. Linebaugh and Rediker, *Many-Headed Hydra,* 128.

78. Alexander Cleeve, Gamboa, September 26, 1686, in *Abstract of Letters Received by the Royal African Company of England From the Coast of Africa so far as relate to the Committee of Correspondence, No. 2, From March the 20th, 1682 to January the 6th, 1698,* PRO, T 70, 11:60.

79. Tattersfield, *Forgotten Trade,* 283–84.

80. Declaration against Thomas Corker in *Copies of Affidavits, Informations & Certificates Rec'd by the Royal African Company of England from Abroad, From January 1698 to March the 25th, 1712,* PRO, T 70, vol. 1434; Declaration by William Norris, ibid.

81. For the June 1716 revolt on the *Selby* (or the *Sylvia*), the September 1716 revolt on the *Anne & Priscilla,* and the October 1716 revolt on the *Sophia,* see letter dated James Fort, Gambia River, December 21, 1716, in *Abstract of Letters Received by the Royal African Company of England from the Coast of Africa, No. 2, From October the 20th, 1714 to December the 5th, 1719,* PRO, T 70, 6:43–44; David Francis, Gambia River, James Fort, December 21, 1716, in *Extracts of Letters Received by the Royal African Company of England so far as relate to the Committee of Shipping From October the 22d, 1705 to February the 3'd, 1719,* PRO, T 70, 26:54; Tattersfield, *Forgotten Trade,* 292–93, 300, 349.

NOTES TO CHAPTER 3

1. Francis Moore refers to what is presumably the same instrument as a "balaseu." See Moore, *Travels into the Inland,* 110. Colin Palmer suggests *balaseu* may be a corruption of *bandore,* a stringed instrument of African origin that is the forerunner of the banjo. See Palmer, "The Slave Trade, African Slavers and the Demography of he Caribbean to 1750," in *General History of the Caribbean,* ed. Franklin W. Knight (London: UNESCO, 1997), 3:32.

2. Deposition of John Tozor, Captain of the *Postillion,* given at Gambia, June 10, 1704, in *Copies of Affidavits, Informations & Certificates Rec'd by the Royal African Company of England from Abroad, From January 1698 to March the 25th, 1712,* PRO, T 70, vol. 1434; letter dated James Island, Gambia River, June 10, 1704, in *Abstract of Letters received by the Royal African Company of England so far as relate to the Committee of Correspondence, No. 5, From May the 31st, 1704 to October the 3'd, 1706,* PRO, T 70, 14:66–67; letter dated Virginia, York River, September 25, 1704, ibid., 14:74.

3. Law and Lovejoy, *Biography of Mahommah Gardo Baquaqua,* 154–55.

4. Mouser, *Slaving Voyage,* 7.

5. Jean Barbot, *Description of the Coasts of North and South Guinea,* quoted in Uya, "Slave Revolts of the Middle Passage," 74; Munford, *Black Ordeal,* 2:280; Greene, "Mutiny," 347.

6. Newton, *Journal of a Slave Trader,* 50.

7. Ibid., 56.

8. Greene, "Mutiny," 348; Munford, *Black Ordeal,* 2:338–39.

9. C. L. R. James, *The Black Jacobins: Toussaint L'Ouverture and the San Domingo Revolution,* 2nd ed. (New York: Vintage Books, 1963), 9.

10. Thomas Phillips, *Abstract of a Voyage,* in Astley, *New General Collection of Voyages and Travels,* 2:407.

11. James, *Black Jacobins,* 9.

12. Svalesen, *Slave Ship* Fredensborg, 102–3.

13. Peleg Clarke to John Fletcher, Christenborg Castle, Accra, December 1, 1776; John Bell to John Fletcher, Cape Coast Road, December 15, 1776; "The Danish Government of Coast of Guina To [illegible] Ship Thames," December 27, 1776; Peleg Clarke to John Fletcher, Cape Coast, January 8, 1777; "Coppy of the Minutes of the Protest Taken onboard 'Thames'"; "A Coppy of Account, of ther Monthly Exspence of Ship 'Thames' and Damages sent the Deans Company at Accra," all in Peleg Clarke Letters, 1774–1782, letter book 76, Newport Historical Society, Newport, RI. See also Donnan, *Documents,* 3:323–24, 325, 331.

14. Svalesen, *Slave Ship* Fredensborg, 103; Harms, *The* Diligent, 310.

15. Mettas, *Répertoire,* 1:576–77; Stein, *French Slave Trade,* 104–5. In Stein's account of this revolt, the ship is referred to as the *Diamant.*

16. Miller, *Way of Death,* 411–12; Suzanne Schwarz, *Slave Captain: The Career of James Irving in the Liverpool Slave Trade* (Wrexham, Clwyd, Wales: Bridge Books, 1995), 16.

17. Mouser, *Slaving Voyage*, 63; Coughtry, *Notorious Triangle*, 72, 153; Svalesen, *Slave Ship* Fredensborg, 92, 106; Harms, *The* Diligent, 251; William Richardson, *A Mariner of England: An Account of the Career of William Richardson from Cabin Boy in the Merchant Service to Warrant Officer in the Royal Navy (1780–1819) as Told by Himself*, ed. Edmund Spencer Eardley Childers (London: Murray, 1908), 49; Falconbridge, *Account of the Slave Trade*, 6.

18. Falconbridge, *Account of the Slave Trade*, 6.

19. Newton, *Journal of a Slave Trader*, 22.

20. Clarkson, *Substance of the Evidence*, in Oldfield, *British Transatlantic Slave Trade*, 3:203–4.

21. Postma, *Dutch in the Atlantic Slave Trade*, 165; Miller, *Way of Death*, 409.

22. Snelgrave, *New Account*, 162–63.

23. Ibid., 172–73.

24. Svalesen, *Slave Ship* Fredensborg, 114.

25. Bolster, *Black Jacks*, 52.

26. Phillip Drake, *Revelations of a Slave Smuggler: Being the Autobiography of Captain Rich'd Drake, an African Trader for Fifty Years—from 1807 to 1857; During Which Period He Was Concerned in the Transportation of Half a Million Blacks from African Coasts to America* (1860; reprint, Northbrook, IL: Metro Books, 1972), 44–45.

27. "Abstract of most Material Occurrences in the District of Sierra-Leone from June 16 to Octo'r 25, and the Minutes Continued from thence to November 28, 1728," entries dated August 2 and 4, 1728, PRO, T 70, 1465:39, 40–41; *Weekly Journal; or, The British-Gazetteer* (London), January 25, 1729.

28. Miller, *Way of Death*, 410.

29. Clarkson, *Substance of the Evidence*, in Oldfield, *British Transatlantic Slave Trade*, 3:221–22, 224.

30. Mettas, *Répertoire*, 2:92–93; Joseph Brugevin, "Journal de traite du vaisseau LA LICORNE de Bordeaux," in *Traite des noirs et navires négriers au XVIIIᵉ siècle*, ed. Patrick Villiers (Grenoble, France: Editions des 4 Seigneurs, 1982), 152. For further information on Makua involvement in shipboard revolts, see Alpers, "Becoming 'Mozambique,'" 4.

31. Rediker, *Devil and the Deep Blue Sea*, 48. For another seventeenth-century observation on the ways in which language differences hindered slave rebelliousness, see Richard Ligon, *A True and Exact History of the Island of Barbadoes . . .* (1657; reprint, London: Cass, 1998), 46.

32. William Smith, *A New Voyage to Guinea: Describing the Customs, Manners, Soil, Climate, Habits, Buildings, Education, Manual Arts, Agriculture, Trade, Employments, Languages, Ranks of Distinction, Habitations, Diversions, Marriages, and Whatever Else is Memorable Among the Inhabitants* (1744; reprint, London: Cass, 1967), 28.

33. Snelgrave, *New Account*, 179.

34. Eltis, *Rise of African Slavery*, 229.

35. Svalesen, *Slave Ship* Fredensborg, 114.

36. Snelgrave, *New Account*, 187.

37. Ibid., 174–85; Peter H. Wood, *Black Majority: Negroes in Colonial South Carolina from 1670 through the Stono Rebellion* (New York: Norton, 1975), 180.

38. Uya, "Slave Revolts of the Middle Passage," 72; Uya, "Middle Passage and Personality Change," 93–94; Wood, *Black Majority*, 180; Sidney W. Mintz and Richard Price, *The Birth of African-American Culture: An Anthropological Perspective* (Boston: Beacon, 1992), 42–44.

39. Emilia Viotti da Costa, *Crowns of Glory, Tears of Blood: The Demerara Slave Rebellion of 1823* (New York: Oxford University Press, 1994), 193.

40. Michael A. Gomez, *Exchanging Our Country Marks: The Transformation of African Identities in the Colonial and Antebellum South* (Chapel Hill: University of North Carolina Press, 1991), 65. See also Eltis, *Rise of African Slavery,* 257.

41. McGowan, "African Resistance," 25–26.

42. José Luis Cortés Lopéz, *La esclavitud negra en la España peninsular del siglo XVI* (Salamanca, Spain: Ediciones Universidad de Salamanca, 1989), 174–75.

43. David Francis, James Fort, Gambia River, December 21, 1716, in *Extracts of Letters Received by the Royal African Company of England so far as relate to the Committee of Shipping From October the 22d, 1705 to February the 3'd, 1719,* PRO, T 70, 26:54.

44. Newton, *Journal of a Slave Trader,* 54–55, 56, 71, 77, 80.

45. Thomas Phillips, *A Journal of a Voyage Made in the* Hannibal *of London, Ann. 1693, 1694 . . . ,* quoted in Mannix and Cowley, *Black Cargoes,* 108.

46. Wadström, *Essay on Colonization,* 85–86.

47. Donnan, *Documents,* 1:462.

NOTES TO CHAPTER 4

1. *Virginia Gazette* (PD) (Williamsburg), May 24, 1770; *New-York Journal; or, the General Advertiser,* June 7, June 21, 1770.

2. Uya, "Slave Revolts of the Middle Passage," 77; Greene, "Mutiny," 347.

3. Cugoano, *Thoughts and Sentiments,* 15.

4. Newton, *Journal of a Slave Trader,* 71.

5. *Gentleman's Magazine* (London), October 1773, 523; *Virginia Gazette* (Williamsburg), December 23, 1773, January 6, 1774. For an account of a revolt on an unnamed vessel that is probably the same, see Searing, *West African Slavery,* 156. See also Inikori, "Measuring the Unmeasured Hazards," 69.

6. Svalesen, *Slave Ship* Fredensborg, 114.

7. William Richardson, *Mariner of England,* 63–4.

8. Atkins, *Voyage to Guinea,* 72–3.

9. *Weekly Journal; or, The British-Gazetteer* (London), July 5, 1729.

10. *Lloyd's List* (London), June 29, 1764.

11. *New York Gazette,* May 12, 1766; *Virginia Gazette* (Williamsburg), May 23, 1766.

12. *Felix Farley's Bristol Journal,* September 13, 1783; *Universal Daily Register* (London), July 1, 1785; Charles Durnford and Edward Hyde East, eds., *Term Reports in the Court of King's Bench* (London: J. Butterworth, 1794), 1:130–31; Merritt M. Robinson, *Reports of Cases Argued and Determined in the Supreme Court of Louisiana and in the Superior Court of the Territory of Louisiana,* annotated ed., vol. 9 (1845; reprint, St. Paul: West, 1911), 144, 155.

13. *Lloyd's List* (London), December 15, 1797; Richard Brooke, *Liverpool as It Was during the Last Quarter of the Eighteenth Century, 1775–1800* (London: J. R. Smith, 1853), 236–37; Williams, *Liverpool Privateers,* 592–93; Christopher Robinson, *Reports of Cases Argued and Determined in the High Court of Admiralty, Commencing with the Judgments of the Right Honourable Sir William Scott, Michaelmas Term, 1798,* 6 vols. (Philadelphia, 1799–1804), 1:322–23.

14. Conneau, *Slaver's Log Book,* 208. In 1845, Brantz Mayer first published Conneau's narrative, but changed many of the names and dates to protect the anonymity of its author. In Mayer's version, the revolt referred to here took place on a vessel known as *La Estrella.* See Mayer, ed., *Captain Canot: or, Twenty Years of an African Slaver* (1845; reprint, New York: Arno, 1968).

15. Peleg Clarke to John Fletcher, Christenborg Castle, Accra, December 1, 1776; John Bell to John Fletcher, Cape Coast Road, December 15, 1776; "The Danish Government of Coast of

Guina To [illegible] Ship Thames," December 27, 1776; Peleg Clarke to John Fletcher, Cape Coast, January 8, 1777; "Coppy of the Minutes of the Protest Taken onboard 'Thames'"; "A Coppy of Account, of ther Monthly Exspence of Ship 'Thames' and Damages sent the Deans Company at Accra," all in Peleg Clarke Letters, 1774–1782, letter book 76, Newport Historical Society, Newport, RI. See also Donnan, *Documents,* 3:323–24, 325, 331.

16. Miller, *Way of Death,* 409; Clarkson, *Substance of the Evidence,* in Oldfield, *British Transatlantic Slave Trade,* 3:248, 259.

17. Newton, *Journal of a Slave Trader,* 55.

18. *Boston News-Letter,* June 21, September 6, 1750; *Boston Post-Boy,* June 25, 1750; *Pennsylvania Gazette* (Philadelphia), July 5, 1750; *Lloyd's List* (London), July 13, 1750; *Maryland Gazette* (Annapolis), November 14, 1750.

19. *Lloyd's List* (London), February 6, 1753; *Felix Farley's Bristol Journal* (England), February 3–10, March 24–31, 1753; *Maryland Gazette* (Annapolis), May 10, 1753.

20. Munford, *Black Ordeal,* 2:339–40.

21. Svalesen, *Slave Ship* Fredensborg, 105.

22. Bosman, *New and Accurate Description,* 365–66.

23. Dow, *Slave Ships and Slaving,* 176.

24. Rediker, *Devil and the Deep Blue Sea,* 237.

25. Conneau, *Slaver's Log Book,* 84.

26. Stein, *French Slave Trade,* 104.

27. For the case of the *Robert,* see Atkins, *Voyage to Guinea,* 72; for the case of the *Elizabeth,* see Snelgrave, *New Account,* 179–80.

28. Clarkson, *Substance of the Evidence,* in Oldfield, *British Transatlantic Slave Trade,* 3:207–8.

29. Behrendt, Eltis, and Richardson have concluded that time of day was not a significant factor in shipboard revolts. See Behrendt, Eltis, and Richardson, "Costs of Coercion," 465; David Richardson, "Shipboard Revolts," 75.

30. Mannix and Cowley, *Black Cargoes,* 108.

31. Snelgrave, *New Account,* 189–90.

32. Dow, *Slave Ships and Slaving,* 271–72. See also Donnan, *Documents,* 3:400.

33. Mettas, *Répertoire,* 1:380–81, 382.

34. Stein, *French Slave Trade,* 104.

35. Munford, *Black Ordeal,* 2:340.

36. *Pennsylvania Gazette* (Philadelphia), September 30, 1756. See also Williams, *Liverpool Privateers,* 480.

37. Dow, *Slave Ships and Slaving,* 176.

38. William Richardson, *Mariner of England,* 59.

NOTES TO CHAPTER 5

1. *Lloyd's List* (London), December 15, 1797; Christopher Robinson, *High Court of Admiralty,* 1:322–23; Williams, *Liverpool Privateers,* 592–93; Brooke, *Liverpool as It Was,* 236–37.

2. Harms, *The* Diligent, 315. See also William Richardson, *Mariner of England,* 61.

3. Mannix and Cowley, *Black Cargoes,* 108.

4. Donnan, *Documents,* 3:374–75.

5. *Supplement to the Cornwall Chronicle* (Montego Bay, Jamaica), December 11, 1790. Thanks to Stephen D. Behrendt for bringing the account of this revolt to my attention.

6. Snelgrave, *New Account,* 167–68.

7. Moore, *Travels into the Inland,* 64–65; *London Evening-Post,* November 13–16, 1731; *Country Journal; or, The Craftsman* (London), November 20, December 18, 1731.

8. Mettas, *Répertoire*, 2:364–65.

9. *Boston Weekly News-Letter*, April 22–29, April 29–May 6, 1731; *New-York Gazette*, May 3–10, 1731; *Pennsylvania Gazette* (Philadelphia), May 6–13, 1731.

10. *Boston Weekly News-Letter*, April 12–19, 1733.

11. Joseph Debat, Edmund Tew, and Samuel Hurst, James Fort, December 20, 1762, PRO, T 70, 31:32. See also *Lloyd's List* (London), April 1, 1763.

12. *New York Gazette*, August 18, 1766; *New London Gazette*, August 22, 1766; *Massachusetts Gazette and Boston News-Letter*, August 28, 1766.

13. Paiewonsky, *Eyewitness Accounts*, 21–23; Philip Quaque to Dr. Daniel Burton, Cape Coast Castle, February 8, 1786, in Margaret Priestley, "Philip Quaque of Cape Coast," in *Africa Remembered: Narratives by West Africans from the Era of the Slave Trade*, ed. Philip D. Curtin (Madison: University of Wisconsin Press, 1967), 133; Postma, *Dutch in the Atlantic Slave Trade*, 166–67.

14. William Richardson, *Mariner of England*, 59.

15. *Memorandum Book Kept at Cape Coast Castle from January the 13th 1703 to January the 2nd 1704*, entry dated November 28, 1703, PRO, T 70, 1463:66.

16. Joseph Debat, Edmund Tew, and Thomas Radcliff, James Fort, December 28, 1761, PRO, T 70, 30:436; *Lloyd's Evening Post and British Chronicle* (London), January 4–6, 1762; *Lloyd's List* (London), January 5, 1762; Melinda Elder, *The Slave Trade and the Economic Development of Eighteenth-Century Lancaster* (Krumlin, Halifax, England: Ryburn, 1992), 53, 55, 175. For additional information on this revolt, see "The widows of sailors killed during the revolt on the Lancaster ship *Mary* (1762) receive alms from the Lancaster Parish, 1762," Merseyside Maritime Museum, Liverpool.

17. Svalesen, *Slave Ship* Fredensborg, 223.

18. Hall, *Africans in Colonial Louisiana*, 91.

19. *Boston News-Letter*, June 21, 1750, September 6, 1750; *Boston Post-Boy*, June 25, 1750; *Pennsylvania Gazette* (Philadelphia), July 5, 1750; *Lloyd's List* (London), July 13, 1750; *Maryland Gazette* (Annapolis), November 14, 1750.

20. Munford, *Black Ordeal*, 2:342.

21. Johannes Rask, *En Kort og Sandferdig Rejse-Beskrivelse til og fra Guinea* (Trondheim, Norway: Jens Christensen Winding, 1754), 75–76.

22. Lt. Dom Jeulin, journal entry quoted in Stein, *French Slave Trade*, 105–6; Mettas, *Répertoire*, 1:205–6.

23. Clarkson, *Substance of the Evidence*, in Oldfield, *British Transatlantic Slave Trade*, 3:208.

24. Harms, *The* Diligent, 272.

25. Atkins, *Voyage to Guinea*, 71–73.

26. Dow, *Slave Ships and Slaving*, 176–77.

27. Mettas, *Répertoire*, 2:199–200.

28. William Page, testimony before the U.S. consul in Rio de Janeiro, February 13, 1843, PRO, FO 84, 563:172–89; *Senate Executive Documents* 28, 30th Cong., 1st sess. (1847), 4:71–77; *House Executive Documents* 61, 30th Cong., 2nd sess. (1849), 148, 220–21; *Irish University Press Series of British Parliamentary Papers*, vol. 29, Class A (1846 session), 513–23. See also Conrad, *Children of God's Fire*, 39–42; Lawrence F. Hill, *Diplomatic Relations between the United States and Brazil* (Durham, NC: Duke University Press, 1932), 134.

29. Bolster, *Black Jacks*, 96.

30. Linebaugh and Rediker, *Many-Headed Hydra*, 49–51.

31. Frank McLynn, *Crime and Punishment in Eighteenth-Century England* (London: Routledge, 1989), xi, 272–74, 280–82; Peter Linebaugh, *The London Hanged: Crime and Civil*

Society in the Eighteenth Century (London: Penguin, 1991), 52–54; J. M. Beattie, *Policing and Punishment in London, 1660–1750: Urban Crime and the Limits of Terror* (Oxford: Oxford University Press, 2001), 304–6.

32. Louis Garneray, *Le négrier de Zanzibar: Voyages, aventures et combats* (Paris: Phébus, 1985), 155–69.

33. Clarkson, *Substance of the Evidence*, in Oldfield, *British Transatlantic Slave Trade,* 3:320.

34. If the number of slave deaths in cases in which an approximate range is given is assumed to be the median of that range, the total for the 170 cases in which a numerical value is given would be 5,501. There are an additional 28 cases where "several," "a number," "many," or "some" slaves died. If we arbitrarily apply a conservative estimate of 5 slaves per incident for each of these revolts, it adds another 140 deaths. In another 3 cases, "all" of the slaves are noted as having died. If we estimate this to be 200 per ship, then this adds another 600, bringing the grand total to 6,241 deaths in 201 cases, or 31 slaves per incident. However, if we assume no slaves died in the remaining 292 slave revolts for which no death toll is known or can be fairly estimated, the number of slaves dying per revolt falls to fewer than 13.

35. Snelgrave, *New Account,* 181–82.

36. Hugh Crow, *Memoirs of the Late Captain Hugh Crow, of Liverpool* (1830; reprint, London: Cass, 1970), 99.

37. Adam Jones, "Brandenburg-Prussia and the Atlantic Slave Trade, 1680–1700" in *De la traite à l'esclavage: actes du Colloque international sur la traite des noirs, Nantes, 1985,* ed. Serge Daget (Nantes: Centre de recherche sur l'histoire du monde atlantique, 1985), 1:289–90. See also Adam Jones, *Brandenburg Sources for West African History, 1680–1700* (Stuttgart: Steiner-Verlag-Wiesbaden, 1985), 180–97.

38. *Felix Farley's Bristol Journal* (Bristol, England), September 13, 1783; *Universal Daily Register* (London), July 1, 1785; Durnford and East, *Term Reports,* 1:130–31; Merritt M. Robinson, *Supreme Court of Louisiana,* 9:144, 155.

39. For the two English vessels, see Clarkson, *Substance of the Evidence,* in Oldfield, *British Transatlantic Slave Trade,* 3:214–16, 314. For the *Vigilantie,* see Postma, *Dutch in the Atlantic Slave Trade,* 166.

NOTES TO CHAPTER 6

1. *Lloyd's List* (London), February 6, 1753; *Felix Farley's Bristol Journal* (England), February 3–10, March 24–31, 1753; *Maryland Gazette* (Annapolis), May 10, 1753.

2. John L. Vogt, "The Early Sao Tome-Principe Slave Trade with Mina, 1500–1540," *International Journal of African Historical Studies* 6, no. 3 (1973), 461. See also Vogt, *Portuguese Rule on the Gold Coast, 1469–1682* (Athens: University of Georgia Press, 1979), 58.

3. For the *Clare,* see *Weekly Journal; or, The British-Gazetteer* (London), August 2, September 6, 1729, and February 28, June 20, 1730; *Fog's Weekly Journal* (London), August 2, September 6, 1729, and February 28, June 20, 1730; *Boston Weekly News-Letter,* September 18–25, 1729; *Pennsylvania Gazette* (Philadelphia), October 9–16, 1729, and January 6–13, 1730. For the *Princess Carolina,* see *Boston Weekly News-Letter,* November 15–22, 1739.

4. Tobias Lisle and William Harvey, James Fort, February 14, 1757, PRO, T 70, 30:179–80; Tobias Lisle, James Fort, Gambia, February 14, 1757, in *Extract of Letters, No. 1: 1751–1757,* PRO, T 70, vol. 1694.

5. For the *Marlborough,* see *Lloyd's List* (London), February 6, 1753; *Felix Farley's Bristol Journal* (England), February 3–10, March 24–31, 1753; *Maryland Gazette* (Annapolis), May 10, 1753. For the *Delight,* see *Virginia Gazette* (PD) (Williamsburg), May 24, 1770; *New-York Journal; or, The General Advertiser,* June 7, June 21, 1770.

6. *Providence Gazette,* August 2, 1800; *Newport Mercury,* August 5, 1800.

7. Mettas, *Répertoire,* 1:516–17, 519, 2:797.

8. Mouser, *Slaving Voyage,* 99.

9. *Newport Mercury,* May 21, 1764; *Pennsylvania Gazette* (Philadelphia), May 31, 1764.

10. Mettas, *Répertoire,* 2:309.

11. *Virginia Gazette* (PD) (Williamsburg), May 24, 1770; *New-York Journal; or, The General Advertiser,* June 7, June 21, 1770.

12. Mettas, *Répertoire,* 1:603–4. See also Stein, *French Slave Trade,* 88.

13. Wadström, *Essay on Colonization,* 2:87.

14. *Lloyd's List* (London), December 15, 1797; Brooke, *Liverpool as It Was,* 236–37; Williams, *Liverpool Privateers,* 592–93; Christopher Robinson, *High Court of Admiralty,* 1:322–23.

15. Mettas, *Répertoire,* 2:319.

16. Bolster, *Black Jacks,* 47–51. As early as the late seventeenth century, an agent for the French Compagnie du Senegal reported seeing African vessels that could carry as many as one hundred men. See Paris, *Voyage to the Coast of Africa,* 31.

17. Atkins, *Voyage to Guinea,* 175.

18. *Virginia Gazette* (Williamsburg), April 18, 1771.

19. *Loudon's New-York Packet,* February 14, 1785; *Providence Gazette and Country Journal,* January 29, 1785.

20. Thomas Bee, *Reports of Cases Adjudged in the District Court of South Carolina* (Philadelphia: William P. Farrand, 1810), 260–62; *The Federal Cases: Comprising Cases Argued and Determined in the Circuit and District Courts of the United States . . .* (St. Paul: West, 1895), 9:275–76.

21. *South-Carolina Gazette* (Charleston), October 24, 1743; *Boston Gazette,* December 20, 1743; *Boston News-Letter,* December 22, 1743.

22. *Newport Mercury,* May 21, 1764; *Pennsylvania Gazette* (Philadelphia), May 31, 1764.

23. Wadström, *Essay on Colonization,* 2:86.

24. *London Times,* June 18, 1858; *New York Times,* June 21, 1858; *Class A Correspondence with the British Commissioners at Sierra Leone, Havana, the Cape of Good Hope, and Loanda; and Reports from British Naval Officers, Relating to the Slave Trade from April 1, 1858, to March 31, 1859* (1859), 225, 245. See also Eltis, *Rise of African Slavery,* 232.

25. Bolster, *Black Jacks,* 80; Rediker, *Devil and the Deep Blue Sea,* 82, 95.

26. Clarkson, *Substance of the Evidence,* in Oldfield, *British Transatlantic Slave Trade,* 3:223.

27. Messrs. Brathwaite, Cruikshank, and Peake, Cape Coast Castle, May 28, 1730, in *Abstract of Letters Received by the Royal African Company of England from the Coast of Africa, No. 3, From January the 12th, 1719 to August the 26th, 1732,* PRO, T 70, 7:164–65; *London Evening-Post,* January 19–21, 1731; *Read's Weekly Journal; or, British-Gazetteer* (London), January 23, 1731. See also *Pennsylvania Gazette,* November 19–26, December 22–29, 1730.

28. *Pennsylvania Gazette* (Philadelphia), June 25, 1772; *Virginia Gazette* (PD) (Williamsburg), July 16, 1772, August 27, 1772. The last account states that the slaves "murdered all the Crew except one little Boy, who begged hard of the Savages for his Life, which they granted him."

29. *Newport Mercury,* May 21, 1764; *Pennsylvania Gazette* (Philadelphia), May 31, 1764.

30. *Pennsylvania Gazette* (Philadelphia), December 9, 1772; *Virginia Gazette* (Williamsburg), December 24, 1772.

31. *Virginia Gazette* (DH) (Williamsburg), January 7, 1775.

32. Munford, *Black Ordeal,* 1:187–88, 2:286–87, 343.

33. Munford, *Black Ordeal,* 2:344.

34. Mettas, *Répertoire,* 1:395–96.

35. Wadström, *Essay on Colonization,* 2:87.

36. Mettas, *Répertoire*, 2:686.

37. *Virginia Gazette* (DH) (Williamsburg), July 1, 1775.

38. David Francis, Gambia River, James Fort, December 21, 1716, in *Extracts of Letters Received by the Royal African Company of England so far as relate to the Committee of Shipping, From October the 22d 1705 to February the 3d 1719*, PRO T 70, 26:53. In another instance of this term being used for crew mutiny, readers were told, "The *William*, late West-cot, from Africa was cut off by the White People, who cut the Captain's Throat and carried the Vessel to St. Jago." *Lloyd's List* (London), April 3, 1767.

39. *Lloyd's List* (London), August 9, 1748.

40. *Lloyd's List* (London), June 21, 1751.

41. *New-York Gazette*, June 15, 1761; *Boston News-Letter*, June 25, 1761. Interestingly, the Boston paper printed an update a month later noting that the ship was not actually "cut off" by the slaves but the captain was able to save his vessel. See *Boston News-Letter*, August 20, 1761.

42. *Lloyd's List* (London), September 13, 1793. See also Durnford and East, *Term Reports*, 7:186–95.

43. *Country Journal; or, The Craftsman* (London), March 24, 1733; *South-Carolina Gazette* (Charleston), July 7–14, 1733.

44. *Lloyd's List* (London), January 14, 1763.

45. *Boston News-Letter*, February 4, 1762. This account has been considered by another historian to in fact be a case of shipboard revolt. See James G. Lydon, "New York and the Slave Trade, 1700–1774," *William and Mary Quarterly* 35, no. 2 (April 1978): 380.

46. *Virginia Gazette* (Williamsburg), April 7, 1774.

47. *Lloyd's Subscription Book*, MS 14931/2 (1775), Guildhall Library, London.

48. *Pennsylvania Gazette* (Philadelphia), September 22, 1768.

49. *Virginia Gazette* (WR) (Williamsburg), June 23, 1768.

50. *Pennsylvania Gazette* (Philadelphia), November 16, 1774.

51. Moore, *Travels into the Inland*, 64–65; *London Evening-Post*, November 13–16, 1731; *Country Journal; or, The Craftsman* (London), November 20, December 18, 1731.

52. *Lloyd's List* (London), June 21, 1765; *Felix Farley's Bristol Journal* (Bristol, England), June 22, 1765, emphasis added.

53. *Pennsylvania Gazette* (Philadelphia), August 9, 1750; *Boston Post-Boy*, August 13, 1750; *Maryland Gazette* (Annapolis), September 5, 1750; *Lloyd's List* (London), August 28, 1750.

54. *Fog's Weekly Journal* (London), August 2 (emphasis added), September 6, 1729; *Weekly Journal; or, The British-Gazetteer* (London), September 6, 1729; *Pennsylvania Gazette* (Philadelphia), January 6–13, 1730 (emphasis added).

55. Messrs. Brathwaite, Cruikshank, and Peake, Cape Coast Castle, May 28, 1730, in *Abstract of Letters Received by the Royal African Company of England from the Coast of Africa, No. 3, From January the 12th, 1719 to August the 26th, 1732*, PRO, T 70, 7:164–65; *Pennsylvania Gazette*, November 19–26, December 22–29, 1730; *London Evening-Post*, January 19–21, 1731; *Read's Weekly Journal; or, British-Gazetteer* (London), January 23, 1731.

56. *Boston Weekly News-Letter*, May 7, 1747; *Pennsylvania Gazette*, May 21, 1747. For an account possibly relating to this rebellion, see also *Pennsylvania Gazette*, July 30, 1747.

57. William Richardson, *Mariner of England*, 57–59.

NOTES TO CHAPTER 7

1. Amasa Delano, *A Narrative of Voyages and Travels, in the Northern and Southern Hemispheres: Comprising Three Voyages Round the World; Together with a Voyage of Survey and Discovery, in the Pacific Ocean and Oriental Islands* (Boston: E. G. House, 1817). See also Jorge Pinto Rodríguez, "Una rebelion de negros en las costas del Pacifico sur: El caso de la

Fragata Trial en 1814," *Historica* (Peru) 10, no. 1 (July 1986): 139–55. Apparently mistakenly, one author refers to this insurrection as occurring on a vessel named *La Prueba*. See Leslie B. Rout Jr., *The African Experience in Spanish America: 1502 to the Present Day* (Cambridge and New York: Cambridge University Press, 1976), 120.

2. Herman Melville's "Benito Cereno" was first published in *Putnam's Monthly Magazine* (New York) in three installments, from October to December 1855. First discovered as the source for Melville's story in 1928, the relevant portion of Delano's narrative was published with commentary by Harold C. Scudder in "Melville's 'Benito Cereno' and Captain Delano's Voyages," *Publications of the Modern Language Association of America* 43, no. 2 (June 1928): 502–32. For criticism of Melville's story, see Joshua Leslie and Sterling Stuckey, "The Death of Benito Cereno: A Reading of Herman Melville on Slavery," *Journal of Negro History* 67, no. 4 (Winter 1982): 287–301; Robert E. Burkholder, ed., *Critical Essays on Herman Melville's "Benito Cereno"* (New York: Hall, 1992); Seymour L. Gross, ed., *A "Benito Cereno" Handbook* (Belmont, CA: Wadsworth, 1965).

3. In Melville's account of the revolt, the *Tryal*'s name was changed to the *San Dominick*.

4. In Melville's account of the revolt, Mure, the leader of the revolt, was given the name Babo.

5. In Melville's account of the revolt, the *Perseverance*'s name was changed to the *Bachelor's Delight*.

6. Delano, *Narrative of Voyages and Travels,* 323–24.

7. Ibid., 324; "Declaration of Benito Cereno," in ibid., 338.

8. Delano, *Narrative of Voyages and Travels,* 328.

9. Atkins, *Voyage to Guinea,* 71–73.

10. Postma, *Dutch and the Atlantic Slave Trade,* 168.

11. Judge Don Juan Martinez de Rozas, sentence of the court, Concepcion, Chile, March 2, 1805, in Delano, *Narrative of Voyages and Travels,* 347–48.

12. Michael Tadman, *Speculators and Slaves: Masters, Traders, and Slaves in the Old South* (Madison: University of Wisconsin Press, 1996), 81; Herman Freudenberger and Jonathan B. Pritchett, "The Domestic United States Slave Trade: New Evidence," *Journal of Interdisciplinary History* 21, no. 3 (Winter 1991): 470. See also Robert H. Gudmestad, *A Troublesome Commerce: The Transformation of the Interstate Slave Trade* (Baton Rouge: Louisiana State University Press, 2003), 27; Walter Johnson, *Soul by Soul: Life inside the Antebellum Slave Market* (Cambridge, MA: Harvard University Press, 1999), 50, 61.

13. Solomon Northup, *Twelve Years a Slave,* ed. Sue Eakin and Joseph Logsdon (1853; reprint, Baton Rouge: Louisiana State University Press, 1968), 42–46.

14. Gudmestad, *Troublesome Commerce,* 25; Ralph Clayton, *Cash for Blood: The Baltimore to New Orleans Domestic Slave Trade* (Bowie, MD: Heritage Books, 2002), 60–61.

15. *New-York Evening Post,* May 26, 1826; *Genius of Universal Emancipation* (Baltimore), January 2, 1827; Clayton, *Cash for Blood,* 71–72; *Christian Inquirer* (New York), December 23, 1826, 394. Woolfolk was a pioneer of sorts in that he built his own slave pen behind his Baltimore residence rather than paying others to imprison slaves for him. See William Calderhead, "The Role of the Professional Slave Trader in a Slave Economy: Austin Woolfolk, A Case Study" *Civil War History* 23, no. 3 (September 1977): 199.

16. *New-York Evening Post,* May 18, May 20, May 23, 1826; *Niles' Weekly Register* (Baltimore), May 20, 1826.

17. *New-York Evening Post,* May 18, May 20, May 23, 1826; *Niles' Weekly Register* (Baltimore), May 20, 1826; *National Gazette and Literary Register* (Philadelphia), May 20, May 23, 1826; *Christian Inquirer* (New York), December 23, 1826, 394–95; *Genius of Universal Emancipation* (Baltimore), January 2, 1827; Clayton, *Cash for Blood,* 71–73.

18. Clayton, *Cash for Blood*, 73; *Christian Inquirer* (New York), December 23, 1826, 395–96.

19. Woolfolk and his family are said to have transported well over two thousand slaves to Louisiana between 1819 and 1832. See Calderhead, "Role of the Professional Slave Trader," 195, 200–201; Gudmestad, *A Troublesome Commerce*, 26, 153–54, 163–64; Clayton, *Cash for Blood*, 66.

20. *Christian Inquirer*, December 23, 1826, 396; *Genius of Universal Emancipation* (Baltimore), January 2, 1827.

21. *Genius of Universal Emancipation* (Baltimore), January 8, January 20, 1827; Merton L. Dillon, *Benjamin Lundy and the Struggle for Negro Freedom* (Urbana: University of Illinois Press, 1966), 118–24.

22. *Genius of Universal Emancipation* (Baltimore), February 24, March 31, 1827; Clayton, *Cash for Blood*, 74.

23. *New York Evening Post*, December 29, 1829; *Genius of Universal Emancipation* (Baltimore), January 1, 1830, 131; *Richmond Enquirer*, January 5, January 28, 1830; *Niles' Weekly Register* (Baltimore), January 9, 1830.

24. *New York Journal of Commerce*, August 31, September 2, 1839; Lewis Tappan, letter extracted in *New York Journal of Commerce*, September 12, 1839, and *The Sun* (New York), September 12, 1839; John W. Barber, *A History of the Amistad Captives* (New Haven, CT: E. L. and J. W. Barber, 1840), 4, 18–20. See also Joseph Sturge, *A Visit to the United States in 1841* (Boston: Dexter S. King, 1842), xlvi; Howard Jones, *Mutiny on the Amistad: The Saga of a Slave Revolt and Its Impact on American Abolition, Law, and Diplomacy* (New York: Oxford University Press, 1987), 14–23; Christopher Martin, *The Amistad Affair* (New York: Abelard-Schuman, 1970), 37; Arthur Abraham, "Sengbe Pieh: A Neglected Hero?" *Journal of the Historical Society of Sierra Leone* 11, no. 2 (1978): 22–30.

25. *The Liberator* (Boston), September 6, 1839; Lewis Tappan, letter dated New Haven, September 9, 1839, printed in *New York Journal of Commerce*, September 10, 1839, and reprinted in *The Sun* (New York), September 12, 1839, and *New York Advertiser and Express*, September 14, 1839; *New York Advertiser and Express*, October 5, 1839; *New-York Commercial Advertiser*, June 10, 1840. See also Howard Jones, *Mutiny on the Amistad*, 5, 23–24, 85, 124.

26. *The Sun* (New York), August 31, 1839; *New York Journal of Commerce*, August 31, September 2, 1839; *The Liberator* (Boston), September 6, 1839; *New York Advertiser and Express*, October 5, 1839; Barber, *History of the Amistad Captives*, 6–8; Sturge, *Visit to the United States*, xlvii–xlviii. See also Howard Jones, *Mutiny on the Amistad*, 24–26.

27. *New York Journal of Commerce* August 30, August 31, September 2, 1839; *The Sun* (New York), August 31, 1839; *The Liberator* (Boston), September 6, 1839; *New York Advertiser and Express*, October 5, 1839; Barber, *History of the Amistad Captives*, 3. See also Howard Jones, *Mutiny on the Amistad*, 26–28.

28. *New York Journal of Commerce*, August 30, 1839, September 21, September 23, September 24, 1839; *The Sun* (New York), August 31, 1839; *New York Advertiser and Express*, August 31, September 14, September 21, 1839; *New-York Commercial Advertiser*, September 2, 1839; *The Liberator* (Boston), September 6, 1839; Barber, *History of the Amistad Captives*, 4–6; Sturge, *Visit to the United States*, xxxiii–xxxv. See also Howard Jones, *Mutiny on the Amistad*, 3–4, 6–7, 28–30.

29. Joshua Leavitt, letter printed in *New-York Commercial Advertiser*, September 6, 1839, reprinted in the *New York Advertiser and Express*, September 7, 1839.

30. Fred J. Cook, "The Slave Ship Rebellion," *American Heritage* 8, no. 2 (February 1957): 104.

31. William Jay, letter dated Bedford, September 7, 1839, printed in *The Liberator* (Boston), September 20, 1839. See also *New York Journal of Commerce*, September 4, 1839.

32. *New-York Commercial Advertiser*, August 26, 1839.

33. *The Liberator* (Boston), September 13, 1839; *New-York Commercial Advertiser*, January 10, 1840; *Niles' National Register* (Baltimore), December 4, 1841; *National Anti-*

Slavery Standard (New York), December 9, 1841, 105–6; Barber, *History of the Amistad Captives*, 20–24; Cook, "Slave Ship Rebellion," 104–6; R. Earl McClendon, "The Amistad Claims: Inconsistencies of Policy," *Political Science Quarterly* 48, no. 3 (September 1933): 388–89; Howard Jones, *Mutiny on the Amistad*, 205. For Adams's argument, see John Quincy Adams, *Argument in the Case of United States vs. Cinque* (1841; reprint, New York: Arno, 1969).

34. Abraham, "Sengbe Pieh," 26–27; Howard Jones, *Mutiny on the Amistad*, 205.

35. Tadman, *Speculators and Slaves*, 80; Freudenberger and Pritchett, "Domestic United States Slave Trade," 470.

36. Merritt M. Robinson, *Supreme Court of Louisiana*, 9:111–14, 164–65; Edward D. Jervey and C. Harold Huber, "The *Creole* Affair," *Journal of Negro History* 65, no. 3 (1980): 196–98; Howard Jones, "The Peculiar Institution and National Honor: The Case of the *Creole* Slave Revolt," *Civil War History* 21, no. 1 (March 1975): 28–29; Maggie Montesinos Sale, *The Slumbering Volcano: American Slave Ship Revolts and the Production of Rebellious Masculinity* (Durham, NC: Duke University Press, 1997), 122–25.

37. Merritt M. Robinson, *Supreme Court of Louisiana*, 9:114–15, 119–20, 164–65; Jervey and Huber, "*Creole* Affair," 198–201; Howard Jones, "Peculiar Institution," 30–31.

38. Merritt M. Robinson, *Supreme Court of Louisiana*, 9:115–84; Jervey and Huber, "*Creole* Affair," 201–8; Howard Jones, "Peculiar Institution," 31–50. See also Helen Catterall, ed., *Judicial Cases Concerning American Slavery and the Negro* (Washington, DC: Carnegie Institution of Washington, 1926–1936), 3:565–69, 4:207; Wilbur Devereux Jones, "The Influence of Slavery on the Webster-Ashburton Negotiations," *Journal of Southern History* 22, no. 1 (February 1956): 48–58.

39. Howard Jones, "Peculiar Institution," 47; "The *Creole* Case," *Southern Quarterly Review* 2 (1842): 55–72.

40. Henry Highland Garnet, *An Address to the Slaves of the United States of America* (1848), reprinted in Sterling Stuckey, *The Ideological Origins of Black Nationalism* (Boston: Beacon, 1972), 172; Frederick Douglass, *The Narrative and Selected Writings*, ed. Michael Meyer (New York: Random, 1984), 299–348. See also Sale, *Slumbering Volcano*, 173–97.

41. William Wells Brown, *The Negro in the American Rebellion: His Heroism and His Fidelity . . .* (Boston: Lee and Shepard, 1867), 28–31; William Wells Brown, *The Black Man; His Antecedents, His Genius, and His Achievements* (New York: T. Hamilton, 1863), 75–85. See also George Hendrick and Willene Hendrick, *The* Creole *Mutiny: A Tale of Revolt aboard a Slave Ship* (Chicago: Dee, 2003), 38–57.

42. Steven Deyle, "The Irony of Liberty: Origins of the Domestic Slave Trade," *Journal of the Early Republic* 12, no. 1 (Spring 1992): 61; Tadman, *Speculators and Slaves*, 17; Frederic Bancroft, *Slave Trading in the Old South* (1931; reprint, New York: Unger, 1959), 19: Johnson, *Soul by Soul*, 5.

43. Johnson, *Soul by Soul*, 72, 76.

44. Gudmestad, *Troublesome Commerce*, 24; Johnson, *Soul by Soul*, 61.

45. *Western Luminary* (Lexington, KY), October 4, 1826. See also *Genius of Universal Emancipation* (Baltimore), October 21, 1826.

46. *Kentucky Reporter* (Lexington), September 25, October 2, 1826; *Western Luminary* (Lexington, KY), September 27, October 4, October 11, 1826; *Niles' Weekly Register* (Baltimore), October 14, 1826; *Genius of Universal Emancipation* (Baltimore), October 14, 1826; *Connecticut Courant* (Hartford), October 16, 1826.

47. *Western Luminary* (Lexington, KY), October 11, 1826.

48. *Kentucky Reporter* (Lexington), September 25, October 2, October 9, 1826; *Western Luminary* (Lexington, KY), October 4, October 11, 1826; *Niles' Weekly Register* (Baltimore), October 14, 1826; *Genius of Universal Emancipation* (Baltimore), October 14, 1826.

49. *Western Luminary* (Lexington, KY), November 1, 1826; *Niles' Weekly Register* (Baltimore), November 18, 1826. See also *Genius of Universal Emancipation* (Baltimore), December 16, 1826. For the court records of this case, see Breckinridge County Archives, Breckinridge County, KY, Circuit Court, book 7, entries dated October 17 (pp. 182–83), October 18 (p. 194), October 19 (pp. 207–8), and October 21 (p. 219), 1826.

50. *Niles' Weekly Register* (Baltimore), December 26, 1829; *Richmond Enquirer,* January 28, 1830.

NOTES TO CONCLUSION

1. Claude McKay, "If We Must Die," in *Black Writers of America: A Comprehensive Anthology,* ed. Richard Barksdale and Keneth Kinnamon (New York: Macmillan, 1972), 493–94.

2. Munford, *Black Ordeal,* 2:338; David Richardson, "Shipboard Revolts," 74.

3. David Richardson, "The Costs of Survival: The Treatment of Slaves in the Middle Passage and the Profitability of the Eighteenth-Century British Slave Trade," in Daget, *De la traite à l'esclavage,* 2:170–73, 176.

4. Eltis, *Rise of African Slavery,* 192.

5. Harms, *The* Diligent, 84; Behrendt, Eltis, and Richardson, "Costs of Coercion," 467–68; Coughtry, *Notorious Triangle,* 99; Frank Worsley and Glyn Griffith, *The Romance of Lloyd's: From Coffee-House to Palace* (New York: Hillman-Curl, 1937), 47. See also A. H. John, "The London Assurance Company and the Marine Insurance Market of the Eighteenth Century," *Economica* 25, no. 98 (May 1958): 139.

6. Merritt M. Robinson, *Supreme Court of Louisiana,* 9:144, 155; Durnford and East, *Term Reports,* 1:130–31; *Universal Daily Register* (London), July 1, 1785. See also Catterall, *Judicial Cases,* 1:19–20.

7. Munford, *Black Ordeal,* 2:338.

8. David Richardson, "Shipboard Revolts," 89; Behrendt, Eltis, and Richardson, "Costs of Coercion," 473, 475; Eltis, *Rise of African Slavery,* 160.

9. David Brion Davis, *The Problem of Slavery in the Age of Revolution* (1975, reprint, New York: Oxford University Press, 1999), 41–49, 82–83, 163–64, 255–63, 455; David Brion Davis, *Slavery and Human Progress* (New York: Oxford University Press, 1984), xvi–xviii, 13–15, 77–80, 108–16, 280–82.

10. Linebaugh and Rediker, *Many-Headed Hydra,* 227; David L. Crosby, "Anthony Benezet's Transformation of Anti-Slavery Rhetoric," *Slavery and Abolition* 23, no. 3 (December 2002): 55. For the revolt on the *Expedition,* see Anthony Benezet, *Some Historical Account of Guinea, its Situation, Produce, and the General Disposition of its Inhabitants, with an Inquiry into the Rise and Progress of the Slave Trade, its Nature, and Lamentable Effects* (London: J. Phillips, 1788), 126–28.

11. Christopher Fyfe, ed., *Anna Maria Falconbridge: Narrative of two Voyages to the River Sierra Leone During the Years 1791–1792–1793, and the Journal of Isaac Dubois, with Alexander Falconbridge: An Account of the Slave Trade on the Coast of Africa* (Liverpool: Liverpool University Press, 2000), 193–94.

12. Falconbridge, *Account of the Slave Trade,* 30.

13. Newton, *Thoughts Upon the African Slave Trade,* in *Journal of a Slave Trader,* 103.

14. Clarkson, *Substance of the Evidence,* in Oldfield, *British Transatlantic Slave Trade,* 3:207.

15. Ibid., 3:203.

16. *General Advertiser* (Philadelphia), February 11, 1794.

17. *Royal Gazette, and Sierra Leone Advertiser* (Freetown), April 2, April 9, 1825; His Majesty's Commissioners to Mr. Secretary Canning, Sierra Leone, April 10, 1825, *Irish University Press Series of British Parliamentary Papers*, vol. 10, Class A (1825–26 session), 9–10; *Genius of Universal Emancipation and Baltimore Courier,* September 24, 1825; *Niles' Weekly Register* (Baltimore), October 1, 1825.

18. *New-York Evening-Post,* December 14, December 15, 1826; *Genius of Universal Emancipation* (Baltimore), January 2, 1827.

19. *National Anti-Slavery Standard* (New York), December 30, 1841, 118.

20. Stein, *French Slave Trade,* 103.

21. Behrendt, Eltis, and Richardson arrive at a similar figure of 25.4 slaves as the average mortality during shipboard revolts and their immediate aftermath. See "Costs of Coercion," 463; David Richardson, "Shipboard Revolts," 74.

22. M. Le Page Du Pratz, *The History of Louisiana, or of the Western Parts of Virginia and Carolina: Containing a Description of the Countries that Lie on Both Sides of the River Mississippi: With an Account of the Settlements, Inhabitants, Soil, Climate, and Products* (1774; reprint, New Orleans: Pelican, 1941), 72; Hall, *Africans in Colonial Louisiana,* 107–9; Daniel H. Usner, "From African Captivity to American Slavery: The Introduction of Black Laborers to Colonial Louisiana," *Louisiana History* 20, no. 1 (Winter 1979): 36–37; Aptheker, *American Negro Slave Revolts,* 182.

23. Douglass, *Narrative and Selected Writings,* 73.

Bibliography

ARCHIVAL SOURCES

England

Guildhall Library, London
Merseyside Maritime Museum, Liverpool
    Transatlantic Slave Trade Exhibit
Public Record Office, Kew, England
    Foreign Office Records, with row and drawer numbers following.
    Records of the Colonial Office
    Publications of the House of Commons
    Treasury Records

United States

Breckinridge County Archives, Hardinsburg, Kentucky
John Carter Brown Library, Providence, Rhode Island
    Brown Family Business Records, with box and folder numbers following.
Newport Historical Society, Newport, Rhode Island
    Peleg Clarke Letters, 1774–1782
    Other items followed by box and folder numbers.
Rhode Island Historical Society, Providence, Rhode Island
    Log of the Ship *Dolphin*, Ship's Logs Collection
Rhode Island State Archives, Providence, Rhode Island
    Moses Brown Papers, with series and folder numbers following.
    Petitions to the Rhode Island General Assembly, with volume and document
    numbers following.
    Public Notary Records

NEWSPAPERS

Annual Register (London)
Boston Gazette

Boston News-Letter

Boston News-Letter and New-England Chronicle

Boston Post-Boy

Boston Post-Boy and Advertiser

Boston Weekly News-Letter

Christian Inquirer (New York)

Connecticut Courant (Hartford)

Country Journal; or, The Craftsman (London)

Felix Farley's Bristol Journal (Bristol, England)

Fog's Weekly Journal (London)

General Advertiser (Philadelphia)

Genius of Universal Emancipation (Baltimore)

Genius of Universal Emancipation and Baltimore Courier

Gentleman's Magazine (London)

Kentucky Reporter (Lexington)

Liberator (Boston)

Lloyd's List (London)

Lloyd's Evening Post and British Chronicle (London)

London Evening Post

London Times

Loudon's New-York Packet

Maryland Gazette (Annapolis)

Massachusetts Gazette (Boston)

Massachusetts Gazette Extraordinary (Boston)

Massachusetts Gazette and Boston News-Letter

National Anti-Slavery Standard (New York)

National Gazette and Literary Register (Philadelphia)

New Lloyd's List (London)

New London Gazette

New York Advertiser and Express

New-York Commercial Advertiser

New York Evening Post

New York Gazette

New York Journal of Commerce

New York Journal, or General Advertiser

New York Times

Newport Mercury

Niles' Weekly Register (Baltimore)

Niles' National Register (Baltimore)

Pennsylvania Gazette (Philadelphia)

Providence Gazette

Providence Gazette and Country Journal

Rhode Island Gazette
Richmond Enquirer
Royal Gazette and Bahama Advertiser (Nassau, Bahamas)
Royal Gazette and Sierra Leone Advertiser (Freetown, Sierra Leone)
Read's Weekly Journal; or, British-Gazetteer (London)
Salem Gazette
South-Carolina Gazette (Charleston)
Sun (New York)
Universal Daily Register (London)
Universal Spectator, and Weekly Journal (London)
Virginia Gazette (Williamsburg)
Virginia Gazette (Williamsburg), published by John Dixon and William Hunter (DH)
Virginia Gazette (Williamsburg)- published by Alexander Purdie and John Dixon (PD)
Virginia Gazette (Williamsburg)- published by William Rind (WR)
Weekly Journal; or, The British-Gazetteer (London)
Western Luminary (Lexington, KY)
Weekly Rehearsal (Boston)

PUBLISHED SOURCES

Abbott, Willis J. *American Merchant Ships and Sailors.* New York: Dodd, Mead, 1908.

Abraham, Arthur. "Sengbe Pieh: A Neglected Hero?" *Journal of the Historical Society of Sierra Leone* 11, no. 2 (1978): 22–30.

Adams, John Quincy. *Argument in the Case of United States vs. Cinque.* 1841. Reprint, New York: Arno, 1969.

Anstey, Roger T., and P. E. H. Hair, eds. *Liverpool, the African Slave Trade, and Abolition.* Liverpool: Historic Society of Lancashire and Cheshire, 1976.

Aptheker, Herbert. *American Negro Slave Revolts.* 1943. Reprint, New York: International, 1993.

Asgarally, Issa. "Les revoltes d'esclaves dans les Mascareignes ou 'l'histoire du silence.'" In *Slavery in South West Indian Ocean*, ed. U. Bissoondoyal and S. B. C. Servansing, 176–88. Moka, Mauritius: Mahatma Gandhi Institute, 1989.

Astley, Thomas, ed. *A New General Collection of Voyages and Travels Consisting of the Most Esteemed Relations which have been hitherto Published in any Language Comprehending Everything Remarkable in its Kind in Europe, Asia, Africa, and America*, 4 vols. 1745–47. Reprint, London: Cass, 1968.

Atkins, John. *A Voyage to Guinea, Brasil, and the West-Indies.* London, 1735.

Bancroft, Frederic. *Slave Trading in the Old South.* 1931. Reprint, New York: Unger, 1959.

Barber, John W. *A History of the Amistad Captives.* New Haven, CT: E. L. and J. W. Barber, 1840.

Barbot, Jean, Jr. *A Supplement to the Description of the Coasts of North and South Guinea* (London, 1746). Reprinted in Churchill and Churchill, *Collection of Voyages and Travels,* 5:497–522.

Barksdale, Richard, and Keneth Kinnamon, eds. *Black Writers of America: A Comprehensive Anthology.* New York: Macmillan, 1972.

Beattie, J. M. *Policing and Punishment in London, 1660–1750: Urban Crime and the Limits of Terror.* Oxford: Oxford University Press, 2001.

Bee, Thomas. *Reports of Cases Adjudged in the District Court of South Carolina.* Philadelphia: William P. Farrand, 1810.

Behrendt, Stephen D. "The Captains in the British Slave Trade From 1785 to 1807." *Transactions of the Historic Society of Lancashire and Cheshire* 140 (1991): 79–140.

———. "Crew Mortality in the Transatlantic Slave Trade in the Eighteenth Century." In Eltis and Richardson, *Routes to Slavery,* 49–71.

Behrendt, Stephen D., David Eltis, and David Richardson. "The Costs of Coercion: African Agency in the Pre-Modern Atlantic World." *Economic History Review* 54, no. 3 (2001): 454–76.

Benezet, Anthony. *Some Historical Account of Guinea, its Situation, Produce, and the General Disposition of its Inhabitants, with an Inquiry into the Rise and Progress of the Slave Trade, its Nature, and Lamentable Effects.* London: J. Phillips, 1788.

Bennett, Lerone, Jr. *Before the Mayflower: A History of Black America.* 5th rev. ed. Chicago: Johnson, 1982. Reprint, New York: Penguin Books, 1984.

Bentley, William. *The Diary of William Bentley, D.D., Pastor of the East Church, Salem, Massachusetts.* Vol. 1. 1905. Reprint, Gloucester, MA: Smith, 1962.

Bettelheim, Bruno. "Individual and Mass Behavior in Extreme Situations." In *Surviving, and Other Essays.* New York: Knopf, 1979.

Blake, W. O. *The History of Slavery and the Slave Trade, Ancient and Modern. The Forms of Slavery That Prevailed in Ancient Nations, Particularly in Greece and Rome. The African Slave Trade and the Political History of Slavery in the United States.* Columbus, OH: H. Miller, 1860.

Bolster, W. Jeffrey. *Black Jacks: African American Seamen in the Age of Sail.* Cambridge, MA: Harvard University Press, 1997.

Bosman, William. *A New and Accurate Description of the Coast of Guinea, Divided into The Gold, The Slave, and The Ivory Coasts.* 1704. Reprint, London: Cass, 1967.

Bradley, Patricia. "The Boston Gazette and Slavery as Revolutionary Propaganda." *Journalism and Mass Communication Quarterly* 72, no. 3 (Autumn 1995): 581–96.

Brawley, Benjamin. *A Social History of the American Negro, Being a History of the Negro Problem in the United States, Including a History and Study of the Republic of Liberia.* 1921. Reprint, New York: Macmillan, 1970.

Brevard, Joseph. *Reports of Judicial Decisions in the State of South Carolina, from 1793 to 1816.* 3 vols. Charleston: W. Riley, 1840.

Brooke, Richard. *Liverpool as It Was during the Last Quarter of the Eighteenth Century, 1775–1800.* London: J. R. Smith, 1853.

Brown, William Wells. *The Black Man: His Antecedents, His Genius, and His Achievements.* New York: T. Hamilton, 1863.

———. *The Negro in the American Rebellion: His Heroism and His Fidelity.* . . . Boston: Lee and Shepard, 1867.

Brue, André. *Voyages and Travels along the Western Coast of Africa, on Account of the French Commerce.* Reprinted in Astley, *New General Collection of Voyages and Travels,* 2:27–158.

Brugevin, Joseph. "Journal de traite du vaisseau La Licorne de Bordeaux." In *Traite des noirs et navires négriers au XVIIIe siècle,* ed. Patrick Villiers, 127–62. Grenoble, France: Editions des 4 Seigneurs, 1982.

Burkholder, Robert E., ed. *Critical Essays on Herman Melville's "Benito Cereno."* New York: Hall, 1992.

Butt-Thompson, F. W. *Sierra Leone in History and Tradition.* London: Witherby, 1926.

Buxton, Thomas Fowell. *The African Slave Trade and Its Remedy.* 1840. Reprint, London: Cass, 1967.

Calderhead, William. "The Role of the Professional Slave Trader in a Slave Economy: Austin Woolfolk, A Case Study." *Civil War History* 23, no. 3 (September 1977): 195–211.

Cappon, Lester J., and Stella F. Duff. *Virginia Gazette Index, 1736–1780.* 2 vols. Williamsburg, VA: Institute of Early American History and Culture, 1950.

Caron, Peter. "'Of a Nation Which the Others Do Not Understand': Bambara Slaves and African Ethnicity in Colonial Louisiana, 1718-60." In Eltis and Richardson, *Routes to Slavery,* 98–121.

Carretta, Vincent. "Olaudah Equiano or Gustavus Vassa? New Light on an Eighteenth-Century Question of Identity." *Slavery and Abolition* 20, no. 3 (December 1999): 96–105.

Carroll, Joseph Cephas. *Slave Insurrections in the United States, 1800–1865.* 1938. Reprint, New York: Negro Universities Press, 1971.

Catterall, Helen, ed. *Judicial Cases Concerning American Slavery and the Negro.* 5 vols. Washington, DC: Carnegie Institution of Washington, 1926-1936.

Chandler, David L. *Health and Slavery in Colonial Colombia.* New York: Arno, 1981.

Churchill, Awnsham, and John Churchill. *A Collection of Voyages and Travels, Some Now First Printed From Original Manuscripts, Others Now First Published in English.* 6 vols. London: J. Walthoe, 1752.

Clarkson, Thomas. *The Substance of the Evidence of Sundry Persons on the Slave Trade.* 1789. Reprinted in Oldfield, *British Transatlantic Slave Trade,* 3:177–320.

Class A Correspondence with the British Commissioners at Sierra Leone, Havana, the Cape of Good Hope, and Loanda; and Reports from British Naval Officers, Relating to the Slave Trade from April 1, 1858, to March 31, 1859. London, 1859.

Clayton, Ralph. *Cash for Blood: The Baltimore to New Orleans Domestic Slave Trade.* Bowie, MD: Heritage Books, 2002.

Coffin, Joshua. *An Account of Some of the Principle Slave Insurrections, and Others, Which Have Occurred, or Been Attempted, in the United States and Elsewhere, during the Last Two Centuries.* New York: American Anti-Slavery Society, 1860.

Cohn, Raymond L. "Deaths of Slaves in the Middle Passage." *Journal of Economic History* 45, no. 3 (September 1985): 685–92.

Collins, Dr. *Practical Rules for the Management of Negro Slaves, in the Sugar Colonies.* London: J. Barfield for Vernor and Hood, 1803.

Conneau, Theophilus. *A Slaver's Log Book; or, 20 Years' Residence in Africa.* London: Hale, 1977.

Conrad, Robert Edgar. *Children of God's Fire: A Documentary History of Black Slavery in Brazil.* University Park: Pennsylvania State University Press, 1994.

Cook, Fred J. "The Slave Ship Rebellion." *American Heritage* 8, no. 2 (February 1957): 61–64, 104–6.

Cooper, Thomas. *Letters on the Slave Trade.* 1787. Reprinted in Oldfield, *British Transatlantic Slave Trade,* 3:19–56.

Cortés Lopéz, José Luis. *La esclavitud negra en la España peninsular del siglo XVI.* Salamanca, Spain: Ediciones Universidad de Salamanca, 1989.

Coughtry, Jay. *The Notorious Triangle: Rhode Island and the African Slave Trade.* Philadelphia: Temple University Press, 1981.

Craton, Michael. "The Passion to Exist: Slave Rebellions in the British West Indies, 1650–1832." *Journal of Caribbean History* 13 (1980): 1–20.

——. *Testing the Chains: Resistance to Slavery in the British West Indies.* Ithaca, NY: Cornell University Press, 1982.

"The *Creole* Case." *Southern Quarterly Review* 2 (1842): 55–72.

Crone, G. R., ed. and trans. *The Voyages of Cadamosto and Other Documents on Western Africa in the Second Half of the Fifteenth Century.* Works issued by the Hakluyt Society, 2nd series, no. 80. London: Hakluyt Society, 1937.

Crosby, David L. "Anthony Benezet's Transformation of Anti-Slavery Rhetoric." *Slavery and Abolition* 23, no. 3 (December 2002): 39–58.

Crow, Hugh. *Memoirs of the Late Captain Hugh Crow, of Liverpool.* 1830. Reprint, London: Cass, 1970.

Cugoano, Quobna Ottobah. *Thoughts and Sentiments on the Evil of Slavery and Other Writings.* Ed. Vincent Carretta. New York: Penguin, 1999.

Curtin, Philip D., ed. *Africa Remembered: Narratives by West Africans from the Era of the Slave Trade.* Madison: University of Wisconsin Press, 1967.

——. *The Atlantic Slave Trade: A Census.* Madison: University of Wisconsin Press, 1969.

Curtin, Philip D., Roger Anstey, and J. E. Inikori. "Measuring the Atlantic Slave Trade: A Discussion." *Journal of African History* 27, no. 4 (1976): 595–627.

Da Costa, Emilia Viotti. *Crowns of Glory, Tears of Blood: The Demerara Slave Rebellion of 1823.* New York: Oxford University Press, 1994.

Daget, Serge, ed. *De la traite à l'esclavage: actes du Colloque international sur la traite des noirs, Nantes, 1985.* 2 vols. Nantes: Centre de recherche sur l'histoire du monde atlantique, 1985.

———. *Répertoire des expéditions négrières françaises à la traite illégale (1814–1850).* Nantes: Centre de recherche sur l'histoire du monde atlantique, 1988.

Davis, Angela. "Reflections on the Black Woman's Role in the Community of Slaves." *Black Scholar* 3, no. 9 (December 1971): 3–15.

Davis, David Brion. *The Problem of Slavery in the Age of Revolution, 1770–1823.* 1975. Reprint, New York: Oxford University Press, 1999.

———. *Slavery and Human Progress.* New York: Oxford University Press, 1984.

Delano, Amasa. *A Narrative of Voyages and Travels, in the Northern and Southern Hemispheres: Comprising Three Voyages Round the World; Together with a Voyage of Survey and Discovery, in the Pacific Ocean and Oriental Islands.* Boston: E. G. House, 1817.

De la Roncière, Charles. *Histoire de la marine française.* Vol. 4. Paris: Plon, 1910.

De l'état actuel de la traite des noirs: extrait des renseignements déposés récemment à ce sujet sur le Bureau de la Chambre des communes d'Angleterre; composant le rapport présenté, le 8 mai, 1821, aux directeurs de l'Institution africaine par le comité spécial nommé à cet effect. London: G. Schulze, 1821.

Degler, Carl N. *Neither Black nor White: Slavery and Race Relations in Brazil and the United States.* Madison: University of Wisconsin Press, 1971.

Deschamps, Hubert. *Histoire de la traite des noirs de l'antiquité à nos jours.* Paris: Fayard, 1972.

Desport, Jean-Marie. *De la servitude à la liberté: Bourbon des origines à 1848.* 2nd ed. Réunion: Océan, 1989.

Deveau, Jean-Michel. *La traite rochelaise.* Pairs: Karthala, 1990.

Deyle, Steven. "The Irony of Liberty: Origins of the Domestic Slave Trade." *Journal of the Early Republic* 12, no. 1 (Spring 1992): 37–62.

Dillon, Merton L. *Benjamin Lundy and the Struggle for Negro Freedom.* Urbana: University of Illinois Press, 1966.

Diouf, Sylviane A., ed. *Fighting the Slave Trade: West African Strategies.* Athens: Ohio University Press, 2003.

Donnan, Elizabeth, ed. *Documents Illustrative of the History of the Slave Trade to America.* 4 vols. Washington, DC: Carnegie Institution of Washington, 1930–1935.

Douglass, Frederick. *The Narrative and Selected Writings.* Ed. Michael Meyer. New York: Random, 1984.

Dow, George Francis. *Slave Ships and Slaving.* Salem, MA: Marine Research Society, 1927.

Drake, B. K. "The Liverpool-African Voyage, c. 1790–1807: Commercial Problems." In Anstey and Hair, *Liverpool, the African Slave Trade, and Abolition,* 126–56.

Drake, Philip. *Revelations of a Slave Smuggler: Being the Autobiography of Captain Rich'd Drake, an African Trader for Fifty Years—from 1807 to 1857; During Which Period He Was Concerned in the Transportation of Half a Million Blacks from African Coasts to America.* 1860. Reprint, Northbrook, IL: Metro Books, 1972.

Du Bois, W. E. B. *The Suppression of the African Slave Trade to the United States of America, 1636–1870.* 1896. Reprint, Baton Rouge: Louisiana State University Press, 1969.

Ducasse, Andre. *Les négriers; ou, Le trafic des esclaves.* 1946. Reprint, Paris: Hachette, 1948.

Dunn, Richard S. *Sugar and Slaves: The Rise of the Planter Class in the English West Indies, 1624–1713.* New York: Norton, 1973.

Durnford, Charles, and Edward Hyde East, eds. *Term Reports in the Court of King's Bench.* Vols. 1 and 7. London: J. Butterworth, 1794, 1802.

Earle, Thomas. *The Life, Travels, and Opinions of Benjamin Lundy; Including His Journeys to Texas and Mexico, with a Sketch of Contemporary Events, and a Notice of the Revolution in Hayti.* 1847. Reprint, New York: Kelley, 1971.

Edwards, Bryan. *The History, Civil and Commercial, of the British Colonies in the West Indies.* 4 vols. Philadelphia: James Humphreys, 1806.

Elder, Melinda. *The Slave Trade and the Economic Development of Eighteenth-Century Lancaster.* Krumlin, Halifax, England: Ryburn, 1992.

Elkins, Stanley. *Slavery: A Problem in American Institutional and Intellectual Life.* 3rd ed., rev. Chicago: University of Chicago Press, 1976.

Eltis, David. *Economic Growth and the Ending of the Transatlantic Slave Trade.* New York: Oxford University Press, 1987.

———. "Mortality and Voyage Length in the Middle Passage: New Evidence from the Nineteenth Century." *Journal of Economic History* 44, no. 2 (June 1984): 301–8.

———. *The Rise of African Slavery in the Americas.* Cambridge: Cambridge University Press, 2000.

Eltis, David, et al., eds. *The Trans-Atlantic Slave Trade: A Database on CD-ROM.* Cambridge: Cambridge University Press, 1999.

Eltis, David, and David Richardson, eds. *Routes to Slavery: Direction, Ethnicity, and Mortality in the Atlantic Slave Trade.* London: Cass, 1997.

Equiano, Olaudah. *Equiano's Travels: The Interesting Narrative of the Life of Olaudah Equiano or Gustavus Vassa, the African.* Ed. Paul Edwards. 1789. Reprint, Oxford: Heinemann, 1996.

Fairfield, William. Letter to Rebecca Fairfield, Cayenne, April 23, 1789. *Essex Institute Historical Collections* 25 (1888): 311–12.

Falconbridge, Alexander. *An Account of the Slave Trade on the Coast of Africa.* London: J. Phillips, 1788.

The Federal Cases: Comprising Cases Argued and Determined in the Circuit and District Courts of the United States. . . . Vol. 9. St. Paul: West, 1895.

Forbes, R. N. *Six Months' Service in the African Blockade, from April to October, 1848, in Command of H.M.S. Bonetta.* 1849. Reprint, London: Dawsons, 1969.

Fortescue, J. W., ed. *Calendar of State Papers, Colonial Series.* Vol. 11, *America and West Indies, 1681–1685.* London: Eyre and Spottiswoode, 1898.

Freudenberger, Herman, and Jonathan B. Pritchett. "The Domestic United States Slave Trade: New Evidence." *Journal of Interdisciplinary History* 21, no. 3 (Winter 1991): 447–77.

Fryer, Peter. *Staying Power: The History of Black People in Britain.* London: Pluto, 1992.

Fyfe, Christopher, ed. *Anna Maria Falconbridge: Narrative of Two Voyages to the River Sierra Leone during the Years 1791–1792–1793, and the Journal of Isaac Dubois, with Alexander Falconbridge: An Account of the Slave Trade on the Coast of Africa.* Liverpool: Liverpool University Press, 2000.

Garneray, Louis. *Le négrier de Zanzibar: Voyages, aventures et combats.* Paris: Phébus, 1985.

Gaspar, David Barry, and Darlene Clark Hine, eds. *More Than Chattel: Black Women and Slavery in the Americas.* Bloomington: Indiana University Press, 1996.

Gemery, Henry A., and Jan S. Hogendorn, eds. *The Uncommon Market: Essays in the Economic History of the Atlantic Slave Trade.* New York: Academic, 1979.

Genovese, Eugene D. *From Rebellion to Revolution: Afro-American Slave Revolts in the Making of the Modern World.* Baton Rouge: Louisiana State University Press, 1979.

——. "Rebelliousness and Docility in the Negro Slave: A Critique of the Elkins Thesis." *Civil War History* 13 (1967): 300–315.

Gomez, Michael A. *Exchanging Our Country Marks: The Transformation of African Identities in the Colonial and Antebellum South.* Chapel Hill: University of North Carolina Press, 1998.

Grant, Douglas. *The Fortunate Slave: An Illustration of African Slavery in the Early Nineteenth Century.* London: Oxford University Press, 1968.

Greene, Lorenzo J. "Mutiny on the Slave Ships." *Phylon* 5, no. 4 (1944): 346–55.

Green-Pedersen, Svend E. "The Scope and Structure of the Danish Negro Slave Trade." *Scandinavian Economic History Review* 19, no. 2 (1971): 149–97.

Gross, Seymour L., ed. *A "Benito Cereno" Handbook.* Belmont, CA: Wadsworth, 1965.

Gudmestad, Robert H. *A Troublesome Commerce: The Transformation of the Interstate Slave Trade.* Baton Rouge: Louisiana State University Press, 2003.

Gueye, Mbaye. *L'Afrique et l'esclavage: une étude sur la traite négrière.* Romorantin, France: Martinsart, 1983.

Haines, Robin, John McDonald, and Ralph Shlomowitz. "Mortality and Voyage Length in the Middle Passage Revisited." *Explorations in Economic History* 38, no. 4 (October 2001): 503–33.

Halasz, Nicholas. *The Rattling Chains: Slave Unrest and Revolt in the Antebellum South.* New York: McKay, 1966.

Hall, Gwendolyn Midlo. *Africans in Colonial Louisiana: The Development of Afro-Creole Culture in the Eighteenth Century.* Baton Rouge: Louisiana State University Press, 1992.

Hansen, Thorkild. *Coast of Slaves.* Trans. Kari Dako. Accra, Ghana: Sub-Saharan, 2002.

Harding, Vincent. *There Is a River: The Black Struggle for Freedom in America.* San Diego: Harcourt Brace Jovanovich, 1992.

Harms, Robert. *The* Diligent: *A Voyage through the Worlds of the Slave Trade.* New York: Basic Books, 2002.

Hart, Richard. *Slaves Who Abolished Slavery.* Vol. 2, *Blacks in Rebellion.* Kingston, Jamaica: Institute of Social and Economic Research, 1985.

Hawkins, Joseph. *A History of a Voyage to the Coast of Africa, and Travels into the Interior of that Country; Containing Particular Descriptions of the Climate and Inhabitants, and Interesting Particulars Concerning the Slave Trade.* Philadelphia, 1797.

Hedges, James B. *The Browns of Providence Plantations.* Vol. 1, *Colonial Years.* Cambridge, MA: Harvard University Press, 1952.

Hendrick, George, and Willene Hendrick. *The* Creole *Mutiny: A Tale of Revolt aboard a Slave Ship.* Chicago: Dee, 2003.

Highfield, Arnold R. "The Danish Atlantic and West Indian Slave Trade." In *The Danish West Indian Slave Trade: Virgin Islands Perspectives,* ed. George F. Tyson and Arnold R. Highfield, 11–32.. St. Croix, Virgin Islands: Antilles, 1994.

Hill, Lawrence F. *Diplomatic Relations between the United States and Brazil.* Durham, NC: Duke University Press, 1932.

Hill, Pascoe G. *Fifty Days on Board a Slave Vessel.* 1848. Reprint, Baltimore: Black Classic, 1993.

Howard, Warren. *American Slavers and the Federal Law, 1837–1862.* Berkeley: University of California Press, 1963.

Iliffe, John. *Africans: The History of a Continent.* Cambridge: Cambridge University Press, 1995.

Inikori, Joseph E., ed. *Forced Migration: The Impact of the Export Slave Trade on African Societies.* London: Hutchinson University Library, 1982.

——. "Measuring the Unmeasured Hazards of the Atlantic Slave Trade: Documents Relating to the British Trade." *Revue Française d'Histoire d'Outre-Mer* 83, no. 312 (1996): 53–92.

Irish University Press Series of British Parliamentary Papers: Correspondence with British Commissioners and With Foreign Powers Relative to the Slave Trade. Shannon, Ireland: Irish University Press, 1968.

James, C. L. R. *The Black Jacobins: Toussaint L'Ouverture and the San Domingo Revolution.* 2nd ed. New York: Vintage Books, 1963.

Jensen, Merrill, ed. *English Historical Documents.* Vol. 9. London: Eyre and Spottiswoode, 1969.

Jervey, Edward D., and C. Harold Huber. "The *Creole* Affair." *Journal of Negro History* 65, no. 3 (Summer 1980): 195–211.

John, A. H. "The London Assurance Company and the Marine Insurance Market of the Eighteenth Century." *Economica* 25, no. 98 (May 1958): 126–41.

Johnson, Walter. *Soul by Soul: Life inside the Antebellum Slave Market.* Cambridge, MA: Harvard University Press, 1999.

Jones, Adam. "Brandenburg-Prussia and the Atlantic Slave Trade, 1680–1700." In Daget, *De la traite à l'esclavage*, 1:283–98.

———. *Brandenburg Sources for West African History, 1680–1700*. Stuttgart: Steiner-Verlag-Wiesbaden, 1985.

Jones, G. I. "Olaudah Equiano of the Niger Ibo." In Curtin, *Africa Remembered*, 60–98.

Jones, Howard. *Mutiny on the Amistad: The Saga of a Slave Revolt and Its Impact on American Abolition, Law, and Diplomacy.* New York: Oxford University Press, 1987.

Jones, Howard. "The Peculiar Institution and National Honor: The Case of the *Creole* Slave Revolt." *Civil War History* 21, no. 1 (March 1975): 28–50.

Jones, Wilbur Devereux. "The Influence of Slavery on the Webster-Ashburton Negotiations." *Journal of Southern History* 22, no. 1 (February 1956): 48–58.

A Journal of an Intended Voyage in the Ship Black Prince *From Bristol to the Gold Coast of Africa.* East Ardsley, England: EP Microform, ca. 1967.

Kaplan, Sidney. "Black Mutiny on the *Amistad.*" *Massachusetts Review* 10, no. 3 (Summer 1969): 493–532.

Kiple, Kenneth F., and Brian T. Higgins. "Mortality Caused by Dehydration during the Middle Passage." In *The Atlantic Slave Trade: Effects on Economies, Societies, and Peoples in Africa, the Americas, and Europe,* ed. Joseph E. Inikori and Stanley L. Engerman, 321–37. Durham, NC: Duke University Press, 1992.

Klein, Herbert S. *The Atlantic Slave Trade.* Cambridge: Cambridge University Press, 1999.

———. *The Middle Passage: Comparative Studies in the Atlantic Slave Trade.* Princeton, NJ: Princeton University Press, 1978.

Klein, Herbert S., and Stanley L. Engerman. "Long-Term Trends in African Mortality in the Transatlantic Slave Trade." In Eltis and Richardson, *Routes to Slavery,* 36–48.

———. "Shipping Patterns and Mortality in the African Slave Trade to Rio de Janeiro, 1825–1830." *Cahiers d'Etudes Africaines* 15, no. 3 (1975): 381–98.

———. "Slave Mortality on British Ships, 1791–1797." In Anstey and Hair, *Liverpool, the African Slave Trade, and Abolition,* 113–25.

Lacroix, Louis. *Les derniers négriers: derniers voyages de bois d'ébène.* Paris: Editions maritimes et d'outre-mer, 1977.

Law, Robin, and Paul E. Lovejoy, eds. *The Biography of Mahommah Gardo Baquaqua: His Passage from Slavery to Freedom in Africa and America.* 1854. Reprint, Princeton, NJ: Wiener, 2001.

Lawrence, A. W. *Trade Castles and Forts of West Africa.* London: Cape, 1963.

Le Page Du Pratz, M. *The History of Louisiana, or of the Western Parts of Virginia and Carolina: Containing a Description of the Countries that Lie on Both Sides of the River Mississippi: With an Account of the Settlements, Inhabitants, Soil, Climate, and Products.* 1774. Reprint, New Orleans: Pelican 1941.

Leslie, Joshua, and Sterling Stuckey. "The Death of Benito Cereno: A Reading of Herman Melville on Slavery." *Journal of Negro History* 67, no. 4 (Winter 1982): 287–301.

Ligon, Richard. *A True and Exact History of the Island of Barbadoes. . . .* 1657. Reprint, London: Cass, 1998.

Linebaugh, Peter. *The London Hanged: Crime and Civil Society in the Eighteenth Century.* London: Penguin, 1991.

Linebaugh, Peter, and Marcus Rediker. *The Many-Headed Hydra: Sailors, Slaves, Commoners, and the Hidden History of the Revolutionary Atlantic.* Boston: Beacon, 2000.

Littlefield, Daniel C. *Rice and Slaves: Ethnicity and the Slave Trade in Colonial South Carolina.* Urbana: University of Illinois Press, 1991.

Lydon, James G. "New York and the Slave Trade, 1700–1774." *William and Mary Quarterly* 35, no. 2 (April 1978): 375–94.

MacInnes, C. M. *England and Slavery.* Bristol, England: Arrowsmith, 1934.

Mackenzie-Grieve, Averil. *The Last Years of the English Slave Trade, Liverpool 1750–1807.* London: Chiswick, 1941.

Mannix, Daniel P., and Malcolm Cowley. *Black Cargoes: A History of the Atlantic Slave Trade, 1518–1865.* New York: Penguin Books, 1978.

Martin, Christopher. *The Amistad Affair.* New York: Abelard-Schuman, 1970.

Martin, Eveline Christiana, ed. *Journal of a Slave-Dealer: A View of Some Remarkable Axcedents in the Life of Nics. Owen on the Coast of Africa and America from the Year 1746 to the Year 1757.* Boston: Houghton Mifflin, 1930.

Martin, Gaston. *Nantes au XVIIIe siècle: l'ère des négriers (1714–1774): d'après des documents inédits avec 7 planches hors-texte.* Paris: F. Alcan, 1931. Reprint as *L'Ere des négriers (1714–1774): Nantes au XVIIIe siècle.* Paris: Karthala, 1993.

Martin, Phyllis M. *The External Trade of the Loango Coast, 1576–1870: The Effects of Changing Commercial Relations on the Vili Kingdom of Loango.* Oxford: Clarendon, 1972.

Mason, George C. "The African Slave Trade in Colonial Times." *American Historical Record* 1, no. 7 (July 1872): 311–19; 1, no. 8 (August 1872): 338–45.

Mattoso, Katia M. de Queiros. *To Be a Slave in Brazil, 1550–1888.* New Brunswick, NJ: Rutgers University Press, 1986.

Mayer, Brantz, ed. *Captain Canot; or, Twenty Years of an African Slaver: Being an Account of his Career and Adventures on the Coast, in the Interior, on Shipboard, and in the West Indies.* 1845. Reprint, New York: Arno, 1968.

McClendon, R. Earl. "The *Amistad* Claims: Inconsistencies of Policy." *Political Science Quarterly* 48, no. 3 (September 1933): 386–412.

McGowan, Winston. "African Resistance to the Atlantic Slave Trade in West Africa." *Slavery and Abolition* 11, no. 1 (May 1990): 5–29.

——. "The Origins of Slave Rebellions in the Middle Passage." In *In the Shadow of the Plantation: Caribbean History and Legacy,* ed. Alvin O. Thompson, 74–99. Kingston, Jamaica: Randle, 2002.

McLynn, Frank. *Crime and Punishment in Eighteenth-Century England.* London: Routledge, 1989.

Mettas, Jean. *Répertoire des expéditions négrières françaises au XVIIIe siècle,* 2 vols. Ed. Serge Daget. Paris: Société française d'histoire d'outre-mer, 1978–1984.

Miller, Joseph C. "Mortality in the Atlantic Slave Trade: Statistical Evidence on Causality." *Journal of Interdisciplinary History* 11, no. 3 (Winter 1981): 385–423.

———. *Slavery and Slaving in World History: A Bibliography, 1990–1991.* Millwood, NY: Kraus International, 1993.

———. *Way of Death: Merchant Capitalism and the Angolan Slave Trade, 1730–1830.* Madison: University of Wisconsin Press, 1988.

Minchinton, Walter, Celia King, and Peter Waite. *Virginia Slave-Trade Statistics 1698–1775.* Richmond: Virginia State Library, 1984.

Mintz, Sidney W., and Richard Price. *The Birth of African-American Culture: An Anthropological Perspective.* Boston: Beacon, 1992.

Moore, Francis. *Travels Into the Inland Parts of Africa.* London: E. Cave, 1738.

Mouser, Bruce L., ed. *A Slaving Voyage to Africa and Jamaica: The Log of the San-down, 1793–1794.* Bloomington: Indiana University Press, 2002.

Mousnier, Jehan, ed. *Journal de la traite des noirs: Dam Joulin, Charles le Breton la Vallée, Garneray, Mérimée.* Paris: Editions de Paris, 1957.

Mullin, Gerald W. *Flight and Rebellion: Slave Resistance in Eighteenth-Century Virginia.* New York: Oxford University Press, 1972.

Munford, Clarence J. *The Black Ordeal of Slavery and Slave Trading in the French West Indies, 1625–1715.* 3 vols. Lewiston, NY: Mellen, 1991.

Newton, John. *The Journal of a Slave Trader (John Newton), 1750–1754, With Newton's "Thoughts Upon the African Slave Trade."* Ed. Bernard Martin and Mark Spurrell. London: Epworth, 1962.

Nørregård, Georg. *Danish Settlements in West Africa, 1658–1850.* Boston: Boston University Press, 1966.

———. "Slaveoproret pa 'Patientia' 1753." *Årbog (Handels-og søfartmuseet på Kronborg)* (Denmark) (1950): 23–44.

Northup, Solomon. *Twelve Years a Slave* (1853). Ed. Sue Eakin and Joseph Logsdon. Baton Rouge: Louisiana State University Press, 1968.

Observations of the Slave Trade and a Description of some Part of the Coast of Guinea, During a Voyage Made in 1787, and 1788, in Company with Doctor A. Sparrman and Captain Arrehenius. London, 1787.

Oldfield, John, ed. *The British Transatlantic Slave Trade.* Vol. 3, *The Abolitionist Struggle: Opponents of the Slave Trade.* London: Pickering and Chatto, 2003.

Owens, William A. *Slave Mutiny: The Revolt on the Schooner* Amistad. New York: Day, 1953.

Paiewonsky, Isidor. *Eyewitness Accounts of Slavery in the Danish West Indies; also Graphic Tales of Other Slave Happenings on Ships and Plantations.* St. Thomas, Virgin Islands: Isidor Paiewonsky, 1987.

Paige, John. *The Letters of John Paige, London Merchant, 1648–1658.* Ed. George F. Steckley. Publications of the London Record Society, vol. 21. London: London Record Society, 1984.

Palmer, Colin. *Human Cargoes: The British Slave Trade to Spanish America, 1700–1739.* Urbana: University of Illinois Press, 1981.

——. "The Slave Trade, African Slavers, and the Demography of the Caribbean to 1750." In *General History of the Caribbean,* ed. Franklin W. Knight, 3:9–44. London: UNESCO, 1997.

Paris, François de. *Voyage to the Coast of Africa, Named Guinea, and to the Isles of America, Made in the Years 1682 and 1683.* Trans. Aimery Caron. Madison: University of Wisconsin Press, 2001.

Park, Mungo. *Travels in the Interior Districts of Africa.* Ed. Kate Ferguston Marsters. Durham: Duke University Press, 2000.

Patterson, Orlando. "Slavery and Slave Revolts: A Sociohistorical Analysis of the First Maroon War, 1665–1740." In *Maroon Societies: Rebel Slave Communities in the Americas,* 2nd ed., ed. Richard Price, 246–92. Baltimore: Johns Hopkins University Press, 1993.

——. *Slavery and Social Death: A Comparative Study.* Cambridge, MA: Harvard University Press, 1982.

——. *The Sociology of Slavery: An Analysis of the Origins, Development, and Structure of Negro Slave Society in Jamaica.* London: MacGibbon and Kee, 1967.

Phillips, Thomas. *Abstract of a Voyage along the Coast of Guinea to Whidaw, the Island of St. Thomas, and thence to Barbadoes, in 1693.* In Astley, *New General Collection of Voyages and Travels,* 2:387–416.

Phillips, Ulrich Bonnell. *American Negro Slavery: A Survey of the Supply, Employment and Control of Negro Labor as Determined by the Plantation Regime.* 1918. Reprint, Baton Rouge: Louisiana State University Press, 1969.

Piersen, William D. "White Cannibals, Black Martyrs: Fear, Depression, and Religious Faith as Causes of Suicide among New Slaves." *Journal of Negro History* 62, no. 2 (April 1977): 147–59.

Pluchon, Pierre. *La route des esclaves: Négriers et bois d'ébène au XVIIIe siècle.* Paris: Hachette, 1980.

Pope-Hennessy, James. *Sins of the Fathers: A Study of the Atlantic Slave Traders, 1441–1807.* London: Weidenfeld and Nicolson, 1967.

Postma, Johannes. *The Dutch in the Atlantic Slave Trade, 1600–1815.* New York: Cambridge University Press, 1992.

——. "Mortality in the Dutch Slave Trade, 1675–1795." In Gemery and Hogendorn, *Uncommon Market,* 239–60.

Powell, J. W. Damer. *Bristol Privateers and Ships of War.* London: Arrowsmith, 1930.

Priestley, Margaret. "Philip Quaque of Cape Coast." In Curtin, *Africa Remembered,* 99–139.

Pruneau de Pommegorge, Antoine Edme. *Description de la Nigritie.* Amsterdam and Paris: Chez Maradan, 1789.

Putzel, Max. "The Source and the Symbols of Melville's 'Benito Cereno.'" *American Literature* 34, no. 2 (May 1962): 191–206.

Rashid, Ismail. "A Devotion to the Idea of Liberty at Any Price: Rebellion and Anti-slavery in the Upper Guinea Coast in the Eighteenth and Nineteenth Centuries." In Diouf, *Fighting the Slave Trade*, 132–51.

Rask, Johannes. *En Kort og Sandferdig Rejse-Beskrivelse til og fra Guinea*. Trondheim, Norway: Jens Christensen Winding, 1754.

Rathbone, Richard. "Some Thoughts on Resistance to Enslavement in West Africa." *Slavery and Abolition* 6, no. 3 (December 1985): 11–22.

Rawley, James A. *The Transatlantic Slave Trade: A History*. New York: Norton, 1981.

Rediker, Marcus. *Between the Devil and the Deep Blue Sea: Merchant Seamen, Pirates, and the Anglo-American Maritime World, 1700–1750*. Cambridge: Cambridge University Press, 1999.

Reis, Joao Jose. *Slave Rebellion in Brazil: The Muslim Uprising of 1835 in Bahia*. Baltimore: Johns Hopkins University Press, 1993.

Reynolds, Edward. *Stand the Storm: A History of the Atlantic Slave Trade*. London: Allison and Busby, 1989.

Richardson, David, ed. *Bristol, Africa, and the Eighteenth-Century Slave Trade to America*. 4 vols. Bristol, England: Bristol Record Society, 1986–1996.

——. "The Costs of Survival: The Treatment of Slaves in the Middle Passage and the Profitability of the Eighteenth-Century British Slave Trade." In Daget, *De la traite à l'esclavage*, 2:169–81.

——. "Shipboard Revolts, African Authority, and the Atlantic Slave Trade." *William and Mary Quarterly* 58, no. 1 (January 2001), 69–92.

——, and Stephen D. Behrendt. "Inikori's Odyssey: Measuring the British Slave Trade, 1655–1807." *Cahiers d'Etudes Africaines* 35, nos. 2–3 (1995): 599–615.

Richardson, William. *A Mariner of England: An Account of the Career of William Richardson from Cabin Boy in the Merchant Service to Warrant Officer in the Royal Navy (1780–1819) as Told by Himself*. Ed. Edmund Spencer Eardley Childers. London: Murray, 1908.

Robinson, Christopher. *Reports of Cases Argued and Determined in the High Court of Admiralty, Commencing with the Judgments of the Right Honourable Sir William Scott, Michaelmas Term, 1798*. 6 vols. Philadelphia, 1799–1804.

Robinson, Merritt M. *Reports of Cases Argued and Determined in the Supreme Court of Louisiana and in the Superior Court of the Territory of Louisiana*. Annotated edition. Vol. 9. 1945. St. Paul: West, 1911.

Rodríguez, Jorge Pinto. "Una rebelion de negros en las costas del Pacifico sur: El caso de la Fragata Trial en 1814." *Historica* (Peru) 10, no. 1 (July 1986): 139–55.

Rout, Leslie B., Jr. *The African Experience in Spanish America: 1502 to the Present Day*. Cambridge and New York: Cambridge University Press, 1976.

Sale, Maggie Montesinos. *The Slumbering Volcano: American Slave Ship Revolts and the Production of Rebellious Masculinity*. Durham, NC: Duke University Press, 1997.

Sanderson, F. E. "The Liverpool Delegates and Sir William Dolben's Bill." *Transactions of the Historic Society of Lancashire and Cheshire* 124 (1973): 57–84.

Saunders, A. C. de C. M. *A Social History of Black Slaves and Freedmen in Portugal, 1441–1555.* Cambridge: Cambridge University Press, 1982.

Scarr, Deryck. *Slaving and Slavery in the Indian Ocean.* Houndmills, Basingstoke, England: Macmillan, 1998.

Schofield, M. M. "The Slave Trade from Lancashire and Cheshire Ports outside Liverpool, c. 1750–c. 1790." *Transactions of the Historic Society of Lancashire and Cheshire* 126 (1977): 30–72.

Schuler, Monica. "Akan Slave Rebellions in the British Caribbean." In *Caribbean Slave Society and Economy: A Student Reader,* ed. Hilary Beckles and Verene Shepherd, 73–86. Kingston, Jamaica: Randle, 1991.

Schwarz, Suzanne, ed. *Slave Captain: The Career of James Irving in the Liverpool Slave Trade.* Wrexham, Clwyd, Wales: Bridge Books, 1995.

Scott, Kenneth. "George Scott, Slave Trader of Newport." *American Neptune* 12, no. 3 (July 1952): 222–28.

Scudder, Harold C. "Melville's 'Benito Cereno' and Captain Delano's Voyages." *Publications of the Modern Language Association of America* 43, no. 2 (June 1928): 502–32.

Searing, James F. *West African Slavery and Atlantic Commerce: The Senegal River Valley, 1700–1860.* Cambridge: Cambridge University Press, 1993.

Sharafi, Mitra. "The Slave Ship Manuscripts of Captain Joseph B. Cook: A Narrative Reconstruction of the Brig *Nancy*'s Voyage of 1793." *Slavery and Abolition* 24, no. 1 (April 2003): 71–100.

Sheridan, Richard B. *Doctors and Slaves: A Medical and Demographic History of Slavery in the British West Indies, 1680–1834.* Cambridge: Cambridge University Press, 1985.

Smith, William. *A New Voyage to Guinea: Describing the Customs, Manners, Soil, Climate, Habits, Buildings, Education, Manual Arts, Agriculture, Trade, Employments, Languages, Ranks of Distinction, Habitations, Diversions, Marriages, and Whatever Else is Memorable Among the Inhabitants.* 1744. Reprint, London: Cass, 1967.

Snelgrave, William. *A New Account of Some Parts of Guinea, and the Slave Trade.* 1734. Reprint, London: Cass, 1971.

Stampp, Kenneth M. "Rebels and Sambos: The Search for the Negro's Personality in Slavery." *Journal of Southern History* 37, no. 3 (August 1971): 367–92.

Steckel, Richard H., and Richard A. Jensen. "New Evidence on the Causes of Slave and Crew Mortality in the Atlantic Slave Trade." *Journal of Economic History* 46, no. 1 (March 1986): 57–77.

Stein, Robert Louis. *The French Slave Trade in the Eighteenth Century: An Old Regime Business.* Madison: University of Wisconsin Press, 1979.

——. "Mortality in the Eighteenth-Century French Slave Trade." *Journal of African History* 21, no. 1 (1980): 35–41.

Stuckey, Sterling. *The Ideological Origins of Black Nationalism.* Boston: Beacon, 1972.

Sturge, Joseph. *A Visit to the United States in 1841.* Boston: Dexter S. King, 1842.

Svalesen, Leif. *The Slave Ship* Fredensborg. Trans. Pat Shaw and Selena Winsnes. Bloomington: Indiana University Press, 2000.

Tadman, Michael. *Speculators and Slaves: Masters, Traders, and Slaves in the Old South.* Madison: University of Wisconsin Press, 1996.

Tattersfield, Nigel. *The Forgotten Trade: Comprising the Log of the Daniel and Henry of 1700 and Accounts of the Slave Trade from the Minor Ports of England, 1698–1725.* London: Cape, 1991.

Thomas, Hugh. *The Slave Trade: The Story of the Atlantic Slave Trade, 1440–1870.* New York: Simon and Schuster, 1997.

Thompson, Vincent Bakpetu. *The Making of the African Diaspora in the Americas, 1441–1900.* Essex, England: Longman, 1987.

Thornton, John Kelly. *Africa and Africans in the Making of the Atlantic World, 1400–1680.* Cambridge: Cambridge University Press, 1992.

——. "African Dimensions of the Stono Rebellion." *American Historical Review* 96, no. 4 (October 1991): 1101–13.

——. "Cannibals, Witches, and Slave Traders in the Atlantic World." *William and Mary Quarterly* 60, no. 2 (April 2003): 273–94.

Treadway, W. R. H. *Reports of Judicial Decisions in the Constitutional Court, of the State of South Carolina; Held at Charleston and Columbia, During the Years 1812, 13, 14, 15 and 16.* Vol. 2. Charleston: W. R. H. Treadway, 1823.

Uring, Nathaniel. *The Voyages and Travels of Captain Nathaniel Uring.* 1726. Reprint, London: Cassell, 1928.

Usner, Daniel H. "From African Captivity to American Slavery: The Introduction of Black Laborers to Colonial Louisiana." *Louisiana History* 20, no. 1 (Winter 1979): 25–48.

Uya, Okon Edet. "The Middle Passage and Personality Change." In *Global Dimensions of the African Diaspora,* 2nd ed., ed. Joseph Harris, 83–97. Washington DC: Howard University Press, 1993.

——. "Slave Revolts of the Middle Passage: A Neglected Theme." *Calabar Historical Journal* 1, no. 1 (June 1976): 65–88.

Van den Boogaart, Ernst, and Pieter C. Emmer. "The Dutch Participation in the Atlantic Slave Trade, 1596–1650," in Gemery and Hogendorn, *Uncommon Market,* 353–75.

Vogt, John L. "The Early Sao Tome–Principe Slave Trade with Mina, 1500–1540." *International Journal of African Historical Studies* 6, no. 3 (1973): 453–67.

——. *Portuguese Rule on the Gold Coast, 1469–1682.* Athens: University of Georgia Press, 1979.

Voyages aux côtes de Guinée et en Amérique faits en 1702. Amsterdam, 1719.

Wadström, Carl Bernhard. *An Essay on Colonization, Particularly Applied to the Western Coast of Africa, With Some Free Thoughts on Cultivation and Commerce; Also Brief Descriptions of the Colonies Already Formed, or Attempted in Africa, Including Those of Sierra Leona and Bulama.* Book 2. 1794. Reprint, New York: Kelley, 1968.

Wadsworth, Alfred P., and Julia De Lacy Mann. *The Cotton Trade and Industrial Lancashire, 1600–1780.* Manchester, England: Manchester University Press, 1931.

Wax, Darold. "The Browns of Providence and the Slaving Voyage of the Brig *Sally,* 1764–65." *American Neptune* 32, no. 3 (July 1972): 171–79.

——. "Negro Resistance to the Early American Slave Trade." *Journal of Negro History* 51, no. 1 (January 1966): 1–15.

——. "A Philadelphia Surgeon on a Slaving Voyage to Africa, 1749–1751." *Pennsylvania Magazine of History and Biography* 92, no. 4 (October 1968): 465–93.

——. "Preferences for Slaves in Colonial America." *Journal of Negro History,* 58, no. 4 (October 1973): 391–99.

——. "Thomas Rogers and the Rhode Island Slave Trade." *American Neptune* 35, no. 4 (October 1975): 289–301.

Weisbord, Robert. "The Case of the Slave-Ship 'Zong,' 1783." *History Today* 19, no. 8 (1969): 561–67.

Wepman, Dennis. *The Struggle for Freedom: African-American Slave Resistance.* New York: Facts On File, 1996.

Westergaard, Waldemar Christian. *The Danish West Indies under Company Rule (1671–1754) with a Supplementary Chapter, 1755–1917.* New York: Macmillan, 1917.

Williams, Gomer. *History of the Liverpool Privateers and Letters of Marque, with an Account of the Liverpool Slave Trade.* 1897. Reprint, New York: Kelley, 1966.

Wish, Harvey. "American Slave Insurrections Before 1861." *Journal of Negro History* 22, no. 3 (July 1937): 299–320.

Wood, Peter H. *Black Majority: Negroes in Colonial South Carolina from 1670 through the Stono Rebellion.* New York: Norton, 1975.

Worsley, Frank, and Glyn Griffith. *The Romance of Lloyd's: From Coffee-House to Palace.* New York: Hillman-Curl, 1937.

UNPUBLISHED SECONDARY WORKS

Alpers, Edward A. "Becoming 'Mozambique': Diaspora and Identity in Mauritius." Paper presented at the Harriet Tubman Seminar, Department of History, York University, Toronto, November 15, 1999.

Behrendt, Stephen D. Personal correspondence with the author, April 17, 1995.

Hamm, Tommy T. "The American Slave Trade with Africa, 1620–1807." Ph.D. diss., Indiana University, 1975.

Postma, Johannes. "The Dutch Participation in the African Slave Trade: Slaving on the Guinea Coast, 1675–1795." Ph.D. diss., Michigan State University, 1970.

Taylor, Eric Robert. "If We Must Die: A History of Shipboard Insurrections during the Slave Trade." Ph.D. diss., University of California, Los Angeles, 2000.

Index

abolitionist movement, 167–69, 224n34; role of newspapers in, 170–72. *See also Amistad*, abolitionist support for rebel slaves of; *Creole*, abolitionist support for rebel slaves of

Account of the Slave Trade, An (Falconbridge), 168

Adams, John Quincy, 155–56

Affriquain, 59; punishment of rebellious slaves aboard, 112

Africa, 79

African, 89

African Americans, 56–57, 143, 145, 146, 175–76; idealization of past in African American historiography, 106; origins of resistance movement and, 81–82

Africans (as slaves), 22, 56–57, 145, 167; branding of, 23; capture and transfer of, from interior of Africa to coast, 17–19; death rates of, 20; diseases among, 20, 22; examinations of, by slavers, 22–23; experience of, in barracoons, 19–23; oral culture of, used to mitigate oppression of slavery, 175–76; treatment of, by slavers, 18–19. *See also* Africans (as slaves), characterizations and stereotypes of; slave ships; slaves/slavery

Africans (as slaves), characterizations and stereotypes of, 60–66; of Angola, 60; of Ardra, 63; of Bonny, 63, 227n72; of Calabar, 60; of Congo, 60; of Fida, 63; of Gaboon, 60; of Gambia, 63–64; of Gold Coast, 61; of Makua, 63; of Oyo, 63; of Senegambia, 63–64, 227nn75–76; of Si-

erra Leone, 63, 64; of Slave Coast, 60–61, 62–63. *See also* Coromantees

Ajax, 151

Alabama, 160

Alexandre, 113

American Negro Slave Revolts (Aptheker), 5

Amistad, 8–9, 146, 157 158; abolitionist support for rebel slaves of, 154–55; legal issues involved in case of, 154–56; revolt aboard, 151–52, 154–56; role of Celestino and Grabeau in revolt aboard, 152; Supreme Court decision concerning, 155–56

Anderson, George, 158

Ann (1750), 47; newspaper accounts of revolt aboard, 134

Ann (1797), capture of, by French, 50–51

Anne & Priscilla, 53–54

Annibal, 111

Anomabu Fort, 20, 65

Antigua, 47

Antigua conspiracy (1736), 61

antislavery movement. *See* abolitionist movement

Apollo, attempt of, to aid *Delight*, 86–87, 125

Aptheker, Herbert, 5

Atkins, John, 127

Attwood, Captain, 148

Aye, 77–78

Bacon, John, 158

Baldy, Captain, 132

Baltimore, 148, 150, 151

banisou, 67, 228n1

"banzo," 32

Baquaqua, Mahommah, 11, 219n33

Barbados, 64, 104

Barbot, Jean, 62–63, 69, 83; instructions of, to ship captains on punishing slave rebels, 113

barracoons, 19–23

barricadoes (slave bulwarks), 74, 76

Beekesteyn, 31

Behrendt, Stephen D., 46, 215n3, 231n5

Benezet, Anthony, 168, 170

Benguela, 19

"Benito Cereno" (Melville), 139, 236nn2–5

Benjamin, 47

Berbice revolt (1763–64), 61

Bienfaisant, 125

Bight of Benin, 64

Bight of Biafra, 41, 54, 63, 65

Black Prince, 123

Blacksmith, Ben, 157

Bonny, 65, 110. See also *Marlborough*, success of revolt aboard

Bosman, Willem, 22, 26, 95

Bowser, William, 147–49; editorial concerning execution of, 171

Branfill, Captain, 9

Brazil, 55, 59, 135; Bahian revolts in, 57

Breckinridge County (Kentucky), 161–62

Bristol, 54

British Emancipation Act (1833), 157, 158

Brome, 80

Brooks, 28

Brothers, 31

Buenos Aires, 31

Bunce, Captain, 133

Cadiz Dispatch, 132

Calabar, 36, 42, 65

cannibalism, 25–26, 219n37, 219–20n40

Cape Coast Castle, 20, 54, 65, 136, 219n22

Cape Horn, 139

Cereno, Benito, 139, 140–41

Charleston, revolt aboard, 15–16, 17

Charlton, 51

Christiansborg (1775), 111

Christiansborg (1786), 62

Cinque, Joseph, 151

Clare, 10, 123

Clarkson, Thomas, 169

Cobb, David, 161–62

Cockburn, Francis, 158

Codd, Captain, 119, 120, 121

Compagnie du Senegal, 55

Conneau, Theophilus, 23, 38, 63, 98, 230n14

Constitution, attempt of, to aid *Decatur*, 148

Coralline, 78

Coromantees, 61–62, 63, 65; revolts of, 61

Cothrington, 64

cotton farming, 160

Coughtry, Jay, 7

Courrier de Bourbon, 13

Cowley, Malcolm, 7

Craton, Michael, 5

Creole, 8, 171; abolitionist support for rebel slaves of, 158–59; revolt aboard, 156–59

Cron-Prindzen, 35, 221n83

Cuffy's plot (1675), 61

Cugoano, Ottobah, 11, 24, 34, 38; plotting of shipboard revolt by, 88–89

Daget, Serge, 7

Davis, David Brion, 167

Davis, Humphrey, 161–62

Decatur, 151, 171; revolt aboard, 147–50; sentencing of rebellious slaves of, 149

Delano, Captain, 140, 141, 236n2

Delight, revolt aboard, 85–88, 92, 109, 124

Demerara, 81

Demerara revolt (1823), 61

Den Keyser, 35

Deux Soeurs, 59; revolt aboard, 170–71

Diligent, 13, 217n30

Dispatch, 38

Dolben's Act (1788), 36

Don de Dieu, 131

Donnan, Elizabeth, 7

Douglass, Frederick, 159; on being a slave, 175

Dove, revolt aboard, 110

Dow, George Francis, 7

Dragon, 64

Draper, Captain, 133

Du Bois, W. E. B., 56

Duke of Argyle, 45

dysentery, 28, 31

Eagle, 11, 45; revolt aboard, 107
East Africa, 63
Edwards, Bryan, 61
Elizabeth, 80; punishment of slave rebels on, 116; revolt aboard, 99
Elkins, Stanley, 13
Ellis Island, 149
Elmina, 20, 64
Elminas. *See* Coromantees
Eltis, David, 8, 46, 165, 215n3
Emilia, 32
Ensor, Robert, 156, 157
Equiano, Olaudah, 11, 217n26, 219–20n40
Ettin, Essjerrie, 62, 142
Exeter, 130
Expedition, 168

Falconbridge, Alexander, 17, 22, 62, 76, 170; antislavery sentiment of, 168; on brutal treatment of sailors, 52–53; on conditions aboard slave ships, 29–30, 33; on torture of slaves to make them eat, 37–38
Feliz Eugenia, 79
Ferrer, Ramon, 152
Ferrers, 81; revolt aboard, 100–101
Finette, 131
"fixed melancholy," 32–33
Flore, 49
Florida, 160
Fly, 133
Flying Fish, 51; revolt aboard, 124
Fort Christiansborg, 21
Fort Fredensborg, 111
Fredensborg, 32, 77–78, 80, 89
French Company of the Indies, 36
Fridericus Quartus, punishment of rebellious slaves on, 112
From Rebellion to Revolution (Genovese), 5

Gambia, 47, 53, 64
Gambia River, 44, 63, 64, 67, 110, 111
Garnet, Henry Highland, 159
Gedney, Thomas, 154
Genius of Universal Emancipation, 149
Genovese, Eugene, 5, 55
Gentleman, 156
Gideon, Captain, 133

Gifford, Zephaniah, 156, 157, 158
Gold Coast, 21, 42, 61, 62, 65, 80, 94, 111, 130. See also *Marlborough,* success of revolt aboard
Golden Age, 116
Gomez, Michael, 81–82
Goree Island, 1, 63
Gould, Captain, 1–2
Grand Terre Island, 42
Gray, James M., 161–62
Great Britain, 155
Greene, Lorenzo J., 7, 71
Grenada, 13
grometto, 78
Guadeloupe, 42, 111
Guinea, 80, 132. *See also* Upper Guinea
Guinea, 12
Guinese Vriendschap, 62
Guyana, 61, 81

Haiti, 148, 150
Hamilton, Captain, 133
Harms, Robert, 23, 63
Harrod, Thomas, 148
Havana, 151
Hawk, attempt of, to aid *Marlborough,* 121, 124
Hawkins, Joseph, 15–16, 18
Henry, 62; revolt aboard, 77
Hercule, 36
Hermosa, 157
Hero, 133
"Heroic Slave, The" (Douglass), 159
Heureux, 52
Hope, attempts by crew of, to cover up murder of captain, 1–2

"If We Must Die" (McKay), 164
Indian Queen, 31; crew member deaths on, 47
Industry, 91
Inikori, Joseph, 7

Jamaica, 32, 47, 55, 61, 135
James, C. L. R., 71
James Fort (James Island), 67, 110, 111
Jane, 102
Jay, William, 155
Jobson, Captain, 64

Johnson, poisoning of crew of, 91

Jolly Prince, 134

Jones, Captain, 133

Katherine, 52

Kentucky, punishment of slave rebels on, 113–14

King David, 94, 111; erroneous newspaper reports concerning, 222n1; illness of crew on, 47; revolt aboard, 41–42, 59

King's Fisher, 132

Koromantyn. *See* Coromantees

La Desirade Island, 42

La Estrella, 230n14

La Prueba, 236n1

La Rochelle, 34

Lady Mary, 32

Lafayette, 156; revolt aboard, 150–51

Le Courrier de Bourbon, 13

Leander, 128

Leusden, 35

Levrette, 101

Licorne, 80

Lima (Peru), 139

Linebaugh, Peter, 61

Liot, Philippe, 34–35

Little Cape Mount, 85

Little George, revolt aboard, 109

London, 111

Londonberry, 132

Louisa, attempt of, to take back *Creole* from rebellious slaves, 158

Luanda, 19

Lundy, Benjamin, 149–50

Mannix, Daniel, 7

Marie-Gabrielle, 47

Marlborough, 56; revolt aboard, 94, 124; success of revolt aboard, 119–22

Martin, Gaston, 7

Mary (1737), 35

Mary (1742), 128

Mary (1761), 111, 232n16

Mary (1796), 34; betrayal of planned revolt on, by slave, 107

Maryland, 49, 150, 160. *See also* Baltimore

Mayer, Brantz, 230n14

McCorty, Dennis, 48

McGowan, Winston, 7

McKay, Claude, 164

measles, 30, 31

Melville, Herman, 139, 236nn2–5

Merritt, William, 156, 157–58

Mettas, Jean, 7

Middle Passage, 2, 3, 11, 23–24, 143, 144, 146–47; mortality rates during, 31, 35–37; psychological trauma of, 13–14, 32–33, 39; total lives lost during, 37. *See also* slave revolts (shipboard)

"Middle Passage: Resistance on the Waves, The" (Munford), 7

Miller, Joseph, 7, 19, 226n57

Misericordia, 123

Mississippi, 55

Mississippi River, 160

Montego Bay, 107

Montes, Pedro, 151–52, 154

Moore, Francis, 44

Morell, Captain, 10

Morris, Elijah, 156–57

Mozambique, 80

Munford, Clarence, 7, 94; on intangibles of shipboard slave revolts, 101

Mure, 139, 140–41

Nancy (1769), illness of crew of, 47

Nancy (1793), 8; justification for revolt aboard, 170

Nancy (1806), 101

Nantes, 7

Nassau (Bahamas), 158

Necessaire, 127

Neptunis, 110

New Britannia, 89

New Calabar River, 79

New Haven, 154

New London, 154

New Orleans, 147, 150, 151, 160

New York City, 148; slave revolt in (1741), 61

Newton, John, 33, 35, 43, 45, 76, 170; antislavery sentiment of, 168–69; on attempted revolt of slaves by spiritual means, 69–70; and frequency of slave revolts, 83

Nicoll, Captain, 132

Norfolk, 150
North Carolina, 91

Ohio River, 160
okofokum, 61
Old Calabar, 41

Pallas, 35
Panchiata, 28–29
Parrey, Captain, 28
Patientia, 8
Patterson, Orlando, 57
Pearl: punishment of rebellious slaves on, 112–13; revolt aboard, 100
Perfect, 45
Perseverance, suppression by, of revolt aboard *Tryal*, 140–41
Phillips, Thomas, 24; precautions taken by, against slave revolts, 83, 105
Phoenix (1762): damage to, by thunderstorm, 49; revolt aboard, 49
Phoenix (1783), 36
Pieh, Sengbe, 151, 152, 154, 156
pirates, racial egalitarianism of, 50
Port Louis, 42
Postillion, 67–68
Postma, Johannes, 7, 215n3
Preest, William, 2; death of, 215n2
Prince of Orange, 12, 217n28
Princess Carolina, 123
privateers, 50–51
Puerto Principe (Cuba), 151

Queen Caroline, successful revolt aboard, 78–79

Rainbow, 78
Rathbone, Richard, 7
Rebecca, 47
Rediker, Marcus, 53, 61
Regina Coeli, 129
Restoration, 134
Richardson, David, 7, 46, 165, 215n3, 216–17n20
Robert (1721), 21; punishment of rebel slaves on, 113; revolt aboard, 90, 99
Robert (1733), 133
Rookes, role of, in *Decatur* affair, 148

Royal African Company, 3, 9, 67, 132; death rates of slaves transported by, 20
Royal Chartered Danish Guinea Company, 72
Ruby (1721), 133, 134, 107–8
Ruby (1787), 95; punishment of rebel slaves on, 113; revolt aboard, 102
Ruiz, Jose, 151–52, 154

St. Domingue, 111
St. Domingue Revolution, 57, 135, 150
St. John Island revolt (1733), 61
St. Kitts, 41
Sainte Hélène, 56
Sally (1764–65), 8; erroneous newspaper reports of deaths on, 224–25n36; revolt aboard, 54
Sally (1775), 133
Sam Christova, 82
Samba, 175
Sandown, 47–48
Santa Maria, 140
Sao Tome Island, 42, 117
Scudder, Harold C., 236n2
scurvy, 27, 31
Senegal, 2, 63, 66, 130, 131, 139
Senegambia, 63–64, 227nn75–76
Shakoe, 78
Sharp, Captain, 133
ship surgeons, 31; involvement of, in punishing slaves, 112–13
Sierra Leone, 21, 47, 59, 63, 64, 90, 129, 170
Sisters, 36
Slave Coast, 62–63
slave revolts, 5, 18, 81; alternatives to, 55, 225n43; in barracoons, 21–22, 58, 218n19; in Brazil, 57; on plantations, 4, 5, 37, 55; and ratio of African-born slaves to American-born, 56–57. *See also* slave revolts (shipboard); *revolts aboard specific ships*
slave revolts (shipboard), 1–3, 42–43, 83–84, 87–88, 137–38; accounts of ships being "cut off," 132–35, 235nn38, 41; accounts of slaves fighting on side of ship's crew, 107–8; acquisition of and types of weapons used by slaves, 95–98; attempts by slaves to run ships aground,

130–31; common characteristics of, 102–3; compassion of rebel slaves for captured crews, 128–30; crew awareness of dangers posed by slaves, 44, 69–70, 82–84; crew responses to, 101–3; definition of, 12–13, 217n28; difficulty of, 37; early studies of, 6–8; effect of, on slave trade, 167–69; fear of, 69–70, 82–83; and feigning of sickness by slaves, 93–94; frequency of, 3, 7, 9, 215n3, 216n19, 216–17n20, 223n11; frequency of, near African coast, 43–44, 46, 172–73, 223n11; and hand-to-hand combat, 96; historical record of, 3–4, 9–11, 136–37; importance of timing to, 98–101, 173, 231n29; influence of, on slaves rebellions on land, 173–75; and mobility of slaves, 88–94; number of, 8, 172–73; number of slaves saved because of, 167; potential for disaster during, 127–28; prevalence of, in different regions of Africa, 62–66; reactions to planning of, 106; reporting of, by ship captains, 3; role of children in, 88–89, 91, 92–93; role of women in, 88–93; scarcity of evidence concerning, 9–11, 136–37; slave deaths resulting from, 115–16, 117, 172, 233n34, 240n21; special environment of, 5–6; as unique phenomenon, 6; whites as chroniclers of, 11–12, 172–73. *See also* slave revolts (shipboard), in the Americas; slave revolts (shipboard), conditions for; slave revolts (shipboard), precautions against; slave revolts (shipboard), reasons for lack of success of; slave revolts (shipboard), success of; *revolts aboard specific ships*

slave revolts (shipboard), in the Americas, 4, 10, 139–43, 223n11; case of the *Amistad,* 151–52, 154–56; case of the *Creole,* 156–59; case of the *Decatur,* 147–50; case of the *Lafayette,* 150–51; on oceangoing vessels, 144–47; in riverine slave trade, 159–62

slave revolts (shipboard), conditions for: African origins of slaves, 56–66; familiarity of slaves with Europeans, 59–60; disunity of crew, 51–53; illness of crew, 46–48; military training of slaves, 59;

negligence of crew, 53–54; numerical advantage of slaves, 54–56; pursuit of ships by pirates and privateers, 50–51; reductions in crew strength, 43–48; shipboard crises, 49–51

slave revolts (shipboard), precautions against, 67–71, 83–84, 122; arming and training of crew, 68–69; controlling of slaves through violence, 71–73; health of crew versus that of slaves, 70–71; language and cultural barriers, 5, 79–82, 229n31; neglecting of slave hygiene, 73–74; ship design, 74, 76; use of spies and informants, 76–79

slave revolts (shipboard), reasons for lack of success of, 104–5, 127–28; assistance of nearby ships, 108–10; assistance of nearby soldiers and forts, 110–11; betrayal of plots by slaves or free Africans, 105–8; brutal punishment for failed revolts as deterrent, 112–18; and psychology of slavers as a "brotherhood of people-buyers," 111–12

slave revolts (shipboard), success of, 56, 173; and capture of vessel, 122–25; life aboard captured slave ships, 125–32; number of shipboard revolts that led to freedom of slaves, 135–38; ships "cut off" ("cut out") on African coast, 12, 132–34, 235nn38, 41. See also *Marlborough,* success of revolt aboard

slave ships, 19, 23–39 *passim;* abuse of female slaves by crew members of, 33–35; accidents on, 35–36, 48; amount of time spent by, on African coast capturing slaves, 45, 223n6; arms carried by, 69; brutal treatment of sailors on, 52–53, 224n34; carelessness of crews of, 95–96, 99; daily routine on, 26–27; design of, 74, 76; diet of slaves on, 26–27; disease on, 28, 30–31, 36, 47–48; disposal of bodies from, by throwing overboard, 48, 223–24n19; exercise of slaves on, 33, 221n71; fear of cannibalism by slaves on, 25–26, 219n37, 219–20n40; food and drink rations for slaves on, 26–28, 146; hardships faced by crews of, 70–71; high cost of operating, 164–67; insurance for,

165–66; jettisoning of slaves from, to save provisions, 31–32; medical care on, 31; mortality rates of crews of, 46–47, 70; mortality rates of slaves on, 31, 35–37, 115, 221–22n92; personality of crews of, 174; psychological ailments of slaves on, 32–33; ratio of slaves to crew on, 55; refusal of slaves to eat on, 37–38; sanitary conditions on, 29–30; ship's "boys" on, 129–30, 234n28; slaves' reaction to boarding, 23–24; sleeping conditions on, 29–30; spoilage of water on, 28; suicide attempts on, 37–39, 43; tactics of crews of, to escape revolts on, 123–24; tendency of captains of, to protect their investment in slaves, 115–16; treatment of slaves on, 24–25; violence among slaves on, 32, 71–73. *See also* slave revolts (shipboard)

slave trade, 121–22, 176–77; Cuban, 151, 155; effect of slave revolts on, 167–69; factors affecting profitability of, 72, 164–67; riverine, 159–62

slaves/slavery, 6–7; in America, 55, 57, 81; in the Chesapeake Bay area, 160; "*ladino*," 59, 226n57; oral culture of slaves, 175–76; plantation, 175–76; sailing and navigation skills of slaves, 127, 234n16; "social death" of slaves, 57. *See also* slave revolts; slave revolts (shipboard); slave ships; slave trade

Sloop Sisters, 9–10

Smith, William, 80

Snelgrave, William, 7, 11–12, 62, 80; on execution of rebellious slaves, 116; use of informants by, 77

Some Historical Accounts of Guinea (Benezet), 168

South Carolina, 55, 160

Spain, 155

speculum oris, 37

Stone, Edward, 161–62

Stone, Howard, 161–62

Substance of the Evidence of Sundry Persons on the Slave-Trade, The (Clarkson), 169, 224n34

Sultane, 58

Surinam, 135

Tacky's rebellion (1760), 61

Taggart, George, 1–2

Tecora, 151, 152

Testing the Chains (Craton), 5

Thames, 54, 105; recapture of, after revolt aboard, 125; revolt aboard, 62, 73

Thomas, 91, 125; revolt aboard, 104–5

Thompson, Vincent Bakpetu, 7

Thoughts Upon the African Slave Trade (Newton), 168

Three Friends, 133

Tomba, Captain, 21, 142

Tozor, John, 67

Trans-Atlantic Slave Trade, The: A Database on CD-ROM (Eltis et al.), 8, 63, 216n19, 217n28

Transport, 151

True Blue, 52

Tryal (1767–69), 76

Tryal (1804), 146, 147, 151, 235–36n1; names of slaves involved in and surviving revolt aboard, 141–42; revolt aboard and suppression of, 139–43; sentencing of rebellious slaves on, 142–43, 149

Upper Guinea, 63, 64

Uya, Okon, 7

Valparaiso (Chile), 139

Venus (1794), 124

Venus (1831), 92, 230n14

Vigilantie, 117

Ville de Basle, 45; revolt aboard, 109

violence, as common to Western Europe, 114–15

Virginia, 110, 159, 160

War of Spanish Succession, 36

Warwick Castle, 117

Washington, Madison, 156–59, 171; fame of, 159

Washington, capture of *Amistad* by, 154

Wasp, 91; insurance for, against revolts, 166; revolt aboard, 117

Wax, Darold, 7

West Africa, 17, 46, 48, 56, 63, 160; militarization of, 61

West Central Africa, 17, 19, 65
West Indies, 151
Whydah, 33, 64, 117
William (1730), revolt aboard, 130, 136
William (1767), 235n38
Wilson, Manuel, 148
Windward Coast, 63, 64, 85, 134
Wish, Harvey, 7

Wolf, 52
Wood, Peter, 81
Woodside, Captain, 158
Woolfolk, Austin, 147, 149–50, 236n15, 237n19

Zanzibar, 66
Zong, 32